World of a Slave

World of a Slave

ENCYCLOPEDIA OF THE MATERIAL LIFE OF SLAVES IN THE UNITED STATES

Volume 1: A–I

MARTHA B. KATZ-HYMAN

and

KYM S. RICE, EDITORS

AN IMPRINT OF ABC-CLIO, LLC
Santa Barbara, California • Denver, Colorado • Oxford, England

Library of Congress Cataloging-in-Publication Data

World of a slave : encyclopedia of the material life of slaves in the United States /
Martha B. Katz-Hyman and Kym S. Rice, editors.
     p. cm.
     Includes bibliographical references and index.
     ISBN 978-0-313-34942-3 (set : acid-free paper) — ISBN 978-0-313-34943-0
(set : ebook)— ISBN 978-0-313-34944-7 (v. 1 : acid-free paper) — ISBN 978-0-313-34945-4
(v. 1 : ebook) — ISBN 978-0-313-34946-1 (v. 2 : acid-free paper) — ISBN 978-0-313-34947-8
(v. 2 : ebook)
     1. Slavery—United States—History—Encyclopedias. 2. African Americans—
Material culture—History—Encyclopedias. 3. Material culture—United States—History—
Encyclopedias. I. Katz-Hyman, Martha B. II. Rice, Kym S.
     E441.W895   2011
     306.3'620973—dc22   2010037597

ISBN: 978-0-313-34942-3
EISBN: 978-0-313-34943-0

15   14   13   12   11   1   2   3   4   5

This book is also available on the World Wide Web as an eBook.
Visit www.abc-clio.com for details.

Greenwood
An Imprint of ABC-CLIO, LLC

ABC-CLIO, LLC
130 Cremona Drive, P.O. Box 1911
Santa Barbara, California 93116-1911

This book is printed on acid-free paper ∞

Manufactured in the United States of America

Contents

Preface

Human beings spend their lives surrounded by things. Sometimes these objects are utilitarian, such as the cars we drive, the beds we sleep on, or the shoes we wear. Others may represent something more unique and personal, like a gift from a beloved friend or relative. Still others reflect the society in which we live or our value systems and beliefs. Whether we are considering the objects that help us to do our work or those that reflect our choices, passions, and decisions, we all understand that these things say something about us and our identity, often more powerfully than words. This encyclopedia tries to capture the material culture of slavery. Until recently, scholars, museums, and the general public thought that little tangible evidence remained from those 200-plus years of U.S. history, other than a detailed documentary record that reflects almost entirely the slaveholders' perspective. Thanks largely to recent archaeological investigations conducted across the plantation South, the Chesapeake, the Upper South, and sites in New England and the Mid-Atlantic, new museum collecting practices, and a renewed interest in and access to the oral histories collected from former slaves by the Federal Writers' Project of the Works Progress Administration in 1936–1938, we know more about what slaves surrounded themselves with than ever before. The entries collected here use objects as a prism for understanding both the complex institution that was American slavery and the individual experiences of the people trapped within it. The items that brought joy and preserved culture get as much attention as those that inflicted cruel punishments or extracted long hours of backbreaking labor.

As much as possible, it is the story of the enslaved that we try to tell, and it is their world that we explore throughout the encyclopedia. The focus is on the enslaved in all of the areas where slavery was to be found, from the North to the South, and west to Texas, and from the 17th century through Emancipation. In addition, many entries discuss how the West and Central African traditions and customs brought by those torn from their homelands continued to manifest themselves in the everyday lives of African Americans even through the difficult years of slavery. This melding of cultural traditions and influences resulted in new practices and beliefs, called creolization, which enabled enslaved Africans to use the objects they found in their new locations and the ideas that they learned to make sense out of experiences that were demeaning and painful, and lives that were marked by unrelenting labor and unpredictability.

Although thousands of books have been published about slavery, this is the first encyclopedia to focus on the material culture of slaves in the United States. It covers the everyday lives of the enslaved: what they wore, saw, and looked at; played and played with; ate and drank and smoked; worked on and in; heard, read, used, made, touched, hid away, lived in, built, were given, slept on, carried, raised, and cultivated; were sold on; and much more. The experiences of the enslaved are the principal topic, but a great deal is revealed about the white and slaveholding society as well. Much of the information contained in the entries has not been published before in this format. Hopefully, this reference will serve as a springboard for future investigations and new discoveries about this important subject.

The encyclopedia includes more than 170 entries arranged alphabetically. Readers also will find a topical list of entries at the front of the book so that they can quickly find topics of interest. Two broad essays on music and dance and on literacy and orality appear before the encyclopedia entries as necessary context for readers to understand the wider material culture. The individual entries include suggestions for further reading, and cross-references are given to related entries, either as bolded topics in the entries or following "*See also*" at the end of the entry. The volume ends with a selected bibliography that will lead readers to substantive books and articles as well as Web sites. Contributors are experts drawn from academia, historical archaeology, museums, and public history who work in this field.

The encyclopedia boasts a large number of images selected from museum and library collections to illustrate the entries. The photographs of now-vanished slave quarter houses, the watercolor portraits of the enslaved, and the archaeological survivals from slave-related sites chosen for this encyclopedia are but a sample of what has survived and been documented for posterity. We have tried to be as wide-ranging as possible, realizing that examples from archives of material slave life are anything but generic; architecture and objects were as varied as the plantations and states in which enslaved African Americans lived. For example, slave housing looked very different in Virginia, New Orleans, and Tennessee and even from plantation to plantation to less grand slaveholdings, depending on local vernacular and resources, degree of wealth, and architectural ambitions.

Many entries are accompanied by sidebars that offer complementary testimony from the Federal Writers' Project slave narratives. The narrative excerpts taken from interviews with former slaves usually were transcribed in vernacular speech with unusual spelling and grammar, and they use language that some modern readers may find offensive. As many historians note, these interviews are problematic in that the individuals who were interviewed for the project were mostly young children as slaves. Their memories were also shaped by the era in which the interviews were conducted, the Great Depression. Many of the people interviewed in 1936–1938 were old, hungry, and living in poverty. The interviewers, most of whom were white, asked leading questions and frequently patronized their subjects. Nonetheless, these accounts often are detailed, and they offer the most direct record that we have of the world of a slave. Fisk University Social Science Institute staff member Ophelia Settle Egypt was a rare example of an African American interviewer. When she interviewed a former slave in 1929 or 1930, she was told, "If you want Negro History, you will have to get [it] from somebody who wore the shoes."* This encyclopedia offers readers a chance to put on those shoes.

---

*In Rawick, George P. *The American Slave: Oklahoma and Mississippi Narratives*, Vol. 7 (Westport, CT: Greenwood Press, 1972), pp. 45–46.

Acknowledgments

Putting together a reference work of this size takes time, patience, and the contributions and assistance of many people. Our thanks first go to our editor, Wendi Schnaufer, who first approached Kym about this project more than four years ago. Kym then recruited Martha to help her, and all along the way, Wendi has been there to encourage, help, and push this encyclopedia to completion. We are most grateful. Our thanks, as well, to Michael Millman, who became our editor during the production of the encyclopedia and smoothed the way to its conclusion.

We acknowledge the contributions of our advisory board: Fath Davis Ruffins, curator, Division of Home and Community Life, National Museum of American History; Theresa Singleton, associate professor of anthropology, the Maxwell School of Syracuse University; and John Michael Vlach, professor of American studies and anthropology at the George Washington University. They reviewed the initial list of entries and made good suggestions regarding topics that the encyclopedia needed to cover.

Our thanks to the following for allowing us to use images from their collections: Roddy Moore, director, Blue Ridge Institute & Museum, Ferrum College; Daniel Ackermann, associate curator, Museum of Early Southern Decorative Arts and the Old Salem Toy Museum; Jill Slaight, rights and reproductions, New-York Historical Society; Leah Stearns, digital services coordinator, Monticello, Thomas Jefferson Memorial Foundation; and especially, Marianne Martin, visual resources librarian, Colonial Williamsburg Foundation, who worked with her colleagues across the Foundation to get us the images we wanted.

We are especially grateful to all of our contributors, many of whom wrote more than one entry—some at the last minute. Many of them responded directly to our personal requests; others responded to our call for contributors. Without their enthusiasm, support, and writing, this project never would have been completed. Their names and affiliations are found in the list of contributors.

Our deepest thanks is reserved for our families. At times this project has taken over our dining rooms, living rooms, and family rooms, not to mention our lives, and they have been very understanding. Tsvi and Mark: thank you.

Martha B. Katz-Hyman
Kym S. Rice

Introduction

The study of human experience through objects and their context is called material culture. According to the pioneering scholar of material culture, Thomas Schlereth, the methodology that underlies the study of material culture is that "objects made or modified by humans, consciously or unconsciously, directly or indirectly, reflect the belief patterns of individuals who made, commissioned, purchased, or used them, and, by extension, the belief patterns of the larger society of which they are a part."[1] In the case of enslaved African Americans, these objects can be as large as a house that survives from the 1800s or as small as a fragment from a ceramic plate recovered from a slave quarter after being buried for more than a century. Some objects are more ephemeral: while they might have survived slavery, their meanings have slipped away in modern life, and archaeologists are only now beginning to unravel them.

This encyclopedia takes a broad look at enslaved experiences over the more than 250 years between the establishment of the first colonial settlements and the Civil War that ended chattel slavery in the United States. The work concentrates on the American South. This is where the largest enslaved African American populations resided, over the longest period of time. By 1861, some 4 million enslaved individuals lived in the region, about half the total population of the South. Our entries try to cover everything used by slaves, whether that is the goods found in their dwellings; their work tools; the furniture, textiles, and other goods used by them in the course of their day; or the houses in which they lived and worked as well as the landscapes in which they were situated; the clothing they wore and how they wore it; their food and how they prepared it; even their hairstyles and oral traditions. From the emerging field of slave archaeology, we find tantalizing evidence that some things, which remained largely invisible to whites, reflected the belief systems that accompanied captive Africans to the Caribbean and Americas, but often were adapted or changed in the face of their altered circumstances. Slaves came into contact with other objects too, ones that we associate with the oppression that marked their chattel status, including those that were used to inflict the cruel punishments that many slaves feared or experienced. For all its bleakness, slavery was far from monolithic. We know that enslaved African Americans were able to purchase fashionable items at stores as consumers as well as make or repurpose objects for themselves. These modest endeavors suggest the ways that material goods added richness and color to an individual's life and contributed in no small measure to creating and maintaining personal and collective identity. All this was a part of "the World of a Slave."

Although the characteristics of enslavement varied from place to place and changed over time, all slaves occupied two distinctive and complex worlds: the one that was dictated to them and controlled by whites, which they needed to traverse and survive daily, and the one that they fashioned for themselves within their families and their communities that existed apart from whites. Our contributors address both the ways that particular objects functioned in these two worlds, and the different kinds of meaning that those items might have embodied for enslaved people.

Nearly 200 years stretch between 1619, when the first Africans arrived in the Virginia colony, and the official end of the U.S. slave trade by Congress in 1807. Although estimates by scholars vary, more than 12 million captive Africans were transported to the Caribbean, South America, and mainland North America over this time span. Still others were brought illegally, despite the ban, right up until the Civil War. This movement of Africans to the Americas has been called the largest forced migration in world history. Some African captives were themselves the victims of tribal wars in their own countries; others were people who had been kidnapped either by slave traders or their African agents and sold into slavery. Most could trace their origins to the wide swath of what is identified in the 21st century as West and Central Africa, although individuals were transported to coastal slave markets from locations much farther away. To a large extent, the Africans who came to what became the United States were from West Central Africa. Yet they spoke assorted different languages and dialects and held many different beliefs and traditions. In fact, it is thought that some already knew a version of the creolized form of English learned from Europeans that is preserved in the Gullah language found in the Georgia and South Carolina Sea Islands. Seeking agricultural workers for their colonial holdings, and especially valuing individuals with experience in the crops that they hoped to exploit like tobacco, sugar, or rice, many European countries, including Great Britain, Holland, France, and Portugal, participated in the African slave trade until well into the 18th century. According to the Trans-Atlantic Slave Trade Database, more than 40,000 voyages from Africa by slave-trading vessels are documented.[2]

Those individuals who survived the terrible trip across the Atlantic known as the Middle Passage spent upward of 45 days together below deck in close quarters with inadequate food, water, and exercise. On some ships, even while outfitted in heavy chains, slaves were forced to dance, sing, or drum for the crew's amusement—and were whipped if they refused. Some captives carried out mutinies against their captors and others jumped overboard in desperation. The trip, too, was subject to the vagaries of weather, including terrible storms. By a recent estimate, some 10.5 million Africans probably survived the Middle Passage.[3] After arriving in the Caribbean or North America, individuals could be sold several times over and travel considerable distances before they reached their final destinations.

The brutality associated with the African slave trade makes it relatively certain that few, if any, enslaved individuals transported personal belongings with them to the New World. Although most captives reportedly were stripped of their clothing before the voyage, a cowry shell tucked away in hair or perhaps a bead necklace might have traveled across the Atlantic Ocean on a slave ship and thus into the colonial South. It is more likely that slaves acquired such items on board ship. Slavers often carried goods for trading that included glass beads. The *Henrietta Marie*, which sunk off the coast of present-day Florida in 1701, had thousands of glass beads in its cargo hold, along with shackles and chains. African women possibly were given beads on board ship as a diversion. James Penny, an English slave trader in the 1770s and 1780s, reported that he furnished captives with pipes and tobacco as well as musical instruments. He noted that "the women are supplied with beads, which they make into ornaments."[4]

With the exception perhaps of some scattered trinkets recovered by archaeologists at different sites associated with slavery, what nearly all Africans brought with them stayed alive only in their memories, perhaps later reinforced by oral traditions that were repeated and passed down within the groups or communities that colonial enslavement created. This included information on how to grow and harvest certain African crops; what foods were preferred and how to cook them; medical and health practices; the shapes and materials that composed once familiar household objects; the perpetuation of sacred forms that were imbued with spiritual meaning and power; and traditions related to the built environment. These were all they had to help them make sense of their lives in a very foreign place, under circumstances that, by and large, robbed them of their names, families, and societies. This process, which, in fact, occurs with all people who move to a new culture, was continuous and changing. Second-, third-, fourth-, and even fifth-generation people of African descent became more and more acculturated, and they were as familiar with their material environment as people in the 21st century are with theirs. Throughout the 18th century, newly arrived Africans brought reminders of old traditions to their new homes, but they soon learned the ways of the European colonists who now owned them and became accustomed within several generations to their new environments.

The material objects that are the easiest to associate directly with American slavery across its entire time span are those related to work. They are the hoes, plows, and other implements that worked the fields, the looms that made cloth, the needles and thread that sewed or repaired clothes, the pots that cooked food and the plates that it was served on, the variety of tools that crafted everything from silver cups to manacles, the chamber pots that had to be emptied each morning, the saddles that needed cleaning or repair—the list goes on and on. Although building techniques and forms varied across the region, from shotgun houses to one-room cabins, enslaved individuals constructed both the buildings in which they lived and those in which they worked.

Slaves used a diverse range of objects to perform work that varied in terms of quality and quantity, depending on their owners' economic level. A farm where two or three slaves resided presented a different living situation and level of material comfort than a plantation with several hundred workers in residence. Similar modifications are found in Southern cities, where most enslaved individuals lived in proximity to their owners. In some cases, enslaved African Americans not only used these objects to do the jobs required of them by whites, but crafted them as part of their labors as trades workers. The domestic workforce handled different objects than did the field hands. Yet, even given these many distinctions, doing work day in and day out for someone else, without choice or precious little recompense, was a condition that all slaves shared. Regardless of location or time period, the white and the black worlds intersected over work. Through their daily use of the implements that performed every type of job imaginable, enslaved African Americans learned much of what they knew about the world of their white masters. And whenever possible or desirable, they acquired or replicated these objects for themselves. The pallets, benches, stools, and iron pots that furnished many slave quarters were homemade or readily available and looked the same as those used by lower-class whites or free blacks.

To many readers, the notion that enslaved people slept in beds, lived in houses with wood floors, cooked with a variety of equipment, and wore clothing that spanned the range from coarse linen shirts and trousers for work in the fields to dresses of printed cottons or suits of fine livery may seem strange. After all, being a slave implies that someone owns not only one's physical body but also anything else that one might have, from the clothing one wears to the food one puts into one's mouth to the bed one sleeps in—whatever that bed might be—to the utensils one cooks with. It implies a material status so low that only the most basic of food, shelter, and clothing is provided. Yet the evidence we have, both archaeological and documentary, shows time and time again that slaves in the 18th century and 19th century lived within a fairly wide range of material levels, from those who truly did have only the most basic of the necessities of life, to those who managed to acquire goods that were equal to or better than those that poor to middling whites could obtain.

How did slaves accumulate these goods? Were they yet another facet of the negotiation historians described that occurred regularly between master and slave that characterizes other aspects of enslavement? If slaves had no legal right to own these items, why were they not required to give them up to their owners? And if American slavery was not denoted by having few, if any, possessions of one's own, then how was it characterized?

The last question is probably the easiest to answer: simply, that these people of African descent were slaves by virtue of laws, enacted beginning in the late-17th century, that delineated their status and reflected long-time prejudices, not because these laws dictated levels of material goods. The law said they were chattel, and the law provided the ways in which they could cease being slaves. Over time, these laws were modified, repealed, and reenacted. Sometimes they specified what slaves could and could not possess, like guns, liquor, or dogs. In these cases, the laws reflect what enslaved individuals actually did possess or had access to and, therefore, what slave owners were unhappy about them possessing and wished to prohibit. But, by and large, these laws were enacted to regulate behavior and legal status, not consumption.

How slaves acquired goods is also relatively easy to answer, because of the wealth of primary sources—letters, diaries, business records, legal records, runaway slave advertisements—that provide the information. Masters issued clothing, blankets, and food on a semiregular schedule: clothing was issued in the spring/summer and fall/winter or once a year on New Year's Day, blankets usually in the fall, and food was distributed weekly as well as seasonally. It appears from the available documentation that, once these goods were issued, masters as well as slaves considered these goods to be the slaves' property. Masters also supplied slaves with the tools necessary to do their jobs, although these remained the property of the master and are the items most likely to be found listed in probate inventories of slaveholders as the property of the deceased's estate.

Although not well documented, some slaves received hand-me-down cooking utensils, furniture, and clothing from their masters. This, however, was not a usual practice. They also picked up items discarded by whites, repaired them and put them to their own purposes. They obtained goods by theft, usually from their owners, a crime for which, if discovered, they were punished and sometimes legally prosecuted. That many masters or overseers kept a close eye on the tools and supplies used by their enslaved workers, scrutinized their return carefully, and kept them under lock and key suggests that stealing was a widespread problem. On the other hand, enslaved individuals understandably displayed little remorse over these appropriations, thinking perhaps that they had earned these items.

Slaves made things for themselves and bartered and sold these goods to their masters, to white neighbors, and on the open market. Especially on rural plantations, slaves had their own plots of land called "patches" and grew their own produce, and they also took advantage of nearby streams, rivers, and woodlands to catch fish and trap animals. Slaves acquired goods by purchasing them with money they earned from tips or gifts, from the sale of produce or animals, primarily chickens, from the sale of their own products, like baskets, or from their own labor. In urban settings, greater opportunities existed for enslaved individuals to earn money, including by selling produce or other items at city markets. By the end of the antebellum period, the hiring-out system had evolved in such a way that many enslaved individuals were permitted to keep some part of their wages. With cash accumulated over many years, some slaves hoped to buy their freedom or that of family members, but many others used their money more immediately, to purchase a variety of goods, ranging from fabrics and ribbons to tools, liquor, and food. These purchases are well documented in surviving store account books; in both early Maryland and Virginia, for instance, these records often appear as credit accounts in the slave's own name. All of these goods were the same types of things bought by whites and free blacks.[5]

As for why slave owners allowed their slaves to keep their goods, one answer may be found in a principle derived from ancient Roman law, called the *peculium*, that was well understood by most slave owners. According to this principle, slaves were allowed to accumulate property but that property was subject to appropriation by the master at any time, although in practice, the appropriation of the goods may have happened infrequently, if at all. Thomas Jefferson makes it clear that he understood this principle in a letter that he wrote to his son-in-law, Thomas Mann Randolph, in 1798, thanking Randolph "for putting an end to the cultivation of tobacco as the peculium of the Negroes. I have ever found it necessary to confine them to such articles as are not raised on the farm. There is no other way of drawing a line between what is theirs and mine."[6] Historian Orlando Patterson writes that the peculium

> solved the most important problem of slave labor: the fact that it was given involuntarily. It was the best means of motivating the slave to perform efficiently on his master's behalf. It not only allowed the slave the vicarious enjoyment of the capacity he most lacked—that of owning property—but also held out the long-term hope of self-redemption for the most diligent slaves. The master lost nothing, since he maintained an ultimate claim on the peculium, and he had everything to gain.[7]

From the point of view of the slave owners' self-interest, allowing slaves to accumulate goods made good management sense: slaves who stood to lose a lot materially by rebelling might think twice about doing so if it meant losing the property they had worked long and hard to accumulate. Therefore, for all practical purposes, it is most likely that slaves' personal goods were considered by both blacks and whites to belong to the slaves and therefore not subject to inventory or other accounting as part of the possessions of the slaves' owner, although the real possibility exists that white slave owners, at least initially, felt that the items owned by their slaves were of no real value.

In the antebellum period, when the institution of slavery came under greater threat, some slaveholders did express concerns about whether enslaved individuals should be allowed to spend the money they earned as they pleased and choose their own possessions. Not only did slaveholders wish to reinforce their control and authority over their slaves whenever possible, but they increasingly perceived that any means by which enslaved individuals could carve out some measure of autonomy for themselves was dangerous to the entire system. "Money is power," an Alabama planter astutely observed in 1858. He suggested "cram[ming] negroes' pockets with strings, old buckles, nails, &c. instead of silver dollars."[8] But by the 1850s, enslaved individuals certainly were too sophisticated as consumers to be satisfied with any old castoffs. Even if the amount of money that slaves had was not great, it still permitted them the ability to acquire possessions that they could use in any way they saw fit. Through goods, enslaved African Americans found one means with which to thwart the threadbare life accorded them by whites and craft a distinctive identity.

While archaeological excavations have found evidence of guns and other weapons in slave quarters, the objects associated with reading and writing that have been uncovered might be considered more seditious. By the outbreak of the Civil War, because Southern whites were increasingly fearful of anything that might provoke dissention or violence among their slaves, enslaved people were legally prohibited from learning to read and write. By these laws, whites hoped to limit slaves' access not only to books, but also to newspapers, auction posters, and the rare anti-slavery tract. Some slaveholders, who were motivated by their religious beliefs, taught their slaves to read the Bible regardless, but undoubtedly some individuals, such as Frederick Douglass, who escaped from slavery in Maryland and went on to become one of the most famous black abolitionists, learned on their own. The pens, pencils, ink bottles, and slates found by archaeologists tucked behind walls and secreted in other locations on slave-occupied sites offer a tantalizing clue that some enslaved individuals pursued these skills, regardless of the risk. It is significant that in their testimony given before the Freedmen's Bureau at the Civil War's end, many former slaves declared emphatically that their first act in freedom was to learn to read and write.

In the words of an ancient Yoruba proverb, "However far the stream flows, it never forgets its sources."[9] Although the Africans who came to the New World as slaves possessed backgrounds as different as the languages that they spoke, they sought and found areas of common ground. Africa clearly provided a critical element that shaped enslaved material culture over several generations. To have some stability in their lives, enslaved people had to make some sense of the chaos around them. One way they did this was to take the objects they had, both manufactured and natural, and impose upon them the usages and meanings that similar objects carried in Africa. They also made objects with materials found in the United States that in form and function resembled those that they knew from their homelands. Archaeological evidence suggests that even as they acculturated, enslaved individuals retained some cultural traditions. While the form and meaning changed over time, ideas about the innate power of certain objects—pierced coins worn as charms, crystals placed under kitchen floors, or pottery marked with cosmogram symbols—and their ability to protect and transform were preserved and handed down to descendants. African elements likewise remained alive in many facets of slave life: in the music they played, the songs they sang, the dances they performed, the food they ate, the stories they told, the hairstyles and adornments they wore, and the ways in which they buried their dead. In areas such as the Sea Islands of South Carolina and Georgia, where enslaved African Americans lived together in large groups with limited contact with whites, these traditions and practices stayed intact into the 20th century.

Many 21st-century Americans recognize that this country is far richer for the contributions made to it by enslaved African Americans. This powerful legacy has transformed American culture. We can see, hear, and taste it every day, through the foods we eat, the landscape that surrounds us, the words we hear, and the music, art, and dance that we enjoy. It is harder to experience enslaved material culture, although it forms a distinctive element in this story of survival and change. While slavery is interpreted at many museums and historic sites in the 21st century, original objects with enslaved provenance are few, and archaeological materials are seldom displayed. Whether they purchased, found, or appropriated them, African Americans adopted the familiar objects that signified the white world and brought them into their lives. Despite the fact that these items made their lives more comfortable and bearable, they must have served as poignant reminders of what free people could possess. At the same time, as terrible as slavery was, it did not truly rub out what enslaved African Americans were as a people. Archaeology in slave sites across the South shows that the old ways persisted in secret, not only because whites found them subversive but also because enslaved individuals thought it was important to preserve them at any cost.

NOTES

1. Thomas Schelereth, *Material Culture Studies in America* (Lanham, MD: AltaMira Press, 1982), 3.

2. Trans-Atlantic Slave Trade Database (www.slavevoyages.org). The number of Africans taken on the voyages documented in the database represents approximately 80 percent of those actually transported.

3. Trans-Atlantic Slave Trade Database (www.slavevoyages.org).

4. Jerome S. Handler, "On the Transportation of Material Goods by Enslaved Africans During the Middle Passage: Preliminary Findings from Documentary Sources," *The African Diaspora Archaeology Newsletter*, 2006. (http://www.diaspora.uiuc.edu/news1206/news1206.html#1). Also, Jerome S. Handler, "The Middle Passage and the Material Culture of Captive Africans," *Slavery & Abolition* 30, no. 1 (March 2009): 1–26.

5. Ann Smart Martin, *Buying into the World of Goods: Early Consumers in Backcountry Virginia* (Baltimore, MD: Johns Hopkins University Press, 2008).

6. Thomas Jefferson to Thomas Mann Randolph Jr., June 14, 1798, Library of Congress, Washington, DC.

7. Orlando Patterson, *Slavery and Social Death: A Comparative Study* (Cambridge, MA: Harvard University Press, 1982), 185–186.

8. Quoted in James O. Breeden, ed., *Advice Among Masters: The Ideal in Slave Management in the Old South* (Westport, CT: Greenwood Press, 1980), 274.

9. Quoted in Charles Joyner, *Down By The Riverside: A South Carolina Slave Community* (Urbana: University of Illinois Press, 1986), xiii.

Alphabetical List of Entries

Topical List of Entries

Dance and Music

Jurretta Jordan Heckscher

Dance and music were activities of life-sustaining importance to the people enslaved in the American South. From the 1620s to the 1860s, on small farms and great plantations, in village workshops and city factories, from southern Delaware to eastern Texas, slaves made music and danced. They sang songs to pace their grinding agricultural labors, remember their ancestors, mourn those who had died or been stolen from them, mock their oppressors, and worship the divine; they danced to strengthen the bonds of kinship and community, to find love and pleasure, and to experience their bodies in ways that did not belong entirely to someone else. To understand what slavery meant to slaves means to understand their dance and music and to understand American dance and music means understanding how much these art forms owe to those who were enslaved in the United States.

SOURCES AND STEREOTYPES

Because most history is based on written records and slaves were legally forbidden to read or write throughout most of the 19th century, the history of slave dance and music depends largely on documents left by white people. The major black sources are slave narratives and the interviews undertaken by the Federal Writers' Project in the 1930s, asking elderly African Americans to recall their early lives in slavery many decades before. Most interviewers were white, and there was plenty of room for misunderstanding on both sides.

Some contemporary white observers were quick to interpret slaves' love of dance and music as evidence that they were happy in slavery. By the antebellum decades, too, a highly popular form of entertainment—the minstrel show—was showcasing stereotypes of contented slaves dancing and singing for white audiences throughout the United States. Theatrical performances and motion pictures projected the same images far into the 20th century.

The former slave and noted abolitionist Frederick Douglass (1818–1895) went to great lengths to set the record straight. It would be a grave mistake to understand slaves' songs "as evidence of their contentment and happiness," wrote Douglass. "But for these [dancing and music], the slaves would be forced to the wildest desperation," Douglass explained; when a slave dances or sings, such expressions "represent the sorrows, rather than the joys, of his heart; and he is relieved by them, only as an aching

"The Old Plantation," unknown artist, probably South Carolina, ca. 1795, watercolor on laid paper. Enslaved men and women dance to the music of a gourd banjo and hollow gourd drum. (Abby Aldrich Rockefeller Folk Art Museum, The Colonial Williamsburg Foundation. Gift of Abby Aldrich Rockefeller.)

heart is relieved by its tears."[1] Careful examination of the evidence confirms Douglass's insight: slaves danced and sang not to express happiness but because life otherwise would have been unbearable.

AFRICAN LEGACIES AND THE 18TH CENTURY

The men and women forcibly enslaved to North America brought with them the cultural diversity of a far-flung range of nations across West and Central Africa. In nearly all these nations, dance and music were essential components both of the great passages in the individual life cycle and of all life in community. The noted African British abolitionist Olaudah Equiano (ca. 1745–1797) summarized the heritage of most Africans when he characterized his ancestral Igbo homeland as "almost a nation of dancers [and] musicians."[2] It is equally certain that these "nations of dancers," diverse though they were, shared deep structural similarities in their dance and music traditions that facilitated the formation of the earliest African American dance and music cultures in the 18th century.

Most important, most traditional African music could not and cannot usefully be distinguished from dance. Musicians and dancers participated equally in a single mutually responsive conversation: dancing made music visible; music sounded the dance; and music-making, whether vocal or instrumental, required intense and skillful bodily engagement that amounted to a form of dancing. The two phenomena essentially were inseparable, and for this reason, it is more historically accurate to speak of African and African-derived dance and music together than separately.

Other widely shared features of dance and music in Africa are as follows: their pervasive presence in everyday life and its importance in building and sustaining community; inclusive performance practices that obliterated distinctions between performers and audience; rhythmic complexity as the dominant structural principle, and the consequent importance of percussive sound and movement; structural formations that emphasized contrastive interchange, rather than unity, among groups or between a group and an individual (men and women danced apart from each other, often interacting playfully without touching, and individuals emerged from group formations to execute solos or lead responsive dialogues as in the musical pattern known as call-and-response); incorporation of a wide and inventive range of textures, dynamics, pitch, and movement scope, from the most subtle to the most virtuosically energetic; angular and asymmetrical dispositions of the body; placement of the body's center of gravity low, in the hips and pelvis, thereby enabling the dancer to emphasize the independence of different body parts and to use them to sustain simultaneous multiple rhythms, or "polyrhythm," with visible precision; high value accorded improvisation within the bounds of tradition and distinctive personal creativity within the framework of the group, principles related to the structural paradox of emphasis by absence, so that, for example, one located the beat through syncopation, or "heard" it best when it was not sounded but shaped in the dancer's gesture or in the hearer's mind. These elements formed the foundation for the development of African American dance and music in slavery and since.

REGIONAL FOUNDATIONS AND HISTORICAL DEVELOPMENT

Although they built on ancient and widely shared African foundations, slave dance and music always varied significantly both geographically and temporally. Nevertheless, the forces of history and geography had converged sufficiently by the time of emancipation to produce something approaching a common Southern black tradition that later became the single greatest influence on the dance and music practices shared most widely among all Americans.

Geographically, slave dance and music developed in three source regions, or "culture hearths," each of which established an important variant tradition. One was Louisiana, where slave culture was influenced by its proximity to French and Caribbean cultures and reshaped by the influx of French Caribbean slaves following the Haitian Revolution of the 1790s. The resulting dance and music culture remained distinct from that of the rest of the slave South. It included both unique creolized dances and dance types—Calenda (or Calinda), Counjaille, Chica (or Bamboula), among others—and uniquely persistent African practices, such as the gatherings at the Place Congo in New Orleans, where well into the 19th century hundreds of slaves assembled on Sundays to dance in ethnic ensembles according to the acknowledged traditions of their ancestors.

A second cultural hearth for slave dance and music was the coastal Low Country of South Carolina and Georgia. Here the demands of rice cultivation concentrated slaves from Senegambia and encouraged the development of large plantation communities where African cultural traditions could persist in relative isolation from white influence. The associated dance and music culture is less visible in the historical record there than in Louisiana, but what may be the richest and most complex of all slave cultural expressions—the sacred dance type known as the Ring Shout—took deepest root in the Low Country and may well have originated there.

Yet Louisiana and the Low Country eventually proved to be historical backwaters to the broad dance and music mainstream emanating from the Chesapeake. That region, bounded on the east by the coast between southern Delaware and the Cape Fear area of North Carolina and to the west by the Appalachians, became the primary cultural hearth for slave dance and music throughout the South.

The reasons for the Chesapeake's preeminence lay first in the region's staple-crop economy of tobacco and, later, wheat. From the beginning, these crops permitted the establishment of small slaveholdings that brought blacks and whites into constant contact, thereby ensuring the earliest and most thorough creolization of European and African cultures in North America. After the American Revolution, tobacco's legacy of soil exhaustion and wheat cultivation's more modest work demands reduced Chesapeake slaveholders' need for labor. They began to sell their "surplus" workers to the Deep South or to immigrate there with their bondsmen, thereby ensuring that the regional Chesapeake slave culture of the 18th century would become the mainstream Southern slave culture of the 19th. By 1845, a white observer could conclude that "[t]he greater portion of our national poetry [art] originates in Virginia, or among involuntary Virginia emigrants," because

> [e]very year thousands are sent to the far south and southwest for sale. The Virginian type of negro character therefore has come to prevail throughout the slave states, with the exception of some portions of Louisiana and Florida. Thus everywhere you may hear much the same songs and tunes, and see the same dances, with little variety, and no radical difference.[3]

Yet the vigor and creativity of Chesapeake slave culture were hardly the inevitable effects of economic necessity. On the contrary, Chesapeake dance and music depended on two definitive leaps of imagination among Africans and their descendants in captivity. The first was their early recognition of the common dance and music practices underlying the diversity of their various African ethnic traditions and their creation of a creolized dance and music culture on that foundation. This primary act of creolization in the 18th century—what writer Ralph Ellison (1914–1994) called "the beginnings of an American choreography"—paralleled those of other slaves throughout the American South and the Caribbean around the same time, but in the Chesapeake, it proved to be the foundation of black dance and music in North America.[4]

The subsequent imaginative achievement of Chesapeake slaves fused the new dance and music culture with European influences. This secondary creolization was a work of the late 18th and early 19th centuries. It had parallels elsewhere, but because of the intensive interaction of blacks and whites in the Chesapeake, it was more complete and fully realized there than anywhere else in the Western Hemisphere. It involved grafting distinctive European forms onto the older African-based foundation: dancing on the balls of the feet; a more exclusively upright posture; a range of set-dance types such as reels, "country dances," and "square dances" that became standards in the black dance repertoire; and—most important, because it represented a major departure from African practices and formed the basis of so much black dancing thereafter—the adoption of the male-female couple as a primary unit of dance.

The earlier, identifiably African elements persisted, however, at the heart of the new Chesapeake slave dance and music tradition, as did an array of skilled steps and choreographic forms—Buck Dancing, Pigeon Wing, Set the Floor, or Dancing on the Spot, among many others—that had no parallel in the European dance lexicon. Nevertheless, they blended with the creolized European elements in ways that remain the hallmarks of African American, and generally American, vernacular dancing, as Southern black dance and music became mainstream American dance and musical expression in the 20th century.

DANCE AND MUSIC IN EVERYDAY LIFE

Dance and music were perhaps the most important means by which American slaves habitually defied slavery. They shaped the arc of life with it, from cradle songs to courtship and wedding dancing to funeral processions. More important, they used dance and music on countless occasions to make their lives their own, if only momentarily, in the daily crucible of bondage. The historical picture is fullest for the 19th century, and the description that follows reflects that time, although much of it applies to earlier periods as well.

Slave life revolved around an exhausting workday that lasted from dawn to dusk, usually in an agricultural setting. Here, work songs, perhaps most often in call-and-response with a leader, set work's pace and rhythm and coordinated physical effort within the group, making the motions of labor akin to dance. Workers who found themselves alone in the fields, or in isolated groups, used wordless "field calls" or "hollers" as vivid emotional expression or to communicate with one another. As slaves returned from the fields at sunset, they often sang also; long after slavery, many white Southerners still vividly recalled the "cadence melancholy and indescribable, with a peculiar pathos" with which their voices sounded.[5]

In these and its other contexts, slave music blurred the distinction between vocal and instrumental music just as it blurred the distinction between music and dance. The voice could sound wordlessly, as an instrument, encompassing a wide range of pitch and timbre from deep guttural to piercing falsetto. It could be used percussively, as in "the curious rhythmic effect produced by single voices chiming in [to a song] at different irregular intervals," as one Northern observer described it.[6] Song lyrics, conversely, sometimes functioned more as pure sound than as specific meaning, being chosen, as the formerly enslaved Solomon Northup (b. 1808) explained, "rather for [their] adaptation to a certain tune or measure, than for the purpose of expressing any distinct idea."[7]

Even the harshest masters generally found it useful to give slaves some regular opportunities for recreation, and certain holidays were decreed by statute. The normal pattern was outlined by a Virginia jurist in 1836:

> The regular holydays are two [days] at Easter, two at Whitsuntide [the Christian feast of Pentecost], and a week at Christmas. These he [the slave] enjoys by prescription, and others, such as Saturday evenings, by the indulgence of his master. He passes them in any way he pleases. Generally they are spent in

visiting from house to house, and in various amusements. His favorite one, if he can raise a violin, is dancing.[8]

The annual agricultural cycle was also punctuated by lively communal gatherings that combined aspects of work and holiday. At "corn-shuckings" (corn huskings), log rollings, and similar events, contests of speed and skill paced by special songs facilitated major seasonal work tasks and culminated in celebratory dances.

The Saturday-night dance in the quarters early became a staple of rural Southern life. Frequently it drew participants from small farms and large plantations throughout the neighborhood, in defiance of the armed "patrollers" who could arrest and punish any slave discovered off his or her slaveholder's property without a written pass. Continuing a widespread African tradition of dance and song that mocked the moral failings of the powerful, slaves satirized whites in song texts and caricatured them in dancing—where they celebrated their ability to evade and discomfit the patrollers.

Whenever it could be arranged, the music at these dance events was furnished by a fiddle: homemade from a gourd and a stick if necessary, fashioned by a fiddle-maker if possible. Slave fiddlers were individuals of particular importance not only within their own communities but also in the white community, where they were the musicians of choice for dance events from the early 18th century to the early 20th. In both settings, they developed the practice of "calling" the dance steps and floor patterns, or "figures," for set dances, thus establishing one of the most distinctive traditions of American social dance.

Drums were banned from slave gatherings in much of the South once slaveholders realized that they could be used for communication, as in Africa, but other instruments often joined the fiddle, singing, and ubiquitous rhythmic hand-clapping in providing music for dances. They included the banjo, an African instrument type that was nearly as important as the fiddle in slave dance and music, and a variety of simple percussive instruments such as animal bones or sticks, pairs of spoons, rattles, and occasionally triangles or tambourines.

Sometimes at formal dance events, however, and typically on informal occasions of slave dancing, no instrumental accompaniment was available. Instead, the musical dimension was furnished by a distinctive form of bodily percussion known variously as "patting," "patting Juba," "Juba beating," or "jubilee beating." Slapping out a rhythm or rhythms on the thighs and perhaps with his feet, as Frederick Douglass explained, "[t]he performer improvises as he beats, and sings his merry songs, so ordering the words as to have them fall pat with the movement of his hands."[9] Patting Juba was both a form of music and a form of dance, and it was almost certainly slave dancing's most frequent accompaniment.

EVANGELICAL TRANSFORMATION AND THE RING SHOUT
Conflict between Protestant Christianity, which provided the religious underpinnings for white Southern culture, and the music and dance traditions of the enslaved existed almost from the outset of Southern slavery. In the 19th century, it became acute in ways that significantly redirected the course of African American dance and music history and brought to the fore a lasting form of Christian sacred dance known as the Ring Shout.

European Protestantism had differentiated itself from Catholicism in part by rejecting the spiritual utility of a great range of expressive culture, including secular music and all dance. Yet because only a minority of slaves had been Christianized by the time of the American Revolution, and much of white Southern culture remained profoundly secular, this striking contradiction between the European and African cultural backgrounds had affected slave culture only minimally. All of that changed in the late 18th and early 19th centuries, particularly under the influence of the Second Great Awakening (ca. 1780–1830) and the general transformation of white Southern culture into an identifiably Evangelical Protestant mode. For the first time, slaveholders made widespread and concerted attempts to convert slaves to Christianity, not least so as to appropriate religion as an instrument in support of slavery. At the same time, slaves were increasingly drawn to Evangelical faith for reasons of their own and chose to convert to Christianity in significant numbers.

Actively joining in new forms of Evangelical worship such as the great outdoor "camp meetings" that electrified the countryside, slaves soon developed a distinctive African American Christianity that was always in tension and often in direct conflict with slaveholders' purposes and practices. And whether from their own sense of Evangelical Christian ethics, or under the standards enforced by pious masters, an unknown but indisputably significant proportion of Southern slaves between the Revolution and the Civil War abandoned or radically reshaped much of the dance and music heritage that had hitherto sustained them in bondage. Many stopped dancing altogether, breaking with centuries and even millennia of African tradition in favor of a Protestant understanding of the sinful nature of dance. Many likewise withdrew from all forms of musical expression not associated with worship or personal piety. In the process, they contributed to an explosion of creativity in African American religious music, including the development of the sacred song type that came to be known as the spiritual.

The Evangelical transformation profoundly altered slave dance and music then, yet it did not change everything. Christianity was pervasive in the slave community by the Civil War, but it is also likely that most slaves never formally converted. Some of those who did nevertheless continued dancing or making secular music. Many slaveholders continued to permit or even encourage dance and music in the plantation setting, whatever their own religious convictions. And slave Christianity found ways to adapt rather than abandon familiar expressive forms: secular song melodies were repurposed for sacred songs, and psalm-singing could function as worksong. Most significant, the growth of Christianity in the slave population coincided not coincidentally with the first appearance in the historical record of the Christian dance and music ritual known as the Ring Shout.

Expressive movement akin to dance characterized much worship in early African American culture, but the Ring Shout made movement the major instrument of approach to the divine. It may have originated in the Low Country, where it is best documented, but it flourished across the South in the antebellum period. In the Ring Shout, participants moved single file in a circle to sacred singing, gradually building in intensity to an ecstatic crescendo in which some worshippers collapsed and others took their place. The ceremony might continue for hours. "The foot is hardly taken from the floor," one white observer noted, "and the progression is mainly due to a jerking, hitching motion, which agitates the entire shouter, and soon brings out streams of perspiration. . . . Song and dance are alike extremely energetic."[10]

Those who worshipped in the Ring Shout insisted vehemently that what they were doing was not dance, because the feet never crossed and scarcely lifted. This claim was a sophistry necessary to span the chasm between African and European understandings of the sacred, and to support what was in fact an enduring revitalization of the African tradition of sacred dance. In its resourcefulness, its resilience, its vitality, and its capacious embrace of history's unbearable contradictions, the Ring Shout might be taken as the culmination of slave dance and music—a creative tradition of profound historical importance that for more than two centuries made, as Douglass said, "[e]very tone . . . a testimony against slavery, and a prayer to God for deliverance from chains."[11]

NOTES

1. Frederick Douglass, *Narrative of the Life of Frederick Douglass, an American Slave, Written by Himself*, ed. Benjamin Quarles (Cambridge, MA: The Belknap Press of Harvard University Press, 1960), 38, 107; Frederick Douglass, *My Bondage and My Freedom* (1855; Reprint, New York: Arno Press and the New York Times, 1968), 99.

2. Olaudah Equiano, *The Interesting Narrative of the Life of Olaudah Equiano, Written by Himself*, ed. Robert J. Allison (New York: Bedford Books of St. Martin's Press, 1995), 36.

3. J. Kinnard Jr., "Who Are Our National Poets?" *Knickerbocker Magazine* 36 (October 1845); reprinted in *The Negro and His Folklore in Nineteenth-Century Periodicals*, ed. Bruce Jackson (Austin: University of Texas Press, 1967), 27.

4. Ralph Ellison, lecture, Harvard University, Cambridge, Massachusetts, December 1, 1973; quoted in Jacqui Malone, *Steppin' on the Blues: The Visible Rhythms of African American Dance* (Urbana: University of Illinois Press, 1996), 38.

5. Page Thacker [Letitia M. Burwell], *Plantation Reminiscences* (n.p., 1878), 46.

6. Lucy McKim Garrison comment cited in William Francis Allen, Charles Pickard Ware, and Lucy McKim Garrison, eds., *Slave Songs of the United States* (1867; Reprint, Bedford, MA: Applewood Books, 1995), vi.

7. Solomon Northup, *Twelve Years a Slave: The Narrative of Solomon Northup, A Citizen of New York, Kidnapped in Washington City in 1841 and Rescued in 1853, from a Cotton Plantation near the Red River in Louisiana* (Auburn, NY: Derby and Miller, 1853), 100; as quoted in Eileen Southern, *The Music of Black Americans: A History*, 3rd ed. (New York: W.W. Norton, 1997), 169.

8. Letter from "a judicial officer of the Superior Court of that state [Virginia]," printed in J. K. Paulding, *Slavery in the United States* (1836; Reprint, New York: Negro Universities Press, 1968), 209.

9. Douglass, *My Bondage and My Freedom*, 252.

10. Description from an article in *The Nation*, May 30, 1867; quoted in Allen, Ware, and Garrison, xiv.

11. Douglass, *Narrative*, 37.

FURTHER READING

Abrahams, Roger D. *Singing the Master: The Emergence of African American Culture in the Plantation South*. New York: Pantheon Books, 1992.

Allen, William Francis, Ware, Charles Pickard, and Garrison, Lucy McKim, eds. *Slave Songs of the United States*. New York: A. Simpson and Company, 1867.

"Born in Slavery, Slave Narratives from the Federal Writers' Project, 1936–1938," American Memory, Library of Congress. At http://memory.loc.gov/ammem/snhtml/.

"The Church in the Southern Black Community." Documenting the American South. At http://docsouth.unc.edu/church/allen/menu.html.

Courlander, Harold. *Negro Folk Music U.S.A.* Rev. ed. New York: Dover, 1992.

Emery, Lynne Fauley. *Black Dance: From 1619 to Today.* Rev. ed. Princeton, NJ: Princeton Book Company, 1988.

Epstein, Dena J. *Sinful Tunes and Spirituals: Black Folk Music to the Civil War.* Urbana: University of Illinois Press, 1977.

Hazzard-Gordon, Katrina. *Jookin': The Rise of Social Dance Formations in African-American Culture.* Philadelphia: Temple University Press, 1990.

Heckscher, Jurretta Jordan. "'All the Mazes of the Dance': Black Dancing, Culture, and Identity in the Greater Chesapeake World from the Early Eighteenth Century to the Civil War." PhD diss., George Washington University, 2000.

Heckscher, Jurretta Jordan. "'Our National Poetry': The Afro-Chesapeake Inventions of American Dance." In *Ballroom, Boogie, Shimmy Sham, Shake: A Social and Popular Dance Reader*, edited by Julie Malnig, 19–35. Urbana: University of Illinois Press, 2009.

Malone, Jacqui. *Steppin' on the Blues: The Visible Rhythms of African American Dance.* Urbana: University of Illinois Press, 1996.

Southern, Eileen. *The Music of Black Americans: A History.* 3rd ed. New York: W.W. Norton, 1997.

"Voices from the Days of Slavery: Former Slaves Tell Their Stories." Library of Congress: American Memory. At http://memory.loc.gov/ammem/collections/voices/.

Literacy and Orality

Antonio T. Bly

Slave literacy and orality (the spoken word) are at once complex and intertwined themes in the history of blacks in the United States. Once designated as chattel, slaves were bound by words on paper. Like typeset or handwritten letters, they were rendered physically trapped within socially constructed molds or artfully stylized characters inscribed on parchment, forged and set by slaveholding grandees. Indeed, as early as 1680, the "generall assembly" of the Virginia colony explained, it was unlawful "for any negro . . . to goe or depart from his master's ground without a certificate."[1]

Such unlawful behavior could carry heavy burdens. Slaves found away from their masters without written consent, for example, received "twenty lashes on the bare back well layd on." Over time, they were taken up and held as fugitives. Taken up a second time, absconded slaves ran the risk of being branded, mutilated, or dismembered.[2] Consequently, for well over 200 years, the written word stood for the planter's power and the slave's confinement.

The boundaries of literacy also consigned slaves to the margins of early American society intellectually. In the Western tradition, people of African descent have been written out of "culture" because they were identified with oral traditions. In that setting, literacy signified reason and civilization. Performance in print earned the "a special distinction" for "the laurel of humanity."[3]

Still, despite attempts to deny them their humanity, blacks persevered. Many learned to read. Others learned how to write. What is more, for slaves like poet Phillis Wheatley, literacy became a form of resistance, a way of snatching the laurel of civilization from Western hands, forcing otherwise silent books to speak.

Wheatley's story began in 1761 when she was kidnapped by Africans from her parents in a Wolof village. Like other captives in the slave trade, she became the property of several others before reaching the Gold Coast and the infamous "door of no return" on Goree Island, Senegal, that marks the symbolic entry into the Atlantic Slave Trade. Only seven years old, she survived her Middle Passage aboard the schooner *Phillis*. She was declared unsalable in the Caribbean, so traders carried the young girl to Boston and sold her for a trifle to Susanna Wheatley.

In the Wheatley household, Phillis thrived as a domestic. Not long after she became a member of the family, Phillis tried to "make letters upon the wall."[4] As a result, her

Poet Phillis Wheatley, servant to John Wheatley of Boston. Engraving by Archibald Bell, London, 1773. (Library of Congress.)

mistress took pity on her, and with the help of her daughter, Mary, began instructing the young bondservant. "In sixteen Months Time," Phillis's master John Wheatley wrote," she mastered "the English language . . . to such a degree, as to read any, the most difficult Parts of the Sacred Writings."[5] Less than three years later, she learned to write. In 1773, a modest volume, Phillis Wheatley's *Poems on Various Subjects, Religious and Moral*, appeared in print.

Not surprisingly, the book aroused many critics. Thomas Jefferson, for one, denounced *Poems* because they punctured the socially grafted veneer of African racial inferiority. In his view, although "religion" could indeed produce "a Phyllis Whately," it could not "produce a poet." Because "the heroes of Dunciad," Jefferson explained, "are to her, as Hercules to the author of that poem."[6] The French philosopher Voltaire disagreed, yet his acknowledgment of Wheatley reflected the deep-seated prejudices of the day nonetheless. "Genius," Voltaire observed in a 1774 letter to Baron Constant de Rebecq, "which is rare everywhere, can be found in all parts of the earth. Fontenelle [French author, 1657–1757] was wrong to say that there would never be poets among Negroes; there is presently a Negro woman who writes very good English verse."[7]

For Wheatley, literacy represented a way to claim humanity; for other slaves, particularly those who were literate yet uneducated, it met the more pragmatic goal of securing liberty. That is, with knowledge of letters, they could pass for free. They could convince others that they owned themselves. Simply put, literacy gave slaves an opportunity to move about more easily, less encumbered by the fear of being captured and returned to slavery.

That was certainly the case of Peter Custis, whose story begins and ends with a runaway advertisement that his master, John Custis, placed in the *Virginia Gazette* in May 1745 for his safe return. Presumably, as a child, Peter received a scar on his forehead after falling into a fire. The accident suggests that the young lad may have been the child of one of Custis's house servants, possibly the slave cook. Like other domestics, he also probably worked about his master's house, performing minor tasks.

By age 30, Peter had clearly grown rebellious. Though bred to be a domestic of some type, he adopted another line of work. Indeed, for a time, truancy became the Virginia-born slave's choice of professions. Not quite a real fugitive, Peter stayed in the vicinity of his master's Williamsburg house. There, he lurked about town and engaged in mischief from time to time. But eventually, like other truants, he returned home, weary or in want of food and shelter.

Not surprisingly, the local residents were not as understanding of Custis's boisterous bondservant. In many of their minds, Peter made a nuisance of himself. Evidently, during a previous escape from Custis, he had been found stealing and slaughtering livestock and committing "other injuries to the inhabitants" of Williamsburg.[8] In retaliation, townspeople went to the local justices and got him officially outlawed as a danger to the community.

Fortunately for Custis, Peter was returned and unharmed. Back in his master's possession, Peter was forced to wear leg irons to reduce his mobility and deter future escapes. Custis, like other slaveholding grandees, received many guests at his home on Francis Street, especially on the Sabbath, so Peter's clothes were altered to preclude alarm. For the sake of politeness, his shackles were disguised to hide the brute facts of power in his master's genteel household. Finally, or so it seemed, Peter's wayward behavior had come to an end. His days of truancy were no more.

Apparently, however, the privilege of domestic work failed to produce a contented slave. Peter escaped again, and within a month after his disappearance, Custis posted an advertisement in the paper for his recovery. The reward was two pistoles, which was a Spanish gold coin worth almost a pound, or a little more than 18 shillings and twice the usual sum in such cases. Clearly, Peter was a valuable as well as troublesome slave. To judge by the few facts in the runaway advertisement, his ability to read and probably write may have made him so.

Considering the number of runaways who appeared in colonial newspapers, the ranks of literate slaves grew. In Massachusetts, Philadelphia, and New York, they represented approximately 10 percent of those who stole away; in Virginia 5 percent. In South Carolina, they barely totaled 1 percent. Geography and the varying nature of work in early America explain in part the disparity in these figures.[9]

Slave rebellions also may explain why more slaves were not literate. In 1740, for example, after the Stono Rebellion in South Carolina, legislators thought it wise to prohibit slave education. Similar legislation emerged in Virginia after Gabriel Prosser's failed attempt in 1800 to free slaves in Richmond County. Increasingly, whites came to believe that education made slaves rebellious. Almost 100 years after Stono, those latent fears became painfully real, when a literate domestic slave by the name of Nat Turner and a group of his supporters took the lives of 55 whites in Southampton County, Virginia. In the wake of the white riots that followed that slave insurrection, whites judged that teaching slaves was a dangerous and therefore illegal enterprise.

In spite of whites' efforts to deny slaves education, blacks pressed on and continued to gain knowledge of reading and writing. Judging from recent archaeological findings unearthed in subfloor pits (probably root cellars) in slave quarters, they may have even redoubled their efforts. Pencil leads, pencil slates, and writing slates found at several sites in the Tidewater and Piedmont regions of the Chesapeake reveal a picture of slaves learning to read and write and teaching one another. As a result, before the Civil War an estimated 10 percent of the enslaved black population in the United States was literate.[10]

Slave spirituals represent another enduring legacy in literacy. Embodying both the rich and complex oral traditions of Africa, where music, song, and story took on multiple meanings, and a selective reading of Christianity, the religious songs of black slaves in 18th- and 19th-century America reveal a deep understanding of the Bible that may reflect their knowledge of letters. For well over 200 years, slaves found solace not so much in the New Testament but in the Old Testament. Believing themselves the modern-day Israelites, enslaved blacks sang songs of deliverance and reproachment. Merging African oral traditions together with Western religion and literacy, they imagined freedom and protested slavery. In "Go Down Moses," for example, they invoked the Exodus story, which resembled their own plight. In "O Daniel," that connection is made even more explicit. Reflecting on the story of Daniel's deliverance from the lion's den, 19th-century slaves pondered aloud: if God could save Daniel "why not deliver me?"[11] In "Didn't My Lord Deliver Daniel," they invoked not only the story of Daniel but also that of Jonah and Shadrach, Meshach, and Abednego. If God could deliver them, they asked, "why not deliver me too?"[12]

Slaves also invoked African traditions in their songs. Like the Wolof, Bambara, and other West African tribes, antebellum slaves held fast to the idea that water separated the living from the dead. In "Roll Jordan Roll," for instance, they sang of passing over the river Jordan to see the Promised Land. In "Trouble of the World," slaves crossed Jordan to escape the horrors of their earthly environment. In "Let God's Saints Come In," water again divided "Canaan land" from "Egyptian land."[13] Clearly, on one level, these songs were based on Western biblical traditions. On another level, they demonstrated slaves' use of older, African traditions in which water separated the living and the dead, the past and the present.

Yet another legacy of African tradition was found in the stories that enslaved African Americans told to each other, to their own children, and to the children of their owners. These stories, couched in language that made them seem to be humorous tales of an enemy tricked by the cleverness of his opponents, or animals acting out stories with all-too-human traits, were not only a way of transmitting communal values but also a method through which the enslaved were able to soften the harshness of their bondage by poking fun at their owners. Although generally difficult to date, two of the earliest stories were recorded by Eugène A. Vail, a young Frenchman who visited Monticello in 1816 and heard them from Martha Jefferson Randolph, who had heard them from her nurse, Ursula. These tales of "Mammy Dinah and Her Three Dogs" and "Mr. Fox Tricks Mr. Rabbit and Is Tricked in Return" were published in Vail's commentary on American arts and letters, *De la Littérature et des Hommes de Lettres des États Unis d'Amérique* (Paris, 1841). They give a glimpse into an oral tradition that sustained and nurtured people who otherwise had little enough of it in their lives.

NOTES

1. William W. Hening, ed., *The Statutes at Large Being a Collection of all the Law of Virginia . . .* (Richmond, VA: Samuel Pleasants Jr., 1819–1823), 2:481. References to the Statutes at Large are abbreviated as *SAL*.

2. Lathan A. Windley, *A Profile of Runaway Slaves in Virginia and South Carolina, 1730–1787* (New York: Garland Publishing, 1995), 4–10.

3. Henry Louis Gates Jr., "Preface: Talking Books," in *The Norton Anthology of African American Literature*, edited by Henry Louis Gates Jr. and Nellie Y. McKay, xxviii (New York: W.W. Norton and Company, 1998).

4. Margaretta Matilda Oddell, *Memoir and Poems of PW, A Native African and a Slave* (Boston: G. W. Light, 1834), 11.

5. John Wheatley to Archibald Bell, TLS, November 14, 1772, in Phillis Wheatley, *Poems On Various Subjects, Religious and Moral* (London: A. Bell, 1773), vi.

6. Thomas Jefferson, *Notes On the State of Virginia* (1794; rpt. New York: Bedford/St. Martin's, 2002), 178.

7. Voltaire, *Oeuves Completes, Vol. XLVIII*, ed. Louis Moland (Paris: Garnier, 1882–1896), 594–595.

8. *SAL*, 3:460–461.

9. Antonio T. Bly, "'Pretend He Can Read': Runaways and Literacy in Colonial America, 1730–1776," *Early American Studies* 6, no. 2 (Fall 2008): 266–271.

10. Bly, "Pretend He Can Read," 280–286.

11. William Francis Allen, Charles Pickard Ware, and Lucy McKim Garrison, eds. *Slave Songs of the United States* (New York: A. Simpson and Company, 1867), 94.

12. Lawrence W. Levine, "Slave Songs and Slave Consciousness: An Exploration in Neglected Sources," in *African American Religion: Interpretative Essays in History and Culture*, edited by Timothy E. Fulop and Albert J. Raboteau, 78 (New York: Routledge, 1997).

13. Allen et al., *Slave Songs of the United States*, 1; 8.

FURTHER READING

Allen, William Francis, Charles Pickard Ware, and Lucy McKim Garrison, eds. *Slave Songs of the United States*. 1867. Reprint, Bedford, MA: Applewood Books, 1996.

Arouet, Francois-Marie. *The Complete Works of Voltaire*, edited by Theodore Besterman. Toronto: University of Toronto Press, 1968.

Berlin, Ira. *Many Thousands Gone: The First Two Centuries of Slavery in North America*. Cambridge, MA: Harvard University Press, 1998.

Bly, Antonio T. "'Pretends He Can Read': Runaways and Literacy in Colonial America, 1730–1776." *Early American Studies* 6, 2 (Fall 2008): 261–294.

Gamble, David P. *The Wolof of Senegambia*. London: International African Institute, 1967.

Gates, Henry Louis, Jr. *The Signifying Monkey: A Theory of African American Literary Criticism*. Oxford: Oxford University Press, 1988.

Gates, Henry Louis, Jr. *Figures in Black: Words, Signs, and the "Racial" Self*. Oxford: Oxford University Press, 1987.

Hall, Gwendolyn Midlo. *Africans in Colonial Louisiana: The Development of Afro-Creole Culture in the Eighteenth Century*. Baton Rouge: Louisiana State University Press, 1992.

Jefferson, Thomas. *Notes on the State of Virginia*. 1794. Reprint, New York: Bedford/St. Martin's, 2002.

Langhorne Elizabeth. "Black Music and Tales from Jefferson's Monticello." In *Journal of the Virginia Folklore Society* 1 (1979): 60–67 (also available at http://faculty.virginia.edu/vafolk/ffv1a.htm).

Levine, Lawrence W. "Slave Songs and Slave Consciousness: An Exploration in Neglected Sources." In *African American Religion: Interpretative Essays in History and Culture*, edited by Timothy E. Fulop and Albert J. Raboteau, 59–88. New York: Routledge, 1997.

Mullin, Gerald W. *Flight and Rebellion: Slave Resistance in Eighteenth-Century Virginia*. New York: Oxford University Press, 1972.

Oddell, Margaretta Matilda. *Memoir and Poems of PW, A Native African and a Slave*. Boston: G. W. Light, 1834.

Parent, Anthony S., Jr. *Foul Means: The Formation of a Slave Society in Virginia, 1660–1740*. Chapel Hill: University of North Carolina Press, 2004.

Shields, John C. *The Collected Works of Phillis Wheatley*. Oxford: Oxford University Press, 1988.

Sobel, Mechal. *The World They Made Together: Black and White Values in Eighteenth-Century Virginia*. Princeton: Princeton University Press, 1987.

Windley, Lathan A. *A Profile of Runaway Slaves in Virginia and South Carolina, 1730–1787*. New York: Garland, 1995.

A

ABOLITION IMAGERY. Abolitionists created images, objects, and performances that portrayed slavery harshly. These images played an important role in both the British and American campaigns to galvanize public opinion against slavery, from the early 1700s to the end of slavery in the United States in 1865. They generated intense opposition from slaveholders and proslavery Northerners, whose demands for the suppression of abolitionist words and images contributed to rising North-South tensions in the 1830s to 1850s. Major themes of abolitionist imagery included the cruelty of slaveholding and its degrading effect upon slaveholders and, correspondingly, depictions of the suffering imposed on slaves, especially regarding the breakup of black families through the slave trade. Abolitionist images also attacked the incongruity of Americans, as a liberty-loving people, continuing the practice of slaveholding. A third type of imagery dwelled on the benefits that would accrue to both black and white people from the emancipation of slaves and the creation of a free and industrious black population. Still others dwelled on the evils of the kidnapping and reenslavement of free people of color.

The intended audience for these abolitionist images were principally nonslaveholding white people and, secondarily, free people of color. Not only men but also women and children were targeted for persuasion by these images. Methods of dissemination included newspapers, pamphlets, and broadsides. Three-dimensional objects such as medals, ceramics, shawls, bonnets or quilts, and even daguerreotypes, jigsaw puzzles, and gummed wafers for sealing envelopes could also be decorated with abolitionist words and images. Performative imagery of abolition included both symbolic action, such as burning the Constitution as a proslavery document, and direct popular action, such as marches and meetings to show support for abolition, and even proabolitionist violence, such as freeing suspected fugitive slaves. After the American Civil War broke out in 1861, abolitionists deployed a wide variety of images to advocate the arming of slaves and ex-slaves in support of the Union war effort.

From its beginnings, abolitionist imagery insisted that slavery rested on violence and that slaveholders sinned by using violence, or threat of violence, to work their will upon slaves. One early abolition imagist, Benjamin Lay, an 18th-century Philadelphia Quaker, made plain his opposition to slavery by a dramatic appearance at a Quaker meeting, ca. 1740. Lay confronted wealthy Quaker slaveholders entering their

Anti-slavery broadside "Am I Not a Man and a Brother?" United States, 1835–1836. The kneeling slave, asking "Am I Not a Man and a Brother?" was the widely recognized emblem of the abolition movement. (The Colonial Williamsburg Foundation. Gift funds from the Joseph R. and Ruth P. Lasser Philanthropic Fund.)

meetinghouse. Producing a Bible in one hand, Lay thrust a short sword through the Bible, piercing a concealed bag full of red pokeberry juice. He then denounced the astonished slaveholders, and even sprayed them with the "blood" of their sins against humanity and Christianity. Lay was a social isolate who did not represent the views of Quakers in his time, but he bespoke an emerging evolution in Quaker views: 30 years later, the Friends had decided that members must either free their slaves or cease being Quakers.

Lay's style of directly challenging slaveholders would retain a place in abolitionist imagery, but emphasis soon shifted to concentrate on the political mobilization of people who owned no slaves. The British anti-slave trade campaigns of the late 18th century produced the single most famous abolitionist image. Josiah Wedgwood, the English ceramic manufacturer, produced a medallion with the image of a chained male slave, kneeling and supplicating with raised and joined hands, captioned "Am I Not a Man and a Brother?" This image, reproduced on plates, cups, metal tokens, pincushions, and fabrics, sought to engage and politicize ordinary Britons to petition, act, and demonstrate in favor of abolition. It would become a staple of American abolitionist imagery, eventually complemented by a female counterpart asking, "Am I Not a Woman and a Sister?" The latter image is associated with Elizabeth Margaret Chandler, an American black opponent of slavery, and dates from the late 1820s.

Other early abolitionist imagery drew on British models, too. One of the most powerful British images was that of the *Brookes*, a "tight-packed" **slave ship**, published by the English abolitionist Thomas Clarkson (1760–1846). Viewers saw, as from above, a cross-section of the hold of a slave-trading vessel, with more than 400 figures of slaves filling all the space below decks. This image appeared in America as early as 1789, in a broadside entitled "Remarks on the Slave Trade," published by Mathew Carey of Philadelphia. Anti-slave trade imagery could play both on the immorality of slaveholding and its inappropriateness in a land dedicated to liberty. Thomas Branagan's "The Penitential Tyrant; or, Slave Trader Reformed," from 1807, portrayed a presumably morally awakened slaveholder saluting an enthroned goddess of Liberty, recognizable by the Liberty pole topped by a Phrygian liberty cap at her side. Such

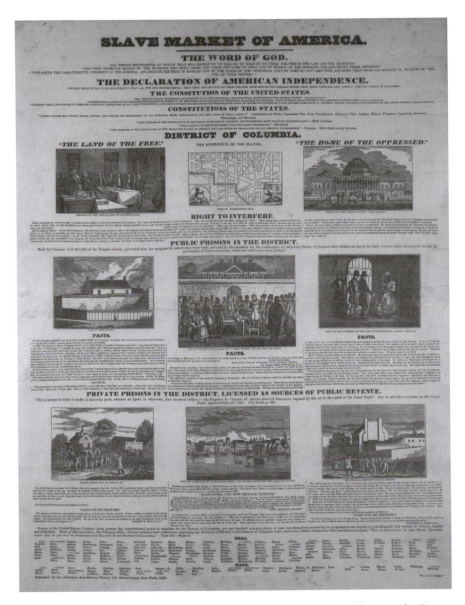

Slave Market of America. Broadside condemning the sale and keeping of slaves in the District of Columbia. The work was issued during the 1835–1836 petition campaign, waged by moderate abolitionists led by Theodore Dwight Weld and buttressed by Quaker organizations, to have Congress abolish slavery in the capital. The text contains arguments for abolition and an accounting of atrocities of the system. At the top are two contrasting scenes: a view of the reading of the Declaration of Independence, captioned "The Land of the Free," with a scene of slaves being led past the capitol by an overseer, entitled "The Home of the Oppressed." Between them is a plan of Washington with insets of a suppliant slave and a fleeing slave with the legend "$200 Reward" and implements of slavery. On the next line are views of the jail in Alexandria, Virginia, the jail in Washington with the "sale of a free citizen to pay his jail fees," and an interior of the Washington jail with imprisoned slave mother Fanny Jackson and her children. On the bottom level are an illustration of slaves in chains emerging from the slave house of J. W. Neal & Co. (left), a view of the Alexandria waterfront with a ship that is being loaded with slaves (center), and a view of the slave establishment of Franklin and Armfield in Alexandria. (Library of Congress.)

images played their part in generating support for the United States' abolition of the African slave trade in 1808.

After 1808, anti-slave trade imagery focused on the evils of the still-licit domestic slave trade, as well as its illegal counterpart, the kidnapping of free people of color to transport and sell them as slaves. Jesse Torrey's "A Portraiture of Domestic Slavery in the United States," published in 1817, showed kidnappers breaking into black homes to seize their victims. Torrey's most dramatic image showed a black woman suspended in midair, just after a desperate leap from a second-story window in Washington, D.C., to evade would-be captors.

From the 1820s onward, the advent of steam-powered presses made it possible to print thousands of copies of images per hour, and abolitionists seized on these new ways to disturb and arouse the public by providing "The Picture of Slavery," an 1838 anti-slavery treatise by George Bourne. By the mid-1830s, groups like the American Anti-Slavery Society published monthly magazines with an image on the cover of each issue showing the evils of slavery in uncompromising terms. Planters or overseers, whip in hand, beat or threatened cowering slaves. Black women often appeared at the moment of being sold, with would-be buyers staring boldly at them. While such images rarely directly suggested the possibility of enslaved women's sexual exploitation, literature that accompanied the images often steered readers to interpret what they saw in that way. Spouses being parted at sale, or most dramatically, mothers grieving over children about to be sold away, made strong emotional appeals against the supposed legitimacy of the "peculiar institution."

Many of these images were produced with children in mind: the American Anti-Slavery Society's "The Slave's Friend," also a monthly, emphasized the cruelties of life for slave children, along with images of kneeling, chained slaves, praying for freedom. Abolitionist images appeared in settings familiar for children, such as rhyming alphabets. "A" could be for abolitionist as well as apple, "S" for slave, and the like.

Images aimed more exclusively at adults frequently drew attention to the incongruity of slavery's existence in America, the fabled land of liberty. Such images could be as simple as a clanging bell, with the Liberty Bell caption, "Proclaim liberty throughout the land," as an eye-catching lead-in to an abolitionist tract. Or they could be far more elaborate. An 1836 broadside entitled "Slave Market of America" drove home this point with nine images calling attention to the prominence of slavery in the District of Columbia. Attentive viewers would learn that slaves were held for sale in jails and sold at auctions within sight of the Capitol. Other images showed slaves erecting public buildings or toiling in a shipyard, illustrating that public funds paid for such slave labor.

By the mid-1830s, abolitionism had become highly controversial, characterized by its opponents as incendiary in nature and threatening to the continuance of the Union. Opposition to abolition sometimes turned violent, and images of such incidents, depicted from an abolitionist vantage point, soon appeared. For example, in 1835, citizens of Charleston, South Carolina, broke into the city's post office to seize and destroy a mass mailing of abolitionist tracts. These Southerners saw themselves as exercising their liberties to preserve life and property from a potential abolitionist-inspired slave insurrection. But a Boston-produced lithograph, labeled "Attack on the Post Office, Charleston, S.C.," showed a mob action, with shadowy figures setting fire to the building and burning the mails. For abolitionists, such images underlined slavery's central reliance on sinful violence. An image carrying the same charge responded to mob actions that destroyed schools for children of color. In "Colored Schools Broken Up, In the Free States," an 1840 woodcut from New York, white assailants hurl paving stones and firebrands at a one-room school, while two terrified black girls flee from the school's side door. When antiabolitionists burned a public auditorium in Philadelphia in 1838 to protest a scheduled meeting of abolitionists, images of unruly rioters soon appeared, with ironic captions that labeled the rioters, rather than the abolitionists, as the real "incendiaries." Abolitionists also rebutted accusations that they sensationalized or misrepresented slavery by reprinting Southern-produced images and reinterpreting them. An image of a slave on an **auction block**, with auctioneer and bidders eyeing him, accompanied by a text denouncing the domestic slave trade could make an abolitionist's point. So, too, could the reproduction of slave sale or **runaway slave advertisements**.

In the 1840s and 1850s, increasing numbers of black people who had escaped from slavery published autobiographies that related their sufferings as slaves, their escapes, and their lives in freedom in the North or in Canada. These **slave narratives** often included powerful illustrations to accompany the story. The images in these books of life in slavery generally conformed to abolitionist themes: slaveholders whip defenseless slaves; families are sold apart; fugitives are shot or attacked by bloodhounds.

But the images in the narratives become more distinctive. Some escapees are shown using force to defend themselves, defy their pursuers, and make good on a bid for freedom. A companion set of images compared life in slavery with life in freedom. An illustration in Henry Bibb's 1849 narrative, entitled simply "Slave State Free State," shows a black man, in the act of shedding his chains, flanked by a slaveholder, in white suit and planter's hat, and a Northern gentleman in frock coat and top hat. The slaveholder's expression suggests anger and frustration at losing valuable property. The Northern man, helping the ex-slave out of one of his fetters, is kindly. Most striking is the black man, who strides purposefully away from the planter and toward freedom. His look is one of resolution, and he thrusts his left hand in the air, pointing skyward. Such portrayals of black independence, self-assertion, and resolution are less common than those of slaves as victims. Henry "Box" Brown (1815–ca. 1870), who escaped from slavery by shipping himself to Philadelphia in a packing crate in 1849, illustrated his resolve with a picture of the "box," carefully specifying its small proportions.

Abolitionist imagery generally shied away from any suggestion of black capability for masculine aggression, with most of the exceptions picturing acts of self-defense. In so doing, abolitionists may have patronized and stereotyped black people as docile or passive. But the abolitionists' selective portrayals of black capabilities also reflect their awareness that a substantial majority of the audience for these images were women, whose concerns centered on family and home, and who might have been repulsed by images of aggressive or assertive black people.

White-produced images of black life were thus incomplete or one-sided. African Americans generated almost no print images recording their perceptions; even the images in the slave narratives were strongly influenced by white publishers. Nonetheless, free African Americans offered their testimony on life in slavery and freedom in a number of ways, including public celebrations of events linked to emancipation. In parades, public meetings, prayer gatherings, and festive outings of all kinds, free people of color created performative images of the meanings of slavery and freedom.

In 1808, the United States outlawed the importation of slaves. In that same year, black groups in Boston, Philadelphia, and New York held ceremonies to commemorate the abolition of the Atlantic slave trade, and these ceremonies would continue for decades. Often held in African American **churches**, the central event might be a sermon or public oration asking the audience to participate in a public thanksgiving to God for the end of the trade. Hymns might be sung, and the agenda might include the public reading of the legislation ending the trade. Speakers might dwell on black accomplishment, for example, contributions to the success of the American Revolution. The prevailing mood was that of sober respectability, temperance, and humility.

By the 1820s, slave trade abolition commemorations began to fade away. In 1827, the ending of slavery in New York generated public celebrations that included parades, public addresses, and picnics. But this local phenomenon was soon subsumed under August 1 Freedom Day celebrations, events that marked the final end of slavery in the British West Indies in 1838. More than 150 such celebrations in more than 50 towns were generally accepted by white people as peaceful and appropriate ways of honoring black emancipation.

These Freedom Day celebrations gradually shifted away from their strong emphasis on middle-class sobriety and respectability. Some events involved steamboat or railroad excursions to picnic grounds where bells were rung, people shot off guns, and couples danced to band music. Parades featured grand marshals in military attire, with marching groups, such as black Masons, Odd Fellows, and Toussaint L'Ouverture Clubs. These celebrations offered images of black people as Americans exercising their rights of public assembly and staking a claim to public attention and space. Abolitionist newspapers published accounts as well as images of these celebrations to show the potential for blacks and whites to live together in freedom.

These celebrations of British abolition and West Indian freedom gave way in the 1860s to celebrations of American emancipation, beginning with the abolition of slavery in the District of Columbia on April 16, 1862, expanding with the issuance of the **Emancipation Proclamation** on January 1, 1863, and culminating with commemorations of the enactment of the Thirteenth Amendment abolishing slavery in 1865. The war years also witnessed the publication of thousands of sketches and photographs of slaves escaping to freedom and black men taking up arms for the Union. These illustrations of black agency and courage helped generate support for creating African American regiments that, in turn, helped win the Civil War.

One final category of abolitionist images appeared after slavery's end, in accounts of the **Underground Railroad**. William Still's mammoth account of the deeds of more than 800 escapees was filled with dynamic images of black people. These images included "Box" Brown emerging from his packing crate, with Still as one of the unpackers. Other images depicted fistfights and shootouts with slavecatchers, including the shooting and killing of William Gorsuch, a Maryland slaveholder killed in pursuit of his "property" at the Christiana Troubles of 1851. Still matched these images with portraits of noted black freedom fighters, ranging from Frederick Douglass (ca. 1818–1895) to the poet and abolitionist lecturer Frances Ellen Watkins Harper (1825–1911). The people in these portraits bristle with intelligence, resolve, and self-respect. Only after slavery's end could all the themes of abolitionist imagery be drawn together.

FURTHER READING

"Documenting the American South: First Person Narratives of the American South." University Library, University of North Carolina at Chapel Hill. At http://docsouth.unc.edu/fpn/.

Jeffrey, Julie Roy. *The Great Silent Army of Abolitionism: Ordinary Women in the Antislavery Movement.* Chapel Hill: University of North Carolina Press, 1998.

Kachun, Mitch. *Festivals of Freedom: Memory and Meaning in African American Emancipation Celebrations, 1808–1915.* Amherst: University of Massachusetts Press, 2003.

Lapsansky, Philip. "Graphic Discord: Abolitionist and Antiabolitionist Images." In *The Abolitionist Sisterhood: Women's Political Culture in Antebellum America*, edited by Jean Fagin Yellin and John C. Van Horne, 201–230. Ithaca, NY: Cornell University Press, 1994.

Margolin, Sam. "'And Freedom to the Slave': Anti-Slavery Ceramics, 1787–1865." In *Ceramics in America 2002*, edited by Robert Hunter, 80–109. Milwaukee, WI: Chipstone Foundation, 2002.

Still, William. *The Underground Railroad.* Philadelphia: Porter & Coates, 1872.

T. Stephen Whitman

ACCORDIONS. The accordion was invented in 1829 in Austria. Initially, competing German and French designs were marketed as parlor instruments on which to perform the popular songs of the day. However, the sudden popularity of the minstrel show, which coincided with the flood of less expensive higher quality instruments, made the accordion an enormously popular instrument in the United States between 1840 and the end of slavery in 1865. Touring across the United States, accordion soloists such as Moody G. Stanwood of the Ethiopian Serenaders nightly demonstrated the instrument's unique combination of volume, durability, and built-in accompaniment. According to one Southern newspaper, the songs they played were those that could be played by everybody "on organs, pianos, **fiddles, banjos, flutes,** accordeons [*sic*], and **guitars**."

The accordion was the first portable manufactured musical instrument targeted to the American masses. It was sold in general stores and at hardware counters in small towns. As accordions spread across the country, they found their way into the hands of slaves, but unlike the other instruments associated with slave society such as the fiddle, banjo, and quills, the technology was not available to make a homemade version of the accordion. In some cases, slaveholding whites played the instrument in the company of enslaved African Americans, as in the case of a Copiah County, Mississippi, mistress who a former slave reported as having played as "good as a man" on the accordion, or the white family of spar cutters who were described as playing dances with the violin and the accordion surrounded by "negroes of all ages." Mary Johnson, interviewed by the Federal Writers' Project in Texas but apparently born on the Mississippi plantation of Florence Walker, recalled a band of musicians on the accordion and fiddle who played waltzes and minuets for white dances. She implied that these were black musicians who also performed for black "frolics." As exclusively store-bought instruments, the accordions used by slaves demonstrate the sophisticated level of economic interplay between freeman and slave.

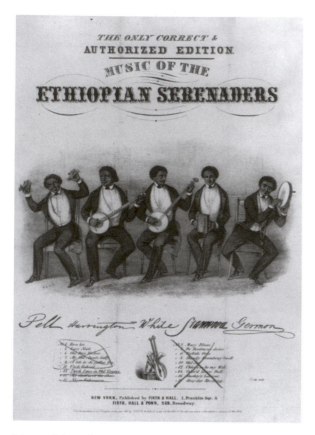

Music of the Ethiopian Serenaders. Music cover, ca. 1847, showing Pell playing bones, Harrington and White playing banjos, Stanwood playing accordion, and Germon playing tambourine. (Library of Congress.)

It was a common tactic of slaveholders to encourage music and dancing as a means of slave management. This extended to the purchase of instruments and, in some cases, lessons or tutoring. The dominant instrument for dance accompaniment in America was the fiddle, but a substantial portion of both black and white Christian society saw it as the instrument of the devil. The accordion, which had no antecedents in the cultures of Europe or Africa, carried none of the cultural stigmas Christianity associated with the fiddle. Early accordion manufactures emblazoned the title "lap organ" next to the brand name, promulgating the idea of the instrument's secular quality.

A surviving portrait in a photographic folio attributed to the Virginia estate of Gen. Robert E. Lee includes a portrait of a formally dressed slave playing a German-style accordion. These accordions were of a simple pine construction that was both hardy and durable. The basic design had ten buttons that each sounded a different note on the diatonic scale (that is, the white keys of the piano) depending on the direction of the bellows. Each note could be sounded by up to four reeds simultaneously, which produced a volume that had no rival short of brass instruments. The hand positions of the man in the Lee photograph are not posed; he clearly knows how to play it. Former slave Abner Griffin from Gold Mines, Georgia, played banjo, fiddle, and accordion at the dances in the area. In neighboring Willington, South Carolina, musician Aaron Washington (1911–unknown) described hearing groups of old people who played "fiddles, banjos, guitars, and accordions." Bessie Jones (1902–1984) recalled that her grandfather played the accordion at frolics in Dawson, Georgia. These were dances with a caller accompanied by accordions and banjos.

A daguerreotype taken in New Orleans in the early 1850s depicts a well-dressed black man playing a French accordion. French accordions were finely crafted with limited volume, a chromatic scale, and a limited accompaniment on the left-hand side of the bellows. In New Orleans, the French accordion, often called the "flutina," continued to be played after the Civil War and several Creole musicians associated with early New Orleans jazz such as Albert Glenny (1870–1958) received musical instruction on it. Early printed songbooks and tutors for French accordion are illustrated with images of young women seated in parlors entertaining friends and family on the accordion. In a portrait commissioned from artist Lilly Martin Spencer (1822–1902) by a plantation family, the child subject appears in a lush outdoor setting where she is entertained by her black nursemaid on a French accordion. A different type of image is found in the wartime (1864) photograph by Mathew Brady (1822–1896) that shows a black man who proudly cradles his French accordion outside a Union barracks in Beaufort, South Carolina.

The distribution of accordions across the slave population is only partially documented in the Works Progress Administration's Federal Writers' Project ex-slave narratives. In a survey of the 504 references to musical instruments in the accounts, only six references were made to the accordion in Louisiana and Mississippi. In Mississippi, these references are clustered in Simpson County, a rural south central Mississippi county with a white population of 3,380 in 1840. Two former slaves, Sylvia Floyd and Wash Hayes, recalled that they attended frolics at which dancers performed squares and sets to the rhythmic instructions of a caller and a band that was composed of accordion, banjo, and fiddle. Jim Brewer, a 20th-century musician from southern Mississippi whose father and uncles played accordions for dances, called the tunes that were played "flang-dang" tunes. The tradition of black accordion playing in Mississippi would survive into the 20th century.

The remaining accordion references in the ex-slave narratives originate from either Louisiana or Texas accounts. At the Forster plantation in Franklin, Louisiana, Virginia Newman, a free-born black woman, recalled the quadrilles danced by the slaves that were led by the accordion. Ex-slave Adeline White in Opelousas, Louisiana, attended big dances at which the band consisted of two violins and an accordion while dancers followed the caller. Leo Mouton from the Pitt Jones plantation in Lake Charles, Louisiana, played accordion with a string bass player and they performed tunes like "Kitty Wells" and "Run, Nigger, Run." Originally from a Baton Rouge parish plantation, Fred Brown heard a combination of banjo and accordion played there.

Slaves commonly called accordions "jammers" and several accounts refer to this. Chris Franklin, born in Caddo Parish in the far northwest corner of Louisiana, danced to the "windjammer," banjo, and fiddle. Caddo Parish resident and well-known musician, Huddie "Lead Belly" Ledbetter (1889–1949) also called his accordion a "windjammer." He played his jammer at local dances or "sukey jumps." From his mother, Lead Belly learned the jig "Diana Got a Wooden Leg," a tune that fiddle and accordion players opened with at the slave dances that Mary Kindred attended in Jasper, Texas. John Sheed also heard the fiddle and accordion played on the Sheed plantation outside of Austin, Texas.

Both enslaved and free black musicians saw the potential of this European invention, which they pulled from the hands of the minstrel musician and made into an expression of black culture. Black musicians heard a potential in the accordion that was hidden to its designers and builders. They transformed that potential into a living, breathing style.

FURTHER READING

Epstein, Dana J. *Sinful Tunes and Spirituals: Black Folk Music before the Civil War.* Urbana: University of Illinois Press, 1977.

Rawick, George, ed. *The American Slave: A Composite Autobiography.* Westport, CT: Greenwood Press, 1972–1979.

Snyder, Jared. "Breeze in the Carolinas: The African American Accordionists of the Upper South." *The Free Reed Journal* III (Fall 2001): 17–45.

Snyder, Jared. "Leadbelly and His Windjammer: Examining the African American Button Accordion Tradition." *American Music* 12, no. 2 (Summer 1994): 148–166.

Snyder, Jared. "Squeezebox: The Legacy of the Afro-Mississippi Accordionists." *The Journal of Black Music Research* (Spring 1997): 37–58.

Winans, Robert B. "Black Instrumental Music Traditions in the Ex-Slave Narratives." *Black Music Research Newsletter* 5, no. 22 (Spring 1982): 2–5.

JARED SNYDER

AFRICAN FREE SCHOOL. The African Free School (AFS) was established by the New York Manumission Society on November 2, 1787, to provide education to slave children and black freemen and prepare them for citizenship. The AFS was a direct descendant of the first slave school in New York City, which offered religious instruction and was operated by Huguenot refugee Elias Neau. Neau ran the school between 1704 and 1722, under sponsorship by the Society for the Propagation of the Gospel, the missionary branch of the Anglican Church in the American colonies.

By the school's founding, after the American Revolution and the birth of the abolitionist movement, many slaveholders already had emancipated their slaves and thought they needed to help them sustain themselves as free people. Established in 1785, the New York Manumission Society actively campaigned for a state law that gradually would abolish slavery in New York State. Its members included famous patriots like James Duane, George Clinton, John Jay, and Alexander Hamilton as well as representatives of the political and economic elite, merchants, bankers, lawyers, and other professionals. Some Quakers, like John Murray Jr. (1758–1819), who financed and founded the AFS, also joined the society and influenced it with their concern for education, moral behavior, and abolition. In 1799, the society managed to have the State Assembly of New York pass the Act for the Gradual Abolition of Slavery, which declared that all children born to slave parents would be free from July 4, 1799, forward. It also outlawed the exportation of slaves out of New York State. The act also stipulated that the children would be required to serve their mother's owner as indentured servants or apprentices until age 28 for males, and age 25 for females. For this reason, the last slaves in the state of New York were not emancipated until July 4, 1827.

Sampler by Mary Ann Cooper, student at an African Free School, possibly New York, February 16, 1841, wool and silk embroidery threads on a linen ground. (The Colonial Williamsburg Foundation.)

The AFS opened in 1787 with 12 students and a white schoolteacher, Cornelius Davis, in a schoolhouse on Cliff Street, near South Street Seaport, and within one year, the school had expanded to 60 students, all free blacks. By 1789, the institution started to admit slave children with the permission of their holders. In 1791, a separate school for girls was opened and conducted first by Davis's wife and then by Abigail Nichols. Because the school was financed by private funds, the society experienced some difficulties in providing a regular wage to its teachers. In 1797, school trustees replaced Davis with William Pirsson, a bookseller, and appointed John Teasman, a free black man, as assistant teacher or usher and later as principal of the school. Born a slave, Teasman was a role model for pupils and parents but, at the same time, whites easily accepted him because of his light **skin**. To supplement their salaries, Pirsson and Teasman instituted an African Evening School for adults in 1801, teaching 36 males and 8 females. In 1809, Teasman was dismissed as head teacher and replaced by Charles C. Andrews, who served until 1831. In the 1810s and 1820s, the school knew real success thanks to an 1810 statute that required slaveholders to teach their enslaved children how to read the Bible. A new building was opened on William Street to house African Free School No. 2, which was financed by New York Manumission Society members. Its enrollment grew to 900 students in 1823, which represented more than half of the city's black youths. By 1832, four more schools had opened to accommodate more than 1,439 students. Many African American children were prevented from going to school because they had to work during the day or could not dress properly. Particularly in the AFS's later years, children were not sent by their parents, who were increasingly involved in conflicts with the school's white administrators.

At the AFS, free and enslaved black children were taught reading, writing, grammar, computation, penmanship, drawing, poetry, arithmetic, and geography. The boys also studied sciences like astronomy that promoted navigational skills: they learned how to read longitude, latitude, and the sun's declination, for many black youths aspired to become seamen. The girls learned domestic skills like **sewing**, knitting, embroidery, quilting, and dressmaking. From 1809 on, the schools employed the Lancasterian system of education (also called the Monitorial System), a movement led by Joseph Lancaster (1778–1838), in which more advanced students taught less advanced ones. The method enabled a small number of adult masters to educate large numbers of students in basic and often advanced skills at low cost. The pupils were also taught public speaking. Indeed, many AFS students went on to become well-known and influential community leaders, entering into careers in medicine, the clergy, scholarship, abolitionism, theater, and business. For instance, James McCune Smith (1813–1865) was the first African American to be licensed as a physician; Henry Highland Garnet was a prominent abolitionist and the first black man to address Congress; Alexander Crummell (1819–1898) was a pioneering minister, professor, and black nationalist; and Ira Aldridge (1805–1867) was the most famous black actor of his day, appearing mainly on the London stage.

Because the school was run by the New York Manumission Society, students were encouraged to speak out for freedom, justice, and equality for their race. They were taught lessons in morals and manners, as it was part of the Society's stated goal to improve the moral behavior of blacks to help them integrate into society. The curriculum aimed at eliminating the vices children supposedly inherited from their slave parents because of a lack of proper education. To control moral behavior, the Manumission Society sent trustees to visit each applicant's family to assess their sobriety, honesty, and orderly living before children could be accepted to the school. In 1788, the Manumission Society established a Committee for Preventing Irregular Conduct in Free Negroes, which could not be maintained because of the lack of staff. The AFS aspired to prove to skeptical and prejudiced New Yorkers that black students were equal to whites in intellect if given equal opportunities. It thus regularly opened its doors to visitors so that students could proudly show off their accomplishments to outsiders.

Before the 1799 "Act for Gradual Emancipation" was passed, African Americans had to cope with the New York Manumission Society's paternalistic attitude. The school appeared to be the only path to better economic conditions for their children, and these families considered education as a means of personal elevation. Blacks were disappointed by the American Revolution's outcome and maintenance of slavery in the Constitution, so in the North, they became very active in the abolitionist movement. Yet, the Manumission Society's emphasis on reforming blacks' moral behavior alienated many blacks and did little to reduce prejudice in society as a whole. By the early 19th century, new independent institutions founded by blacks began to emerge. The African Methodist Episcopal Zion Church opened two schools for blacks that were in direct competition with the AFS. Founded in 1808, the African Society for Mutual Relief was organized by Teasman and many former AFS students. These institutions proudly bore the name "African" in their title to emphasize their African ancestry. Nevertheless, pride in their identity did not mean that they wished to return to Africa. Indeed, in the 1820s, many AFS students expressed their discontent with the growing colonization movement, which promoted the resettlement of blacks in Africa. Advocates of colonization claimed that free blacks could never live together peacefully with whites in the United States. In 1832, 150 black students left the school in protest against the movement, and Charles Andrews, the school's principal and an active proponent of colonization, was forced to resign. Blacks had by then recognized the political role of education for their community, and they had achieved enough cohesion to be able to handle their schools in administration and curriculum policies. The Manumission Society no longer offered education to free blacks, and by 1834, the AFS became part of the New York public school system. That year, more than 1,400 students were taught in the seven school buildings around the city. The AFS remains the most famous early school for blacks in the nation.

FURTHER READING

Andrews, Charles C. *The History of the New-York African Free Schools from Their Establishment in 1787 to the Present Time, Embracing a Period of More Than Forty Years: Also a Brief Account of the Successful Labors of the New-York Manumission Society: With an Appendix.* New York: M. Day, 1830.

Gellman, David Nathaniel. *Emancipating New York: The Politics of Slavery and Freedom, 1777–1827.* Baton Rouge: Louisiana State University Press, 2006.

Hodges, Graham Russell. *Root & Branch: African-Americans in New York & East Jersey, 1613–1863.* Chapel Hill: University of North Carolina Press, 1999.

Jones-Wilson, Faustine C. *Encyclopedia of African-American Education.* Westport, CT: Greenwood Press, 1996.

Swan, Robert J. "John Teasman: African-American Educator and the Emergence of Community in Early Black New York City, 1787–1815." *Journal of the Early Republic* 12, no. 3 (Autumn 1992): 331–356.

Woodson, Carter Godwin. *The Education of the Negro Prior to 1861.* New York: Arno Press, 1968.

ANNE-CLAIRE FAUCQUEZ

ANIMAL TRAPS. Several lines of evidence suggest that enslaved blacks used a variety of handmade traps and possibly steel traps to procure wild game for meat and pelts. Trapping is a specialized means of hunting that does not require the presence of the hunter. Trapping was suited to slave schedules because the traps worked while the slaves were toiling elsewhere. Traps could be checked in the early morning or evening. Unlike rifles and shotguns, traps were not perceived as a possible threat to the planters.

Traditional traps—snares, deadfalls, gums, and eel/fish pots—are known in many West African cultures. In addition, Indians of the southeastern United States—many of whom were enslaved with blacks—had a well-developed trapping technology.

Snares are fiber or wire loops that generally ensnared an animal around its neck, and were used for capturing everything from weasels to white-tailed deer. Deadfalls rely on a heavy object falling on the animal, thereby breaking its neck or back. Gums are hollow sections of gum tree trunk, with an end piece and a trip stick to live-capture rabbits, opossums, or raccoons. Eel pots and fish **baskets** are woven devices with baffles that capture the prey once they are baited into the interior of the device. Traditional traps generally were made of wood and fiber and did not survive well archaeologically. Surviving slave decorative arts show a high level of woodcarving skill, and such carvers would have had no problem making traditional traps. Recent research suggests that traditional traps were often as productive as steel traps.

Steel traps also may have been used by slaves. The steel, leg-hold trap was not mass produced until 1832 and remained somewhat expensive through the time of emancipation. The leg-hold trap is used in established trails or in conjunction with bait; when the prey steps on the trap, steel springs close the jaws on the leg of the prey. Certain slaves, including Harriet Tubman as a young girl, were required to set and check steel traps for their masters.

When archaeological remains recovered from slave contexts include species that are difficult to hunt because they are nocturnal or aquatic, the evidence suggests that traps were used. For example, raccoon and opossum are commonly represented in slave faunal assemblages (animal bones and other remains), yet it is unlikely that slaves had the hounds, **firearms**, and freedom to roam that are necessary for the hunting of these species. Likewise, hunting skunks can be an unpleasant experience, but skunks can be captured without spraying in deadfalls or snares.

Oral history suggests that slaves were skilled trappers. Fish traps are mentioned as one of the products of the Sea Island basket makers. The rabbit gum is mentioned in the Br'er Rabbit stories, which derive from the slave tales of the Gullah/Geechee. The oral history of Moor communities in Delaware, where blacks and Indians formed multiracial populations, indicates that trapping was an important part of subsistence, that pelts provided a valuable source of cash income, and that traditional traps were used into the 20th century.

See also Faunal Remains.

FURTHER READING

Espenshade, Christopher T. "Trapping: The Forgotten Provider." *Bulletin of Primitive Technology* 30 (2005): 36–42.
Speck, F. G. *Catawba Hunting, Trapping, and Fishing.* Joint Publications. Museum of the University of Pennsylvania and the Philadelphia Anthropological Society No. 2. Philadelphia: University Museum, 1946.
Speck, F. G., R. B. Hassrick, and E. S. Carpenter. *Rappahannock Taking Devices: Traps, Hunting, and Fishing.* Joint Publications, Museum of the University of Pennsylvania and the Philadelphia Anthropological Society No. 1. Philadelphia: University Museums, 1946.

CHRISTOPHER T. ESPENSHADE

ARMORIES. An armory is any building dedicated to the housing of weapons, especially **firearms**. From the colonial period through the Civil War, armories commonly held the weapons for state and local militias. The term "armory" was sometimes used interchangeably with "magazine," which refers specifically to a building or structure that houses a store of gunpowder. Armory may also refer to an "arsenal," which is a facility for the production, repair, and storage of firearms. Armories played an important role in the maintenance of the institution of slavery, and thus became a target for slave revolts as well as a factor in political controversies concerning slavery.

The architectural design of armories varied greatly. They could be freestanding structures or a part of larger buildings like town halls, forts, or batteries. Although some were merely timber, the best armories were made of brick or stone to provide security and carefully sealed to prevent unwanted moisture. The interiors typically included large gun racks for various firearms, most commonly muskets or rifles. Along with the storage of firearms, armories often held large powder stores that could spoil if they became wet. Armories' valuable contents were usually subject to around-the-clock guards and were secured with heavy **locks** to prevent the seizure of weapons.

Armories took on particular importance in slaveholding colonies and states because they often were the central weapons cache for militias charged with policing slaves. Along with providing the necessary equipment to repel a Native American raid or a foreign invasion, the weapons in armories also provided communities with the arms needed to carry out slave patrols or slave-catching raids, as well as the means to put down a full-scale slave rebellion. Militia armories were sometimes used by slave patrol members, especially in cases in which citizens were exempted from required militia service in exchange for patrol work. One reason often given for such patrols was to search traveling slaves for firearms and seize the guns if necessary. For these reasons, the maintenance and control of armories often figured prominently in the minds of both slaveholders and potential slave conspirators.

Armories were important structures in many Southern colonial communities. The powder magazine in Charleston, South Carolina, provides a useful example. A smaller brick building with thick walls to keep out moisture, the 1713 structure had a cleverly vaulted roof designed to collapse inward in the event of an accidental explosion, thus preventing the spread of any fire. The Charleston magazine was situated along one of the town's central avenues to provide access in the event it was necessary to transport powder from the magazine to cannon along the city walls.

Molding Iron

Emanuel Elmore's father worked in the Cherokee Iron Works in South Carolina:

I used to go and watch my father work. He was a moulder in the Cherokee Iron Works, way back there when everything was done by hand. He moulded everything from knives and forks to skillets and wash pots. If you could have seen Pa's hammer, you would have seen something worth looking at. It was so big that it jarred the whole earth when it struck a lick. Of course it was a forge hammer, driven by water power. They called the hammer "Big Henry." The butt end was as big as an ordinary telephone pole.

The water wheel had fifteen or twenty spokes in it, but when it was running it looked like it was solid. I used to like to sit and watch that old wheel. The water ran over it and the more water came over, the more power the wheel gave out.

At the Iron Works they made everything by hand that was used in a hardware store, like nails, horse shoes and rims for all kinds of wheels, like wagon and buggy wheels. There were moulds for everything no matter how large or small the thing to be made was. Pa could almost pick up the right mould in the dark, he was so used to doing it. The patterns for the pots and kettles of different sizes were all in rows, each row being a different size. In my mind I can still see them.

Hot molten iron from the vats was dipped with spoons which were handled by two men. Both spoons had long handles, with a man at each handle. The spoons would hold from four to five gallons of hot iron that poured just like water does. As quick as the men poured the hot iron in the mould, another man came along behind them and closed the mould. The large moulds had doors and the small moulds had lids. They had small pans and small spoons for little things, like nails, knives and forks. When the mould had set until cold, the piece was prized out.

Pa had a turn for making covered skillets and fire dogs. He made them so pretty that white ladies would come and give an order for a "pair of dogs," and tell him how they wanted them to look. He would take his hammer and beat them to look just that way.

Rollers pressed out the hot iron for machines and for special lengths and things that had to be flat. Railroad ties were pressed out in these rollers. Once the man that handled the hot iron to be pressed through these rollers got fastened in them himself. He was a big man. The blood flew out of him as his bones were crushed, and he was rolled into a mass about the thickness and width of my hand. Each roller weighed about 2,000 pounds.

Source: George P. Rawick, ed. *The American Slave: South Carolina Narratives*, Vol. 2. Westport, CT: Greenwood Press, 1972.

Another surviving example of a colonial armory is the magazine at Williamsburg, Virginia. This building was also centrally located, about halfway between the College of William and Mary and the colonial capitol at opposite ends of the Duke of Gloucester Street. Although there are earlier references to magazines in the town, the surviving structure was built in 1715, the year after the Virginia General Assembly had voted for the construction to house a gift of powder and muskets given to the colony by England's Queen Anne. Virginia's governor Alexander Spotswood personally designed the magazine with an octagonal shape, stretched to two stories high, and capped with a peaked roof. The magazine walls were red brick, again of considerable thickness, but designers added a few refinements, including relatively elegant arched windows on the top level. The structure was financed in part using taxes on imported slaves. In addition to firearms, the magazine also held the militia's stores of **military equipment**, as well as other weapons like swords and pikes. The building became a major center for arms and powder storage during the Seven Years' War (1756–1763), and so a wall was added around the perimeter to protect the magazine's valuable contents. By the time of the American Revolution, the magazine could hold as much as 60,000 pounds of gunpowder.

The Williamsburg magazine played a significant role in a slave controversy that drove many Southern colonists closer to rebellion against Great Britain. In April of 1775, afraid that the magazine's sizeable holdings might fall into the hands of American rebels, Virginia Lt. Gov. John Murray, the Earl of Dunmore, ordered agents to quietly empty the armory. Many local colonial leaders were outraged, including those who believed the powder's removal had made them more susceptible to a slave rebellion. In the following weeks, locals spurred on by leaders like Patrick Henry organized a mob that drove Governor Dunmore from office in Williamsburg.

Armories figured prominently in a number of major American slave rebellions. Slaves in the 1739 South Carolina Stono Rebellion seized guns from a small rural armory to begin their revolt. Gabriel Prosser (1776–1800) planned a similar tactic during his revolt in 1800, but the plot was discovered before his men could seize the Richmond, Virginia, armory. A few decades later, the free black Denmark Vesey (ca. 1767–1822) planned a slave revolt that also targeted a state armory in South Carolina. When the Virginia slave Nat Turner (1800–1831) led his rebellion in 1831, he and his men set out to seize firearms from the armory in nearby Jerusalem but ultimately were put down by the militia.

The most famous attempt to take an armory occurred during abolitionist John Brown's raid on Harpers Ferry in 1859. Harpers Ferry was properly a federal arsenal, one of two in the United States along with that in Springfield, Massachusetts. The two armories were charged with the production and storage of firearms for the U.S. armed forces. Brown targeted the arsenal at Harpers Ferry because of its huge cache of firearms, which included nearly 100,000 muskets and rifles. He hoped that when he and his party of white abolitionists, free blacks, and escaped slaves captured the arsenal, slaves from the surrounding counties would escape to join his effort, helping him to set off a chain of rebellions in the South, supported with the stolen arms.

The arsenal itself was a large complex of many buildings. It began modestly as a single structure operation in the 1790s but underwent a significant renovation in the 1840s and 1850s. Improvements included new workshops with brick walls over an iron framework and featuring sheet metal roofs, as well as the installation of additional turbines along an enlarged river canal to generate power. By that time the site included a variety of workshops, grinding and sawmills, warehouses, and separate offices. Nearly 400 workers labored on more than 100 machines by the time of Brown's raid. On October 16, 1859, despite armed resistance, Brown's party took the armory, but local townspeople surrounded his position the following day. Amid small skirmishes, Brown withdrew to a small fire-engine house after the town militia had taken the Potomac bridge that led to the arsenal, pinning Brown's party inside the complex. The engine house was a small brick building with a rectangular plan, with three large arches, each with large barn doors and flanking pane windows. Eventually, federal forces took the engine house and captured Brown as a prisoner. The structure later became known as "John Brown's Fort," hosted a memorial ordered by abolitionist Frederick Douglass, and was dismantled and shipped for exhibition at the 1893 Chicago World's Fair.

In some instances, slaves and free blacks made use of armories themselves when fighting as soldiers. Large numbers of African Americans fought in the Revolutionary War on both sides, particularly slaves who escaped to fight for the British in return for their freedom. In desperate circumstances, masters occasionally armed their own slaves to defend themselves and their property against the enemy. This practice was especially common in Spanish Florida where slaves were regularly armed in the event of foreign invasions, and free blacks, many of them escaped slaves from neighboring British colonies, served in the militia and regular army units. During the Civil War, some former slaves made use of armories first as illicit contributors and later as regular soldiers. Many of the rifles these soldiers used had been manufactured at the two federal arsenals.

See also Abolition Imagery.

FURTHER READING

Hadden, Sally. *Slave Patrols: Law and Violence in Virginia and the Carolinas.* Cambridge, MA: Harvard University Press, 2001.
Lenman, Bruce. "The Magazine at Colonial Williamsburg." *History Today* 44 (1993): 63–64.
"Magazine." Colonial Williamsburg. At www.history.org/Almanack/places/hb/hbmag.cfm.
Smith, Merrit Row. *Harpers Ferry Armory and New Technology.* Ithaca, NY: Cornell University Press, 1980.

JAMES COLTRAIN

AUCTION ADVERTISEMENTS. Although dependent on enslaved men, women, and children to work in their fields, houses, taverns, and shops, at times slaveholders had to sell either all or part of their labor force to raise money to pay their debts or the money owed by a deceased family member. When this occurred, many individuals then placed advertisements about the slave auction in a newspaper. Slaveholders posted information about sales on the walls of taverns or in other public spaces. Masters included details—such as a slave's age, gender, and skills—in the printed or handwritten notices to attract potential purchasers.

From the beginning of North American slavery in the 17th century to the 1865 passage of the Thirteenth Amendment, slaveholders sold their enslaved laborers if the proceeds from the sale would benefit the white family. The decision to sell a slave could indicate that a master did not require the individual's labor on a plantation, that the slave was a troublemaker, or that the master needed to raise money to pay off

Slave auction house in Atlanta, 1864. (Library of Congress.)

debts. The officials of a county court could step in and order a decedent's slaves to be sold to the highest bidder to have funds to repay that person's financial obligations.

Either an owner or members of a county court placed an announcement of the upcoming slave auction in the newspaper. Printed advertisements spread the news of the sale and to persuade people to attend the auction and to place high bids on the available slaves. The authors of the announcements began many of these notices with details about the place of the auction. Often, this information appeared in bold, italicized, or large text because the people who wrote the advertisements wanted to ensure that their readers knew the location of the auction, whether it was near a warehouse, on the steps of a **courthouse**, in front of a popular tavern, or at an individual's home. They also included the date and time of the public sale.

Next, the authors turned to information about the slaves to be sold. Potential purchasers might read about the number of male and female slaves to be auctioned, the ages of the enslaved laborers and their place of birth, the family connections that joined the slaves to one another, and the skills possessed by the available slaves. Many auction advertisements concluded with information about when those who placed the highest bids would be required to pay for the slave or slaves whom they purchased.

On the day of the auction, the auction master led enslaved men, women, boys, and girls to an elevated location. Few owners actually participated in the auction, although they, or a surrogate, were in attendance. It was easier for the bidders to see the slaves if they stood on a block or on the steps of a tavern, courthouse, or dwelling. Once the potential purchasers had a chance to look at a slave, the auction master asked the crowd to begin bidding on the individual. The highest bidder gained possession of the enslaved person. As the purchaser began to make arrangements to pay for the slave, the auction master started the bidding on the next person to be sold. The auction continued until each of the enslaved laborers was conveyed to a new owner or, if not sold, returned to the slaveholder.

Auctions were just one way in which a person could sell an enslaved laborer to another person. Some slaveholders decided to have a lottery to raise funds to cover their debts. These individuals divided their slaves into lots (groups) and used printed notices in newspapers to inform readers that they could buy a ticket for a specified price and what they might gain if their ticket was drawn on the day of the lottery. Those who announced lotteries wanted to encourage people to buy tickets. To do so, they included

"Miss Fillis and child, and Bill, sold at publick sale. . . ." From *Sketchbook of Landscapes in the State of Virginia* by Lewis Miller, Virginia, 1853–1867, watercolor and ink on paper. (Abby Aldrich Rockefeller Folk Art Museum, The Colonial Williamsburg Foundation. Gift of Dr. and Mrs. Richard M. Kain in memory of George Hay Kain.)

details about the date, time, and place of the drawing. Next, the slaveholders listed information about available slaves. These details included a slave's gender, age, skills, family connections, and value. The announcement concluded with a list of lottery managers, a group of individuals who collected money from those who purchased tickets and distributed the slaves to those whose tickets were drawn on the day of the lottery.

Whether sold at an auction or in a lottery, the slaves who were transferred to new owners were forced to leave their family members and friends and move to different plantations, sometimes very far away. By the third quarter of the 18th century, a number of planters in Tidewater Virginia and Maryland realized that they did not have enough work for their labor force. Many of the purchasers at auctions and lotteries were planters from the western part of these colonies, men who needed laborers.

After the end of the American Revolution, the transfer of slaves from the eastern portion of the country to the western and southern areas continued. The number of slaves forced to move from the Upper South to the Lower South increased dramatically after the invention of the **cotton** gin made cotton a highly profitable crop. Planters in the Lower South increased the number of laborers on their plantations so they could make more money from their cotton or **sugar** crops. During the 19th century, slave traders and agents moved hundreds of thousands of enslaved men, women, boys, and girls in the domestic (also called the "intrastate") slave trade.

Slave traders and agents read auction advertisements and announcements about lotteries to locate masters who wanted to sell some or all of their labor force. They attended auctions in Virginia and Maryland and bought lottery tickets to acquire enslaved laborers to sell to planters in the Lower South.

Having purchased slaves, the traders and agents moved these men, women, boys, and girls to slave markets in southern cities. Some traders shackled slaves together at their hands and feet before forcing them to walk hundreds of miles in groups called **coffles** to cities in Alabama, Mississippi, or Louisiana where they would be sold. Other traders compelled slaves to walk many miles before they loaded the enslaved people on flatboats that carried this cargo down one of the many rivers and streams that flowed into the Mississippi River. Once they reached the Mississippi, this river carried the slaves to New Orleans. Slave traders also chained men, women, and children before putting them on vessels in Baltimore, Richmond, Norfolk, or Charleston. Ship captains guided the boats southward on the Atlantic Ocean and docked in the harbors of cities in the Lower South.

Once a slave trader arrived at the appointed destination with a group of enslaved laborers, this individual placed a notice of the upcoming auction in the newspaper and posted announcements near the city's slave market. The authors of 19th-century auction advertisements included the same details that appeared in announcements from the colonial and early national periods. Slave traders began their notices with the date, time, and location of the auction. Often this information was in bold, italicized, or text to catch the reader's attention. Next, they turned to information about the enslaved laborers to attract people who would bid on the slaves. The traders included details about the number of available laborers as well as the quantity of men, women, and children to be auctioned. Additional information included the ages of the enslaved workers, the state where the slaves had lived and worked, and the skills possessed by the laborers.

On the day of the auction, the traders led men, women, boys, and girls from the pens in which they had been held and led them to the auction blocks. Whites gathered in the slave markets in New Orleans, Natchez, Charleston, Savannah, and other cities in the Lower South to bid on enslaved laborers. For a master, the auction was an opportunity to add to a labor force and raise the level of production on a plantation. Proceeds from the sale of a larger crop helped to increase the wealth of white families. For the slaves, the auction meant a transfer to a new owner and plantation where they might be forced to learn how to use different agricultural implements to tend a different crop and create a new life as enslaved blacks had done since the first slave auction in the 17th century.

FURTHER READING

"Auctions." Broadsides Collection, New York Public Library. At http://digitalgallery.nypl.org/nypldigital/dgkeysearchresult.cfm?word=Auctions&s=3&notword=&f=2.

Berlin, Ira. *Generations of Captivity: A History of African-American Slaves.* Cambridge, MA: Belknap Press of Harvard University Press, 2003.

"Enslavement—Sale." Toolbox Library, Primary Resources in U.S. History and Literature. At http://nationalhumanitiescenter.org/pds/maai/enslavement/text2/text2read.htm.

Franklin, John Hope, and Alfred A. Moss Jr. *From Slavery to Freedom: A History of African Americans.* 8th ed. New York: Alfred A. Knopf, 2003.

Handler, Jerome S., and Michael L. Tuite Jr., eds. "Slave Sales and Auctions: African Coast and the Americas." The Atlantic Slave Trade and Slave Life in the Americas: A Visual Record. At http://hitchcock.itc.virginia.edu/Slavery/index.php.

JULIE RICHTER

AUCTION BLOCKS. The auction block has become a modern symbol for black slavery in America and a metaphor for slavery and slave sales. A slave auction block traditionally was a raised platform used to display human chattel to be sold to the highest bidder. In the context of the American slavery system, auction blocks were commonly elevated spaces in auction houses or outside in town or city squares where enslaved human beings were made to stand to be visually evaluated from three sides by potential buyers during the bidding process. In the 1860s, one South Carolinian woman wrote of the slave auction block arrangement, "stand 'em up on a block three feet high."

Old slave block in St. Louis Hotel, New Orleans, ca. 1900. (Library of Congress.)

Potential buyers could also examine slaves for sale on the block before an auction commenced.

A wide variety of materials were used for making auction blocks, and many different objects were used for improvised auction blocks. Wood was the most common material. Many mid-19th-century slave auction illustrations show raised box-like structures that extended several feet in length and were narrower in depth and height and resembled small stages with a set of stairs to one side. The ubiquitous wooden platform appears in slave markets, store fronts, town squares, ports, hotels, and train depots. An auctioneer generally stood to one side of the platform. Historical accounts also refer to tree stumps, open wagons, and large stones or boulders being used as auction blocks. In rural areas, slave auction sites were arranged wherever suitable space was found, such as on a knoll on a plantation or farm. **Courthouses**, which were centrally located and accessible to slave traders and buyers, were often sites for slave auctions. Courthouse steps served as auction blocks. Notices of public auctions typically were posted in local newspapers, in local taverns, and on courthouse doors and walls.

During auctions, slaves stood in a variety of formations, sometimes in family groups, in lineups, or as individuals one by one, as an auctioneer chanted the bidding bridge. Enslaved persons were instructed to take particular postures while standing on the auction block. An ascending chant acknowledging higher and higher bids was shouted out by an auctioneer according to what buyers were willing to pay for a slave, or a

Eyewitness to an Auction

North Carolina slave W. L. Bost witnessed slaves sold on the auction block in Newton, North Carolina:

I remember when they put 'em on the block to sell 'em. The ones 'tween 18 and 30 always bring the most money. The auctioneer he stand off at a distance and cry 'em off as they stand on the block. I can hear his voice as long as I live.

If the one they going to sell was a young Negro man this is what he says: "Now gentleman and fellow-citizens here is a big black buck Negro. He's stout as a muls. Good for any kin' o'work an! he never gives any troubles. How much am I offered for him?" And then the sale would commence, and the nigger would be sold to the highest bidder.

If they put up a young nigger woman the auctioneer ery out, "Here's a young nigger wench, how much am I offered for her?" The pore thing stand on the block a shiverin' an' a shakin' nearly froze to death. When they sold many of the pore mothers beg the speculators to sell 'em with their husbands, but the speculator only take what he want. So meybe the pore thing never see her husban' agin.

Source: George P. Rawick, ed. *The American Slave: North Carolina Narratives,* Vol. 14. Westport, CT: Greenwood Press, 1972.

group of slaves, until no more bids were made. Sold and unsold slaves were led off the auction block to wait in a holding area until the sales were final and the sold slaves were then legally given to their new owners.

Selling slaves by auction became commonplace in the United States by the second half of the 18th century. Selling slaves from the auction block was a fast and efficient means for slaveholders and slave traders to collect cash and to circulate enslaved populations. By the middle of the 19th century, the largest slave markets with the highest concentration of auction blocks were likely to have been New Orleans, Louisiana; Natchez, Mississippi; Charleston, South Carolina; Richmond, Virginia; Baltimore, Maryland; St. Louis, Missouri; and Lexington, Kentucky.

See also Auction Advertisements; Slave Pens, Slave Jails, and Slave Markets.

FURTHER READING

Davis, Ronald, L. F. *The Black Experience in Natchez 1720–1880: A Special History.* Natchez, MS: Eastern National, 1994.

Johnson, Walter. *Soul by Soul: Life Inside the Antebellum Slave Market.* Cambridge, MA: Harvard University Press, 1999.

JULIA ROSE

B

BALAFONS. The balafon is a kind of xylophone developed by the Mandinka people of the western Sudan region. Metal xylophones probably originated in Indonesia, but evidence suggests that traders brought them to Africa as early as 1000 BCE. By the 14th century, the balafon played a central role in Mandinka musical culture. The Mandinka empire was the dominant empire in Mali, and although by the 16th century it had lost its superiority, its cultural and musical traditions had spread throughout many West African societies in Senegal, The Gambia, Guinea-Bissau, Guinea, Burkina Faso, Ghana, the Ivory Coast, Sierra Leone, and Mali. Many of these and other African societies created and developed their own style of xylophones over time.

In Mandinka vocabulary, *bala* means "wood," and *fo* means "to speak." In Africa, the instrument is most often called the balofou or balo (or bala); Europeans referred to it as the balafon. The frame generally was made of bamboo or wood, and its top featured a keyboard consisting of wooden or iron keys. Between the top and bottom of the frame were different sizes of **gourds**, scaled to produce particular sounds and ranges of octaves. The musician would strike the keys with sticks, and the sound resonated from the gourds. The balafon was a large and sophisticated instrument to make. Mandinka balafons most often had 19 keys, although some had as many as 22 and others as few as 17.

The balafon was, and still is, an instrument that spoke for the people. The instrument was played by elite professional musicians, known as "jail" or "jeli," who were the society's historians and praise singers. When they performed, either individually or in a group, their purpose was to offer praise for collective political events, funerals, marriages, or initiation rites, and in so doing, they were engaging in ceremonies and rituals essential for the society's self-renewal. The balafon retains its central place in musical culture particularly in Mali and Sierra Leone.

That slaves constructed and played balafons on plantations is a testament to how they retained African musical traditions even in servitude. In colonial and antebellum Virginia, balafons served as prime instruments in singing and dancing entertainments; American versions had between 15 and 19 keys. The vibraphone, an instrument developed in the United States in the early 20th century and central to jazz, also can be linked to the balafon.

See also Cemeteries.

FURTHER READING

Epstein, Dena J. *Sinful Tunes and Spirituals: Black Folk Music to the Civil War*. Urbana: University of Illinois Press, 1977.

Jessup, Lynne. *The Mandinka Balafon: An Introduction with Notation for Teaching*. La Mesa, CA: Xylo Publications, 1983.

LINDA E. MERIANS

BANJOS. The banjo is a stringed musical instrument of African origin. Its African forebearer was constructed of a round or oblong hollow body made from a **gourd** or calabash used as a resonating chamber. A skin, usually antelope hide, was stretched tightly across the gourd body, covering an opening similar to the body of a drum. The neck, often made from a wooden pole or sometimes a piece of bamboo, was attached to the body of the instrument. Gut strings made from animal intestines were then stretched between the gourd body and the neck. This instrument could have as many as three to five strings that were plucked with the fingers or strummed with one hand, depending on the cultural norms of the community. The other hand was used to dampen the strings up and down the neck to produce different individual or combined pitches. In some African American communities, the banjo included a wooden bridge to raise the strings whose vibrations produced the sound.

While the banjo can be played as a solo instrument, its greatest strength during the period of African enslavement was its value as an expression of cultural identity, community cohesion, and musical innovation. Its role in defining the slave experience is undeniable. Although accounts of blacks playing the **fiddle** come earlier, its use was not identified or mentioned in conjunction with the black community as often as the banjo. The banjo is among the very few instruments that can claim diasporic roots that began in Africa, moved to other colonies such as Martinique, Jamaica, and Barbados, and then appeared in enslaved communities in the American South.

Many communities claim kinship with the banjo, but its roots originate in the Senegambia of West Africa. Music historians trace the banjo's beginnings to West African lute and harp-like instruments, among them the ngoni (Wasulu), akonting (Jola), and xalam (Wolof). Each community added its unique interpretation and method of playing the instrument. The ngoni traditionally was played by the "jeli," a combination of musician and storyteller. The akonting comes from the Jola people near the Casamance river in Senegal, West Africa, and the syncopated, rhythmic, drum-inspired

"Banjar Player and Jig Dancer," [*sic*], ca. 1815. (© Blue Ridge Institute and Museum. Used by permission.)

traditions that have become part of folk banjo playing can be attributed, in part, to their traditions. The xalam has contributed a rich melodic tradition as well as vocal accompaniment. It was played by griots, or storytellers, at special occasions such as weddings and naming ceremonies.

As enslaved Africans arrived in the Caribbean, their traditions of banjo-like instruments came with them. There, it was known by various names: banza (Martinique), bangil (Jamaica), strum strum (Jamaica), bangelo (Sierra Leone), and banshaw (St. Kitts and Nevis).

Because of the constraints of slavery in the West Indies, the average life span of enslaved Africans averaged 6 to 10 years. Brought to these islands as captives, Africans worked in the many **sugar** plantations that existed on most of these islands. This constant importation of new Africans resulted in the slave communities of the Caribbean having a more consistent and direct connection to their native land. As a result, their cultural expressions, beliefs, and music were linked more closely to their "African" beginnings, and thus their musical retentions were connected more directly to African traditions and the specific cultures from which they came.

The Colonies

In 1749, slaveholder George Croghan advertised for the return of "a Negroe man, named Scipio, [who] is of short stature, plays on the Banjo, and can sing." Five years later, in July 1754, a **runaway slave advertisement** in the *Maryland Gazette* describes Prince, "a pert lively Fellow and plays well on the Banjer." Twenty years later, Nicholas Cresswell, a young Englishman who had come to America with the intention of settling there permanently, observed a banjo being played at a "Negro Ball" in Nanjemoy, Maryland, in 1774: "Mr. Bayley and I went to see a Negro Ball, Sundays being the only days these poor Creatures have to themselves, they generally meet together and amuse themselves with Dancing to the Banjor." Earlier that same year, in Virginia, Philip Vickers Fithian, the tutor to the children of Robert Carter of Nomini Hall, described an incident he witnessed involving the banjo: "This Evening in the School-Room, which is below my Chamber, several Negroes & Ben & Harry are playing on a Banjo & dancing!" Other documentary sources, including travelers' accounts, personal journals, and newspapers, all document the banjo as a principal musical instrument in the black community and a legitimate expression of secular black folk music of the period. Perhaps the best-known mention of the banjo during the 18th century is that made by Thomas Jefferson. In his *Notes on the State of Virginia*, published in 1781, he stated that "the instrument proper to them [the enslaved] is the banjar, which they brought hither from Africa, and which is the original of the guitar, its chords being precisely the four lower chords of the guitar." Jefferson, along with other colonial citizens, travelers, and observers of the period, firmly set the banjo, its cultural legitimacy, its construction, its style of playing, and its popularity squarely in the world of the enslaved community.

One of the best-known images of the 18th-century South is a watercolor entitled "The Old Plantation," found near Columbia, South Carolina. In its depiction of a group of presumably enslaved African Americans, it points to the centrality of the banjo as a representation of musical traditions brought from Africa that found expression in America. Finally, a banjo-like instrument was included in a painting by American artist

Samuel Jennings in 1792. The painting, *Liberty Displaying the Arts and Sciences, or The Genius of America Encouraging the Emancipation of the Blacks, 1792*, which was commissioned by the Library Company of Philadelphia as a symbol of the anti-slavery movement, is among the earliest artistic representations in support of the abolition of slavery. One of the scenes in the painting is of a black man standing on the shore playing a banjo with a black child at his side, and what could be interpreted as **slave ships** in the background. The musician seems to be playing music for a small group of blacks, some of whom appear to be dancing to its music. The banjo in the painting looks remarkably like a slightly modified akonting.

Although the banjo was primarily a solo instrument, documentary sources also note the pairing of the banjo and the fiddle at dances, both formal and informal, during harvest season as well as at weddings and gatherings during the colonial period. Because the African American banjo playing tradition was improvisational—not tied to formal musical notation or the level of education or sophistication of the player— it was thus as individual as the person who played it. In 18th-century America, its music provided a temporary escape from the realities of broken families, violence, death, dismemberment, disease, and the loss of freedom that was part of the system of chattel slavery.

But just as there were those who condemned enslaved Africans to the lowest form of humanity during the colonial period, there were those who considered the banjo to be the instrument of the lower class with no redeeming qualities. For an unknown author in Jamaica in 1740, the banjo seemed to insult European sensibilities: "On Sundays . . . towards the Evening . . . some hundreds of them will meet together, according to the Custom of their own Country with Strum-Strums and Calabashes, which they beat and make a horrid Noise with." In French-speaking areas of the Caribbean, the banza (the term used most consistently by the French during the colonial period) was seen as an example of African barbarism: "They play on this instrument tunes composed of three or four notes, which they repeat endlessly; this is what Bishop Grégoire calls sentimental and melancholy music; and which we call the music of savages." In 1796, English physician George Pinkard was in the West Indies and had the opportunity to see a slaving vessel. He wrote to a friend,

> In the day time they were not allowed to remain in the place where they had slept, but were kept mostly upon the open deck, where they were made to exercise, and encouraged, by the music of their beloved banjar, to dancing and cheerfulness. . . . Their song was a wild and savage yell, devoid of all softness and harmony, and loudly chanted in harsh monotony.

But whether the comments were rife with condescension, racist hyperbole, or uninformed ethnocentricity, all recognized the significant role the banjo played in the lives of Africans and African Americans. Diarists, journalists, travelers, and artists of the period all saw the banjo as the instrument that spoke to and for the African American experience.

From the Plantation to the Parlor

By the 19th century, the banjo was moving from the plantations and farms of the South to the minstrel stage, and then finally into "respectable" American homes. In a period during which blacks began the struggle for freedom and American citizenship, the banjo increasingly gained legitimacy as a quintessential American instrument. But that legitimacy would take time to develop. The banjo's form and construction, its methods of being played, its geography, its audience, and ultimately its status all underwent significant change by the end of the 19th century.

In those years, not only did the banjo continue to be associated with the enslaved, but it also became a symbol of Southern culture in general and plantation slavery in particular. But beyond its connections to the enslaved community, it also gained considerable popularity as a folk instrument in the mountains of Appalachia, particularly in Kentucky, North Carolina, Ohio, Virginia, and West Virginia. But before it gained respectability in the parlors and living rooms of polite society, it had to become a "white" instrument.

In 1830, a white performer, Thomas Dartmouth Rice (1808–1860), created a character he dubbed "Jim Crow." Rice wore ragged clothes and performed songs and dances "of the Plantation darky" in makeup known as "blackface." In blacking their faces, white performers were able to present as authentically black the caricatured facial features, mannerisms, songs, and dance of both enslaved and free blacks. Such performances gave white audiences a glimpse of what they thought was black life and culture, incorporating burlesque, slapstick, pratfalls, and horseplay as its main elements. The popularity of the minstrel show was an example of the great interest white audiences, especially those in the North, had in knowing more about black culture. So popular were these shows, with their primary subjects depicted as self-indulgent, easily misled, thieving, and sexually permissive, that they drew mass audiences and dominated American theater for much of the 19th century. One of its chief musical symbols was the banjo. It was through this genre of entertainment that the banjo began its transfer from the black community to the white community. As newly emancipated blacks left their enslavement behind, the banjo lost much of its influence and popularity.

Joel Walker Sweeney (1810–1860) and Dan Emmett (1815–1904) were the two most prominent and influential white banjo players of the early 19th century, and both learned to play the banjo from blacks. As popular entertainment began to grow in the United States, so, too, did the interest in Southern culture, and in particular, plantation slavery. Sweeney, Emmitt, Bill Whitlock (1813–1878), Thomas Rice, and a host of others took full advantage of that trend.

Sweeney is credited with beginning the transformation of the banjo from an exclusively black instrument to one that was increasingly identified with whites. Daniel Decatur Emmett was an American songwriter and performer who founded the nation's first minstrel troupe, the Virginia Minstrels, who performed for the first time in 1843. Emmett and the Virginia Minstrels launched shows that were so successful they traveled abroad and performed for royalty. So popular were the minstrel shows that many were included as parts of circus entertainment and eventually spawned a new stage genre called "vaudeville."

See also opening essay "Dance and Music."

FURTHER READING

Carlin, Bob. *The Birth of the Banjo: Joel Walker Sweeney and Early Minstrelsy.* Jefferson, NC: McFarland and Company, 2007.

Conway, Cecelia. *African Banjo Echoes in Appalachia: A Study of Folk Traditions.* Knoxville: University of Tennessee Press, 1995.

Epstein, Dena J. "The Folk Banjo: A Documentary History." *Ethnomusicology* 19, no. 3 (September 1975): 347–371.

Epstein, Dena J. *Sinful Tunes and Spirituals: Black Folk Music to the Civil War.* Urbana: University of Illinois Press, 1977.

Gura, Philip F., and James F. Bollman. *America's Instrument: The Banjo in the Nineteenth Century.* Chapel Hill: University of North Carolina Press, 1999.

Linn, Karen. *That Half-Barbaric Twang: The Banjo in American Popular Culture.* Urbana: University of Illinois Press, 1991.

REX ELLIS

BARTER GOODS. Bartering, defined as the exchange of products without the use of money, was one way that enslaved men and women obtained goods for themselves. This method served both master and slave very well, even though slaves might have preferred cash over goods, as bartering enabled each party to get something that they wanted without having to use cash, which was in limited circulation well into the 19th century. Bartering was commonly used by store owners, tradespeople, and craftsmen as a way of obtaining needed products in a time when paying cash for goods was difficult.

In general, enslaved men and women used agricultural products and their own labor in these bartering transactions, with slaveholders offering **clothing** or sometimes even **liquor** in trade. Landon Carter (1710–1778), a member of one of Virginia's most prominent families, wrote in his diary in 1777 that "My Poor Slaves raise fowls, and eggs in order to exchange with their Master now and then." Francis Taylor (1747–1799), a plantation owner in Orange County, Virginia, often obtained some of his produce from various slaves by means of barter. In August 1788, he "bought some Grass seed of Col Taliaferro's Jack for Pr breeches." And in March 1790, "Reu Taylor's Sam brought some Timothy seed for which I [Taylor] gave him a Jacket." In July 1795, Taylor "bought 1 doz chickens of Col Willis's Phil he had a pair Breeches & to pay me 1/6 worth more." In an interesting exchange in August 1798, Taylor gave "old Joe a quart whisky for a peck onions."

Bartering persisted into the 19th century. Amos Clark, interviewed in Waco, Texas, in 1937 at the age of 96 as part of the Federal Writers' Project slave narratives effort, told his interviewer, "An old Indian come to help us hunt. He'd work a week if Marse Ed give him some red calico or a hatchet. Old Miss done bring a dozen hens and a bag of seeds, and folks come ridin' twenty miles to swap things." Bill Austin was interviewed in Florida between 1936 and 1938 and it was noted that

> Bill's father Jack was regarded as a fairly good carpenter, mason and bricklayer; at times his master would let him do small jobs of repairing of building for neighboring planters. These jobs sometimes netted him hams, bits of corn-meal, cloth for dresses for his wife and children, and other small gifts; these he either used for his own family or bartered with the other slaves.

See also Chickens; Corn.

FURTHER READING

"Born in Slavery: Slave Narratives from the Federal Writers' Project, 1936–1938," American Memory, Library of Congress. At http://memory.loc.gov/ammem/snhtml/.

Carter, Landon. *The Diary of Colonel Landon Carter of Sabine Hall, 1752–1778*, edited by Jack P. Greene. Richmond: Virginia Historical Society, 1987.

Forret, Jeff. "Slaves, Poor Whites, and the Underground Economy of the Rural Carolinas." *The Journal of Southern History* 70, no. 4 (November 2004): 783–824.

Taylor, Francis. *Diary, 1786–1799*. Microfilm 18710. Miscellaneous reel 114. Richmond: Library of Virginia.

MARTHA B. KATZ-HYMAN

BASKETS AND BASKET MAKING. People of African descent enslaved on plantations across the American South made many types of basketry from a diversity of natural fibers. Forms and techniques depended largely on the crops they grew and the availability of particular basket-making materials. Harvesting **cotton** and **corn** required large splintwork hampers woven of hardwood. For winnowing and storing small grains such as **rice**—the staple that made slaveholders along the South Atlantic coast the

Newly freed men and women planting sweet potatoes on James Hopkinson's plantation, Edisto Island, South Carolina, April 1862, five months after the Union army liberated Port Royal Sound. The photo by Henry P. Moore is the earliest known photograph of a coiled basket in use in South Carolina. (Collection of the New York Historical Society.)

Making Baskets

George Briggs, formerly enslaved in South Carolina, began making baskets and other woven or wooden articles as a young child:

When I got big and couldn't play 'round at chillun's doings, I started to platting cornshucks and things fer making hoss and mule collars, and scouring-brooms and shoulder-mats. I cut hickory poles and make handles out of dem fer de brooms. Marse had hides tanned, and us make buggy whips, wagon whips, shoe strings, saddle strings and sech as dat out of our home-tanned leather. All de galluses dat was wo' in dem days was made by de darkies.

White oak and hickory was split to cure, and we made fish baskets, feed baskets, wood baskets, sewing baskets and all kinds of baskets fer de Missus. All de chair bottoms of straight chairs was made from white oak splits, and de straight chairs was made in de shop. You made a scouring brush like dis: (He put his hands together to show how the splits were held.) By splitting a width of narrow splits, keep on till you lay a entire layer of splits; turn dis way; den dat way, and den bind together and dat hold dem like you want dem to stay. Last, you work in a pole as long as you want it fer de handle, and bind it tight and tie wid de purtiest knots.

Source: George P. Rawick, ed. *The American Slave: South Carolina Narratives*, Vol. 2. Westport, CT: Greenwood Press, 1972.

---

wealthiest people in the nation—coiled baskets made from tightly sewn bundles of grass or sedge were best.

In preindustrial times, basket making was a necessary skill. Regarded as a seasonal farm chore, it lacked the prestige of other artisan trades, such as coopering, carpentry, **sewing**, or blacksmithing, but people with the know-how to make baskets were in demand and the ability was often cited by plantation owners as a selling point. A notice in the Charleston *Gazette and Advertiser* in February 1791, for example, announced the public auction of "A Negro Man, who is a good jobbing carpenter and an excellent basket maker, sold for no fault, but that of having a sore leg."

Types of basketry produced on Southern plantations included agricultural work baskets, carrying trays, hampers, sleeping mats and floor mats, chair seats, hats made of plaited palmetto or coiled rush, **brooms**, fly whisks, thatching, **fish** traps, and poultry cages. White oak splintwork was the most widespread material and technique. Dependent on metal tools introduced by European settlers, basketry quickly crossed regional borders and cultural boundaries. An earlier and more tenacious tradition was African inspired and geographically concentrated in the rice-growing region known as the Low Country, now officially designated by the National Park Service as the Gullah/Geechee Cultural Heritage Corridor, stretching from Wilmington, North Carolina, to Jacksonville, Florida.

Arguably the oldest of African American arts, coiled baskets were made in the colony of Carolina at least as early as 1690, when European settlers reported "plausible yields" of rice. As the plantation routine developed, dozens of wide, flat "fanner" baskets would be produced at winnowing time to "clean" the crop. At all times of year, in and around the slave quarters, people would pound rations of rice in wooden mortars to break the husk, and "fan" away the chaff by throwing the pounded grain in the air or dropping it from a basket. Fanners filled other functions, such as sifting **sesame** or "benne" seed; "raking" grits; carrying shelled corn, peas, and other produce; and even cradling babies at nap time. In both the slaveholder's Big House and slave cabins, coiled baskets might serve as trays, **sewing** or cord baskets, and fruit or bread baskets. Vegetable venders balancing huge coiled "head tote" baskets, in the African manner, became an everyday sight on the streets of Charleston and Savannah.

As plantation agriculture spread, people kept moving—north, south, west, and east— and the tradition of coiled basketry that had taken hold along the coast moved with them. Rice production expanded into Georgia and North Carolina in the 18th century as South Carolina planters resettled crews of experienced "hands" to break new ground and plant the crop. By the mid-1840s, the Rice Kingdom extended from the Lower Cape Fear in North Carolina to the St. Johns River in northern Florida, and the range of the basket followed suit. Evidence indicates that the tradition migrated west into Alabama, Mississippi, Tennessee, Louisiana, Arkansas, and Texas, and east to the Bahamas, where Low Country planters who had sided with England fled after the American Revolution, taking their slaves with them. To this day, on the Caicos Islands southeast of the Bahamas, descendants of this forced migration continue to make coiled grass baskets suggestively similar to South Carolina work.

On the western frontier, African American basketry met up with the traditions practiced by remnants of the Native American peoples who already had been removed from the eastern states. Though southeastern Indian tribes are better known for their plaited cane basketry than for their coiled work, Seminoles, Creeks, Koasatis, and Choctaws made coiled baskets. Europeans had a strong coiled rye straw tradition, which crossed the Atlantic with German immigrants who settled in Pennsylvania and trekked south down the Appalachian spine on the Great Wagon Road. Whatever contributions may have come from other cultures, the coiled tradition has been carried on by African Americans continuously for more than 300 years and has become the preeminent symbol of Gullah-Geechee culture.

From the beginning, coiled basketry incorporated one distinctly American element. On mainland plantations, the preferred "binder" or stitching element of coiled grass baskets was a thin splint of white oak. Some basket makers made both coiled and splint baskets. Indeed, some baskets were a hybrid of the two traditions. Coiled carrying baskets might have a splint handle lashed onto the sides, and large, coiled, two-tiered work baskets sometimes were set on incised wooden legs.

Allen Green, the best-known basket maker on Sapelo Island, Georgia, learned the trade from his grandfather, Allen Smith, who during slavery made "all class of baskets" on a cotton plantation near Macon—coiled grass fanners, plaited palmetto forms, and various sizes of split oak containers. "He make rice fanner," Allen Green reported in a 1985 interview, "quart, peck, half-a-peck—didn't have no scale—made quart, bushel basket. He made all class."

Similarly, John Haynes made splint baskets from white oak and coiled baskets from bulrushes stitched with saw palmetto. A "Negro basket maker" living near Old Fort, he told researchers from the Savannah Unit of the Georgia Writers' Project in the late 1930s that he was "carrying on the tradition of his ancestors." For generations, the men of his family had engaged in wood carving, basket making, and weaving, crafts passed from father to son. His stock-in-trade included a variety of forms—"hampers, flat clothes baskets, farm and shopping baskets, and the popular 'fanner' which the Negro venders balance gracefully on their heads as they walk about the city, displaying a colorful array of merchandise."

Owners and overseers of rice plantations sent their workers into the woods and marshes to procure supplies for making baskets used in processing the crop. Collecting materials might occupy a group of men for several days, whereas sewing baskets might take two or three weeks late in summer as the harvest approached, or in winter before planting the new crop. In February 1836, Charles Drayton II wrote from Drayton Hall on the Ashley River to his son, Charles Drayton III, who managed a plantation on the Satilla in Georgia, instructing him to "have rushes and oak got that you might have some baskets made while you are on the place." Three months later he reminded young Charles to "leave strict orders about having baskets made during the summer and fall, & also a quantity of rushes must be laid up for winters work."

Eyewitnesses provide occasional glimpses of the basket makers gathering rushes, sewing baskets, wearing rush hats. "Jacob and Jim getting stuff for baskets," a Berkeley County, South Carolina, planter wrote in his journal on August 27, 1836. "Jacob was occupied 3 weeks in making baskets." Basket making might be assigned to workers no longer fit for field labor. In March 1846, Thomas B. Chaplin of St. Helena Island "put old May to making baskets, 2 a week," although what kind of baskets Chaplin does not say. Workers also produced baskets on their own time, either for sale or for personal use. "After one or two o'clock," wrote Daniel Elliott Huger Smith, recalling his youth at Smithfield, a Combahee River rice plantation, "the hands had the rest of the day to themselves and could work their own fields and gardens, or idle at their will. Many of them were expert basket-makers for which on every plantation there was a demand."

Once the rice was threshed and ready for pounding and winnowing, fanner baskets would be issued by the dozen to the field hands. On Argyle plantation in the Savannah River basin, beginning in November, more than 50 hands were engaged in "thrashing and winnowing rice." These men and women appear only as numbers in the daily entry, but are listed by name under the heading "Disbursement of tools and baskets" at the end of the overseer's report.

Because large quantities of fanner baskets were produced year after year, many examples have survived in barn lofts and attics and several have made their way into museum collections. Other coiled forms from the plantation era that have been preserved include vegetable baskets, covered work baskets, trays and hot plates, bowl-shaped baskets, as well as a few examples of double sewing baskets, described in detail by Santee River rice planter David Doar. This intricate antebellum form is still made by older sewers in Mount Pleasant, South Carolina, although only on commission.

Even in unconditional servitude, workers were able to use basket-making skills as bargaining chips, to make baskets for their own use, or to sell or carry goods to exchange in the open market or the underground economy. At times, baskets served as agents of liberation. Sixteen runaways were able to stay at large by gathering black moss, making baskets, and carrying their handcrafts to town in **boats**, according to an ad that appeared in the *Charleston Courier* on May 28, 1825. A basketry boat made headlines in the summer of 1864 when the northern press learned of Jack Frowers's escape to the Union side of Port Royal Sound in a vessel he had made from coarse grass twisted into a rope and "bound round, or, as the sailors would term it, 'served' with other grass." When the boat was ready, Frowers hid out one more day and then paddled to freedom.

The tradition of coiled grass basketry can be viewed as a tree with two branches. Making agricultural or field baskets was generally men's work on rice plantations; making household baskets, often made of a finer, more flexible grass, was considered women's work. "There were men on the places who were good handicraftsmen," wrote Doar. "They made all the baskets (out of river rushes cured and sewed with white oak strips) that were used on the place."

North of the Santee River, on Waccamaw Neck in Georgetown County, Welcome Beese, who had been born in slavery on Oatland plantation perhaps as early as 1834, was still making baskets in 1938 when A. H. "Doc" Lachicotte opened the Pawley's Island Hammock Shop. Known as a master carpenter as well as an expert basket maker, he is pictured in the shop's first brochure sitting next to a wooden mortar and pestle and seven of his rush baskets.

A hundred miles south of the Santee, on St. Helena Island near the town of Beaufort, bulrush basket making was also relegated to men, as Principal Roosa Cooley was to discover when she introduced basketry into the women's curriculum at the Penn School, an abolitionist enterprise established in 1862. At Penn, the connection with Africa was direct. The school's first basket-making instructor was Alfred Graham, whose African father had taught him, and Graham passed the practice along to his nephew George Browne.

The last known maker of old-style Sea Island bulrush baskets was Jannie Cohen of Hilton Head Island. Cohen began sewing baskets at the age of 10 or 12 under the tutelage of her father, Edward Green, who had been born in slavery in 1856. Besides coiled rush baskets, Green made palmetto hats, drying the leaf before he "knit it." He taught Jannie and her younger brother David to harvest and prepare saw palmetto and rushes, and using an interlocked stitch, attach each new binder with a knot. Jannie learned to make fanners, "egg" baskets (oblong in shape), and monumental "trash" baskets, which by the last decade of the 20th century were coveted collectors' items.

The African roots of coiled basketry have never been disputed, but the European origins of splintwork have been challenged by historians who point out that Native Americans were making splint baskets from ash and river cane when the first Europeans stepped onto their land. Certainly, Africans arriving in America already knew how to work with flexible splints. What were quickly adopted were European metal tools—axes, wedges, sledgehammers, drawknives, or froes (used to make shingles)—and European forms, such as carrying baskets with handles. In the 21st century, white oak basket makers are descended from Appalachian hill farmers, Cherokees and other native peoples, or African Americans whose ancestors practiced the trade on cotton plantations across the South.

Although Native Americans helped spread oak splintwork west, African Americans were largely responsible for its dissemination across the plantation South. From the Sea Islands to East Texas, and south to North Florida, known locally as "South Georgia," field hands made baskets for harvesting cotton, corn, and **yams**, market and feed baskets, hampers, and fish traps from light and extremely durable white oak splints. "I helped make the baskets for the cotton," Mary Ann Kincheon Edwards, told Federal Writers' Project field researchers from the Works Progress Administration who interviewed her near Austin, Texas, in the 1930s. "The men get white oak wood and we lets it stay in the water for the night and the next morning and it soft and us split it in strips for making of the baskets. Everybody try to see who could make the best basket."

Andrew Goodman of Smith County, Texas, recalled his master, Robert Goodman, buying "cornshuck horse collars and all kinds of baskets" from his slaves. "What he couldn't use, he sold for us. We'd take post oak and split it thin with drawing knives and let it get tough in the sun and then weave it into cotton baskets and fish baskets and little fancy baskets. The men spent they [basket] money on whiskey."

In the early 1800s, blacks carried the splintwork tradition as far north as Halifax, Nova Scotia, where basket maker and historian Joleen Gordon has identified "frame baskets almost identical with the Appalachian ones." The bearer of the Halifax tradition is Edith Clayton, among whose maternal forebears was an African American taken by the British during the War of 1812 and carried to Nova Scotia. Apparently the captive had acquired basket-making skills on an American plantation. Clayton learned splintwork from her mother, who learned from her mother, and so on back through the generations. The family sold their baskets, made of swamp maple, in Halifax City Market.

See also Blacksmith Shops; Chickens; Cooperage; Punkahs and Fly Brushes; Woodworking Tools.

FURTHER READING

Burrison, John A. *Handed On: Folk Crafts in Southern Life.* Atlanta: Atlanta Historical Society, 1993.

Coakley, Joyce V. *Sweetgrass Baskets and the Gullah Tradition.* Charleston, SC: Arcadia Publishing, 2006.

Rosengarten, Dale. *Row Upon Row: Sea Grass Baskets of the South Carolina Lowcountry.* 1986. Reprint, Columbia: McKissick Museum, University of South Carolina, 1994.

Rosengarten, Dale. "Social Origins of the African-American Lowcountry Basket." PhD diss., Harvard University, 1997.

Rosengarten, Dale, Theodore Rosengarten, and Enid Schildkrout, eds. *Grass Roots: African Origins of an American Art.* New York: Museum for African Art, 2008.

Rosengarten, Theodore. *All God's Dangers: The Life of Nate Shaw.* 1974. Reprint. Chicago: University of Chicago Press, 2000.

Savannah Unit, Georgia Writers' Project, Work Projects Administration. *Drums and Shadows: Survival Studies among the Georgia Coastal Negroes.* 1940. Reprint, Athens: University of Georgia Press, 1986.

Stanton, Gary, and Tom Cowan. *Stout Hearts: Traditional Oak Basket Makers of the South Carolina Upcountry.* Columbia: McKissick Museum, University of South Carolina, 1988.

Vlach, John Michael. *The Afro-American Tradition in Decorative Arts.* 1978. Reprint, Athens: University of Georgia Press, 1990.

Vlach, John Michael. *By the Work of Their Hands: Studies in Afro-American Folklife.* Charlottesville: University Press of Virginia, 1991.

Wood, Peter H. *Black Majority: Negroes in Colonial South Carolina from 1670 through the Stono Rebellion.* New York: Alfred A. Knopf, 1974.

DALE ROSENGARTEN

BEADS. Among enslaved blacks, beads were culturally dynamic objects typically made of glass, metal, precious stones, and shell. They were strung, sometimes singly, and worn on various parts of the body, including the ears, hair, neck, wrist, and waist. On occasion, beads were used as barter, gaming pieces, sewn to cloth or hide as part of a garment, or grouped together with an anomalous assortment of objects into a spiritual cache or ancestral altar. Based on ethnological, historical, and archaeological research, the function of beads in enslaved black culture originated in Africa and was defined by daily social interaction, physical placement on the body or within a space, and the bead's material, form, and style. Depending on these factors, a single bead could function as a symbol or sign of adornment, trade, commerce, identity, and religious ideology, and could be imbued with the power to protect, heal, attract mates, and bring luck. Some scholars have labeled such beads as African American ethnic markers, but this is an oversimplification. The reality is that beads were symbolic pawns within the underlying cultural process of creolization, which is the interaction and exchange of objects, foodways, technology, and ideology between two or more cultures. This process results in the formation and transformation of a new ethnic group, like African Americans.

Beads have been a common object of material culture for most societies throughout history, but each culture has imbued them with their own cultural meanings and functions. The use of beads among enslaved blacks can be linked to their ancestral origins in West and Central Africa, where beads were interlaced with nearly all aspects of society, including beautification, age, kinship, marital status, gaming, commerce, rank, rituals, and religious beliefs. Beads were most frequently used in concert with other forms of body adornment or modification, ranging from temporary hairstyles, clothing, and body painting to permanent techniques of **scarification**, head deformation, and filing of teeth.

Beads used in Sub-Saharan Africa were obtained from local craftspeople and through trade with Europe and the Middle East. These ornate objects were made of a single element or a combination of bone, ceramic, fossils, glass, hair, hide, metal, precious stones, seeds, **shells**, and wood. When the transatlantic slave trade began in the 16th century, European-made beads, particularly from Venice, were already being

---

How Beads Were Worn

According to Cicely Cawthorn, a former Georgia slave, beads were worn around the neck of many enslaved individuals or used in other decorative ways:

In them days all darkies wore beads. Babies wore beads around their necks. You wouldn't see a baby without beads. They was made of glass and looked like diamonds. They had 'em in different colors too, white, blue, and red, little plaited strings of beads. When their necks got bigger, they wore another kind, on 'till they got grown. They trimmed hats with beads, ladies and chillun too.

Source: George Rawick, ed. *The American Slave: Georgia Narratives* Supp. Ser. 1, Vol. 3, Part 1. Westport, CT: Greenwood Press, 1978.

used as barter by European and African slave traders to acquire Africans, who were forced into servitude through warfare, kidnapping, or indebtedness. The journey of the Middle Passage from Africa to the Americas stripped these enslaved people of family, friends, homeland, and humanity. The only remembrance of home and self was limited to their memories and the clothing on their backs. This likely included beads around their necks, waist, ankles, or in their hair. Once in the Americas, this jewelry may have taken on a more significant cultural meaning, connecting them to their ancestors and cultural identity.

In the United States, the best evidence for bead use and their symbolic meaning by enslaved blacks comes from archaeological research. Beads have been recovered from burials, **subfloor pits**, caches, and general activity areas around **slave quarters**. These have included glass beads and shells as well as objects transformed into beads or pendants, like pierced **coins** and chandelier crystals. Interpretations of these artifacts have associated them with beautification, gender, prestige, ethnic identity, and most frequently with **charms**, and amulets.

The use of beads as protective charms originates from a belief system in West and Central Africa that people can be harmed and/or become sick through natural illness, a conjurer's curse or hex, or evil spirits or ghosts entering the body. Within a slave community, one person typically served as both a religious leader and healer. If one became sick, this respected person often would prescribe both herbal remedies and a protective charm to wear and also could perform a countercurse. Personal charms were worn to ward off evil, to foster good luck, and to attract the opposite sex. They were not meant to be seen by the living and were hidden around ankles, inside **shoes**, or sewn on the interior of a garment. These charms were frequently made of objects with reflective properties, like metal, glass, crystals, and **mirrors**, because they could deflect or trap any harmful spirits or curses. Similarly, the color of a bead may have been selected for its unique characteristics. It has been statistically shown that enslaved blacks preferred blue beads over other colors. One explanation from oral tradition suggests that blue was important because it is the same color as the sky, which is where heaven and the almighty being reside. Thus, if a slave wore something blue, then evil spirits would be afraid to go toward them or the blue would help protect them from harsh treatment by their masters. In the 21st century, the significance of blue is still evident in the Deep South with door and window frames of some African Americans' homes painted blue to prevent specters (ghosts) or thieves from entering.

In 1991, the African Burial Ground, a 17th- and 18th-century black **cemetery** in Lower Manhattan, New York, was uncovered during excavations before the construction of a new federal building. This cemetery was used from approximately 1650 to 1795 for the final resting place of both free and enslaved people of African descent. A total of 376 burials were recovered and these individuals and the associated grave offerings and hardware were then analyzed at Howard University in Washington, D.C. Only 30 of these individuals were interred with objects of adornment, including beads, **buttons**, cowrie shells, cufflinks, rings, pendants, and possibly earrings. A total of 147 glass beads was collected, representing 15 types, with blue and blue-green the most common color. The bead assemblage of one woman (Burial 340), who was buried with a bracelet and a strand around her waist, consisted of 111 European-made glass beads of blue and yellow hues, 1 red agate bead, and 7 cowrie shells (*Cypraea moneta*). A waist strand was commonly worn by women in West and Central Africa. It was used in daily adornment and was rarely removed except for restringing. It served as an underbelt to tuck and secure a wrapper, a style of garment in West Africa worn around the woman's waist to conceal her body shape. This specific waist strand may have traveled with her during the Middle Passage and may symbolize cultural ties to kinship and ethnic identity.

The seven cowrie shells on this same strand are native to Indo-Pacific tropical waters and were utilized in Africa for centuries as adornment or gaming pieces, in rituals, and as currency. Shell beads and shells in general have been linked to life after death in West Africa and consequently by some people of African descent in the Americas. For example, additional graves at the African Burial Ground in New York contained local mussel shells, and some West African and African American graves in the Deep South still have shells placed as grave offerings in the 21st century. Shell in West Africa was associated with water and a deceased spirit's journey into the afterlife. When people die, their spirits travel to the underworld located at the bottom of the ocean. The shell provided a protective and peaceful space for the deceased ancestor's passage. The wearing of shell beads or placing a shell on or in a grave would ease a restless spirit and protect the living.

In Annapolis, Maryland, and in the surrounding Chesapeake Bay region, beads have been identified as part of house caches or bundles within the living or work space of enslaved blacks. These bundles were buried in the floor near entryways and openings, sometimes arranged in specific cardinal directions, and included a wide array of objects. The most frequent artifacts were straight pins, buttons, wire, animal bones, beads, **nails**, crystals, discs, buckles, coins, bottles, and ceramics. Individually, these objects may be considered inconsequential, but bound together and with a distinctive spatial placement, this suggests a West African origin as house charms or ancestral altars. These caches were either used to appease and communicate with the ancestral spirits that occupied their living and working space or to prevent unwanted spirits from entering. The strength of these bundles lay in their ménage of objects, which provided multiple layers of defense.

The range of bead forms reflects the resourcefulness of African Americans and the creolization process by which enslaved Africans adapted to their new surroundings by sharing and mixing material objects, technology, and ideas from European and Native American cultures into a new African American identity. Within ritual and burial contexts, bead use and meaning were creolized between African traditions and newly introduced Christian ideology. By 1800, graves of enslaved blacks still included glass beads and pierced metal discs, but now they frequently were included as part of a rosary with a **cross** or a metal medallion embossed with a patron saint that provided protection.

See also Faunal Remains; Hair and Hairstyles; Herbs; Shrines and Spirit Caches.

FURTHER READING

Dubin, Lois Sherr. *The History of Beads: 30,000 B.C. to the Present*. New York: H. N. Abrams, 1987.

Heath, Barbara J. "Buttons, Beads, and Buckles: Contextualizing Adornment Within the Bounds of Slavery." In *Historical Archaeology, Identity Formation, and the Interpretation of Ethnicity*, edited by Maria Franklin and Garrett Fesler, 47–69. Williamsburg, VA: Colonial Williamsburg Research Publications/Colonial Williamsburg Foundation, 1999.

LaRoche, Cheryl J. "Beads from the African Burial Ground, New York City: A Preliminary Assessment." *Beads: Journal of the Society of Bead Researchers* 6 (1994): 3–20.

Stine, Linda France. "Blue Beads as African-American Cultural Symbols." *Historical Archaeology* 30, no. 3 (1996): 49–75.

TIMOTHY E. BAUMANN

BEDS. Beds and bedding were an important part of the material world of American slaves. Specific sleeping arrangements and furniture forms varied over time, from region to region, and between urban and rural locations, but in general slaveholders throughout the period of American slavery provided enslaved men, women, and children with basic bedding and a place to sleep.

The living conditions of the first generations of American slaves differed little from those of indentured servants and even some free men and women. Bedsteads (the frames on which bedding was placed) typically were reserved for the master and mistress. Servants, enslaved and indentured, slept on **pallets** consisting of a coarse linen tick stuffed with straw or whatever material happened to be available. Depending on the size of the house and household, they might sleep on the floor by the fire, in a back room, or in **lofts**. Privacy was an infrequent luxury in the 17th century, and several slaves, servants, and children might share the same sleeping space.

As the slave system became more codified, sleeping spaces and bedding for the enslaved began to be differentiated from those of the rest of the household. One Long Island estate described a "room of 14 by 16 foot for white servants, over it lodging rooms and a back stairs; behind it a kitchen with a room fit for negroes." A 1711 inventory of Bacon's Castle, in Surry, Virginia, specifically mentions "Negroes bedding" in the still house. Slaves still slept wherever space was available, but increasingly, Southern plantation owners built freestanding slave quarters to house growing communities of agricultural slaves.

Throughout the 18th century and into the 19th, most slaves continued to sleep on pallets stuffed with straw, or piles of straw covered with a sheet. Sometimes the straw would be contained in a wooden box creating a crude bedstead. Slaveholders typically provided the adult slaves on their plantation with a single blanket yearly, usually made of coarse wool. One description written by Ferdinand-Marie Bayard in 1791 paints a particularly grim picture of the conditions in which most slaves lived:

> A box-like frame made of boards hardly roughed down, upheld by stakes, constituted the nuptial couch. Some wheat straw and cornstalks, on which was spread a very short-napped woolen blanket that was burned in several places, completed the wretched pallet of the enslaved couple.

Josiah Henson similarly described his experience as a slave in the late 18th century in his autobiography *Uncle Tom's Story of His Life*:

> Our beds were collections of straw and old rags, thrown down in the corners and boxed in with boards; a single blanket the only covering. Our favourite

way of sleeping, however, was on a plank, our heads raised on an old jacket and our feet toasting before the smouldering fire.

Compared with the living conditions of even the poorest whites, these sleeping arrangements were primitive at best.

But not all slaves lived in squalid surroundings. Conditions varied from plantation to plantation, and even within plantations and households. Domestic servants and personal slaves often had access to a much higher standard of material goods than did agricultural workers. For example, Major Joseph Ball made special arrangements for a favored slave, Aron Jameson. Ball instructed his steward to provide Jameson with "one of the worst of my old Bed steads cut short & fit for his Mattress, and have a cord and hide to it." Jameson had an assortment of fine bedding, including "a Large mattress stuffed well with flocks and stiched with tufts, and a bolster filled with feathers, the Mattress & Bolster both besides their Ticks having Ozenbrigs cases; and two new coverleds, and other old Bedcloths." Compared with the sleeping arrangements described by Bayard and Henson, Jameson enjoyed considerable luxury in his bedding.

In urban areas, the enslaved often lived in even more crowded quarters than their rural counterparts did. With little space for freestanding slave quarters, enslaved men and women slept wherever they could. James Stuart, who traveled to the United States in the 1830s, arrived at a Charleston hotel to find "the male servants of the house . . . already laid down for the night in the passages with their clothes on. They had neither beds nor bedding, and you may kick them or tread upon them (as you come in) with impunity." He found a similar arrangement in New Orleans. A lucky few urban slaves, mostly those who had been hired out for industrial work, were able to live independently, but most found themselves crammed into **kitchens**, attics and back rooms, or sleeping in hallways, corners, and closets.

As the 19th century progressed, it became more and more common for slaves, particularly those living on large plantations, to be housed in single-family dwellings. Surviving documents, particularly the ex-slave narratives compiled by the members of the Federal Writers' Project in the 1930s, provide a particularly complete picture of the sleeping arrangements of enslaved African Americans in the antebellum South. By the mid-19th century, most married adult slaves slept in raised bedsteads rather than pallets on the floor. Furniture forms varied regionally and from plantation to plantation, but the majority can be classified as either freestanding bedsteads or so-called Georgia beds.

The term "Georgia bed" or sometimes "Alabama bed" refers to a furniture form found only in slave contexts. These beds were built directly into the side or corner of the cabin, typically consisting of a wooden plank or box supported by one or two legs. Former slave Malindy Maxwell described such an arrangement from her Mississippi plantation childhood:

Colored folks' bed had one leg. Then it was holes hewed in the wall on the other three sides and wooden slats across it. Now that wasn't no bad bed. Some of them was big enough for three to sleep on good. When the children was small four could sleep easy cross ways, and they slept that way.

Another description comes from John F. Van Hook of Georgia:

> The beds used by most of the slaves in that day and time were called "Georgia Beds," and these were made by boring two holes in the cabin wall and two in the floor, and side pieces were run from the holes in the wall to the posts and fastened; then planks were nailed around the sides and foot, box-fashion, to hold in the straw that we used for mattresses.

Georgia beds were particularly common not only in Georgia but also in other Deep South states like Alabama and Arkansas.

Although common, Georgia beds were considered inferior to freestanding bedsteads. Frank Patterson of Arkansas recalled: "The best experienced colored people had these tester beds. Didn't have no slats. Had ropes. They called 'em cord beds sometimes." Rope beds typically consisted of a simple wooden frame with crisscrossed ropes providing support for a mattress. As the ropes stretched out and the bed sagged, they could be tightened using a wooden key. Green Willbanks, enslaved in Georgia in the 1850s, described such a bed:

> To make a bed they first cut four posts, usually of pine, and bored holes through them with augers; then they made two short pieces for the head and foot. Two long pieces for the sides were stuck through the auger holes and the bedstead was ready to lay on the mats or cross pieces to hold up the mattress. The best beds had heavy cords, wove crossways and lengthways, instead of slats. Very few slaves had corded beds.

A few former slaves also described slat bedsteads, which replaced the rope support system with flat planks and therefore did not require tightening.

Bedsteads were topped with a linen tick filled with straw, broken up **corn** cobs, unsalable **cotton**, or whatever material was readily available on the plantation. Willbanks noted that "Mattresses were not much; they were made of suggin sacks filled with straw. They called that straw 'Georgia Feathers.' Pillows were made of the same things. Suggin cloth was made of coarse flax wove on a loom." True feather pillows and mattresses were reserved for plantation owners.

Children often slept wherever there was room. Where extra bedsteads were available, they slept several to a bed. Others slept on pallets on the floor or in lofts, or on short trundle beds that fit beneath their parents' bedsteads. Thomas McIntire, who was enslaved in Bath County, Kentucky, recalled that "We had a ladder nex' to de side of de cabin, en us chillum climb up in de lof' en slep' on straw ticks laid on de floot [sic]. Manys de time I waked up en foun' snow all on our bed, done sifted t'rough de tracks in de ceiling.'" Children in training as personal servants might also sleep in the "Big House." Betty Cofer of North Carolina recalled: "I waited on [Miss Ella] an' most times slept on the floor in her room."

Most nuclear families slept together in a single cabin. Unmarried adults, or those with families living on another plantation, slept wherever there was room. Sometimes this meant sharing living quarters with another family, other times being housed in groups in small cabins or dormitories. Either way, space was often at a premium and two or three adults might share a single bed, with additional individuals sleeping on pallets on the floor.

Sleeping arrangements also changed to reflect the seasons. Charles Green, interviewed in Ohio, recalled that "Us all slep' in de kitchen en de winter, but wen de weather got warm nough us slep' out on er porch." Slaves living in freestanding quarters may have slept outdoors in the heat of summer or moved their bedding closer to the fire in the winter.

See also Blankets; Linen Fabrics; Slave Housing.

FURTHER READING

"Born in Slavery: Slave Narratives from the Federal Writers' Project, 1936–1938," American Memory. Library of Congress. At http://memory.loc.gov/ammem/snhtml/.

Campbell, Edward D. C., Jr., and Kym S. Rice, eds. *Before Freedom Came: African American Life in the Antebellum South*. Richmond, VA: The Museum of the Confederacy, 1991.

"Documenting the American South: First Person Narratives of the American South." University Library, University of North Carolina at Chapel Hill. At http://docsouth.unc.edu/fpn/.

McDaniel, George W. *Hearth & Home: Preserving a People's Culture*. Philadelphia: Temple University Press, 1982.

Taylor, Yuval, ed. *I Was Born a Slave: An Anthology of Classic Slave Narratives*. 2 vols. Chicago: Lawrence Hill Books, 1999.

"WPA [Works Progress Administration]. Ex-Slave Narratives, 1937–1938." The African-American Experience in Ohio 1850–1920, Ohio Historical Society. At http://dbs.ohiohistory.org/africanam/mss/gr7999.cfm.

CATHERINE E. DEAN

BELLS AND HORNS. Slaveholders in the United States and the West Indies used bells and horns to control the actions of their slaves and to direct and regulate their labor. The use of horn and especially bell signals to govern people within a given community was a long-standing Western tradition to which slaves were forced to conform. Although many Africans communicated information from place to place through sounds, most notably through **drum** language, they did not use auditory signals to send directives to others.

Most masters apparently used either a bell or a horn to issue signals to their slaves, but some had both and used them to issue different kinds of signals. Despite the differences between the two kinds of instruments, there was no apparent pattern of preference for bells over horns or vice versa; slaveholders suited themselves in choosing instruments and using them to their liking.

Manufacture

Most bells were made of bronze, and they were professionally cast at a bell-foundry. Slaveholders who used bells had to pay for the cost of the material, production labor, and shipping from the bell-foundry. Horns, however, could be made extremely cheaply. While some were made of metal, usually tin, they also could be carved from wood, animal horn, or even conch **shells**. Slaves probably were responsible for making many of the horns that their masters used to command them.

Time Discipline and Control

In both plantation and factory settings, strict time discipline was important, and bells and horns imposed it on the enslaved workforce. Factories that employed slave laborers used bell signals to transmit the daily work schedule to them. On plantations, either the slaveholder, an overseer, or a black driver (a lower-order overseer, usually a slave) rang a bell or blew a horn to tell slaves when to get up, when to go to work, when to begin and end meal breaks, and when they could stop work for the day, and to announce an evening curfew. Sometimes, slave managers used bell or horn signal sounds to tell nursing mothers when they could break from work to suckle their children. On each plantation, the same daily work schedule generally applied both to field hands and slaves skilled in a particular craft, such as blacksmithing. Domestic servants, on the other hand, usually were allowed to rise half an hour later than other slaves, but their duties frequently were regulated by a bell system mounted near the kitchen or located in rooms throughout the house. On Saturdays, slave managers also rang a bell or blew a horn to summon slaves to receive

Former slave with horn used to call the slaves, near Marshall, Texas, 1939. (Library of Congress.)

their weekly **rations**. Individual masters set different schedules for their workforces; an especially demanding master might require his slaves to rise hours earlier than those on neighboring plantations.

Because bell and horn sounds carried across space, slaveholders could command their slaves at a distance. But this also gave the slaves some privacy. Both on plantations and in urban areas, slave cabins usually were located behind and at a distance from their master's house. Even house servants usually slept outside the Big House (the slaveholder's home) in the **slave quarters**. Although hand bells could be used inside the house to call maids or other servants who worked inside it during the day, most servant bells were located on the rear exterior wall of the Big House, where servants working in the detached kitchens and other outbuildings could hear them. Wires connected the servant bells to bell-pulls inside the Big House. The separation meant that enslaved servants were not always available at night. On the other hand, some slaveholders kept personal body servants (valets and maids) close by at night to ensure that they were available at all times; such servants usually slept on the floor by their master's or mistress's bed or on **pallets** in nearby hallways.

The big bells used to direct field hands and plantation artisans usually were mounted outside the master's or overseer's house or, on large plantations, at the end of a lane of cabins in the slave quarters. Several paintings by the French émigré artist Marie Adrien Persac (1823–1873) illustrate the latter arrangement on Louisiana **sugar** plantations. Slaveholders or overseers usually kept horns in their houses, and unlike the large heavy bells, slave managers could carry their horns with them during the day.

Slaves Disciplining Each Other

Black drivers were co-opted into the system of slavery and often issued the bell or horn signals used to wake their fellow slaves and send them to work each day. Cooks, too, were granted the privilege of sounding mealtime signals. Although some of these elite slaves abused their authority, most were more loyal to the slave community than to their masters and used their privileged positions to help fellow slaves if possible. But **slave drivers**, especially, were held accountable for the behavior of those under them, and sometimes they had to be punitive, whipping slaves who rose late in the morning or were caught out after curfew, both to avoid punishment themselves and to retain their precarious status. Many found this deeply demoralizing.

Resistance

Because plantation managers usually adhered to a rigid daily schedule, slaves knew when it

Bell rack shown on model, ca. 1937. This contraption was used by an Alabama slave owner to guard a runaway slave. This rack originally was topped by a bell that rang when the runaway attempted to leave the road and go through foliage or trees. It was attached around the neck. A belt passed through the loop at the bottom to hold the iron rod firmly fastened to the waist of the wearer. (Library of Congress.)

was safest for them to flout plantation discipline. The best time for slaves to slip off the plantation, visit friends, hold religious meetings, or otherwise break plantation rules was after sundown, when the curfew bell or horn had already sounded. To avoid punishment, transgressing slaves had to be careful not to be caught by white patrollers, who circulated through neighborhoods at night looking for slaves out without permission, and to be back in time for the morning wake-up call.

Punishment

Among the cruelest punishment inflicted on slaves involved fitting them with a "bellrack," an iron frame that was welded around the slave's upper body, which held a bell or set of bells suspended over his or her head. The bell rack usually was used on attempted runaways; because the bells rang every time they moved, it was very difficult for them to slip away. **Slave collars** with bells worked similarly. Even if the individuals

Call to Work

Isaiah Butler, formerly enslaved in South Carolina, recalled the horns that sounded work and rest times. When a slave refused to work when the horn sounded, he risked being sold. Butler remembered when a fellow slave who had been sent to another plantation refused to work when the horn sounded on a Sunday:

> In slavery time de slaves wuz waked up every morning by de colored over-driver blowin' a horn. Ole man Jake Chisolm wuz his name. Jes' at day-break, he'd put his horn through a crack in de upper part of de wall to his house an' blow it through dat crack. Den de under-driver would go out an' round 'em up. When dey done all dey day-work, dey come home an' cook dey supper, an' wash up. Den dey blow de horn for 'em to go to bed. Some-time dey have to out de fire an' finish dey supper in de dark. De under-driver, he'd go out den and see who ain't go to bed. He wouldn't say any t'ing den; but next mornin' he'd report it to de overseer, an' dem as hadn't gone to bed would be whipped.
>
> My mother used to tell me dat if any didn't do dey day's work, dey'd be put in de stocks or de bill-bo. You know each wuz given a certain task dat had to be finish dat day. Dat what dey call de day-work. When dey put 'em in de stocks dey tie 'em hand and foot to a stick. Dey could lie down wid dat. I hear of colored folks doin' dat now to dere chillun when dey don't do. Now de bill-bo wuz a stabe [stave] drove in de ground, an' dey tied dere hands and den dere feet to dat, standin' up. Dey'd work on Saturday but dey wuz give Sundays. Rations wuz give out on Mondays. Edmund Lawton went over to Louisiana to work on de Catherine Goride place, but he come back, 'cause he say dey blow dey horn for work on Sunday same as any other day, and he say he wa'n't goin' to work on no Sunday. Dey didn't have a jail in dem times. Dey'd whip 'em, and dey'd sell 'em. Every slave know what, "I'll put you in my pocket, sir!" mean.

Source: George P. Rawick, ed. *The American Slave: South Carolina Narratives*, Vol. 2. West-port, CT: Greenwood Press, 1972.

Reuben Fox remembered the clanging of the large freestanding bell on a Mississippi cotton plantation:

> The place was not very large so Master George looked after it hisself. The big bell was in the yard. He rang it before day every morning for everybody to get up and out. I is knowed them to work as late as ten o'clock at night, when it was the light of the moon, and they was behind with the cotton picking.

Source: George P. Rawick, ed. *The American Slave: Mississippi Narratives*. Supp. Ser. 1, Vol. 7, Part 2. Westport, CT: Greenwood Press, 1978.

were out of sight, they were not out of the range of their master's hearing. Bell racks were uncommon, but a number survive, together with slave collars, in museums as testaments to some slaveholders' determination to utterly possess and control.

Other Signals

Besides keeping slaves working to a tight schedule, slaveholders used bells and horns to sound alarm calls when they needed neighbors to come help them, for example, if a building caught fire or a slave escaped. The signal sounds could carry several miles in every direction. Bells generally could be heard over greater distances than horns. Whites feared the possibility of slave insurrections and considered the hours of darkness especially propitious for illicit slave meetings. In large towns and cities, the white population principally used bells to impose a curfew upon their slaves, although bells also rang to announce the openings of slave auctions. Any slave, and sometimes free blacks as well, caught out on the streets after the curfew bell rang was liable to be imprisoned and whipped. Escaped slave Harriet Jacobs remembered that in Charleston, South Carolina, whites also worried that slaves might take advantage of the distraction a fire offered to meet and plot an insurrection. All slaves therefore were expected to respond to the sound of a fire bell and to assemble and carry water through the streets to the site of conflagration.

Different Perspectives

Slaveholders believed that auditory signals preserved the kind of order and control they desired and maximized productive labor. On the other hand, many ex-slaves expressed deep resentment over having been made to obey auditory signals, thinking they symbolized enslavement's debasing and dehumanizing methods. There was, however, one occasion that many former slaves recalled hearing their master's bell or horn with pleasure: that was when their owners, or in some cases Union Army officers, called them together for the last time to tell them they were free.

See also Blacksmith Shops; Whips; Work Routines.

FURTHER READING

Breeden, James O., ed. *Advice among Masters: The Ideal in Slave Management in the Old South.* Westport, CT: Greenwood Press, 1980.

Gates, Henry Louis, Jr., ed. *The Classic Slave Narratives.* New York: Penguin, 2002.

Murtha, Hillary. "Instruments of Power: Sonic Signaling Devices and Antebellum Labor Management." PhD diss., University of Delaware, 2010.

Rawick, George P., ed. *The American Slave: A Composite Autobiography.* Westport, CT: Greenwood Press, 1972–1979.

Smith, Mark M. *Listening to Nineteenth-Century America.* Chapel Hill: University of North Carolina Press, 2001.

Van Deburg, William. *The Slave Drivers: Black Agricultural Labor Supervisors in the Antebellum South.* Westport, CT: Greenwood Press, 1979.

Vlach, John Michael. *Back of the Big House: The Architecture of Plantation Slavery.* Chapel Hill: University of North Carolina Press, 1993.

HILLARY MURTHA

BENEVOLENT ASSOCIATIONS. Benevolent associations developed in the late-18th century as Americans, regardless of race, addressed social and economic problems.

In the North and the Upper South, gradual manumission practices inspired by the American Revolution created a growing African American population who confronted the challenge of establishing lives as freed people in a racially divided society. Guided by an ethic of mutual responsibility, African American men and women established benevolent societies to provide food, shelter, and **clothing** to their community's neediest members. In turn, these groups provided valuable leadership opportunities for the free black population. Significantly, northern African American benevolent associations were committed to racial uplift and the abolition of slavery.

Benevolence

In the first quarter of the 19th century, American society was overwhelmed with the profound economic, social, and cultural changes caused by the "market revolution," which marked a shift from the traditional household economy of the 18th century to large-scale manufacturing typical of industrialization. The "market revolution" influenced the development of an urban working class. This shift to a wage-labor economy, aided in part by the abolition of slavery in Northern states, meant more men and women than ever were dependent on wages rather than living as self-sufficient farmers. Thus, industrialization intensified economic instability for all members of society, especially African Americans and poor whites.

At the turn of the 19th century, cities such as Boston, New York, and Philadelphia witnessed the beginnings of benevolent organizing among white and black residents. Early associations specifically targeted poor women and children and sought to provide temporal and spiritual relief. Americans typically organized benevolent associations within their local communities, maintaining in their associations distinct boundaries between gender and race. Although African American and white societies developed simultaneously, benevolence took on different meanings in these communities that reflected contemporary racial ideas.

In the 1790s, white women organized associations within **churches** and local communities. Associations such as the New York Society for the Relief of Poor Women with Small Children (1797); the Boston Female Asylum (1800); the Association for the Relief of Respectable, Aged, Indigent Females (1814); the Female Hebrew Benevolent Society (1819); and the Boston Children's Friend Society (1833) were established to care for women and children overlooked by existing social programs. Benevolent women did not seek dramatic changes in American society; rather they worked within existing ideas about class, race, and gender to provide material and spiritual comfort to those who needed it. As privileged Christian and Jewish women, they believed they were responsible for helping the less fortunate of their community.

In the 1820s, as industrialization intensified and community needs increased dramatically, men and women shifted from charitable assistance to reform. The spread of evangelicalism in this period reinforced this change as revivalists such as Charles Finney (1792–1875) and Lyman Beecher (1775–1863) emphasized individual action in achieving salvation. Associations formed by white men and women in the 1820s promoted temperance, public education, and abolition of slavery in an effort to remove sin and reform American society. Because these organizations sought to reform society, men and women often attempted to organize across lines of race, class, and gender beginning in the 1830s.

Benevolence and the Black Community

Like whites, black men and women often established separate associations. African American men in Philadelphia established the Free African Society in 1787 to provide mutual aid for the free black community of Philadelphia. The Society also provided leadership development and aided ex-slaves who were transitioning from slave labor to wage labor. In other New England communities, African Americans established similar associations such as the African Society of Boston (1796); the African Benevolent Society of Newport, Rhode Island (1808); and the African Society for Mutual Relief of New York City (1808). Organizers consciously adopted the use of "Africa" in their associations' names. Many members were either from Africa or were only one or two generations removed from Africa.

In addition to charity, black benevolent societies played an important role in other areas of community life. For example, the Free African Society of Philadelphia petitioned the city in 1790 for land to be reserved for a black **cemetery**. In the same year, a group of elite free mulattos in Charleston, South Carolina, founded the exclusive Brown Fellowship Society, in which membership was based on (light) **skin** color and economic status. It handled members' funerary arrangements as well as provided support for social and educational activities. African American societies also provided vital support for the development of African American churches and schools. Prominent Philadelphia ex-slaves Richard Allen (1760–1831) and Absalom Jones (1746–1818), founders of the Free African Society, were instrumental in establishing black churches in the city. Jones opened a school for black children in his African Episcopal Church of St. Thomas in 1800. For blacks, education was foundational for freedom and racial uplift.

Black women were equally busy establishing benevolent associations. Like male associations, these groups emphasized community aid, racial betterment, and abolition of slavery. For example, the constitution of the Afric-Female Intelligence Society of America, established in Boston in 1831, emphasized the well-being of the members of its communities as well as the abolition of slavery. The African Dorcas Association of New York City made and distributed garments to their neighbors and friends. The association developed out of members' concern that poor black children could not attend school because of the lack of adequate clothing and **shoes**. In addition to self-help activities such as **sewing**, black women also formed literary societies. For example, by 1849, the city of Philadelphia had 106 black literary societies with membership including more than one-half of the area's black population. Literary clubs raised funds to build schools and libraries for the black community. Indeed, the Ladies Educational Society in Ohio was responsible for opening more black schools than any other American organization, black or white.

Abolitionism

Free black men and women influenced the rise of radical abolitionism in the 1820s, particularly through their opposition to the American Colonization Society (ACS). Founded in 1817 by white Americans who opposed slavery but feared a larger national free black population, the ACS promoted plans for establishing an American colony in Africa for freed slaves and free blacks. The ACS supporters believed removing the free black population from the United States would promote the eventual abolition of slavery. Blacks, however, noted the racist sentiments of colonization supporters and feared that the movement would lead to forced emigration of all blacks. Blacks also believed that the presence of a free black population in the United States would aid abolition in the form of continued activism and practical aid to newly freed slaves. In Maryland, Virginia, and Delaware, free blacks worked more cautiously against colonization throughout the antebellum period.

Blacks in the North organized racially segregated and integrated anti-slavery societies. In 1832, black women in Massachusetts formed the first female anti-slavery organization in the United States, the Female Anti-Slavery Society of Salem. In 1833, women organized the Philadelphia Female Anti-Slavery Society and the Boston Female Anti-Slavery Society. Black women were essential in the establishment and activities of both organizations. Although black and white women worked together in these associations, the two groups differed in their views of abolitionism. While white women emphasized moral suasion, black women promoted a broader agenda, including racial uplift with abolitionism.

The passage of the Fugitive Slave Act of 1850 led blacks to step up their efforts to aid fugitive slaves. Black men and women established benevolent associations in Canada to provide clothing, housing, and food to newly arrived fugitives. Black abolitionists Henry (1815–1854) and Mary Bibb (1820–1877) established the Refugee Home Society in 1851 to raise money, collect clothing and other material goods, and purchase land to develop black settlements in Canada. Other organizations such as the Victoria and the Daughters of Prince Albert were established by black women to aid black Canadian communities in caring for the sick and the poor and burying the dead.

During the American Civil War, blacks continued to rely on established patterns of benevolence. With the exception of the navy, black men were not allowed to enlist in the early years of the war so black women in the North did not face dramatic changes in their domestic arrangements. When the Emancipation Proclamation took effect on January 1, 1863, and northern black men were recruited into the Union military, black women formed organizations to aid black soldiers and their families. Black soldiers were paid less than whites and all soldiers received pay only after considerable delay; thus, black families faced significant economic hardships that were compounded by the lack of jobs for black women. Associations also provided clothing and other provisions for soldiers, aided fugitive slaves, and sent teachers to the South to work with freed slaves. After passage of the Thirteenth Amendment and the end of the Civil War, black benevolence remained an important resource for the black community.

See also African Free School.

FURTHER READING

Boylan, Anne. *The Origins of Women's Activism: New York and Boston, 1797–1840*. Chapel Hill: University of North Carolina Press, 2002.

Cott, Nancy, ed. *No Small Courage: A History of Women in the United States*. New York: Oxford University Press, 2000.

Dorsey, Bruce. *Reforming Men and Women: Gender in the Antebellum City*. Ithaca, NY: Cornell University Press, 2002.

Horton, James Oliver, and Lois E. Horton. *In Hope of Liberty: Culture of Community, and Protest among Northern Free Blacks, 1700–1860*. New York: Oxford University Press, 1997.

Johnson, Michael P., and James L. Roark. *Black Masters: A Free Family of Color in the Old South*. New York: W.W. Norton & Company, 1986.

Quarles, Benjamin. *Black Abolitionists*. New York: Oxford University Press, 1969.

Silber, Nina. *Daughters of the Union: Northern Women Fight the Civil War*. Cambridge, MA: Harvard University Press, 2005.

Winch, Julie. *Philadelphia's Black Elite: Activism, Accommodation, and the Struggle for Autonomy, 1787–1848*. Philadelphia: Temple University Press, 1988.

Yee, Shirley J. *Black Women Abolitionists: A Study in Activism, 1828–1860*. Knoxville: University of Tennessee Press, 1992.

JULIE HOLCOMB

BIBLE. During slavery in the United States, slavery proponents used the Bible to justify human bondage and enforce slave subordination. Enslaved blacks responded to this in various ways, some with acceptance, others with defiance. At the same time, American slaves also developed their own interpretation of biblical passages, which not only reflected their disdain for slavery but also provided them with emotional comfort.

From the colonial to the antebellum period, slavery proponents rationalized the institution using the Bible. They argued that people of African descent were inherently inferior to whites because of the "the curse of Ham" (Genesis 9:20–27). Because Ham had witnessed Noah's nakedness, Noah cursed Ham's descendants, through his son Canaan. Though the Bible does not specify that Canaan was "black," many white people came to identify him as such because they associated blackness and darkness with evil. As a result, these individuals also identified Noah's "accursed" descendants as people with dark skin, or Africans. Proslavery proponents also cited other Old Testament passages to support slavery, such as Genesis 14:14, which refers to Abraham's slaves, and Exodus 20:17 and Deuteronomy 5:21, which refer to the Ten Commandments' admonition against coveting another's "manservant or maidservant." To slaveholders, these passages clearly illustrated that the Bible, and, subsequently, God, sanctioned the practice.

Although many justified slavery through the words in the Bible, many North American slaveholders had little interest in sharing the book with their slaves. Despite laws to the contrary, some slaveholders believed that slaves who accepted Christianity would be entitled to freedom. Still others were concerned that religious activities would distract slaves from their temporal duties or fill slaves' minds with thoughts of equality and freedom, making them more difficult to control. Other slaveholders, who were not religious themselves, placed little importance on religious instruction for their slaves.

Nevertheless, some white Americans actively sought to convert the enslaved population. The Massachusetts Congregationalist minister Cotton Mather (1663–1728), for example, wrote an appeal to his fellow colonists in 1706, as well as a catechism, which he hoped would convince them to share Christianity with their "servants," black and white. Organizations such as the Anglican Society for the Propagation of the Gospel in Foreign Parts (SPG) also sent missionaries to North America in the 18th century, some of whom spent considerable time teaching small numbers of slaves to read religious works such as the Bible. Reverend Alexander Garden (ca. 1685–1756) of South

Carolina, for example, obtained funds from the SPG to purchase two enslaved boys, whom he baptized and catechized. One of the slaves, Harry, became a teacher at Garden's school for blacks, which served Charleston from 1743 to 1768. Another missionary society, the Associates of Thomas Bray, founders of the **Bray schools**, sometimes worked with the SPG to provide the colonies with **books**—including Bibles, spelling books, testaments, and catechisms—for slave instruction. The Associates also paid for schools and catechists, or teachers, for slaves, such as Joseph Ottolenghe (ca. 1711–1775), who catechized slaves in Georgia through the support of the Associates and the SPG.

By the 19th century, a stronger religious movement arose toward sharing the Bible with the enslaved, although some slave masters were still wary of providing slaves access to Christianity. Many made similar arguments to their colonial counterparts, but 19th-century slavery proponents were increasingly concerned over the rise in slave rebellions based on religious messages, such as the Denmark Vesey conspiracy of 1822 in Charleston, South Carolina. Although it never came to fruition, many believed that this conspiracy was based on Vesey's interpretations of the Bible. In 1831, Nat Turner's rebellion terrified Southampton County, Virginia, when slave preacher Turner led slaves in killing 59 whites before the revolt fell apart. Turner argued that God had supported his actions through a series of visions. As a result of Vesey, Turner and other insurrections, antebellum whites throughout the South passed strict legislation forbidding slaves from learning to read. Ministers and other religious Americans, however, still pushed for slaves' greater access to the biblical teachings, arguing that if slaves were "properly" instructed in the Bible, they would learn that God approved of slavery, which would prevent future conspiracies and rebellions. Such beliefs on the part of religious whites led to the creation of antebellum missions to enslaved populations, where slaves were taught the catechism and the Bible by white missionaries, ministers, or even by their white "family" members, such as masters and mistresses. For example, Louisa Maxwell Cocke, the evangelical Protestant mistress of Bremo, Fluvanna County, Virginia, taught her slaves to read the Bible. Benevolent associations such as the American Bible Society and the American Tract Society published Bibles for use among African Americans, although slave masters often continued to deny their slaves direct access to the text.

More than just white intervention led slaves to Christianity. Many enslaved Americans learned about Christ and the Bible from friends, parents, or elderly slaves who had charge of the young. Some slaves directly appealed to their white families to read them the Bible. Slaves themselves held religious gatherings in praise houses, their own houses of worship on the plantation, or in brush (or hush) arbors, outdoor shelters made up of branches and brush. Such meetings were frequently led by slave preachers chosen from among their brethren because of the preachers' knowledge of the scriptures and their ability to inspire the crowd.

Even as more and more African American slaves adopted Christianity during the 19th century, the vast majority of them still could not read their faith's most important text. Historians estimate that only some 5 to 10 percent of approximately 4 million Southern slaves were literate by the time of the Civil War. Whether they could read or not, however, slaves continued to place a great value on the Bible. They frequently memorized Biblical verses that they had heard in **churches and praise houses** or learned in catechism classes, Sabbath school, or at informal gatherings where slaveholders offered religious instruction.

Slaves reacted to their religious lessons in a variety of ways. When preachers, even enslaved preachers, extolled the need for slave subordination and obedience, some slaves accepted the messages as part of their faith. Still more, however, outright rejected such lessons as whites' distortions of Christ's true message. Those individuals who refused to accept white interpretations of slavery as God's will found justification for their own interpretations in the Bible, most notably in Old Testament books about slavery and freedom, such as Exodus. It is in Exodus that Moses, under God's command, led the enslaved Israelites out of Egyptian bondage. Many American slaves believed this story demonstrated a divine hatred of slavery that eventually would bring them, too, out of their bondage. Other Bible stories further encouraged slaves to struggle through life's hardships because, in return, God would reward their faith and fortitude. Such stories include that of Daniel, who continued to pray to God despite laws opposing prayer and therefore survived being thrown to the lions, and Noah, who faced ridicule for believing God's message of a flood, but survived the deluge because of his faith. Other slaves, particularly those who did not have access to the Bible, completely rejected Christianity because they could not find any redeeming qualities in what they had learned from others. Whether they were reinterpreting the Bible or rejecting it entirely, slaves who held such opinions frequently avoided airing them in front of whites because of the backlash that could come from disagreeing with white society's proslavery Bible-based argument.

In addition to valuing the content of the Bible, slaves also cherished the book itself as a tangible, holy object. Accounts relate that slaves who had access to Bibles sought spiritual comfort by searching the text for the one or two words they may have known, such as "Jesus" or "Spirit," or by holding the book in front of them and reciting memorized verses to themselves and to others. Other statements indicate that runaway slaves who had access to Bibles often included them among the few belongings that they carried with them into freedom. Some slaves so valued books and reading that they placed an almost religious value on secular texts, such as spellers, as well, as disclosed in firsthand accounts that describe slave children attending funerals, carrying schoolbooks as they would a religious text. Thus, many enslaved individuals placed great value on both the book itself and its message. They viewed the Bible as containing God's true feelings toward slavery and delivering promises of future freedom.

See also African Free School; Bray Schools.

FURTHER READING

Callahan, Allen. *The Talking Book: African Americans and the Bible*. New Haven, CT: Yale University Press, 2006.

Cornelius, Janet Duitsman. *Slave Missions and the Black Church in the Antebellum South*. Columbia: University of South Carolina Press, 1999.

Frey, Sylvia R., and Betty Wood. *Come Shouting to Zion: African American Protestantism in the American South and British Caribbean to 1830*. Chapel Hill: University of North Carolina Press, 1998.

Genovese, Eugene D. *Roll, Jordan, Roll: The World the Slaves Made*. New York: Vintage Books, 1976.

Mathews, Donald G. *Religion in the Old South*. Chicago: University of Chicago Press, 1977.
Raboteau, Albert J. *Slave Religion: The "Invisible Institution" in the Antebellum South*. 1978. Reprint, New York: Oxford University Press, 2004.

TAMMY K. BYRON

BLACKSMITH SHOPS. Blacksmiths, metalworkers who work iron and steel by heating the metals and hammering them into useful shapes, were among the first European settlers to arrive in the United States because of the great need for iron objects. Historically, blacksmiths were found in most urban centers and scattered throughout the rural countryside, providing tools and hardware for everyday activities.

Large numbers of slaves were trained as blacksmiths within the mid-Atlantic plantation economy, providing goods and services necessary for the success of agricultural enterprise and producing additional income by doing work for neighboring farms. Within a plantation economy, training could be accomplished in a number of ways. A young slave could be formally apprenticed to a commercial shop and return to the plantation as a skilled workman at the end of the apprenticeship; an indentured servant skilled in the work could train the slave as a smith during the course of his indenture, or a slave could learn by working in a shop with other skilled slaves. Once a skilled labor base was established, it became self-perpetuating within the plantation with one generation training the next. Most of the work done in these rural shops was utilitarian in nature. Common plantation shops repaired tooling, shod horses, and manufactured farm implements and simple household goods much like their urban counterparts.

In larger urban centers such as Baltimore, New Orleans, Charleston, and Philadelphia, slave smiths were exposed to more formal architectural **ironwork**, such as gates, railings, and sign brackets that adorned homes and businesses of the wealthier residents. Vestiges of that early traditional architectural work can still be seen on early buildings in cities like Charleston and New Orleans where a rich heritage of African American ironwork developed among the slave population.

Tools from the Blacksmith Shop

On the North Carolina plantation where Doc Edwards was enslaved, some tools were made of wood and others were made by the blacksmith:

> We hed big work shops whare we made all de tools, an' even de shovels was made at home. Dey was made out of wood, so was de rakes, pitchforks an' some of de hoes. Our nails was made in de blacksmith shop by lan' an' de pisks an' grubbin' hoes, too.

Source: George P. Rawick, ed. *The American Slave: North Carolina Narratives*. Vol. 14. Westport, CT: Greenwood Press, 1972.

African Traditions

While West Africans had developed highly sophisticated ironworking traditions in their homelands, African-born slaves do not seem to have been chosen and marketed specifically for their knowledge or skill as ironworkers. Newly arrived slaves were not identified by the skills that they brought, as was often the case with newly arrived English indentured servants. Most were simply sold as laborers, the younger and healthier being more highly valued. Succeeding generations of American-born slaves were trained in skilled trades such as blacksmithing, and these skilled slaves were advertised as such when being sold, commanding higher prices than common laborers or household workers.

The work of slave blacksmiths rarely exhibits direct links to African tradition. In many West African communities, blacksmiths were thought to have mystical powers and the ability to control forces of the natural world, influencing the lives and futures of those that sought the smith's advice. Smiths produced potions and amulets to heal physical ailments or to control positive and negative forces in the natural world. Little material evidence exists from early American settlements to suggest that these traditions of power and influence were bestowed on slave smiths. Functionally, objects like agricultural tools are nearly identical in North America and in Africa, yet African styles and methods of manufacture show distinct differences from the European-style tools that dominate in North America. Great differences are evident in work methods as well. African smiths traditionally work in a squatting position with the forge and anvil set at ground level, whereas European smiths work standing erect at an elevated hearth and anvil. Slaves were most often acculturated into the European methods and produced European-styled implements for their masters.

Iron Production

The iron-smelting industry was the largest user of slave labor after agriculture. Slaves were found at all levels of the industry, including common laborers in the **mines**, wood cutters and charcoal burners, carters hauling materials, and charging the furnace. Slaves were found in highly skilled positions overseeing the operation of the furnace, where one individual was capable of controlling the success or failure of the entire operation. Skilled furnace operators were highly valued and as such were frequently allowed benefits not normally given to common slaves. In the dispersal of a defunct ironworks, the furnace operators and finers (ironworkers) often were sold in a family unit, whereas common laborers usually were sold off individually.

The work of a blacksmith might vary considerably depending on geographic location and time period. Geography influenced the size of the population locally and the type of industry found nearby. The range and types of work were defined by local demand. Iron objects made by blacksmiths can be categorized by function into several distinct groupings. Building hardware includes **nails**, hinges, door latches and **locks**, gates, railings, weathervanes, and lightning conductors. Tools used in nearly every trade were made from iron and steel, as well as household furnishings like fireplace tools and cooking utensils. Agricultural implements like axes, **hoes**, rakes, ploughs, and harvesting knives traditionally have been the staple of a rural smith's work. A considerable quantity of iron is used in transportation: horseshoes and hardware for wagons and ships. Finally, weaponry such as guns and swords were necessary for sport, fashion, and defense.

See also Auction Advertisements; Charms; Fetishes; Firearms; Legal Documents; Shrines and Spirit Caches.

FURTHER READING

Christian, Marcus. *Negro Ironworkers of Louisiana, 1718–1900*. Gretna, LA: Pelican Publishing, 1972.

Deas, Alston. *Early Ironwork of Charleston*. Fresno, CA: Linden Publishing, 1997.

Dew, Charles B. *Bond of Iron: Master and Slave at Buffalo Forge*. New York: W.W. Norton, 1994.

Gill, Harold. *The Blacksmith in Eighteenth-Century Williamsburg*. Williamsburg, VA: Colonial Williamsburg Foundation, 1978.

McNaughton, Patrick R. *The Mande Blacksmiths: Knowledge, Power, and Art in West Africa*. Bloomington: Indiana University Press, 1988.

KENNETH SCHWARZ

BLANKETS. After **food**, blankets were the commodity most commonly distributed to the enslaved. In general, blankets were distributed once a year or every two years, although some masters only gave them out every three years, and women who gave birth received a blanket even if it was not the regular time for their distribution. Procurement and cost of blankets were constant concerns of slaveholders, who gave their agents and overseers precise instructions regarding the quality, size, and source of the blankets they wished to have. Blanketing was imported in quantity from England and Europe in the years before the American Revolution, but this trade was suspended during the war years, forcing slaveholders to find other sources for blankets, including producing them on their own plantations or purchasing them from local sources. By the mid-19th century, enslaved women were producing most of the blankets that they and their masters used.

The blankets themselves were of types that were available to all, both enslaved and free persons. They were made from wool and in a variety of sizes, from 56 inches to 86 inches wide (with most between 66 inches and 72 inches wide), and 69 inches to 96 inches long (with most between 78 inches and 84 inches long). Some slaveholders describe the fabric as Kendall (also Kendal) **cotton**, which was not cotton but a type of coarse wool. In the midst of the Revolutionary War, George Washington, writing to Clement Biddle, the deputy quartermaster-general of the Continental Army, asked that Biddle purchase and send to Mount Vernon "200 (Dutch) Blankets for my Negros. . . . The Blankets which I used to Import for my Negros came under the description of Dutch Blankets, abt. 15 in a piece, striped large and of the best quality, such I now want." In December 1815, Martha Ogle Forman, who lived at "Rose Hill" in Cecil County, Maryland, wrote in her diary that she and her enslaved women "cut out 13 home made twilled blankets." Interviewed in Arkansas sometime between 1936 and 1938 as part of the Federal Writers' Project, "Aunt" Susie King remembered, "I had a good mother. She wove some. We all wove mos' all of the blankets and carpets and counterpans and Old Missey she loved to sit down at the loom and weave some."

Weaving Blankets

In North Carolina, Tempie Herndon Durham remembered the blankets and other textiles made on the plantation:

My white fo'ks lived in Chatham County. Dey was Marse George an' Mis' Betsy Herndon. Mis Betsy was a Snipes befo' she married Marse George. Dey had a big plantation an' raised cawn, wheat, cotton an' 'bacca. I don't know how many field niggers Marse George had, but he had a mess of dem, an' he had hosses too, an' cows, hogs an' sheeps. He raised sheeps an' sold de wool, an' dey used de wool at de big house too. Dey was a big weavin' room whare de blankets was wove, an' dey wove de cloth for de winter clothes too. Linda Harnton an' Milla Edwards was de head weavers, dey looked after de weavin' of de fancy blankets. Mis' Betsy was a good weaver too. She weave de same as de niggers. She say she love de clackin' soun' of de loom an' de way de shuttles run in an' out carryin' a long tail of bright colored thread. Some days she set at de loom all de mawnin' peddlin' wid har feets an' her white han's flittin' over de bobbins.

De cardin' an' spinnin' room was full of niggers. I can hear dem spinnin' wheels now turnin' roun' an' sayin' hum-m-m-m, hum-m-m-m, an' hear de slaves singin' while day spin. Mammy Rachel stayed in de dyein' room. Dey wuzn' nothin' she didn' know 'bout dyein'. She knew every kind of root, bark, leaf an' berry dat made red, blue, green, or whatever color she wanted. Dey had a big shelter whare de dye pots set over de coals. Mammy Rachel would fill de pots wid water, den she put in de roots, bark an' stuff an' boil de juice out, den she strain it an 'put in de salt an' vinegar to set de color. After de wool an' cotton done been carded an' spun to thread, Mammy take de hanks an' drap dem in de pot of boilin' dye. She stir dem 'roun' an' lif' dem up an' down wid a stick, an' when she hang dem up on de line in de sun, dey was every color of de rainbow. When dey dripped dry dey was sent to de weavin' room whare dey was wove in blankets an' things.

Source: George P. Rawick, ed. *The American Slave: North Carolina Narratives.* Vol. 14. Westport, CT: Greenwood Press, 1972.

In the 18th and early 19th centuries, many slaveholders were concerned that blankets be distributed on a regular schedule and before cold weather arrived. In July 1787, Washington wrote to another deputy quartermaster-general to find out whether he had been able to find the blankets he needed, noting that "the Season in which these will be wanted is now fast approaching and against which they must be provided for the accomodation [*sic*] of my Negros." Three months later, in September 1787, he asked his nephew, George Augustine Washington, to send me the number of New blankets your Aunt has in her store room. They are not to be had here but in high terms, and yet this is the year that *all* my people are entitled to receive them, except the Women who have had children and been supplied on that occasion.

Other slaveholders were not as concerned with the welfare of their enslaved men and women as George Washington. Abolitionist Frederick Douglass wrote in his *Narrative of the Life of Frederick Douglass, An American Slave* that at the plantation in Talbot County, Maryland, where he was born

There were no beds given the slaves, unless one coarse blanket be considered such, and none but the men and women has these. This, however, is not considered a very great privation. They find less difficulty from the want of beds, than from the want of time to sleep; for when their day's work in the field is done, the most of them having their washing, mending, and cooking to do, and having few or none of the ordinary facilities for doing either of these, very many of their sleeping hours are consumed in preparing for the field the coming day; and when this is done, old and young, male and female, married and single, drop down side by side, on one common bed,—the cold, damp floor,—each covering himself or herself with their miserable blankets; and here they sleep till they are summoned to the field by the driver's horn.

In 1839, abolitionists Theodore Weld (1803–1895); his wife, Angelina Grimke (1805–1879); and her sister, Sarah Grimke (1792–1873), gathered the testimony of Northern travelers to the South about slavery and the enslaved and published this evidence in *American Slavery As It Is: Testimony of a Thousand Witnesses*. One contributor stated that in Mississippi, "a small poor blanket is generally the only bed-clothing, and this they [slaves] frequently wear in the field when they have not sufficient clothing to hide their nakedness or to keep them warm."

See also Beds; Bells and Horns; Wool Textiles.

FURTHER READING

"Born in Slavery: Slave Narratives from the Federal Writers' Project, 1936–1938," American Memory, Library of Congress. At http://memory.loc.gov/ammem/snhtml/.
Forman, Martha Ogle. *Plantation Life at Rose Hill: The Diaries of Martha Ogle Forman, 1814–1845*. Edited by W. Emerson Wilson. Wilmington: The Historical Society of Delaware, 1976.
"George Washington Papers at the Library of Congress 1741–1799," American Memory, Library of Congress. At http://memory.loc.gov/ammem/gwhtml/gwhome.html.
Weld, Theodore. *American Slavery As It Is: Testimony of A Thousand Witnesses*. New York: American Anti-Slavery Society, 1839. "Documenting the American South: North American Slave Narratives." At http://docsouth.unc.edu/neh/weld/menu.html.

MARTHA B. KATZ-HYMAN

BOATS. Almost from the beginning of slavery in North America, black slaves worked as riverboatmen, handling small boats in the Chesapeake region, introducing

African boatways to South Carolina, and serving in military capacities on American rivers throughout the colonial era and during the American Revolution. Slaveholders worried about employing slaves on rivers, for the waterways provided avenues of escape for slaves and the slave riverboatmen gained knowledge about the countryside and its hideaways, information that might be turned against slaveholders during a slave revolt. The exigencies of moving staples to market, however, overrode planters' fears about losing control over slaves plying skiffs, dugouts, rafts, **canoes,** or larger craft on the rivers. Slaves as riverboatmen remained ubiquitous but hardly noticed throughout the South.

Nowhere were the presence and importance of slave riverboatmen more profound than on the Mississippi River. As early as 1733, French officials were using Africans to row military bateaux between settlements in lower Louisiana. These slaves made excellent boatmen. They no doubt had civilian counterparts. Under Spain, Louisiana's population created a large demand for food staples, and the flat-boat-keelboat era began in earnest. Blacks, slave and free, manned such boats in significant numbers. Frequently, slaves were both cargo and crew, moving with owners to resettle or with dealers for resale. Sometimes escaped slaves became river pirates.

Flatboat commerce continued to employ slaves until Emancipation. From Natchez, Mississippi, Simon Gray and other slaves transported numerous flatboats of lumber and huge log rafts downriver. They enjoyed considerable responsibility, mobility, and economic opportunity. Gray even bossed white crews and handled large sums of cash. Despite his position, hard work and fevers wrecked his health.

Probably more blacks worked on steamboats than on other river craft; indeed, crews without blacks were rare. In personal services, blacks functioned as waiters, cooks, maids, dishwashers, stewards, barbers, and musicians. From these ranks emerged such postwar leaders as P. B. S. Pinchback, Reconstruction governor of Louisiana, and R. R. Church, a wealthy Memphis civic leader.

Roustabouts performed the heavy labor. In port or taking on fuel, they did hurried, body-racking work. Under way, however, they enjoyed relative ease when not stoking the furnaces. Their storytelling and singing later became blues music.

Slaves also worked dredge-boats and snagboats. They tended **ferries** and maintained levees. Many joined the Union's Civil War fleets. Slave contributions to river transport were far-reaching but, ironically, have been unsung.

See also Shipyards.

FURTHER READING

Baldwin, Leland. *The Keelboat Age on Western Waters.* Pittsburgh: University of Pittsburgh Press, 1941.

Kinnaird, Lawrence, ed. *Spain in the Mississippi Valley, 1765–1794: Translations of the Materials from the Spanish Archives in the Bancroft Library.* 3 vols. Washington, DC: U.S. Government Printing Office, 1946–1949.

McPherson, James M. *The Negro's Civil War: How American Negroes Felt and Acted during the War for the Union.* New York: Vintage Books, 1965.

Moore, John Hebron. "Simon Gray, Riverman: A Slave Who Was Almost Free." *Mississippi Valley Historical Review* 49 (1962): 472–484.

Surrey, Nancy M. *The Commerce of Louisiana during the French Regime, 1699–1763*. New York: Columbia University Press, 1916.

Thwaites, Reuben Gold, ed. *Early Western Travels, 1748–1846*. 31 vols. Cleveland, OH: A. H. Clark, 1904–1907.

JOHN E. HARKINS

BOOKS. Schooling for persons of African descent in North America was limited from colonial times onward, but literacy among enslaved and free blacks—even in the South—has a longer, more nuanced history than conventional wisdom suggests. Only two mainland British colonies, South Carolina (1740) and Georgia (1755), passed laws against slave literacy. A few slaves and free blacks acquired basic reading and simple arithmetic via instruction arranged by slaveholders or during apprenticeships in skilled trades. Well before prohibition of slave ownership by the Society of Friends, slaveholding Quakers in the colonies promoted general welfare and some schooling for their enslaved workers.

A significant source of instruction for African Americans came with late 17th- and early 18th-century concern that enslaved persons in the colonies be converted to Christianity. For example, the Virginia legislature in 1667 and bishops of London after 1720 encouraged slaveholders to allow for religious training and baptism of their human property. Reading skills were thought to greatly improve understanding of Christian principles for blacks and whites, but many slaveholders balked at the idea. Learning and religion were believed to engender prideful behavior among enslaved

---

A Will to Learn

Laura Thornton's brother, enslaved in Arkansas, taught himself to read:

> I never learnt to read and write. In slave time, they didn't let you have no books. My brother though was a good reader. He could write as well as any of them because he would be with the white children and they would show him. That is the way my brother learnt. He would lay down all day Sunday and study.

Source: George P. Rawick, ed. *The American Slave: Arkansas Narratives*, Vol. 10, Parts 5 and 6. Westport, CT: Greenwood Press, 1972.

On Louisa Adams's North Carolina plantation and on many others, books were forbidden:

> Lawd, you better not be caught wid a book in yor han'. If you did, you were sold. Dey didn't 'low dat.

Source: George P. Rawick, ed. *The American Slave: North Carolina Narratives*. Vol. 14. Westport, CT: Greenwood Press, 1972.

---

workers, and literacy often made the difference between a successful or failed escape attempt. In 1723, a Virginia slave wrote to the bishop of London in affecting if broken English about slaveholders' demeaning treatment of slaves and their reluctance to allow for religious training.

Anglican minister William Dawson wrote from Virginia to England in 1743 for a copy of school rules "which, with some little Alteration, will suit a Negro School in our Metropolis [Williamsburg]." Rev. Alexander Garden (ca. 1685–1756) established a short-lived "Negro school" in Charleston supported by the Anglican Society for the Propagation of the Gospel in Foreign Parts until the government intervened in 1755. In contrast to many Anglican ministers, Presbyterian Rev. Samuel Davies (1723–1761) judged African-born and Virginia-born blacks capable of learning to read. He and several associate ministers in Hanover County from about 1755 added literacy to their conversion ministry among slaves. Davies supplied **Bibles**, various catechisms, Watts's prayers for children and *Psalms, Hymns, and Spiritual Songs*, and spelling books at his own expense until the nondenominational Society for Promoting Religious Knowledge among the Poor began sending him books.

Schools for enslaved slave children were established in both the North and South by the Associates of Dr. Bray in Philadelphia (1758); Williamsburg, Virginia (1760); New York (1760); Newport, Rhode Island (1762); and Fredericksburg, Virginia (1765). A philanthropic organization allied with the Anglican Church in England, the Associates dedicated themselves to converting blacks in the colonies to Christianity but like Anglican ministers, the bishop of London, and Samuel Davies, the Associates did not call for an end to slavery as unchristian. Materials sent from England for the **Bray schools**' teachers included beginning English primers and catechisms for children, sermons, and bishops' pastoral letters.

By 1760, Davies and his associates used literate slaves to teach other slaves in Hanover and Louisa counties to read. Anglican Rev. Jonathan Boucher was not able to establish a Bray school in King George County, Virginia, but with books from the Associates, he also "employ'd a very sensible, well-dispos'd negro belonging to a Gentleman who lives about a Mile from Me, to endeavour at instructing his poor fellow Slaves in Reading and some of the first Principles of Religion." He told the Associates that it might surprise them if he were "to relate to You some of the Conversations I have had with Negroes to whom I had given Books." A 19th-century writer claimed that black parents who had been instructed by Davies in turn taught their children and passed on to them books from Davies. A 19th-century Baptist historian reported in 1810 that a church book was kept by early members of the black Baptist church founded in Williamsburg in the last quarter of the 18th century, further evidence for a subculture of literate slaves. Slaves who were moved to Missouri in the early 19th century wrote letters back to Williamsburg inquiring after relatives from whom they had been separated. But schooling for African Americans in the South was the exception, not the rule, from colonial times through the Civil War. What toleration there had been for slave literacy evaporated in the early 19th century as fear of slave rebellion spawned laws designed to discourage it. An 1831 Virginia statute banning the gathering of free blacks to learn to read was representative of increasingly draconian slave codes from about 1830 to the Civil War.

In Northern cities and towns until well into the 19th century, if education for African American students was offered at all, it was in separate schools, often supported by philanthropic organizations such as the New York Manumission Society or the Society of

Friends (Quakers). The earliest of these, the New York **African Free School** established in 1787, won high praise from visitors, but most students' failure to find professional employment afterward sent many to sea or into employment as waiters, coachmen, barbers, servants, and laborers. In the common school era in the 1840s and 1850s, some of these schools in the Northeast and Midwest were desegregated. In 1850, the Massachusetts Supreme Judicial Court, in the face of charges that segregated schools stigmatized black children, upheld Boston's power to segregate black children in separate schools.

Blacks' marked desire for education and access to the printed word within the institution of slavery cannot be underestimated. Davies noted that slaves in his Presbyterian congregations in colonial Virginia often expressed to him their need for more books. In the early 19th century, some free black parents in the South, at some danger to themselves, paid for lessons for their children at home. And later, educator Booker T. Washington (1856–1915) wrote that escaping slaves during the Civil War and freed men and women after the Civil War were "a whole race trying to go to school" as Northern missionary societies sent teachers South to teach slaves who had escaped to federal lines and the Freedmen's Bureau established schools.

See also Writing Tools.

FURTHER READING

Coleman, Mary Haldane Begg. *Virginia Silhouettes: Contemporary Letters Concerning Negro Slavery in the State of Virginia*. Richmond, VA: Press of the Dietz Printing Company, 1934.

Costa, Tom. "Advertisements." The Geography of Slavery in Virginia. At www2.vcdh.virginia.edu/gos/explore.html.

Ingersoll, Thomas N. "'Releese us out of this Cruell Bondegg': An Appeal from Virginia in 1723." *William and Mary Quarterly* 3rd ser., 51 (1994): 777–782.

Jones-Wilson, Faustine C., et al. *Encyclopedia of African-American Education*. Westport, CT: Greenwood Press, 1996.

Richards, Jeffrey H. "Samuel Davies and the Transatlantic Campaign for Slave Literacy in Virginia." *The Virginia Magazine of History and Biography* 111 (2003): 333–378.

Stanton, Lucia. *Free Some Day: The African-American Families of Monticello*. Charlottesville, VA: Thomas Jefferson Foundation, 2000.

Van Horne, John C., ed. *Religious Philanthropy and Colonial Slavery: The American Correspondence of the Associates of Dr. Bray, 1717–1777*. Urbana: University of Illinois Press, 1985.

LINDA H. ROWE

BOTTLE TREES. A bottle tree is a living or dead tree usually located in front **yards** or **gardens** with glass bottles of various colors stuck on the end of its branches or hanging from its limbs by string or wire. Additional objects were also suspended from trees, including tinfoil, metal disks, and sometimes animal bones. Historically, tree ornamentation originated in West Africa to protect home and field from evil spirits and thieves. This custom was transported to the Americas by enslaved Africans and concentrated in the Deep South. This practice evolved from a similar tradition of grave decoration to appease deceased spirits.

The Kongo peoples of West Africa traditionally used bottle gourds, glass bottles, and ceramics hanging from trees outside of homes and on the edge of cultivated fields to protect them from specters (ghosts) and trespassers. The evil spirits would be attracted to the dancing sunlight passing through the bottles and, upon entering, they would be trapped and prevented from harming the household or its possessions and products. Thieves would see these trees and would be afraid to enter, believing that they would be cursed. Accounts are recorded of enslaved African Americans using similar methods in their gardens to prevent stealing or damage and to ensure a bountiful harvest.

Cedar trees and blue glass were the preferred mediums, but any species of tree and color of bottle could be used. In some cases, the trees and adjacent rocks also were whitewashed, which designated sacred ground. The interior of the glass bottle was sometimes painted and could be partially filled with water, stones, sticks, **nails**, pins, or dirt from a graveyard. The bottle lip could be lined with grease. This bottle preparation would attract spirits inside and prevent them from escaping.

Bottles and other objects also could be placed on porches, near entryways, or throughout the yard and garden. Other forms of yard decoration have included plates nailed to trees or placed on pointed sticks, wheels, flashing or reflective objects, personal materials of the deceased, and broken or inverted artifacts. Circular artifacts represented the cycle of life, death, and rebirth. The reflective pieces, such as **mirrors**, could deter evil spirits or symbolize the light of heaven. Personal relics such as the tools of ancestors and chairs symbolizing thrones often were placed strategically within an area where the ancestor was active for protection or as a form of ancestor veneration.

Such yard ornamentation customs evolved from a similar tradition of grave decoration. West African and African American graves often were covered with a wide assortment of material objects, including **shells**, white rocks, ceramics, lamps, clocks, mirrors, wooden sculptures, and toys, which to the untrained eye can be viewed as trash. Many of these things are the personal or the last touched objects of the deceased and were left on the grave to comfort them in the afterlife and prevent them from haunting the living. Many of these grave offerings were purposely broken to symbolize the passing of the individual and encourage their spirit to pass into the afterlife where things were made whole again. The ancestors could then help those left in the living world.

In the 21st century, bottle trees are seen across the country in the yards and gardens of both white and black households. The modern forms of these trees are more often viewed as yard art and may be constructed of wood or metal stands resembling a Christmas tree.

See also Shrines and Spirit Caches.

FURTHER READING

Thompson, Robert Farris. *Flash of the Spirit: African and Afro-American Art and Philosophy.* New York: Vintage Books, 1984.

TIMOTHY E. BAUMANN

BRANDS. Branding irons were used to mark enslaved Africans before leaving Africa as the property of a particular owner and to mark those both free and enslaved who were convicted of certain felonies and who then claimed "benefit of clergy" and were set free.

The brands used to mark enslaved Africans were of several types. Some were wrought-iron letters or symbols or a combination of both, specific to a particular owner, and attached to a wood handle. As described in the instructions to captains of **slave ships** and in 19th-century narratives of slave traders, some brands were made of silver wire formed into specific shapes, and some were just a simple metal pipe. All were heated in a fire until hot and then applied to the skin of the enslaved person. The heat caused a blistering of the skin in the pattern of the brand, and it was this pattern that was used by at the ship's final destination to distinguish one slaveholder's property from another's.

It is unclear how common branding was among American slaveholders. In an early example of branding, in 1766, "twenty-four prime Slaves, six prime women Slaves, being mark'd and number'd as in the margin [of the captain's instructions]" were sent to "Georgey, in South Carolina" aboard the *Mary Brow*. Branding was more common in the earliest years of the slave trade, primarily for those enslaved Africans destined for the West Indies or South America. Although the practice fell into disuse after England and the United States abolished the legal importation of enslaved Africans in 1807 and 1808, branding was revived after 1820 with the onset of the illegal slave trade to Cuba, Brazil, and the American South. In what was clearly intended as a cruel reference to slave branding, the abolitionist Capt. Jonathan Walker's hand was branded "SS" (slave stealer) when he was found guilty for trying to help seven Pensacola, Florida, slaves escape in 1844. The infamous case inspired John Greenleaf Whittier's poem, "The Branded Hand."

The "benefit of clergy" plea was an English common law and statute law practice carried into the British colonies in the 17th century and used in Virginia even after the American Revolution. Briefly, it involved a legal fiction whereby those convicted of certain crimes could, by reading a verse from the **Bible**, be considered members of the clergy and thus could escape being punished for certain felonies. If the plea was accepted by the court, which it usually was, the convicted persons were branded at the base of the left thumb with an "M" for manslaughter or a "T" for various kinds of theft. This branding was meant to discourage the felons from committing further crimes and also served to mark them in case they were ever brought to court again on a felony and wished to plead benefit of clergy again. In Virginia, the requirement to read a verse from the Bible was abolished by law in 1732, and the same law made white women equally eligible for benefit of clergy as white men. It also specified that "any negro, mulatto, or Indian whatsoever" was eligible for benefit of clergy, but the list of offenses for which they could receive this benefit was severely limited in comparison to those allowed for white men and women. But even though severely limited, this still represented an improvement over previous law, which had no such exceptions.

FURTHER READING

"Atlantic Slave Trade to Savannah." The New Georgia Encyclopedia. At www.georgiaencyclopedia.org/nge/Article.jsp?id=h-686.

Canot, Theodore. *A Slaver's Logbook: or 20 Years' Residence in Africa: The Original Manuscript.* Englewood Cliffs, NJ: Prentice-Hall, 1976.

Rediker, Marcus. *The Slave Ship: A Human History.* New York: Viking, 2007.

Rowe, Linda. "The Benefit of Clergy Plea." Colonial Williamsburg. At http://research.history
.org/Historical_Research/Research_Themes/ThemeReligion/Clergy.cfm.
"Voyage 91133, Mary Brow (1766)." The Trans-Atlantic Slave Trade Database. At http://slave
voyages.org/tast/database/search.faces?yearFrom=1700&yearTo=1800&anyowner=Strong&ship
name=Mary+Brow.

MARTHA B. KATZ-HYMAN

BRAY SCHOOLS. Laws in almost all the Southern colonies before the American Revolution made it illegal for enslaved persons to be taught to read. In Virginia, however, although most black Virginians were not educated, it was not against colonial Virginia law for slaves to know how to read and write. The occasional slaveholder paid to have an enslaved child schooled for a year or two, the small number of enslaved apprentices were supposed to get basic reading and figuring, and even organized elementary instruction for black children was known in Virginia and its capital, Williamsburg.

In 1743, the Rev. William Dawson (d. 1752), Church of England (Anglican) minister of Bruton Parish Church in Williamsburg and president of the College of William and Mary, wrote to England for a copy of school rules "which, with some little Alteration, will suit a Negro School in our Metropolis [Williamsburg], when we shall have the Pleasure of seeing One established." Whether Dawson envisioned occasional Anglican catechism classes is unclear, but he later wrote that he visited three of these schools in his parish.

More significant for its longevity, continuity, and scope was a school in Williamsburg for enslaved children founded by the Associates of the Late Dr. Bray, a philanthropic organization in London closely allied with the Church of England. In the early 1700s, Thomas Bray (1658–1730) had played a leading role in emerging Anglican missionary efforts such as the Society for the Propagation of the Gospel in Foreign Parts. One of Bray's long-time goals was the Christian conversion of slaves in North America. After his death in 1730, the Bray Associates sought to fulfill Bray's vision by underwriting schools for young slaves in Virginia, Pennsylvania, New York, and South Carolina. Neither Bray nor the Associates called for an end to slavery.

The Bray Associates established a school in Williamsburg in 1760. The charity school (or Bray School as it is sometimes known) ran at capacity, 25 to 30 students at a time, for 14 years. Colonial officials, tavern keepers, and tradesmen were among the broad range of slaveholders, both men and women, in Williamsburg who enrolled enslaved children from 3 to 20 years of age for all or part of the three years of instruction the Associates wanted for each child. A small number of free black children also attended this school.

The Bray school in Williamsburg was administered by local trustees appointed by the Associates. The longest serving of these was Robert Carter Nicholas (1728–1780), the treasurer of Virginia, assisted by the current rectors of Bruton Parish Church. Ann Wager (1716–1774), a widow of modest means, was appointed schoolmistress. At the time she applied for the position, Wager was the much admired teacher of 12 white children in Williamsburg and a former tutor to the Burwell children at Carter's Grove plantation a few miles from town.

Wager taught from a curriculum based almost entirely on the **Bible**, Anglican catechisms, religious tracts, sermons, and bishops' pastoral letters shipped from London to Williamsburg by the Associates. The students assembled at Wager's rented home at

6:00 A.M. in the warmer months, 7:00 A.M. in the winter. She was to accompany the children to Bruton Parish Church when special services occurred during the school day, for example, on saints' days. She taught her pupils "the true Spelling of Words, make them mind their Stops & endeavour to bring them to pronounce & read distinctly." Pupils received a *Book of Common Prayer* upon completion of an examination on the catechism by the church rector. Girls also learned to knit and sew.

Children of African descent in 18th-century Virginia usually learned by doing alongside their parents on plantations or in shops and houses in urban settings. Anglican clergymen cooperated with slaveholders. Although kindly disposed toward her students at the Bray School, Wager undoubtedly reinforced the message of keeping to one's place. Still, the schooling black children received from her via the Bray Associates may have had unintended consequences: Wager taught her students rules of behavior, correct enunciation, and, most important, to spell and read. These were tools resourceful slaves could use to advantage in a society that offered them little formal protection.

See also Books; Writing Tools.

FURTHER READING

Van Horne, John C. *Religious Philanthropy and Colonial Slavery: The American Correspondence of the Associates of Dr. Bray, 1717–1777.* Urbana: University of Illinois Press, 1985.

LINDA H. ROWE

BROOMS. Brooms are objects most often associated with sweeping and cleaning. In the everyday lives of enslaved African Americans these objects served a dual purpose. Brooms were used to sweep and clean debris, but also were used in nonutilitarian ways. They were used in wedding ceremonies and in other rituals associated with beliefs about keeping away enemies, spirits, or bad luck. Although brooms commonly are used by an array of cultural groups for sweeping and cleaning, and some cultural groups use them for rituals, many of the rituals in which enslaved African Americans across the southeastern United States used brooms seem to share common ideologies concerning protection of their home lives. Many of these ideas are similar to practices that are present in Africa and regions in the Caribbean where Africans were shipped as slaves.

Broom Making

Brooms were initially made of organic materials, so they typically have not survived into the 21st century. What is known about brooms and how the enslaved living on plantations used them survives in the form of oral histories and photographs and through African American traditions that persist. Oral accounts that document the use of brooms—such as that by the Mars Bluff farming community of descendants of slaves located in the piedmont region of South Carolina—indicate that at least two types of brooms were made within their community: a straw broom for sweeping the house and a brush broom for sweeping the yard. The brush brooms often were made from dogwood tree branches and wrapped with a strip of cloth or wire if available. Straw brooms were made with a stiff grass or straw. Some accounts suggest that sorghum (*Sorghum vulgare technicum*) was used to make these types of brooms. Sorghum,

---

Brooms and Weddings

As Paul Smith, a former slave in Georgia relates, broomsticks played an important role in many slave marriage ceremonies:

> When a slave man wanted to git married up wid a gal he axed his marster, and if it was all right wid de marster den him and de gal come up to de big house to jump de broomstick fore deir white folkses. De gal jumped one way and de man de other. Most times dere was a big dance de night dey got married.

Source: George P. Rawick, ed. *"The American Slave: Georgia Narratives*, Vol. 13. Westport, CT: Greenwood Press, 1972.

Another former slave in Georgia, James Bolton, elaborated on the weddings:

> Folkses diden' make no big to-do over weddings lak they do now. When slaves got married, they jes' laid down the broom on the flo' an' the couple jined hands an' jumped bakkuds over the broomstick. Ah done seed 'em married that way many a time. Sometimes mah marster would fetch Mistess down to the slave quarters to see a weddin'. Effen the slaves gittin' married was house servants sometimes they married on the back porch or in the back yahd at the big 'ouse, but plantation niggers, whut was fiel' hands, married in they own cabins. The bride an' groom jes' wo' plain cloes, kyazen they didn' have no mo'.

Source: George Rawick, ed. *The American Slave: Georgia Narratives*, Supp. Ser. 1, Vol. 3, Part 1. Westport, CT: Greenwood Press, 1978.

---

often referred to by slaves as broom corn, is a grass that can be processed and used to make sorghum molasses, a task that slaves often were required to perform. When this plant was dried out, the grass stiffened, making it ideal for use as broom straw. Some accounts by slaves suggest that certain types of grasses or straws were available only in certain seasons, and, therefore, the brooms in use at any particular time likely reflected seasonal vegetation changes. The materials used to make brooms varied regionally and were dependent on the availability of raw materials.

In some instances, broom making might have been a task that was required of slaves by the plantation overseer, but it is likely that this was something slaves did regardless, after daily tasks were completed. Plantation inventory records suggest that, much like **baskets** or **colonoware**, slaves were making brooms to take to market to be sold or traded, although it is unclear whether slaves or the plantation overseers received the profit.

Rituals

Ex-slave narratives often reference the use of brooms as instruments of protection and control. Brooms were thought to effectively protect the house from unwanted guests and the troubles of the outside world. A broom placed near a doorway would keep unwanted guests from entering the house. If salt was swept over the path of an unwanted guest by a broom, it was thought that the guest would stay away and not interfere with the lives of those inside the house. Because enslaved African Americans accorded the broom certain supernatural powers, it was important to treat it with respect. In African American folklore, it was considered bad luck if sweeping was done in the presence of guests. It was considered disrespectful and brought bad luck if a broom was stored with broom straw on the ground.

In many areas of West Africa and in the Caribbean, it is a common practice to keep the areas in front of a house clean of debris. Individuals often viewed the front yard areas as an extension of the house, where most of the daily domestic activities outside of work occurred. By keeping the outside areas around the house clean of debris, unwanted materials that may have been harmful to one's health were prevented from entering the home and therefore a swept yard was a means of protection from the outside world. Women and children were often the ones who took on the duty of sweeping the **yards**. This practice took place on plantations and is still practiced in some African American communities in the 21st century.

Slave narratives often refer to the use of broomsticks during plantation wedding ceremonies that involved slaves. Although laws at the time prohibited marriage between slaves, some slaveholders allowed their slaves to marry, and most often they or a plantation overseer performed the wedding ceremony. The practice of jumping over a broomstick, with several variations recorded, often was part of the marriage ceremony. Some slaves recalled that the man placed his broom on the ground in front of the woman and the woman then placed her broom on the ground in front of the man, they both faced each other, and then simultaneously jumped over the broom that was positioned in front of them. Another account mentions that an individual had to jump over the broom three times to be married. In one instance, the slaveholder held the broomstick off the ground and then the bride and groom jumped, separately, over the broomstick backward. Whoever made it over without touching the handle of the broomstick became head of the household. As slave marriages were not legal, the broom jumping was thought to provide the symbolic action of being married, and when it occurred, the event signified marriage. Varied accounts all reference crossing over the broom.

The origins of "jumping the broom" are unclear, and it is unknown whether the custom of jumping the broom at weddings originated with slaves or their holder. It is possible that a special broom was made for the occasion or the broom was provided by the overseer or slaveholder. The tradition of jumping the broom during wedding ceremonies is a practice that continues among many members of the African American community who want to maintain a link with their African heritage. The ritual usually is performed at the end of the wedding or at the reception and involves all of the guests present. Typically, the history of the event is told as another guest places a broom on the floor, everyone present counts to three, and then the couple jumps the broom.

Broomsticks were used by blacks on Sapelo Island, a Sea Island located off the coast of Georgia, during a dance called the "Buzzard Lope." The Buzzard Lope dance celebration, often called a "shout" by members of the community, was performed to the beat of a broomstick. During the dance, the men first threw a handkerchief on the floor and then danced around it in a circle to the beat of the broomstick on the floor. The motions of the men mimicked a buzzard hunting its prey.

A late 18th-century watercolor entitled "The Old Plantation," painted by an anonymous artist and thought to have been created in South Carolina, shows a group of men and women on a plantation with scarves or handkerchiefs along with instruments, who appear to be dancing. The man in the center holds a long stick in his hand and the painting's activities may represent a broomstick-jumping ceremony or a variation of the Buzzard Lope celebration. The presence of what appears to be a broomstick in the painting hints at the varied use of the broomstick in the lives of enslaved blacks.

The use of brooms in rituals suggests that slaves had traditions and practices beyond those simply ascribed by the plantation owner, and their continuation through slavery and beyond indicates their importance to African American heritage. When enslaved blacks gathered materials for brooms and then crafted them, they had the opportunity to make choices that reflected ideas about their importance.

FURTHER READING

Bailey, Cornelia Walker, with Christena Bledsoe. *God, Dr. Buzzard, and the Bolito Man: A Saltwater Geechee Talks about Life on Sapelo Island.* New York: Anchor Books, 2000.

Bird, Stephanie Rose. *Sticks, Stones, Roots & Bones: Hodoo, Mojo & Conjuring with Herbs.* St. Paul, MN: Llewellyn Publications, 2004.

Genovese, Eugene D. *Roll, Jordan, Roll: The World Slaves Made.* New York: Random House, 1974.

Georgia Writers' Project, Savannah Unit, Works Progress Administration. *Drums and Shadows: Survival Studies among the Georgia Coast Negroes.* Athens: University of Georgia Press, 1940.

Vernon, Amelia Wallace. *African American at Mars Bluff, South Carolina.* Columbia: University of South Carolina Press, 1993.

STACEY L. YOUNG

BUTTONS. Buttons have a long history as objects of decoration, utility, value, play, and even spirituality. In ancient Egypt, Greece, and Iran, button-like objects made of gold, earthenware, bone, and glass were used as ornaments, seals, or badges to indicate status, wealth, or rank, but most probably were not used as clothing fasteners, although period images of Greek and Roman clothing indicate the use of fasteners of some type in holding garments together. Some of the earliest evidence of button manufacture comes from 13th-century Paris, France, where laws regulating the operation of craft guilds were established by the city's provost (mayor); among the guilds to be regulated was the one to which the buttonmakers of the city belonged. At about the same time, Crusaders returning from the Middle East brought with them the idea of a deliberately made slit in clothing through which a fastener could be inserted, making buttons more useful as a way to hold pieces of clothing together.

Buttons became sought-after clothing accessories. During the Renaissance, buttons were used as ornamentation on men and women's **clothing**, with some men's coats having hundreds of decorative buttons. By the 17th century, buttons made of bone, wood, cloth, thread, silk, wool, and metal were readily available, with the less expensive types of buttons used on clothing worn by the poor and middle classes, and the most expensive types used on clothing of the gentry and aristocracy.

Buttons and buckles found by archaeologists in a subfloor pit at Carter's Grove slave quarter, Williamsburg, Virginia. (The Colonial Williamsburg Foundation.)

During the 18th century, the production of buttons of all types exploded. French manufacturers sold buttons embroidered in silks, or with gold decoration, as well as ones covered in lace or studded with jewels. English manufacturers became specialists in metal buttons of silver, pewter, brass, and steel; cut steel buttons were especially popular. Although some types of women's clothing in this period did include buttons, by far the greatest use of buttons was on men's clothing: shirts, waistcoats, vests, breeches, trousers, and coats. The buttons ranged from the strictly utilitarian cloth or plain metal buttons on a craftsman's coat, to the highly ornamental embroidered or precious metal buttons on an aristocrat's coat, which were meant to be worn only at court or on important occasions, to the die-stamped brass buttons used on military uniforms.

For the most part, the enslaved wore clothing that was similar in style to that worn by whites and free blacks, and thus the buttons on their clothing would have been identical. Studies of Virginia **runaway slave advertisements**, many of which describe the clothing of those men and women who made their escape from slavery, indicate that the buttons were of some type of metal. They might also have been **cloth**, as these were often used on the clothing worn by the lower class. An important exception to this were the buttons used on suits of **livery** worn by enslaved men in gentry and upper-class households who worked in highly visible positions such as waiters or footmen inside the house or coachmen and postillions for those wealthy enough to own coaches or other wheeled vehicles. These suits included a coat, waistcoat, and breeches of quality wool complete with elaborate edging and fancy buttons. Being able to clothe a slave in such a fashion was a sign of the slaveholder's elevated economic status.

Typically, many of these articles of clothing—breeches, trousers, shirts, waistcoats, coats—would wear out before the buttons would, so often the buttons would be retained. It is not unexpected, therefore, that buttons of many types have been found in some quantity at known slave quarters. The reasons for their being retained are not clearly understood, however. Some of the archaeologists who did the initial excavations at known slave quarters, such as Monticello and Mount Vernon, in the 1980s thought that the buttons might have been removed from discarded clothing during the process of making pieced quilts, but more recent analysis by other archaeologists suggests that enslaved men and women purchased more fashionable buttons for their

---

Buttons Brought Good Luck

According to Mollie Dawson, a former Texas slave, young enslaved women wore button strings for good luck:

> Most all de young girls had what we called a charm string. Every one of deir friends and kinfolks dey would see dey would ask them for a pretty button ter put on dis charm string. I has seed some of dem charm strings five feet long, and some of de prettiest I ever seed in my life, dey was a lot prettier den dese beads dat we buys at de store now. Dis charm string was supposed ter bring good luck ter de owner of it.

Source: George P. Rawick, ed. *The American Slave: Alabama and Indiana Narratives*, Vol. 6. Westport, CT: Greenwood Press, 1979, 1119–1159.

---

clothing, which would have necessitated removing the older ones. These older buttons may have been retained and used for other purposes, as suggested by other scholars, who think that these buttons were either saved for ornament to replace the **beads** and **shells** most Africans used for adornment or were the only surviving parts of clothing that was hidden or stored in the root cellars. The buttons may have been retained for other reasons as well: for use as toys for children, as game pieces in various games, as decorations on other clothing, or as objects used in African religious ceremonies.

Buttons from the 19th century have been found in other slave-related contexts. For example, archaeological excavations at the Hermitage, Andrew Jackson's home in Nashville, Tennessee, revealed a large quantity of buttons associated with a large triple housing unit that may have been the residence of Gracy, the plantation's seamstress. This indicates that, in some instances, the buttons simply might be the discards from regular **sewing** activities at a slave quarter.

See also Subfloor Pits.

FURTHER READING

"Archaeology." The Hermitage, Home of Andrew Jackson, Archaeology. At http://thehermitage .com/index.php?option=com_content&task=view&id=96&Itemid=118.

Baumgarten, Linda. "'Clothes for the People'—Slave Clothing in Early Virginia." *Journal of Early Southern Decorative Arts* 14, no. 2 (1988): 27–70.

Epstein, Diana, and Millicent Safro. *Buttons*. New York: Harry N. Abrams, 1991.

Heath, Barbara J. "Buttons, Beads, and Buckles: Contextualizing Adornment within the Bounds of Slavery." In *Historical Archaeology, Identity Formation, and the Interpretation of Ethnicity*, edited by Maria Franklin and Garrett Fesler, 47–69. Williamsburg, VA: Colonial Williamsburg Research Publications/Colonial Williamsburg Foundation, 1999.

Kelso, William M. "The Archaeology of Slave Life at Thomas Jefferson's Monticello: 'A Wolf by the Ears.'" *The Journal of New World Archaeology* 6, no. 4 (June 1986): 5–20.

Samford, Patricia M. *Subfloor Pits and the Archaeology of Slavery in Colonial Virginia*. Tuscaloosa: University of Alabama Press, 2007.

MARTHA B. KATZ-HYMAN

C

CANOES. Canoes were the main personal water craft associated with southeastern coastal United States and Caribbean plantations during the 17th, 18th, and 19th centuries. When roads were few and often impassable, canoes served as a means of transportation for both people and goods. Canoes used in the Southeastern United States and Caribbean were initially based on Native American designs and often were built by slaves who had been taught European crafting techniques. In addition, canoes were used for both work and trade or provided an opportunity for recreation, entertainment, and subsistence. Rarely were they used to escape from bondage in the United States, although they were known to have provided means to freedom in the Caribbean.

Before the importation of large numbers of African slaves, Europeans were introduced to local canoe-building techniques by Native Americans. The use of available local resources and the techniques taught to the first Europeans by the Native Americans subsequently were adopted and improved on by later generations of craftsmen using European techniques and designs. Generally, the practice of canoe manufacture in the Southeastern United States involved selecting a large cypress tree trunk to use as the hull of the canoe. Native Americans used fire to soften the interior and then worked the wood with stone or shell tools, hollowing out the interior to create the watercraft. Felled trees would be shaped by burning the interior and scraping out the charred sections to achieve a dugout canoe. Europeans continued this practice but used metal tools to hasten the process. The use of metal tools allowed the crafting of finer canoes that were less bulky in design and eventually eliminated the need of fire reduction. Added to the design were braces and seats to shore up the canoes. Over time, as large cypress trees began to disappear from the environment in the Southeastern United States, different techniques were developed. Some of these techniques had the added benefit of streamlining the watercraft even further and increasing the occupant capacity. In the Caribbean, the overuse of wood, for canoes and other objects, deforested many islands.

Traditionally, there were two types of canoes. The first was the standard canoe known in the 21st century. Long, narrow, and capable of carrying two to three people and a variety of goods, these canoes were widely used for all manner of activity along the rivers and bays. The second type of canoe is called a "periagua" (also called "periauger" or "pirogue"). The periagua is a larger version of the standard base design. Early periaguas were just larger dugouts, reinforced with strakes and internal knees. Later a larger version was created using more than one log. The first log was shaped to create a keel, and the second log was then split in half, with each half hollowed and reattached to the keel. This design created a large open cargo vessel with a shallow draft. By adding oarlocks and a mast, it could be sailed or rowed up and down local rivers while carrying large cargoes. In addition to river trade, this vessel could make short trips up and down the coast or to nearby islands, making trade with other ports possible. This basic shallow design was carried over to the small coasting schooner that, instead of a solid hull, would have traditional European construction with a planked hull.

Little is known about how African designs influenced local boatbuilding traditions. Certainly areas of West Africa had a strong tradition of boatbuilding, although little work has been done to study these connections. This lack of clear evidence may be due to the tradition of plantation owners apprenticing young slaves to white craftsmen. These apprenticeships would have included master shipbuilders and blacksmiths. In addition, those slaves who survived the Middle Passage with such skills would have been sent or loaned to master craftsmen to learn European methods of construction. Because the canoe is a simple water craft and has been used throughout the world, the style developed over and over again with regional variation, including differences in construction material and methods of construction, as well as fore and aft design variations. Slaves making such boats would not have been constructing these craft for personal use or ownership but instead would have been building them for the market or plantation owners' needs and thus would have followed European traditions.

Slaves most often used canoes during the course of their work. Slaves frequently were used as rowers on large canoes or periaguas for shipping goods both up- and downstream or from island to island. Some slaves were held by businesses that specialized in transporting goods and were used strictly for this purpose. Before the development of railroads, most goods were shipped via rivers to major ports such as New York or Charleston from where the goods would be exported. This practice was especially true in the Southeastern United States, where coastal **rice** plantations would ship tons of rice yearly to ports for exportation. Ferry services would be used to deliver such goods or plantation owners could outfit their own canoes and deliver the goods themselves. In addition to the delivery of goods and people, canoes were heavily used in the coastal southern United States and Caribbean for transportation of people. These personal transportation canoes would be generally powered by slave labor. In addition, slaves who worked on rice plantations frequently used canoes, periaguas, and flatboats to move around the plantation's intricate canal systems. In coastal regions, slaves worked as fishermen to provide **fish** to local markets and supplement the food stores of the entire plantation.

The use of canoes on rice plantations also led to a sport that both entertained slaveholders and supplied a source of personal income for some slaves. In the 19th century, boat races often were held in which plantations would field their fastest canoes and rowers. These rowers often competed in front of large audiences for cash prizes and sometimes were dressed in exotic uniforms to add to the entertainment and spectacle of the race. Skilled crews thus were showcased for their ability to quickly get valuable goods to market before the competition.

Aside from work, slaves often had access to canoes for hunting and fishing. Slaves who worked on rice plantations under the task system frequently had free time at the end of each day for personal activities, as opposed to enslaved workers on **cotton** plantations where the work was done from sunup to sundown, who thus had few opportunities to hunt and fish unless directed to. But when an opportunity presented itself in either situation, slaves could use canoes to both hunt and fish outside of the plantation. Extra foodstuffs were a welcome addition to the limited diet of most plantation slaves.

Canoes were not used as a typical means of escaping bondage in the Southeastern United States because few rivers provided the opportunity to truly escape to freedom and instead only led to other plantations. In the Caribbean, however, many slaves attempted to paddle, row, and sail to other islands to escape. Slaves with maritime skills also escaped by disguising themselves as emancipated slaves and signing on to outgoing cargo ships. As the Caribbean was controlled by many different European powers, a slave lucky enough to escape to an island controlled by another foreign power could not be easily retrieved without international repercussions.

See also Boats; Ferries; Fish and Shellfish; Work Routines.

FURTHER READING

Amer, Christopher. *The Malcomb Boat (38CH803): Discovery, Stabilization, Excavation, and Preservation of an Historic Seagoing Small Craft in the Ashley River, Charleston County, South Carolina.* Research Manuscript Series No. 217. Columbia: South Carolina Institute of Archaeology and Anthropology, 1993.

Doar, David. *Rice and Rice Planting in the South Carolina Low Country.* Charleston, SC: The Charleston Museum, 1970.

Fleetwood, Rusty. *Tidecraft: The Boats of Lower South Carolina and Georgia.* Savannah, GA: Coastal Heritage Society, 1982.

Harris, Lynn. "Canoes and Canoe-built Vessels in the Lowcountry." Occasional Maritime Research Papers Maritime Research Division. Columbia: South Carolina Institute of Archaeology and Anthropology, University of South Carolina. At www.cas.sc.edu/sciaa/mrd/documents/canoe.pdf.

Smith, Julia Floyd. *Slavery and Rice Culture in the Low Country Georgia, 1750–1860.* Knoxville: University of Tennessee Press, 1985.

DANIEL HUGHES

CARICATURES. Caricatures are literally "loaded images"; the English word "caricature" derives from the Italian *caricatura*, which means "the act of loading." Caricatures initially began as an art of the graphic exaggeration of facial and bodily features for an intended comic, political, or satiric effect but now encompass all visual and textual representations of a person or thing in which the writer or artist deliberately exaggerates either physical characteristics or aspects of a person's personality to ludicrous ends.

Caricatures, or grotesque likenesses, can range from those that are meant to insult, critique, and poke fun to those that are used for political or polemical purposes, to those created to compliment and entertain. How a caricature is interpreted, however, depends on the context; while a caricature of a person or thing that in one context might be humorous and entertaining, in another context, it might be disparaging and insulting. Thus, the humor in a caricature is both culture and period specific. Caricatures are inherently ephemeral; they must not only be read in context, but also the

"Reply to Bobalition of Slavery, 1819." One of several racist parodies of black American illiteracy, dialect, and manners issued in Boston at various times between 1819 and 1832. The broadsides are in the form of burlesque reports and letters relating to the annual July 14 celebrations among Boston's black residents of the anniversary of the abolition of the slave trade. The text comprises a "Dialogue between Scipio and Cato, and Sambo and Phillis, occasioned by reading the account of Bobalition proceedings, as detailed in a letter from Cesar Gobbo, to his friend Marco Mushy. . . ." The two vignettes illustrate the respective conversations, and the conversants are portrayed as well-dressed, free blacks. (Library of Congress.)

context is needed to understand and interpret the image. The best examples of caricature can be read as both art and social commentary; the worst reveal the artist or period's stereotypes and assumptions, often negative, about a given person or group of people.

Dating back to at least to the 16th century, the art of caricature was popularized in print during the 18th and 19th centuries as a form of public comment on current events. English artists William Hogarth (1697–1764) and George Cruikshank (1792–1878) as well as the French artist Honoré Daumier (1808–1879) and French writers Charles Baudelaire (1821–1867) and Honoré de Balzac (1799–1850) became well known in this period for their political prints, caricatures, and satirical novels. While political caricature in Europe has a long and distinguished history, in America, with the exception of a few political cartoons, caricatures were rare and did not come into widespread use until the 1760s.

The caricatures of African Americans produced from 1620 to 1865 inherently were tied to the visual representation of slaves and slavery and often personify racial oppression or bigotry in the United States. This history is incredibly complex and contains images, which though at one time may have seemed humorous or satiric to some, are offensive to many in the 21st century. These images were circulated widely in a variety of media, from broadsides and newspapers to paintings.

In general, caricatures made of blacks were not exaggerated likenesses of individuals, but instead were rather generalized and clichéd representations based on racist stereotypes of blacks, which often revealed more about the white mind than they revealed of blacks. Such stereotypes both reflected prejudices and the fear of the other, and justified slavery and subjugation in the United States.

In his famous essay "The Negro and Psychopathology" (1952), African American philosopher Frantz Fanon showed how Western children of all races have assimilated racist stereotypes through the consumption of paintings, prints, and especially comics, movies, cartoons, and popular media. The most common caricatures depicted blacks as grotesque buffoons, menial servants, comic entertainers, and even as threatening and dangerous subhumans through various racist types, including coons, darkies, minstrels, pickaninnies, as well as the **banjo**-playing "Sambo," "Uncle Tom," "Mammy," "Aunt Jemima," and "Jim Crow," and the extent to which these images are both familiar and mainstreamed is striking. These caricatures often exaggerated physical attributes assumed to be representative of African Americans, including extremely dark skin, kinky hair, large red lips around bright white teeth, or bulging eyes, and additionally may depict blacks variously playing a banjo, dancing a jig, or eating **watermelon**.

Caricatures of blacks and slaves have existed from the beginning of the slave trade. Among the earliest visual representations are maps of slave trade routes and depictions of **slave ships**. In the late 18th century, English painter George Morland (1763–1804) produced a series of popular sentimental oil paintings on the slave trade, including his *Execrable Human Traffic* (1788) and *African Hospitality* (1791). English artist Thomas Stothard (1755–1834) was one of the first to engrave an image of the "Sable Venus," in which the black slave woman's experience of the Middle Passage is depicted as a version of the *Birth of Venus*. This "Black Venus" came to symbolize all African female slaves that were brought across the Atlantic by means of the slave trade. In this iconography, the slave ship becomes the scallop shell on which she stands.

The most well-known painted representation of slavery in 19th-century Western culture is Joseph M. W. Turner's 1840 *Slavers Throwing Overboard the Dead and Dying: Typhoon Coming On* (more popularly known as *The Slave Ship*), which depicts the true story of the slave ship *Zong* whose captain, in 1781, threw sick and dying slaves overboard so that he could collect insurance money available only for slaves "lost at sea." In the first decade after the American Revolution, two major anti-slavery images appeared in America, though both originated in England as part of the burgeoning abolitionist movement. The first image, which initially appeared in October 1787, was the seal created by the English Committee for Effecting the Abolition of the Slave Trade and popularized by Josiah Wedgwood (1730–1795) through a mass-produced ceramic medallion. The image shows a kneeling African slave, hands in chains, supplicating, with his hands toward heaven, asking "Am I Not a Man and a Brother?" Frequently used in many anti-slavery publications both in England and the United States, this representation of a kneeling, enchained, and docile male slave, and later, a female slave as well, was reproduced on mastheads of anti-slavery publications, stationery, **books**, prints, oil paintings, newspapers, fabric, **coins**, and even ceramic tea services. The second was the image of a slave ship, based on the English slave ship, the *Brookes*, showing the dreadful conditions under which enslaved Africans were transported. Philadelphian Mathew Carey reprinted this image as a broadside, and it also appeared as a book illustration.

Another popularly reproduced image of slaves was the largely standardized representation of the runaway slave that developed from the conventional images of runaway white indentured servants that existed in 18th-century colonial America and in Europe. This modified stock image depicts a black man running and carrying a bundle of goods on a stick while passing a tree. The female version of this stock image shows a runaway slave woman sitting, resting, and holding a bundle in her hand. Other popular images circulated at the time included the stock image of the contented slave or the "happy slave" as part of plantation scenes, as well as images of the flagellation of a female slave.

Caricatured representations of blacks are found in "genre paintings," or the scenes of everyday life that were popular in antebellum America. Such paintings used character types—including country folk, dandies, easterners, westerners, beggars, merchants, slaves, and minstrels—to tell stories that supposedly represented everyday life in the United States. As many scholars have shown, however, such images were idealized or sanitized versions of reality constructed by artists to appeal to an emerging middle-class audience. In paintings by artists such as William Sidney Mount (1807–1868), one may find images of blacks playing instruments, dancing in barns, or inhabiting plantation scenes.

In what has been called the "plantation formula," artists stereotyped slave life by means of a standardized setting. Used as a backdrop of sorts for both visual representations and early minstrel shows, the plantation became the predominant site in which blacks were shown dancing, singing, and often playing banjos. Such picturesque treatments of plantation life essentially caricatured the types of places that blacks actually inhabited and reinforced notions that Southern plantations were populated with happy, contented slaves, a stereotype that lingered on into the 20th century through Hollywood films representing the Old South.

Another caricature that appeared in both 19th-century popular prints and genre paintings was the sleeping black man, reclining in a sleeping faun pose drawn from classical antiquity. This image of the sleeping African American has been interpreted in various ways, but it probably contributed to the stereotyping of black people as lazy and idle.

Between 1830 and 1850, visual representations of slaves altered in America. A key text that provides an index of racial stereotypes is also the book that would become a major source for one of the most popular caricatures in connection with African Americans, Harriet Beecher Stowe's *Uncle Tom's Cabin* (1852). The character of Uncle Tom is one of the first literary and visual examples that demonstrate how ideas about black inferiority can be fully incorporated into popular culture. From this book, two stereotypical figures emerged: Tom and Topsy. They not only become part of literary history, but their caricatured images abound through illustrated versions of Stowe's novel by British cartoonist George Cruikshank (1792–1878) and American artist Charles Howland Hammatt Billings (1818–1874) as well as in ceramic figural groups and in decorated plates, mugs, and other ceramics manufactured in England and exported to America.

In 1857, with the introduction of illustrated journals, newspapers, and weeklies, including *Harper's Weekly, Frank Leslie's Illustrated Newspaper*, and the *New York Illustrated News*, African American caricatures and stereotypes that began as stock characters in genre paintings were spread even more widely. For example, from the 1850s to the 1870s, the popular print makers Currier and Ives distributed scenes of Southern life that further reinforced stereotypes about the happy slaves on plantations. Currier and Ives also produced a popular series of images based on minstrel shows called the *Darktown Comics* (1877–1894) that again repeated negative stereotypes regarding African Americans. Frederick Opper's 1893 engraving *Darkies Day at the Fair (A Tale of Poetic Retribution)* similarly used dehumanizing imagery to illustrate turn-of-the-century sheet music. Not only do such images deny the individuality and dignity of blacks but they also continue to reinforce tired prejudices.

The grotesque caricature of Saarjite Baartman, who became known as the "Hottentot Venus," is an example of a racist caricature. Baartman, a native of what is now the Eastern Cape of South Africa, had *statopygia* (enlarged buttocks), and was brought to England in 1810 by a visiting ship's surgeon so that he could publicly exhibit her unusual physique. First in London and then in Paris, she was displayed like an exotic animal, and forced to endure vulgar epithets shouted at her. When questioned by abolitionists who wished to stop this public display, she told them that she had agreed to come to England, which complicates how one both understands and interprets such images.

The most common caricatures of African Americans came out of minstrelsy. Blackface minstrelsy, which first emerged in the United States in the 1820s, has its roots in plantation entertainment, developed into theatrical conventions by the 1840s, and remained incredibly popular through the Civil War and into the 20th century. Its popularization developed and solidified a number of exaggerated African American stereotypes, including the pompous, overdressed dandy, the country bumpkin, and the banjo-playing minstrel. The grinning black banjo player, often depicted wearing a top hat or dancing a jig, became the most recognizable and clichéd image associated with minstrelsy. The banjo occupies a problematic position in American iconography because of this association.

Caricatures associated with minstrelsy additionally reinforce negative notions of the black man as buffoon or clown or entertainer. These are highly problematic and complicated images, especially as most minstrel performers were whites in blackface. Even in the 20th century, the 1920s radio program *Amos 'n' Andy* borrowed from the minstrel genre and featured two white men performing in black dialect.

These slavery stereotypes persisted well into the 20th century, and additional images were created during Jim Crow and segregation. During the Harlem Renaissance in the 1920s and 1930s, many artists and black intellectuals voiced concerns regarding racist caricatures in art and in the mass media and called for new forms of literary and visual representations of African Americans. Alain Locke (1885–1954), author of *The New Negro*, specifically condemned racial stereotypes and thought that artists, by creating realistic and more sensitive images of blacks, could change negative perceptions about African Americans. Even African American artists such as Palmer Hayden and Archibald Motley Jr., came under critique for their renderings of blacks with bulging eyes, enlarged lips, and musical settings that were associated with minstrel figures.

Throughout the 20th century, African American caricatures were reinforced by their appearance on everyday household items like cookie jars and salt and pepper shakers made for the kitchen. Most common were the "Mammy" and "Uncle Tom" caricatures, but derogatory "coon" caricatures also were depicted on food packaging, including the popular image of Aunt Jemima on syrup bottles and pancake mixes.

Writer Alice Walker (1944–) has described how caricatures and ethnic stereotypes functioned as prisons for African Americans, but contemporary artists, writers, and filmmakers have found ways to interrogate and challenge such racist imagery through the appropriation and reuse of stereotypical representations in their art. For example, artist Betye Saar (1926–), in *The Liberation of Aunt Jemima* (1972), subverts the black mammy stereotype by juxtaposing a raised clenched fist, a symbol of black power, with three different images of Aunt Jemima to express her feelings about racial stereotypes. Contemporary artist Kara Walker (1969–) has used caricatures of African Americans in her works to critique and question issues of race, gender, and sexuality. In her work, she uses the traditional Victorian medium of the silhouette to reproduce racist imagery taken from popular culture. In her *Darkytown Rebellion* of 2000, for example, colored light shone down on the exhibition space. When museum-goers entered the installation, their shadows were forced to interact with Walker's silhouettes, thereby implicating the viewer as part of the scene. Finally, Spike Lee's 2000 film *Bamboozled*, a biting satire of a modern-day minstrel show, explores the proliferation of racial images in American culture and challenges people to think about the power of such imagery and how such caricatures both linger and continue to affect 21st-century society.

See also Abolition Imagery; Runaway Slave Advertisements.

FURTHER READING

Cassuto, Leonard. *The Inhuman Race: The Racial Grotesque in American Literature and Culture.* New York: Columbia University Press, 1997.

Goings, Kenneth W. *Mammy and Uncle Mose: Black Collectibles and American Stereotyping.* Bloomington: Indiana University Press, 1994.

Gombrich, E. H., and Ernst Kris. *Caricature.* Harmondsworth, England: Penguin Books, 1940.

Hofmann, Werner. *Caricature from Leonardo to Picasso.* New York: Crown Publishers, 1957.

Lott, Eric. *Love and Theft: Blackface Minstrelsy and the American Working Class.* New York: Oxford University Press, 1993.

Margolin, Sam. "'And Freedom to the Slave': Anti-Slavery Ceramics, 1787–1865." In *Ceramics in America 2002*, edited by Robert Hunter, 80–109. Milwaukee, WI: Chipstone Foundation, 2002.

Mazow, Leo G. *Picturing the Banjo.* University Park: Pennsylvania State University Press, 2005.

McElroy, Guy C. *Facing History: The Black Image in American Art, 1710–1940.* Washington, DC: Corcoran Gallery of Art, 1990.

Morgan, Jo-Ann. *Uncle Tom's Cabin as Visual Culture.* Columbia: University of Missouri Press, 2007.

Parry, Elwood. *The Image of the Indian and the Black Man in American Art, 1590–1900.* New York: George Braziller, 1974.

Pieterse, Jan Nederveen. *White on Black: Images of Africa and Blacks in Western Popular Culture.* New Haven, CT: Yale University Press, 1992.

Savage, Kirk. *Standing Soldiers, Kneeling Slaves: Race, War and Monument in Nineteenth-Century America.* Princeton, NJ: Princeton University Press, 1997.

Wechsler, Judith, ed. "The Issue of Caricature." Special issue. *Art Journal* 43, no. 4 (Winter 1983): 317–385.

Wonham, Henry B. *Playing the Races: Ethnic Caricature and American Literary Realism.* Oxford: Oxford University Press, 2000.

Wood, Marcus. *Blind Memory: Visual Representations of Slavery in England and America, 1780–1865.* New York: Routledge, 2000.

MELISSA RENN

CAST IRON POTS. Cast iron pots and kettles were the mainstays of 17th-, 18th-, and 19th-century **kitchens**. Manufactured in a wide variety of sizes, they were used by every level of society, including enslaved cooks, for culinary and other household purposes, such as holding hot water for cleaning and washing clothing and household **textiles**. Slaveholders provided pots for their enslaved workers, and they were included as part of the basic equipment specified in overseers' contracts. The same

Uses for Pots

According to former Georgia slave Ed McCree, meals were cooked directly in fireplaces in large iron pots and skillets:

> Most times dere was poke sallet, turnip greens, old blue head collards, cabbages, peas, and 'taters by de wholesale for de slaves to eat and, onct a week, dey rationed us out wheat bread, syrup, brown sugar, and ginger cakes. What dey give chillun de most of was potlicker poured over cornbread crumbs in a long trough. For fresh meat, outside of killin' a shoat, a lamb, or a kid now and den, slaves was 'lowed to go huntin' a right smart and dey fotch in a good many turkles (turtles), 'possums, rabbits, and fish. Folks didn't know what iron cookstoves was dem days. Leastwise, our white folks didn't have none of 'em. All our cookin' was done in open fireplaces in big old pots and pans. Dey had thick iron skillets wid heavy lids on 'em, and dey could bake and fry too in dem skillets. De meats, cornbread, biscuits, and cakes what was cooked in dem old skillets was sho' mighty good.

Source: George P. Rawick, ed. *The American Slave: Georgia Narratives*, Vol. 13. Westport, CT: Greenwood Press, 1972.

As Rev. W. B. Allen recalled, in Georgia many enslaved individuals believed that an overturned cast iron pot offered protection from white interference by muffling the sounds of secret meetings:

> My father was once attending a prayer meeting in a house which had only one door. The slaves had turned a large pot down in the center of the floor to hold the sounds of their voices within. (No sounds can escape from a closed room, if a big pot be turned down in the middle of it). But, despite their precaution, the patrolers found them and broke in. Of course, every Nigger present was "in" for a severe whipping, but the Lord must have spoken to my father. Thinking fast and acting quickly (as if he were inspired), my father stuck a big shovel in the fireplace, draw out a peck or more of hot ashes and cinders and flung them broadcast into the faces of them patrolers. The room was soon filled with smoke and the smell of burning clothes and white flesh and, in the confusion and general hubbub that followed, every Negro escaped.

Source: George P. Rawick, ed. *The American Slave: Georgia Narratives* , Supp. Ser. 1, Vol. 3, Part 1. Westport, CT: Greenwood Press, 1978.

types of pots were found in elegant mansions, dirt hovels, and every type of dwelling in between. Probate inventories of household goods indicate that even some of the poorest members of society usually owned at least one cast iron pot or kettle. Extremely wealthy households often had a number of different cast iron culinary utensils as well as those made from copper and brass.

Cast iron pots that were used for laundry at the Thornhill plantation, Watsonia, Alabama, in slave times. (Library of Congress.)

Early colonists brought cast iron pots and kettles with them to the New World, but by the mid-17th century, iron furnaces throughout the colonies were turning out goods for local consumption. While ships from England and other European ports still continued to carry ironware to the colonies, the American iron industry flourished. Pots, kettles, skillets, griddles, ladles, and other kitchen equipment made from cast iron were created in two-part molds filled with a special type of sticky sand. Each half of the mold consisted of a box-like frame that was filled with the molding sand. A wooden pattern shaped like the pot or kettle was pressed into the sand and then the two parts of the mold were brought together, creating an impression of the object in the sand. The two halves were separated, the pattern removed, and then the two pieces rejoined. The void was filled with molten iron. Once the iron cooled, the two parts of the mold were once again separated, revealing the finished piece.

Cast iron is heavy. A small pot standing 7 or 8 inches tall with a 9- or 10-inch diameter typically weighed about eight pounds. By contrast, a copper kettle of a similar size might weigh only two or three pounds. Because of its solid nature, a cast iron vessel appears indestructible. It will not dent, scratch, or tarnish like copper, brass, or tin. It is, however, quite brittle and will break or shatter under the right circumstances. Its surface is liable to rust if not cared for properly. Cooks and housekeepers were repeatedly warned to wash and dry their ironware carefully and to store it in a dry location to prevent rust from forming. Continual exposure to fire also damaged the bottoms of these vessels.

During the 17th, 18th, and early 19th centuries, most **cooking** in America was done over a wood fire built in a fireplace, although in hot weather food sometimes was cooked outside over a campfire. This manner of food preparation is known as open-hearth cooking. As long as food was cooked over open fires, the shape of most cast iron vessels did not change. Pots, which were sometimes referred to as cauldrons, were bulbous in form. They had rounded bottoms and sides that bulged out and then narrowed in toward the neck only to flare out at the lip. Kettles had straight sides that often tapered slightly toward a flat bottom. Both pots and kettles had two small handles known as "ears" just below their upper edge on opposite sides of the vessel. The shape of these ears changed over time. In the 17th and 18th centuries, they tended to be almost triangular in form, but by the mid-19th century they were more rounded, looking a little like cow horns. Most pots and kettles had a bail handle that attached to the ears, allowing the vessel to be picked up or hung over the fire. Earlier handles were made from wrought iron, whereas later ones tended to be wire. Most pots and kettles had three evenly spaced legs that provided balance when the vessel was set down.

Cooking over an open fire required skill. It took practice to learn how to regulate and manage the fire to produce the correct amount of heat and to know where to place the pot so that the food cooked properly. Some foods like **stews**, soups, and other one-pot meals were cooked with the pot suspended above the fire; others were cooked on the hearth over small piles of hot coals. Most fireplaces were equipped with either an iron crane or a lug pole. The lug pole was mounted in the chimney and spanned the horizontal width of the hearth. The crane was hinged to brackets embedded in the masonry on one side of the fireplace interior. Cranes could be swung into different positions, enabling the cook to take advantage of different parts of the fire. The lug pole was fixed in place. Pots and kettles were suspended from either the lug pole or the crane by pot hooks, chains, or trammels. Other cast iron cooking vessels such as skillets and Dutch ovens, also known as bake ovens, were used only on the hearth. Hot coals were raked from the main fire into small piles supplying individual sources of heat to these vessels. In the case of the Dutch oven, coals were heaped on the lid, so that the heat came from above as well as below.

By the second quarter of the 19th century, cookstoves began to replace the open hearth. With the fire now contained in a cast iron firebox and no longer visible, cooks needed to learn new methods of regulating the heat and of cooking. This new technology required new forms of cookware. Stove tops had removable round cast iron disks that, when removed from the surface of the stove, created "boiling holes" in which the pot or kettle was placed. The traditionally shaped vessels with legs used for open hearth cooking were incompatible. The newer style of pots and kettles was shaped on the bottom so that they sat snuggly in the boiling hole. Stoves usually were sold with a set of cookware that fit the diameter of that particular manufacturer's boiling holes. As pieces broke and were replaced, it was important to buy the correct size vessel for the stove.

Cooking on an open hearth was physically demanding and potentially hazardous work. Although a well-constructed chimney drew the smoke up and away, frequently the cook had to contend with heat, smoke, steam, cinders, burning hot coals, and, at times, chimney fires. While some foods were cooked in pots hanging from pot hooks above the fire, much of the cooking took place on the hearth over small piles of hot coals. The cook was constantly bending over or squatting down next to the pots.

Women (most cooks were female) risked scorching the hems of their petticoats or aprons. Hot, heavy iron pots might easily tip, sending their scalding hot contents down the front of the cook's shins and across the feet. The transition to stove cooking generally resulted in improved working conditions. Cooks no longer needed to bend or squat by the hearth; instead they stood upright. The stove provided a physical barrier between the fire and the cook, although when the stove was in use, the entire surface was hot and visually it looked no different from when it was cold. Cinders and soot no longer landed in the food, but accidents resulted when spilled liquids sent steam billowing up, engulfing the cook. Smoke was drawn directly from the firebox into a pipe and whisked away.

Cast iron vessels had other uses in the domestic setting beyond cooking. During the 17th, 18th, and early 19th centuries, all hot water used by a household was heated in pots or kettles in the fireplace. Laundresses boiled garments and household linens in large pots or cauldrons. They might also place the laundry into wooden tubs and pour the hot water over it. Cast iron pots and kettles were used to make soap and candles, both hot, dangerous tasks involving the rendering of fats. In rural settings, certain aspects of the butchering process used large cast iron pots as well. Beyond the domestic setting, cast iron pots also were found in a number of commercial or industrial settings.

Cast iron pots assumed a unique role among the enslaved who repurposed them as a protective object. Always on guard against any opportunities for rebellion or resistance, slaveholders and their overseer-surrogates routinely forbade their slaves from attending unsupervised meetings. These gatherings, which included praying for freedom, took place nevertheless, usually in secret, at night, and sometimes brought in enslaved individuals from neighboring plantations. Throughout the South, many former slaves later recalled in Works Progress Administration interviews that cast iron pots were overturned at these meetings, which were held both inside and outdoors, because people believed that they muffled the sounds of talking, singing, praying, or shouting and kept the enslaved community free from white interference. As ex-slave Mary Scott from Arkansas observed, "I don't know how they found out the iron pot would take up the noise. They had plenty of em settin' round in them days. Somebody found it out and passed it on." Forbidden from praying, Emma Tidwell, formerly enslaved in Arkansas, remembered that she and others prayed into the ground under an overturned large iron pot normally used for laundry "an de sound wud go up under de pot an ole boss couldn' hear us." In Tidwell's case the sound actually might have been stifled, but in most cases, the pots' use was largely symbolic. In North Carolina, former slave Charity Austin recalled that even though the "pots [were] turned down to kill de soun' o' de singin'," the slaves were overheard having a prayer meeting and singing "I Am Glad Salvation's Free." Because the song mentioned freedom, everyone caught attending the meeting was soundly whipped the next morning.

Pots were used in any number of West African ceremonies and practices among many different cultural groups. Pots frequently embody the gods. For example, among the Yoruba peoples, river water is considered especially powerful and pots are carried into homes filled with river water and therefore river spirits and then are overturned on the floor to protect the house and its occupants. In the American enslaved context, however, the pot's meaning clearly morphed significantly over time, although it remained an object imbued with great power. Its widespread use among American slaves suggests that traditional African practices were carried across the Atlantic to the Americas and then assimilated, probably over several generations. By the 19th century, although the use of the pot had lost its original meaning, it had been transformed and given a new significance that better suited the circumstances.

See also Shrines and Spirit Caches.

FURTHER READING

Brewer, Priscilla. *From Fireplace to Cookstove: Technology and the Domestic Ideal in America.* Syracuse, NY: Syracuse University Press, 2000.

Carlo, Joyce. *Trammels, Trencher, & Tartlets: A Definitive Tour of the Colonial Kitchen.* Old Saybrook, CT: Peregrine Press, 1982.

Eveleigh, David. *Old Cooking Utensils.* Aylesbury: Shire Publications, 1986.

Harrison, Molly. *The Kitchen in History.* New York: Charles Scribner's Sons, 1972.

Rawick, George P. "West African Culture and North American Slavery: A Study of Culture Change among American Slaves in the Ante-Bellum South with Focus upon Slave Religion." In *Migration and Anthropology*, edited by Robert F. Spencer, 149–164. Seattle: University of Washington Press, published for the American Ethnological Society, 1971.

Rose, Peter, ed. *The Sensible Cook: Dutch Foodways in the Old and the New World.* Syracuse, NY: Syracuse University Press, 1989.

Tyler, John D. "Technological Development: Agent of Change in Style and Form of Domestic Iron Castings." In *Technological Innovation and the Decorative Arts*, edited by Ian M. G. Quimby and Polly Anne Earl, 141–163. Charlottesville: University Press of Virginia, published for the Henry Francis du Pont Winterthur Museum, 1974.

ROBIN CAMPBELL

CEMETERIES. Cemeteries are cultural landscape features that are composed of groups of **graves**: each grave represents an individual subsurface deposit that contains the dead. They are, however, more than just burial sites; they frequently serve as a means of social and cultural communication.

Death is among the most disruptive natural phenomena in human societies. Loss of a community member from death removes both their physical and intellectual contributions, such as labor, genes, experience, and wisdom, as well as their social resources, including status, kinship ties, and wealth, from the community. To cope with death, humans developed funerary rituals. Funeral rituals that emphasize burial serve two purposes: (1) they remove the potentially biologically hazardous remains from the living community and permanently place them in a protected subsurface environment, and (2) they address the social voids created by death by reestablishing the social order among the survivors. This latter purpose includes transforming the formerly dynamic living social identity into a static permanent record of how the community wished to remember the decedent. The grave is a primary end-point in the social ritual associated with death: it is frequently used as the vehicle to transmit information about the deceased to all who view the grave site across time.

Markers and other objects found on grave sites do more than just identify where the dead are buried; they provide a tangible record of the decedent's existence and hints of who they once were. When more than one grave is present, and hence more than one grave site ritual is available for interpretation, the audience learns about more than just the individual: they learn about the community that the deceased belonged to and about how that community viewed the world and their place in it. These assemblages are essentially what constitute a cemetery. Cemeteries are features in the cultural landscape that use the dead, and the burial practices related to them, to convey information about communities. They provide cultural links between social identities in the community's past and those still present among the living.

In Africa, different cultures exhibited a wide variety of highly developed funeral rituals that were designed to meet the needs of the survivors. These traditions served as the foundation for a new suite of mortuary practices when the African arrived in the United States. The newly enslaved frequently found themselves in the company of Africans from many different cultures. To develop support networks among themselves, burial traditions that were common to and most meaningful to the greatest number of Africans tended to see more widespread use. Enslaved Africans also came in contact with Euro-American and Native American mortuary ideologies. They frequently assisted in these funeral rituals, which provided a means for them to learn and eventually acculturate these practices. Finally, the dominant Anglo-American Judeo-Christian culture tended to view traditional African belief systems as less civilized, pagan, and even blasphemous. Slaves were encouraged to abandon their traditional mortuary traditions in favor of those followed by their overseers. The burial traditions that developed among enslaved African Americans therefore were unique blends of ideas; these rituals were distinctly different from any in use around them and served as the foundation for many unique features that still dominate modern African American funerals and cemeteries.

Most slaveholders recognized that their charges would not completely abandon their African funerary traditions. Attempts to forcibly dissolve the enslaved's mortuary rituals resulted in instability and revolt. Slaveholders came to believe that slaves were happier and more productive if allowed some control over the dispensation of their dead, but they typically maintained control over aspects of the funerary ritual. Open disregard for the slave as a human being sometimes resulted in open-air abandonment of the body. In other cases, the dead were sometimes provided with an impromptu, on-the-spot burial, frequently in proximity to the place of death. Isolated slave interments occurred in and around fields and work areas. Permitting burials near to the slave's house lots or domestic areas consciously or unconsciously provided links to African homeland traditions.

More commonly, slaveholders set aside land parcels for their slaves' burial purposes. For example, a former slave cemetery with nearly 100 burials has been identified at the McLeod plantation on James Island, South Carolina, near Charleston, and another slave cemetery is located near Nomini Hall, the home of Robert Carter III in Westmoreland County, Virginia. On smaller holdings, slaves were interred outside or adjacent to the slaveholder's burial area. These graves often were located outside of walls and other formal cemetery boundaries. While the slave was recognized as a social personage, the grave location marked their social positions as subservient to those of the owner. On larger landholdings, parcels of less productive land, visually and spatially set apart from domestic and work areas, were dedicated as slave burial grounds. In more urban settings, public lands were set aside for the interment of all African Americans, both free and enslaved. In other cases, some urban slaves were interred in poorly marked graves discreetly placed on the slaveholder's lot. In some communities, **churches** and other social welfare organizations recognized the African American as worthy of burial rites. They encouraged slaveholders to allow slaves to be buried on their grounds in their cemeteries. These burial areas tended to be segregated, and burial rites rarely reflected the dead person's cultural heritage.

In African American culture, the cemetery was considered a place of spiritual pacification. Unlike Judeo-Christian ideology, where a more clearly defined division exists between the world of the dead and the world of the living, West African theologies tended to view the burial place as a conduit between these two worlds. Spirits of the dead were capable of focusing their attention on the living from the cemetery; if they were not properly pacified, this attention could be deleterious. Much of the material symbolism seen in African American cemeteries has its origin in appeasing and controlling the dead or in protecting the dead from other malevolent supernatural forces. Placement of personal items, the last utensils used by the dead, **medicines**, and **food** offerings were all means of providing the dead with the material objects that they might need in the spirit world. Many of these objects intentionally were broken to symbolically release their spirits and to break the dead individual's bonds with the living world. Glass shards, silver **coins**, and shiny metallic objects that shimmered in the sunlight were thought to provide vision into the spirit world; they also frequently were left on graves to guide the dead away from the world of the living. Cemeteries therefore were places that contained considerable supernatural energy for enslaved blacks. For some individuals, these were forces that needed to be harnessed. Objects illicitly retrieved from the cemetery, such as coffin **nails** or grave dirt were seen as important sources for supernatural power. For many people, however, cemeteries were best avoided whenever possible.

Because many African concepts of life and death were discouraged by slaveholders, cemetery form and material representation was limited to what was considered acceptable by the overseeing community. This was accomplished in two ways: (1) representations were scaled back to forms that either the overseeing community considered harmless, quaint, or provincial, or (2) burials were given meanings that meant one thing to the dominant Anglo-American community but carried a different meaning for the blacks. One of the best examples of this latter phenomenon was orientation of the grave. In Christian theology, burial of the dead facing east meant that the dead were buried to face Jesus when he returned. In most African cultures, however, this orientation placed the dead in alignment with the rising and the setting of the sun, which meant that the dead were aligned with the order of the African universe. Graves surrounded by bottles or covered in ceramic shards may have appeared to imitate Anglo-American grave edgings and covers, when in reality they followed African traditions to keep the spirit from haunting the living. The placement of pitchers and other liquid containers may have appeared to indicate placement of flowers on the grave, but they also contained water—an African symbol of the transition between the worlds of the dead and the living. Conch or whelk grave markers and other sun-bleached sea **shells** may have emphasized this symbol of transition, as well as the addition of white, the traditional African color of death. The white-flowering yucca and giant reed may have been planted on or near the grave as attractive foliage, but they symbolized plants that were common to those found in West Africa.

Cemetery organization reflected important aspects of the slave community. Paramount among these was kinship. Slaves made great efforts to ensure that, whenever possible, they were buried with their family members. In larger cemeteries, families would form discrete clusters. While marriage was frequently banned, enslaved couples tried to ensure that they and their children were buried together whenever possible.

Because most slaves lacked command of the written word, any grave inscriptions were ineffective at communicating information to the community. Knowledge of the dead was largely passed on as part of the community's oral tradition. Inscribed markers were extremely rare and usually were donated by the slaveholder as a reward for a life of good service. More often, grave sites were identified with simple wood or fieldstone markers. In some communities, wooden markers took on anthropomorphic and animal forms. These and other distinctive features of the grave were important mnemonics to help the living identify the dead. Being remembered past death was critical to the slave psyche. Despite living in a world that devalued the slave's presence in society, the cemetery provided a means through which the slave's identity was able to survive as part of their community's heritage.

See also Charms; Coffins and Caskets; Conjure Bags; Pottery; Shrines and Spirit Caches.

FURTHER READING

Holloway, Joseph E., ed. *Africanisms in American Culture*. Bloomington: Indiana University Press, 2005.

Orser, Charles E. *Encyclopedia of Historical Archaeology*. New York: Routledge, 2002.

Thompson, Robert Farris. *Flash of the Spirit: African & Afro-American Art & Philosophy*. New York: Vintage Books, 1984.

Vlach, John Michael. *The Afro-American Tradition in Decorative Arts*. Cleveland: Cleveland Museum of Art, 1978.

HUGH B. MATTERNES

CHAMBER POTS AND PRIVIES. Chamber pots and privies were the conventional means of collecting and disposing of human waste during the almost 250 years of legal slavery in what is now the United States. Chamber pots and privies were used by people of every economic and social level, including the enslaved.

Slave quarters privy at Melrose, Natchez, Mississippi, photo ca. 1930s. (Library of Congress.)

Chamber pots are bowl-shaped containers, usually with handles and flat rims, that were used to receive human waste. They were made in a variety of ceramic materials, including salt-glazed stoneware, redware, tin-glazed earthenware, creamware, pearlware, and **colonoware**, as well as pewter and, rarely, silver. Individual ceramic chamber pots were used primarily in bedchambers and other private spaces, where they were usually kept under **beds** for use at night or at other times when using freestanding exterior facilities was not possible or when such facilities did not exist. Some chamber pots were stored in nightstands,

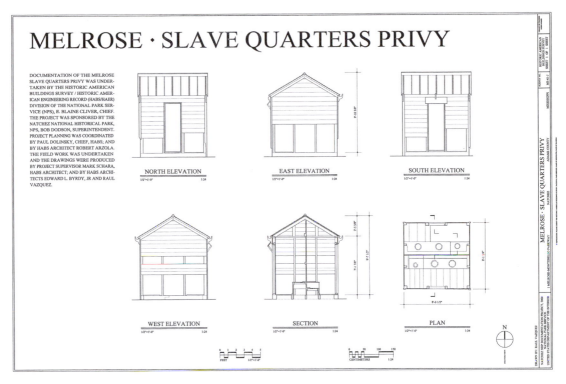

MELROSE · SLAVE QUARTERS PRIVY

DOCUMENTATION OF THE MELROSE SLAVE QUARTERS PRIVY WAS UNDERTAKEN BY THE HISTORIC AMERICAN BUILDINGS SURVEY / HISTORIC AMERICAN ENGINEERING RECORD (HABS/HAER) DIVISION OF THE NATIONAL PARK SERVICE (NPS), E. BLAINE CLIVER, CHIEF. THE PROJECT WAS SPONSORED BY THE NATCHEZ NATIONAL HISTORICAL PARK, NPS, BOB DODSON, SUPERINTENDENT. PROJECT PLANNING WAS COORDINATED BY PAUL DOLINSKY, CHIEF, HABS; AND BY HABS ARCHITECT ROBERT ARZOLA. THE FIELD WORK WAS UNDERTAKEN AND THE DRAWINGS WERE PRODUCED BY PROJECT SUPERVISOR MARK SCHARA, HABS ARCHITECT; AND BY HABS ARCHITECTS EDWARD L. BYRDY, JR AND RAUL VAZQUEZ.

NORTH ELEVATION   EAST ELEVATION   SOUTH ELEVATION

WEST ELEVATION   SECTION   PLAN

Privy plans from Melrose, Natchez, Mississippi. (Library of Congress.)

and some were found in commode chairs (also called "close stools"), which were pieces of seating furniture with removable seats under which was a frame designed to hold a chamber pot. When it was necessary to use the commode chair, the seat cover would be removed, the chair would be used, and, after its use, the chamber pot would be removed, emptied, and cleaned, and the chamber pot returned to its place to be ready for subsequent use.

For those enslaved men and women who were house servants, part of their regular duties included the emptying and cleaning of chamber pots. The pots might be emptied in an outside facility or in a pit, dumped into a nearby river or stream, or used as fertilizer for the garden. After cleaning, the pots would be returned to the house to be ready for their next use.

Privies, also called "necessary houses," were small buildings constructed at some distance from the main house. Inside the privy was a bench seat in which one or more holes were cut to accommodate users. Some privies had covers for the holes. Most privies were constructed so that they could be cleaned out periodically; again, this was a task often performed by slaves. The type of construction ranged from the basic to the elaborate. There was a privy along Mulberry Row at Monticello, where most of Thomas Jefferson's enslaved workers lived, and it is presumed that it was erected for their use. It was described in an insurance plat from 1796 as "a necessary house of wood 8. feet square." Contrasting with this simple structure was the seven-seat brick privy built at Drayton Hall along the Ashley River near Charleston, South Carolina. It was probably constructed between 1738 and 1742, and archaeologists have found a tunnel underneath the building that may have led to a drainage ditch that ultimately would have drained into the Ashley River. Such an arrangement would have reduced the necessity for enslaved workers to clean out the accumulated waste.

FURTHER READING

Noël Hume, Ivor. "Through the Lookinge Glasse: or, the Chamber Pot as a Mirror of Its Time." In *Ceramics in America 2003*, edited by Robert Hunter, 139–172. Milwaukee, WI: Chipstone Foundation, 2003.
Olmert, Michael. "Necessary and Sufficient." *Colonial Williamsburg Journal* 24, no. 3 (Autumn 2002): 33–38.
"Privies." Th: Jefferson Encyclopedia. At http://wiki.monticello.org/mediawiki/index.php/Privies.
"Uncovering the Past through Archaeology." Drayton Hall. At www.draytonhall.org/preservation/archaeology/.

MARTHA B. KATZ-HYMAN

CHARMS. Charms are spiritually empowered rituals, objects, and groups of objects used by enslaved blacks for protection, to promote health and well-being, to invoke harm, or to influence the future. Charms offered the enslaved a means of empowerment when facing the unpredictable and a method of resistance to the harsh realities of daily life. Charms were historically referred to as "charms," "hands," "tobies," "mojos," "jacks," "gris-gris," and "wangas." Charms could be articulated verbally, through ritual practices, in material form, or through a combination of these means. Virtually any type of object could be transformed into a charm, although some materials were used more frequently than others. Roots, minerals, animal parts, and artifacts commonly were used as charms, both independently and in composite.

Sources of evidence for use of charms by enslaved African Americans include archaeological evidence, folklore, and historical documents, such as Works Progress Administration interviews with former slaves, court records, and planters' journals and correspondence. Archaeologists have found evidence of charm use at several sites associated with enslaved laborers. Because any object could be used as a charm, context is critical to determining charm use in the archaeological record.

Spiritual practitioners known as conjurers usually created charms. Conjuring involves intervening with spiritual forces through ritual practices to elicit healing, protection, or success, or to invoke or prevent harm. African American conjuring had its roots in West and Central African spiritual practices and supernatural beliefs. Anthropologists, historical archaeologists, and art historians have documented the roots of BaKongo, Igbo, and Mande belief systems and practices within African American conjuring traditions. Several scholars have particularly noted the similarities between African American composite charms and BaKongo minkisi, sacred materials and material bundles activated through spiritual empowerment. African conjuring practices and charm use were creolized in the Americas over time through the influence of European and Native American spiritual traditions.

Charms were produced and used for specific purposes. The conjurer or the individual who sought to cast the spell selected particular objects for significant characteristics and associations with the problem being addressed or affinities with the evoked spirits. Graveyard dust was a frequent component because of its association with the dead power

Types of Charms

Many former slaves, including Adam Smith from Mississippi, described the use of charms:

> Dey all believed in charms and hants and everybody wore a rabbit foot and all de women tied up dere hair in strings to keep off witches and wore dimes around dere ankles if dey could git em to keep off evil sperrits. Sho I seen hants jest lots of times and all of us carried charms and de little niggers wore asfedita round dere necks to keep off chills. Some of de women made cunger bottles and put em under de steps and sprinkled rattle snake ashes in de pool but I didn't believe in dat stuff much.

Source: George P. Rawick, ed. *The American Slave: Mississippi Narratives*, Supp. Ser. 1, Vol. 10, Part 5. Westport, CT: Greenwood Press, 1978.

According to former South Carolina slave Sylvia Durant, some slaves wore pierced coins for protection:

> Yes, mam, I see plenty people wear dem dimes round dey ankle en all kind of things on dey body, but never didn' see my mother do nothin like dat. I gwine tell you it just like I got it. Hear talk dat some would wear dem for luck on some tote dem to keep people from hurtin dem. I got a silver dime in de house dere in my trunk right to dis same day dat I used to wear on a string of beads, but I took it off.

Source: George P. Rawick, ed. *The American Slave: South Carolina Narratives*, Vol. 2. Westport, CT: Greenwood Press, 1972.

Abram Sells, a former Texas slave, remembered various charms and ways of conjuring:

> There's allus some old time nigger what knowed lots of remedies and knowed all dif'rent kinds of yarbs and roots. My grand-daddy, he could stop blood, and he could conjure off the fever and rub his fingers over warts and they'd git away. He make ile out'n rattlesnake for the rheumatis'. For the cramp he git a kind of bark offen a tree and it done the job, too. Some niggers wo' brass rings to keep off the rheumatis' and punch hole in a penny or dime and wear that on the ankle to keep off sickness.

Source: George P. Rawick, ed. *The American Slave: Texas Narratives*, Vol. 5, Parts 3 & 4. Westport, CT: Greenwood Press, 1972.

ultimately derived from the spiritual realm. Some objects were chosen for their metaphorical associations. For example, an African American tradition called for placing a knife under the bed of a woman giving birth, to "cut" the pain of childbirth. Sympathetic magic was also important. Human exuviae, such as hair or fingernails, were powerful charm components when the goal was to influence a particular person's behavior. Other objects were chosen because their names were cognates of the attribute one was trying to obtain. Natural objects with unusual forms, such as twisted roots, quartz crystals, and smooth stones, were also common charm objects. Insect parts, **nails**, pins, **mirrors**, prehistoric tools, **buttons**, and gunflints were regular material components of composite charms.

Composite charms were placed in bottles or wrapped in **cloth**, leaves, or clay and bound with thread or human **hair**. The materials used to encapsulate and contain the charms, and the symbolism of binding, were as significant as the materials contained within. Former slaves recalled the significance of particular types of cloth, such as red flannel, and particular colors of thread, as necessary elements for the effectiveness of charms. Composite charms were often a mixture of roots, natural materials, and objects. The material composition of objects and their color was often as significant as, and sometimes more significant than, their shape or original function. Sometimes the number of items was significant because some numbers, such as nine, were considered lucky.

The two general types of charms were household charms and personal charms. Household charms were placed within the house or **yard**. These were often placed in particular locations, such as underneath and above doorsills and windowsills and within, above, or below hearths, to prevent malevolent spirits from crossing these entryways to harm residents. Household charms could be individual objects, composite groupings of artifacts, or even paint of a particular color. Anthropologists and folklorists noted that blacks in Georgia and South Carolina painted doors and windows blue to keep out harmful spirits.

Personal charms were worn on the body, usually on the neck, waist, wrist, or ankle. Marinda Singleton, formerly enslaved in Virginia, recalled that slaves hid charms under their clothing to avoid detection by their masters who did not approve of charm use. Glass **beads**, which could be worn as personal adornment or personal charms, probably were overlooked by masters who did not perceive their dual function. Scholars have demonstrated that Africans and African Americans in the past and present used glass beads for medicinal and spiritual purposes. For example, particular types of beads were and are used in Ghana to cure and prevent illness in children. The presence of similar types of beads in burials of enslaved black infants, worn on the same parts of the body, suggest a similar practice in 18th-century New York and 19th-century Virginia. The preponderance of glass beads found at many sites associated with enslaved blacks is blue. Archaeologists debate about the significance of blue glass beads or whether the color was indeed significant at all.

Animal bones were used as personal charms. Archaeologists have recovered raccoon bacula, associated with virility, at Andrew Jackson's Hermitage, Mount Vernon, and Fairfield. The example from Mount Vernon has an incised line on the distal end, likely produced as a result of wear when the object was worn as a pendant. Former slaves noted that rabbit feet, mole feet, **chicken** breastbones, and bones of black cats and other bones worked as charms. Conjurers also used animal bones of various types when they created "mojos" or "hands," which were packets of materials used as composite charms.

"Hand charms," small, stamped brass alloy objects in the shape of a right hand clenched into a fist, may be evidence of sympathetic magic, valued for the hand symbol that had a corresponding linguistic reference to a general good luck or protection charm. These objects originally were mass-produced clothing fasteners that were likely worn as pendants by the enslaved. Archaeologists have recovered nine hand charms in Tennessee, Virginia, and Maryland, all at sites associated with antebellum enslaved blacks.

Archaeologists have proposed various interpretations of the meaning of hand charms. Some scholars note the similarity of hand charms to Latin figas and Islamic Hand of Fatima symbols, making them attractive as charms to individuals who came from those regions. It has also been argued that the abstract shape created by the hand within the circle is significant because of its similarity to the BaKongo **cosmogram**. Hand charms may be an expression of Igbo ideology. For the Igbo, the right hand symbolized power. Hand charms also may serve as signals for the enslaved to communicate resistance or abolitionist ideas. Although the exact meanings of hand charms for their users is unclear, their regional distribution suggests the widespread transmission of a shared cultural practice.

Artifacts sometimes bear evidence of their probable use as charms in the form of modification. Archaeologists have recovered pierced **coins**, modified ceramic shards, and various objects incised with Xs, such as **colonoware** bowls, spoons, **marbles**, coins, and tailor's wax. Most of the pierced coins recovered from slave sites are silver; Spanish *reales* are particularly common. Enslaved blacks used pierced coins for protection and to detect conjure. *Reales* were probably preferred because they were silver. Folklorists and interviews with former slaves indicate the significance of silver for creating many types of charms. The X formed by the divisions on the coat of arms on the reverse of the *reale* may have been appealing. Some excavated coins were inscribed with additional Xs.

The inscribed X marks found on various types of artifacts are evidence of the significance of the X, or crossroads, to enslaved blacks. Some scholars argue that the X symbol is an abstraction of the BaKongo cosmogram. This cosmogram signified a connection between the worlds of the living and the dead. Creating this symbol imbued an object or location with spiritual power. Blacks created X marks to ward off bad luck in the early 20th century. Therefore, inscribing objects with Xs may have transformed them into amulets.

See also Conjure Bags; Fetishes; Shrines and Spiritual Caches; Subfloor Pits.

FURTHER READING

Edwards-Ingram, Ywone. "African-American Medicine and the Social Relations of Slavery." In *Race and the Archaeology of Identity*, edited by Charles Orser Jr., 34–53. Salt Lake City: University of Utah Press, 2001.

Fett, Sharla. *Working Cures: Healing, Health, and Power on Southern Slave Plantations.* Chapel Hill: University of North Carolina Press, 2002.

Leone, Mark, and Gladys-Marie Fry. "Conjuring in the Big House: An Interpretation of African American Belief Systems Based on the Uses of Archaeology and Folklore Sources." *Journal of American Folklore* 112 (1999): 372–403.

Puckett, Newbell. *The Magic and Folk Beliefs of the Southern Negro.* Mineola, NY: Dover, 1969.

Russell, Aaron. "Material Culture and African American Spirituality at the Hermitage." *Historical Archaeology* 31, no. 2 (1997): 63–80.

Stine, Linda, Melanie A. Cabar, and Mark D. Groover. "Blue Beads as African American Cultural Symbols." *Historical Archaeology* 30, no. 3 (1996): 49–75.

LORI LEE

CHICKENS. The chicken (*Gallus gallus domesticus*) is a domesticated bird originally from southeastern Asia raised for its meat and eggs. In ancient times, the chicken spread widely across the Eastern Hemisphere, arriving in Africa from various points east and north. Chickens were introduced into Egypt as early as 1400 BCE and spread throughout the continent thereafter. Although the chicken is not indigenous to Africa, it figures prominently in many creation myths and spiritual traditions and is a part of most traditional rural homesteads in West and Central Africa. It is one of the few species of livestock that can be raised without fear of the tsetse fly, which attacks large mammals living in the transitional and tropical zones as one approaches the Atlantic coast. In West and Central Africa, it shares the category of poultry with the indigenous guinea fowl and on occasion ducks and even turkeys, which came to Africa from the Western Hemisphere via European explorers.

In traditional West African culture, chickens are frequently used in ancestor worship, divination, and propitiatory sacrifice. Throughout Africa they served as the most common animal sacrifice, and their eggs also were used in religious ceremonies. In Ghana, for example, metal sculptures illustrate traditional priests using chickens in rituals or offering them to the *abosom* or deities of traditional Akan religion. The head of the household in traditional Akan homes would offer chicken eggs at the household altar of the family compound. The eggs offered to the ancestors are often cooked and placed on altars dedicated in their honor. This spiritual work, coupled with the affection lavished on the home compound chicken flock, call to mind similar

---

Stealing a Chicken

Former Texas slave Millie Williams stole a chicken from her owner:

> Sometimes massa fed good and den 'gain he didn't, but dat 'cause of de War. We has cornbread and milk and all de coffee you would drink. On Sundays we fills de pot half full of meat and shell peas on top de meat.
>
> I 'member de time we steals one of massa's big chickens and its in de pot in de fireplace when we seed missy comin'. I grabs dat chicken and pot and puts it under de bed and puts de bedclothes top dat pot. Missy, she come in and say, 'I she' de smell somethin' good.' I say, 'Whar, Missy Ellis?' She don't find nothin' so she leaves. When she's gone I takes dat chicken and we eats it in a hurry.

Source: George P. Rawick, ed. *The American Slave: Texas Narratives*, Vol. 5, Parts 3 & 4. Westport, CT: Greenwood Press, 1972.

traditions known among enslaved African Americans who transformed the chicken into "the preacher's bird," as well as raising chickens and other poultry to participate in local economies despite the constrictions of enslavement.

Chickens also were considered to be a special dish in traditional West African cuisine. A welcome addition to a primarily vegetarian diet, the use of chickens as sacrificial animals inevitably varied the common diet. Chickens were broiled with spices, fried in palm oil and then added to **stews**, or simply boiled with other meats, vegetables, or **fish** into a soup. Pieces of chicken fried in oil sold on the street, chicken and groundnut stew, chicken stew with **yams**, and spicy chicken broiled over aromatic wood or roasted while wrapped in banana leaves would all leave their mark on the developing cuisine of the early South.

Early European settlers brought chickens into the South. These first varieties of chickens, such as black-and-white speckled Dominiques (also known as "Dominickers") and other "dunghill fowl," would become legendary parts of enslaved people's lore about life in the rural South. In the slave quarter, chickens served as both alarm clocks and security alarms. Their presence was a welcome opportunity to enjoy a rare occasional meal of home-raised fresh meat. The eggs were rarely part of the diet with the exception of special occasions, when they might be incorporated into richer flavored baked goods such as cornbread or, rarely, wheaten breads.

By the 1730s, travelers began to note that enslaved blacks were raising and selling poultry in the Carolina Low Country. In the colonial Chesapeake, the relationship between enslaved people and poultry was strong. Because slaves were mostly denied the privilege of raising larger and more lucrative livestock, chickens, guineas, ducks, turkeys, and geese clucked and pecked across special poultry yards that appended slave cabins. In the often-quoted words of John Mercer from 1779, "I know already that chickens or other fresh meat can't be had but in exchange, & bacon to spare will allow me preference with the country people or rather Negroes, who are the general chicken merchants." The leading families of Virginia—the Washingtons, Carters, Lees, Jeffersons, and Randolphs—all recorded transactions between the Great House and the slave quarter and witnessed the provisioning of the Great House table with their chickens, ducks, eggs, and other poultry products. Landon Carter noted in his diary,

> Nat brought me 6 chickens this day. . . . My poor slaves raise fowls, and eggs in order to exchange with their masters now and then; and though I don't value the worth of what they bring, yet I enjoy the humanity of refreshing such poor creatures in what they (perhaps though mistakenly) call a blessing.

Among enslaved African Americans the sale or exchange of chickens led to greater social autonomy and financial empowerment, and allowed individuals and households to acquire cast-offs, money, and dry goods that otherwise were unavailable to enslaved blacks. George Washington's enslaved community complained bitterly when the switch was made from whole **corn** to ground cornmeal in their rations; he surmised that this meant that the scraps that fell out of the mortar and pestle could no longer be used as chicken feed.

This heritage of selling chickens was extended to cooked **foods**. A 19th-century pen and ink drawing depicting an enslaved girl "vulgarly" selling rolls and chicken legs at the train station in Richmond, Virginia, documents the trade in fried chicken conducted by black women at the train-side. In Gordonsville, Virginia, northwest of Richmond, black women "waiter-carriers" allegedly served the world's best fried chicken to white passengers captive inside the trains. This thriving trade in fried chicken furthered the power of the African American women who were at once both the caretakers of the region's poultry and the means by which the poultry became transformed into culinary art.

Although chicken was clearly secondary to pork in terms of meat consumption, a number of chicken dishes emerged as popular in the enslaved community. Whole chickens were wrapped in large cabbage leaves, tied and roasted in the coals of the hearth. Broiling chickens required few utensils save a green stick of wood that could be placed in the fireplace or near the fire to ensure an even cooking temperature. Sometimes chickens were barbecued in methods similar to pork. Chicken pot pies and chickens stewed with dumplings were English and German dishes that diffused into black communities during slavery and remained important dishes for special occasions. As evidence of the creolization of Atlantic African food in the South, chickens were incorporated into several important stews and soups, including **okra** soup, groundnut (**peanut**) soup, benne soup, **gumbo**, Brunswick stew, burgoo, and chicken stewed with sweet potatoes, a recipe recorded by Mary Randolph in a later edition of her cookbook, *The Virginia Housewife*. *The Virginia Housewife* also gave America its first published recipe for fried chicken, a Southern treat since the late 17th and early 18th centuries. Several formerly enslaved African American women left their own recipes for the delicacy born out of African deep frying techniques, seasoning styles, and related recipes from England and Scotland. Anna Wright, a formerly enslaved woman from North Carolina, recalled, "Fried chicken wus seasoned, drapped in flour, and den simmered in a big pan of ham gravy wid de lid on hit until it was tender. Den de lif was tuk off, an' de chicken was fried a golden brown, as quick as possible." Contrary to popular opinion, fried chicken was a rare dish in the enslaved community. Chickens were valuable merchandise, the amount of lard needed to fry the chicken was fairly difficult to come by, and white flour, salt, and black pepper were scarce and had to be acquired through purchase, **barter**, or trade.

Part of the lore of the chicken in enslaved communities was the consistent use of racially charged images of blacks as chicken thieves. Cartoons, postcards, folksongs, and the writings of local "colorists" depicted black men sneaking up on chickens to strangle them and take them home for a clandestine meal. The images are partly based in stories from slavery when "broiling stray chickens" in secret was one of the pastimes of enslaved life. According to educator Booker T. Washington (1856–1915),

One of my earliest recollections is that of my mother cooking a chicken late at night, and awakening her children for the purpose of feeding them. How or where she got it I do not know. I presume, however, it was procured from our owner's farm. Some people may call this theft. If such a thing were to happen now, I should condemn it as theft myself. But taking place at the time it did, and for the reason that it did, no one could ever make me believe that my mother was guilty of thieving. She was simply a victim of the system of slavery.

To 19th-century whites, chicken stealing was a sign of African American moral failure, but to enslaved African Americans forced to pilfer for their survival, there was a fine line between theft for the sake of committing a "sin," and theft for the sake of feeding oneself in the face of brutality and malnutrition.

Chickens retained their association with spiritual work, as chicken bones associated with spiritual caches or chicken remains strategically buried at plantations like the Levi Jordan property in Texas attest. As enslaved people transitioned into their own sense of freedom, the chicken became "the preacher's bird," and if available, a Sunday dinner or family celebration was not complete without some sort of chicken dish, usually fried or stewed. Stereotypes of black cuisine aside, for generations, owing to slavery and its after-effects, these were delicacies.

See also Caricatures; Charms; Conjure Bags; Food and Foodways; Pigs and Pork; Subfloor Pits; Yams and Sweet Potatoes.

FURTHER READING

Carter, Landon. *The Diary of Colonel Landon Carter of Sabine Hall, 1752–1778*, edited by Jack P. Greene. 2 vols. Charlottesville: Published for the Virginia Historical Society by the University Press of Virginia, 1965.

Harris, Jessica B. *The Welcome Table: African American Heritage Cooking*. New York: Fireside, 1995.

Hilliard, Sam Bowers. *Hog Meat and Hoecake: Food Supply in the Old South, 1840–1860*. Carbondale: Southern Illinois Press, 1971.

McLeod, Malcolm D. *The Asante*. London: Trustees of the British Museum by British Museum Publications, 1981.

Morgan, Philip D. *Slave Counterpoint: Black Culture in the Eighteenth-Century Chesapeake and Lowcountry*. Chapel Hill: University of North Carolina Press, 1998.

Randolph, Mary. *The Virginia Housewife: With Historical Notes and Commentaries by Karen Hess*. Columbia: University of South Carolina Press, 1984.

Rawick, George P. *The American Slave: Kansas, Kentucky, Maryland, Ohio, Virginia and Tennessee Narratives*, Vol. 16. Westport, CT: Greenwood Press, 1972.

Washington, Booker T. *Up from Slavery*. Oxford: Oxford University Press, 1995.

Williams-Forson, Psyche. *Building Houses Out of Chicken Legs: Black Women, Food and Power*. Chapel Hill: University of North Carolina Press, 2006.

MICHAEL W. TWITTY

CHURCHES AND PRAISE HOUSES. The first black churches in America were established after 1770 as a result of evangelistic efforts by Methodists and Baptists during the period known as the First Great Awakening. In the South during the 19th century, Christian slaves also began to build small informal churches, known as Praise Houses, on their plantations. Forged in racism, these churches and praise houses became centers for communities of enslaved and freed blacks and fostered distinct African American theologies and worship styles that continue in the 21st century.

As with nearly every aspect of slave history and material culture, a full understanding of black churches and praise houses requires nuanced attention to historical contexts and the limitations placed on African Americans by racism and enslavement. Moreover, depending on factors like region, historical period, work performed, gender, and the size of an owner's slave population, slaves experienced a wide range of working conditions and relationships with whites that affected their material culture and religious experiences. For example, slaves in the North were converted to Christianity far earlier than slaves in the South and were more likely to be allowed to purchase their freedom or be freed by their owners. Therefore, most black churches started before the Civil War are found in the North. To understand the circumstances under which people of African descent became Christians and established churches, it is necessary to first consider the history of the praise house as a phenomenon on Southern plantations and then discuss the history of independent black churches in the North and South.

Praise Houses and the Christianization of American Slaves

In the South, the period known as the Second Great Awakening (ca. 1790–1840) marked an upsurge in missionary evangelism that resulted in the conversion of nearly all African American slaves by 1860. While mainline Christian churches like the Episcopalians, Lutherans, Congregationalists, and Presbyterians were open to converting slaves, Baptist and Methodist missionaries focused intensely on the South and its huge population of unconverted blacks. At the beginning of this effort, missionaries faced significant resistance from slaveholders, Christian and non-Christian, who feared that slaves who became Christians would become "uppity," disobedient, or feel entitled to equal treatment or freedom. Missionaries intent on reaching slaves were faced with the task of converting owners and convincing them to allow access to their slaves. For this reason, missionaries emphasized the ways that Christianity could support the institution of slavery by encouraging obedience, dutifulness, and heavenly rewards. Traveling from plantation to plantation, missionaries taught slaves about Christianity, appointed leaders, and established congregations. Because plantations were far apart, churches were few, and missionaries were in short supply, success depended on the ability of a community to remain cohesive after the missionary moved on. It was common for a missionary to return to a plantation and find his former converts lapsed.

The lack of a physical structure to house new slave congregations and the ministers to lead them concerned missionaries, who desperately wanted to be successful. Depending on attitudes of slaveholders and geographic proximity, converted slaves may or may not have attended formal church services. In cases in which masters were supportive of slave conversion, regular Sunday services might be held in the home or slaves might be taken to a local church where a white preacher would encourage slaves to please God by obeying their masters and fulfilling their earthly roles. On plantations where slaveholders were not supportive of conversion efforts, Christian slaves were forced to hold religious meetings in secret.

As more slaves became Christians, the demand for places of worship in the South increased and, in response, plantation owners began to allow their slaves to build small

First African Church in Richmond, Virginia, 1865. (Library of Congress.)

Worship

The field hands held their own religious services on Rebecca Jane Grant's South Carolina plantation, while the household and skilled slaves went with the slaveholders to the white church:

Didn't have no colored churches. De drivers and de overseers, de houseservants, de bricklayers and folks like dat'd go to de white folk's church. But not de field hands. Why dey couldn't have all got in de church. My marsa had three or four hundred slaves, himself. And most of the other white folks had just as many or more. But them as went would sing! Oh they'd sing! I remember two of 'em specially. One was a man and he'd sing bass. Oh, he'd roll it down! The other was a woman, and she'd sing soprano! They had colored preachers to preach to de field hands down in de quarters. Dey'd preach in de street. Meet next day to de marsa's and turn in de report. How many pray, how many ready for baptism and all like dat. Used to have Sabbath School in de white people's house, in de porch, on Sunday evening. De porch was big and dey'd fill dat porch! They never fail to give de chillun Sabbath School. Learn them de Sabbath catechism. We'd sing a song the church bells used to ring in Beaufort. You never hear it any more. But I remembers it.

Source: George P. Rawick, ed. *The American Slave: South Carolina Narratives*, Vol. 2. Westport, CT: Greenwood Press, 1972.

In Mississippi, Robert Weathersby attended church with his masters but also worshipped secretly with the other slaves:

We went to meeting at de white folks meeting house an' sat in de back part, an' us had to wait on de white folks too. Had to see 'bout de horses an' buggies an' take 'em water an' keep de fires a gwine if it wuz cole weather. When we wanted to have our own services we collected up an' went to de woods an' built big brush arbors an' at nite we'd build great big fires an' had sho' nuf services. We could sing an' shout, an' dats what we wanted to do. Dey would hum an' morn all through de services. De preachers didn't hab no book learning but when a darkie wanted to preacher, he wuz give a try out, by gitting up an' trying to preach a time or two an' if he suited de folks an' they thought he could preach, dey would say fer him to preach an' if he didnt suit 'em dey would say fer him not too.

Source: George P. Rawick, ed. *The American Slave: Mississippi Narratives*, Supp. Ser. 1, Vol. 10, Part 5. Westport, CT: Greenwood Press, 1978.

buildings for worship that came to be known as "praise houses." Praise houses were built primarily because slaves wanted to hold worship throughout the week and not just on Sundays. Prior to the construction of praise houses, slaves would regularly leave the plantation to meet other Christian slaves for worship at night. Slaveholders, concerned about the potential for rebellion and collaboration that unsupervised off-plantation meetings presented, believed that they would be able to exact more control over their slaves if they offered them a place of their own to worship on the plantation. Responding to such concerns, missionaries encouraged slaveholders to fund or allow praise houses to increase their control and demonstrate paternalistic benevolence. Missionaries saw praise houses as a way to grow and sustain the religious communities they established. Indeed, by 1860 competing evangelistic efforts by traveling missionaries resulted in many instances in which several praise houses, each affiliated with a distinct Christian denomination, were established on the same plantation. Although praise houses appeared all over the South, they were particularly prevalent among the Gullah of South Carolina and Georgia.

Architecturally, praise houses were simple spaces with little ornamentation and few religious artifacts. Praise houses generally had only one room and one door and would be located near slave quarters. The lack of furnishings of the praise house was an economic, rather than theological, phenomenon. To make praise houses more comfortable and conventional, slaves would use discarded materials to create religious art and artifacts such as **crosses**. Funded by missionaries or by savings from outside work, slaves sometimes built altars, pulpits, and pews, although it was not uncommon for a praise house to remain a small, empty one-room building. Although praise houses were centers of black Christianity, slaves still were expected to attend their master's church every Sunday. Indeed, the designation of a plantation slave church as a "praise house" rather than a church is directly related to the racist belief by whites that slaves could not conduct church services on their own or be in charge of a church. Praise houses were built as a supplement to church services that were controlled and supervised by whites. For whites, praise houses did not have the same kind of authenticity or power as a church but were necessary to keep slaves content and allow them to worship throughout the week. For Christian slaves, the praise house operated as a church and, indeed, the true center of their religious life. The praise house offered slaves opportunities to escape the white gaze, challenge white authority, sustain community and culture, and reinvent the Christianity they were taught to conform with their lives and experiences.

In the praise house, black Christians integrated religious expressions familiar to them and their families in Africa. During services with whites, or overseen by whites, slaves would listen to sermons that taught that heavenly rewards could be attained only if they were obedient to their masters and dutifully performed their work. Within the praise houses, slaves practiced a Christianity that identified black slaves with the ancient Israelites, a chosen people led by Moses out of bondage. Through identification with Israel, slaves were able to make sense of their suffering and maintain hope that justice ultimately would be done. Forbidden to learn to read and write, blacks who secretly were literate used the space of the praise house to teach others and offer alternative interpretations of sacred Christian texts. Slave spirituals and "call and response" songs also were central to praise house worship, which was marked by the integration of African beliefs and practices into Christianity. For example, the practice of the "ring shout" (*see also* opening essay "Dance and Music") generally took place in forums outside of the formal church. During the ring shout, blacks embraced an ecstatic and embodied worship by moving together in a counterclockwise circle. As the ritual progressed, participants moved with increasing speed to summon ecstatic religious experience and connection with the supernatural. Scholars have noted the important parallels between the ring shout and African spirit possession. Indeed, while the ring shout was commonly used in a Christian context, throughout the period of enslavement, people of African descent consistently incorporated forms of expression derived from Africa. In the praise house, it would not be uncommon to witness spirit possessions, ecstatic shouting and dancing, or conjurers offering their services. In the praise house, such syncretistic religious expressions were performed without judgment or fear from whites who often found worship by blacks to be overly emotional and expressive.

Not all black Christians worshiped in praise houses, and many did not have physical structures to house their religious services. For this reason, a full understanding of black churches during slavery must include what has been called "the invisible institution." The invisible institution refers to the practice of slave Christianity in forums beyond white scrutiny: the secret and hidden practice of slave Christianity in informal and makeshift environments and communities. It has been argued that Christianity as practiced by slaves was a predominantly covert phenomenon aimed at undermining the control and authority of whites over Christianity and black religious practice. Slaves were able to undermine this religious authoritarianism by secretly "stealing away" to prohibited services in the middle of the night. These services were led by black preachers who embraced religious themes of liberation and identified enslaved African Americans with enslaved Israelites in the Hebrew **Bible**.

Such furtive church services frequently were held near physical landmarks between plantations, clearings in the woods, or in **slave quarters** with furnishings rearranged to accommodate group worship. Even though they did not always have access to purpose-built structures designed for religious practice, slaves nonetheless reimagined physical spaces designed for other purposes, such as their living quarters or other outdoor spaces, as places for religious devotion. In these "hush arbors" or "praying grounds," magical and practical measures were taken to ensure privacy and conceal the slaves' illegal activity. For example, overturned pots or pots filled with water might be placed around a meeting area or in the rafters of slave quarters. Slaves believed that the pots could muffle the noise of worship. Similar patterns can be seen in the Caribbean where barracoons, large warehouse-style sleeping quarters, would be transformed into spaces for dancing, preaching, drumming, and celebration.

Diversity of Black Churches

Worship communities of blacks who identified themselves as independent churches existed in Maryland, Virginia, and the Carolinas before the American Revolution. These communities rarely were recognized as independent churches by white denominational authorities, and they did not construct church buildings. Nearly all churches that claim to be one of the earliest black churches in the country trace their origins back to a congregation that waited decades before building or buying a church. For this reason, dozens of churches claim to be the first, or one of the first, black churches in the country. For example, Silver Bluff Baptist Church in Aiken County, South

Carolina, has been identified by some scholars as the first independent black congregation in America. Silver Bluff Baptist Church was started in 1773 by a few blacks who decided to establish a plantation church. However, Silver Bluff did not have a church building until 1847 and, therefore, was little different from the hundreds of other black church congregations formed throughout the South on plantations. Although the title of "first" is sought after by many early black churches, formally acknowledging one congregation over another as first ignores the many churches that existed but remained hidden from view and lost to the historical record because of slavery and racism. For this reason, tracing and verifying claims to primacy have proven difficult and have led to dozens of competing claims that too often overlook the agency of blacks throughout the South who formed churches.

While it is certain that black churches have existed for as long as black people have been Christians, before the Civil War it was exceptionally rare for a black church to own a church building because black Christians almost never had the means or resources necessary to house independent congregations in church buildings without the cooperation of white church members. In a few instances, overcrowding in churches shared by whites and blacks led a church that was once interracial to split. The separate black churches formed from these schisms always were overseen by whites. First African Baptist Church of Richmond, Virginia, is an important example. In 1841, the white congregants of First Baptist Church of Richmond sold their church to the black congregants, who then formed First African Baptist Church of Richmond. Using the money from the sale, the white congregants built a new church for themselves, and First African Baptist Church of Richmond remained under the control of a white board of directors and pastor.

Whites were often fearful of relinquishing control over black believers. Indeed, the issue was so heated that in 1838 the Virginia Legislature passed a law making it illegal for blacks to establish an independent church. Although churchgoing blacks continued to attend white churches throughout the period before the Civil War, there was marked discontent with second-class treatment and increasing emphasis on segregation during services. In the North, where free blacks had greater access to resources and the support of abolitionists, blacks worked together to translate this growing discontent with white Christianity and racism into the establishment of the first black churches recognized by major denominations, and the formation of the first black denomination: the African Methodist Episcopal Church.

The African Methodist Episcopal Church was born out of the turbulence created when Philadelphia's St. George's Methodist Episcopal Church chose to sequester blacks in the gallery of the church and prohibited them from worshiping in the main sanctuary. After years of discrimination and paternalistic supervision, black congregants, including Richard Allen (1760–1831) and Absalom Jones (1746–1818), left the church when praying members were forcibly removed because they refused to be segregated in an upstairs gallery. In 1794, Richard Allen opened Mother Bethel African Methodist Episcopal Church, the first denomination to be founded solely on the basis of race. The church building was dedicated in that year and is located at the corner of Sixth and Lombard Streets in Philadelphia, Pennsylvania. The church remains a national historic landmark and the oldest continuously black-owned property in America. That same year, Absalom Jones also opened the doors of the African Episcopal Church of St. Thomas in

Philadelphia at the corner of 5th and Adelphi Streets. Both churches have a history of humanitarian outreach and operated as both a church and a community center that provided economic and social support for the entire black community in Philadelphia.

One of the most remarkable accounts of the creation of a church during slavery comes from the story of First African Baptist Church in Savannah, Georgia, one of the first formal churches to be established and built by blacks in America. The church and its membership evolved from communities of blacks, slave and free, brought together by the efforts of black Christian leaders George Liele (1750–1820) and Andrew Bryan (1737–1812). In 1794, Bryan led the construction of a makeshift church structure named Bryan Street Baptist. After internal tensions resulted in a schism, the majority of the community relocated to Franklin Square, where, for $1,500 they bought a church with money the congregants had saved to purchase their freedom. But the congregation wanted a church of their own that had never been owned by whites, and the members of First African Baptist began constructing a new church in the 1850s. Since nearly all of the members were enslaved, the church was built during the night when the slaves were permitted to leave their homes. During the years of construction, and until emancipation, the First African Baptist Church was a major stop on the **Underground Railroad**. Indeed, the building was specifically designed to hide and house escaped slaves underneath the floor of the sanctuary. Black workers had drilled air holes into the sanctuary floor, disguised as an African tribal design. Pews built by the slaves during this period were engraved with tribal symbols, illustrating the continuing syncretic nature of black Christianity.

The praise houses and early black churches that remain standing in the 21st century are a testimony to the creativity and persistence of enslaved people who overcame nearly insurmountable conditions to develop a religious world of their own.

See also Cast Iron Pots; Conjure Bags; Drums.

FURTHER READING

Frey, Sylvia R. *Come Shouting to Zion: African American Protestantism in the American South and British Caribbean to 1830.* Chapel Hill: University of North Carolina Press, 1998.

Newman, Richard. *Freedom's Prophet: Bishop Richard Allen, the AME Church, and the Black Founding Fathers.* New York: New York University Press, 2008.

Raboteau, Albert J. *Slave Religion: The "Invisible Institution" in the Antebellum South.* Updated ed. New York: Oxford University Press, 2004.

KATIE HLADKY

CLOCKS AND WATCHES. Clocks and watches were the tools by which slaveholders regulated the lives of the men and women whom they held in bondage. Whether it was the sound of a horn in the morning to signal the time to awaken, or a **bell** to announce a break for a quick meal, or a watch held in an owner's hand to measure productivity, time—its measurement and its regulation—lay at the heart of chattel slavery.

Through most of the 17th century, most Europeans measured time by the natural cycles of sunrise and sunset, the phases of the moon, and the change of the seasons, not by the clock. Bells did call worshipers to church, but daily tasks were done without regard to the exact time of day or how long a particular task might take. Similarly, Africans used the same cycles to order their days and their lives. But the advent of clocks and watches that could keep more accurate time, and the increased emphasis on making "every day count" and using time in a "proper" manner, inevitably led to a clash between those who measured time using a timepiece—the clergy, the gentry, and the tradesmen—and those who worked for them who measured time in less structured ways.

Many elite white Virginians were obsessed with keeping time and making sure that their slaves made good use of time. They had tall case clocks, table clocks, and watches and made sure that they were always in good repair.

Virginia slave owner Landon Carter rode out to observe his field slaves several times a day, watching them work for a couple of hours each day to make sure that they spent their time productively. Thomas Jefferson carefully calculated how many **nails** were made in a day by the boys and men who worked in his nailery and made sure that the bell of the great clock he designed for the entrance hall at Monticello could be heard anywhere on the farm so that he could better regulate the working hours of his enslaved laborers. Charlie Davenport, interviewed in Mississippi in 1937 for the Federal Writers' Project, said that, after he was freed, he got somewhat carried away with his freedom because, "Aint no marster gwine a-say to you, 'Charlie, you's got to be back when de clock strikes nine.'"

Enslaved blacks thought about time in entirely different ways, using natural events such as a meteorite shower to indicate a specific date or how many seasons or months had gone by, to indicate the passage of time, or to estimate how long ago or when something had happened. Sandy, a slave of Thomas Wilson in Middlesex County, Virginia, who ran away in 1768 and was caught, told the sheriff that "he [had] made two crops for his master, and [had] been absent for two moons." Samuel Scomp, a Philadelphia runaway who was kidnapped and ended up in New Orleans, from which he was sent back to Philadelphia, testified in 1826 that he was kidnapped the previous year "in water melon and peach time." Another formerly enslaved man, interviewed in Tennessee, stated, "I was a young man when the stars fell; and you know that was a long time ago. I seen them; they just fell and went out before they hit the ground."

Many masters complained that their enslaved workers would not do their work in a timely manner, but what was timely to masters and what was timely to the enslaved depended how one looked at the matter. For slaveholders, getting work done efficiently with little wasted time was essential to the success of the plantation, farm, or trade. Time spent doing a job slowly was time wasted: it cut production and profits. But for the enslaved, when left to their own devices, work was done in the amount of time it took to do it, not by some externally applied measure of time governed by a clock or watch. Different ways of organizing that work depended on how one looked at time: for those slaveholders who used the gang system, a certain amount of work had to be done within a specific amount of time, but for those slaveholders who used the task system, it did not matter how long it took to complete the task, as long as it was completed that day. Different ways of looking at time resulted in different ways of doing work.

See also Work Routines.

FURTHER READING

Blassingame, John W., ed. *Slave Testimony: Two Centuries of Letters, Speeches, Interviews, and Autobiographies*. Baton Rouge: Louisiana State University Press, 1977.

"Born in Slavery: Slave Narratives from the Federal Writers' Project, 1936–1938," American Memory, Library of Congress. At http://memory.loc.gov/ammem/snhtml/.

Carter, Landon. *The Diary of Colonel Landon Carter of Sabine Hall, 1752–1778*, edited by Jack P. Greene. 2 vols. Charlottesville: Published for the Virginia Historical Society by the University Press of Virginia, 1965.

Rawick, George, ed. *The American Slave: Unwritten History of Slavery (Fisk University)*, Vol. 18. Westport, CT: Greenwood Press, 1972.

Sobel, Mechal. *The World They Made Together: Black and White Values in Eighteenth-Century Virginia*. Princeton, NJ: Princeton University Press, 1987.

MARTHA B. KATZ-HYMAN

CLOTH. Cloth was far more than fabric in a slave's world. It was the catalyst for European contact with Africa and a commodity used for both trade and barter in the intra-Africa and trans-Atlantic slave trades. The demand for the cultivation of fibers, the raw materials for the manufacture of cloth, created a need for cheap labor ultimately fulfilled by enslaving Africans and transporting them to North America. On a more basic level, cloth provided garments to protect slaves from the elements. It supplied a means of creativity and identity by creating unique **clothing** items and household goods, such as bedding and head coverings. Above all, cloth was a tool, a visible symbol used to distinguish the free from the slave.

When England and the rest of Europe emerged from the late Middle Ages after 1500, new economic forces were at work. A growing European economy prompted seismic shifts in the agricultural economy of Elizabethan England. Driven by demand for English **wool** fabrics in continental markets, landowners enclosed common pasture and began raising sheep commercially. Local and regional artisans turned the raw material into cloth, and merchants shipped it to newfound customers. Mercantile companies formed, seeking to expand markets beyond Europe. They followed trade routes established by the Portuguese and others down the west coast of Africa. There, English merchants found new opportunities in a thriving **cotton** cloth economy and a well-established slave trade.

English merchants and adventurers entered the West African slave trade in the mid-16th century. They exchanged cloth of European manufacture and other **barter goods** for slaves in established markets and quickly transported them to Spanish settlements in the Caribbean and Central America. Purchased by local planters, these West African slaves, still carrying their cultural connection to cloth cultivation and production, were put to work on cotton and **indigo** plantations.

England established permanent settlements in North America beginning in 1607. The first slaves arrived in 1619. Thousands more arrived in subsequent decades from the Caribbean and West Africa to provide labor for the burgeoning **tobacco** economy of Virginia and Carolina. Their direct connection to the cotton cloth culture of their homelands, but not cloth itself, slipped away.

Cotton regained its significant role in the lives of slaves in the Deep South after the American Revolution. Encouraged by the invention of the cotton gin in 1793, which mechanized the process for removing the seeds from the newly picked cotton bolls, and driven by demand for raw materials from the newly flourishing textile industry in the northern United States and abroad, planters made cotton their primary cash crop. The importation of West African slaves increased to meet the increasing need for workers in the cotton fields on new and expanding plantations. Cut off from all but the cultivation aspect of the familiar cloth culture of West Africa, like their 17th-century counterparts, newly arrived slaves had to find means of integrating it into their lives in bondage.

This was a daunting prospect. England maintained a stranglehold over colonial markets. Cotton, indigo, and other items had to be transported to and sold in England. This discouraged the establishment of large-scale cloth production in the North American colonies. Colonists of all economic levels relied heavily on cloth imported from England through the 17th and early 18th centuries.

Throughout the tenure of slavery in the United States, slave clothing and textiles for slave households were made from inferior fabrics, collectively known as "slave cloth" or **Negro cloth**. Manufactured from lower-grade coarse fibers, slave cloth was **linen**, wool, or cotton. Until the mid-18th century, many slaveholders imported Negro cloth from England. When political and economic conflict erupted between England and her American colonists in the 1750s, households large and small began to produce their own cloth at home. Farmers and planters increased their flax and cotton crops and kept larger flocks of sheep to provide needed raw materials. Larger plantation establishments built weaving and **spinning houses** to accommodate the high quantity of textile production necessary to clothe hundreds of slaves.

The production of cloth, clothing, and household textiles was the responsibility of the farm wife or plantation mistress. She assembled a disparate team to complete this task. This team included her female relatives, skilled female slaves trained as carders, spinners, and occasionally weavers, usually men, and local white artisans. Under her supervision, carders combed raw fibers into batts (matted rolls). Spinners spun batts into yarn, called homespun, on the spinning wheel. Others dyed the yarn in large pots, and weavers wove yarn into fabric on large looms. The fabrics they produced ranged from fine linens for their master's family to coarse Negro cloth for field hands to materials for sheeting, **blankets,** and bed coverings. The plantation mistress reserved some homespun yarn for knitted items, such as stockings.

Making and distributing slave clothing turned on summer and winter **clothing allotments**. Enslaved men, women, and children routinely received two gender-specific outfits, plus stockings, footwear, and blankets, from each allotment. A slave's status determined what each received individually and for their families. Sometimes, slave children received no clothing at all. House servants had better-quality clothing than did field hands. The garments each group received were identical in style and color. They allowed little leeway for individual style or taste.

The size of the slave population determined the system for making garments at each establishment. On smaller farms and plantations, mistresses gave equivalent fabric and yarn allotments to slave women, expecting them to cut, sew, and knit for their own families. At larger establishments, mistresses, with slave hierarchies to consider and hundreds to clothe, ran more complex operations. Individual tasks, such as cutting and stitching garments, went to slave and free artisan specialists. Female members of the owners' family, including the mistress, and young slave girls often did the knitting.

Slaves frequently considered their clothing and household textile allotments inadequate. Stranded economically, with few resources of their own, they worked the system to improve their situations. Many cut clothing too generously and saved the scraps from the sewing of garments to obtain extra fabric. Slave women recycled old garments and blankets and used hand-me-downs from more generous owners. Seamstresses turned these into garments for unclothed children and needed items for themselves. They created distinctive **headwraps** and other decorative items evoking their West African design traditions and connecting them to their original cloth culture.

The system for producing cloth, which dominated the work lives of many female slaves, became antiquated a half-century before the end of slavery in the United States. Inexpensive manufactured cotton textiles, from newly developed textile factories in New England, were readily available on the American market after 1820. Farmers and planters supplied raw cotton to these mills, and then purchased their products which were in turn made into clothing. The presence of a skilled and enslaved labor force that they had to clothe, keep busy, and retain prevented the introduction of this and other labor-saving devices into plantation life. The demand for cloth, initially a catalyst for slavery in the United States, became a stumbling block to its end.

FURTHER READING

Allen, Gloria Seaman. "'For the People': Clothing Production and Maintenance at Rose Hill Plantation, Cecil County, Maryland." *Historic Alexandria Quarterly* (Winter 2003). At http://oha.alexandriava.gov/oha-main/haq/pdfs/haqwin03.pdf.

Baron, Robert C., ed. *The Garden and Farm Books of Thomas Jefferson.* Golden, CO: Fulcrum, 1987.

Berlin, Ira, Marc Favreau, and Steven E. Miller, eds. *Remembering Slavery: African Americans Talk about Their Personal Experiences of Slavery and Emancipation.* New York: New Press, 1998.

Birmingham, David. *Trade and Empire in the Atlantic, 1400–1600.* London: Routledge, 2000.

Clinton, Catherine. *The Plantation Mistress: Woman's World in the Old South.* New York: Pantheon Books, 1982.

Dalzell, Bert F., Jr., and Lee Baldwin Dalzell. *George Washington's Mount Vernon: At Home in Revolutionary America.* New York: Oxford University Press, 1998.

Davies, K. G. *The Royal African Company.* London: Longmans, Green and Company, 1957.

Harmer, Cricket. "The Effects of 'Cloth Politics' in the Trans-Atlantic Slave Trade: Cause, Cash, Commodity and Comfort." Vanderbilt University/Jean and Alexander Heard Library. At http://discoverarchive.vanderbilt.edu/xmlui/handle/1803/3095?show=full.

Morgan, Edmund S. *American Slavery, American Freedom: The Ordeal of Colonial Virginia.* New York: W.W. Norton & Company, 1975.

Phillips, Ulrich B. *Life and Labor in the Old South.* 3rd ed. Boston: Little, Brown and Company, 1963.

Spruill, Julia Cherry. *Women's Life and Work in the Southern Colonies.* 2nd ed. New York: W.W. Norton & Company, 1972.

Woodward, C. Vann. *Mary Chesnut's Civil War.* New Haven, CT: Yale University Press, 1981.

SUSAN ATHERTON HANSON

CLOTHING ALLOTMENTS. Colonial and, later, state laws required owners to clothe their slaves. They mostly did so through a system of clothing allotments.

Usually twice yearly, enslaved men, women, and children received two gender-specific outfits, plus stockings, **shoes, blankets,** and sometimes hats as their individual allotments. A slave's status determined what each received individually and for their families. Sometimes, slave children received no clothing at all. House servants had better-quality clothing than field hands. The garments each group received were usually identical in style and color. They allowed little leeway for individual style or taste.

The wives and daughters of slaveholders oversaw the production of **cloth**. They often helped to make slave clothing and household **textiles** with the assistance of slave seamstresses and artisans. The time and effort involved to produce garments and other items needed for each allotment date was enormous and went on at many plantations year-round.

Slave clothing was made from inferior fabrics, collectively known as slave or **Negro cloth**. Manufactured from lower grade coarse fibers, slave cloth included **linen, wool, cotton,** or a form of linen called oznaberg. Many slaveholders imported Negro cloth from England until political and economic conflict erupted between England and her American colonists in the 1750s. Afterward, households large and small began to produce their own cloth at home. In the 19th century, Negro cloth was specially manufactured for the Southern market in New England textile mills.

Slaves frequently considered their clothing and household textile allotments inadequate. This was a greater concern in the colonial period when cloth was expensive and imported from England. It improved in the early decades of the 19th century after cotton became the cash crop on many plantations.

Slaves, without resources of their own, worked the system to improve their situations. Enslaved women recycled old garments and **blankets** and used hand-me-downs from more generous owners. They saved the scraps from the sewing of garments, turning them into garments for unclothed children, distinctive **headwraps, quilts,** and other needed items for themselves.

The clothing allotment system created resentment and anger among both slaves and their owners. Slave clothing consumed a great deal of resources, human and financial, on plantations. It cut into the owner's profit and represented a large fixed expense. For slaves, clothing allotments were yet another way that slave masters enforced their inferior social and economic status.

FURTHER READING

Allen, Gloria Seaman. "'For the People': Clothing Production and Maintenance at Rose Hill Plantation, Cecil County, Maryland." *Historic Alexandria Quarterly* (Winter 2003): 1–9. At http://oha.alexandriava.gov/oha-main/haq/pdfs/haqwin03.pdf.

American Anthropological Association. "Government: 1600–1775: Colonial Authority." RACE. At www.understandingrace.com/history/gov/colonial_authority.html.

Baron, Robert C., ed. *The Garden and Farm Books of Thomas Jefferson.* Golden, CO: Fulcrum, 1987.

Baumgarten, Linda. "'Clothes for the People': Slave Clothing in Early Virginia." *Journal of Early Southern Decorative Arts* 14, no. 2 (November 1988): 26–70.

Baumgarten, Linda. *What Clothes Reveal: The Language of Clothing in Colonial and Federal America: The Colonial Williamsburg Collection.* Williamsburg, VA: Colonial Williamsburg Foundation, 2002.

Berlin, Ira, Marc Favreau, and Steven E. Miller, eds. *Remembering Slavery: African Americans Talk About Their Personal Experiences of Slavery and Emancipation*. New York: New Press, 1998.

Clinton, Catherine. *The Plantation Mistress: Woman's World in the Old South*. New York: Pantheon Books, 1982.

Dalzell, Bert F., Jr., and Lee Baldwin Dalzell. *George Washington's Mount Vernon: At Home in Revolutionary America*. New York: Oxford University Press, 1998.

SUSAN ATHERTON HANSON

CLOTHING AND FOOTWEAR. Historic illustrations of slaves in the U.S. mainland often presented figures trudging through fields in drab, rough, monochromatic attire. Barefoot and ragged, these slaves projected a picture of uniformity. Clothing was both a common necessity and an avenue of expression for the enslaved. Slaveholders relied on the cheapest, sturdiest fabrics they could find and saved their fanciest clothing for house servants. Although slaveholders often saw clothing their property as the duty of a responsible owner, slaves earned their attire through their labor, sometimes growing the raw materials that would eventually become their wardrobe. Enslaved people also used clothing to express themselves by individualizing their everyday attire with accessories or color or by investing in higher quality apparel.

Resources for Clothing

The clothing of the enslaved in the United States became more uniform as the system of chattel slavery further entrenched itself in the Southern economy. In the 18th century, diaries, letters, and account books indicate that most slaves were clothed in fabrics imported from England and Germany, although some favored slaves were given second-hand clothing passed down from their owners. With the rise of **cotton** production in the antebellum period, planters had access to several sources for what was called **Negro cloth**. Textile mills in England and the northern United States produced yards of this cheap undyed cloth specifically for the Southern market. By the 1830s and 1840s, the ready-made clothing industry was established enough to provide for an export market. Plainly constructed shirts were the most commonly and cheaply available item.

Slave Labor and Clothing

Throughout the antebellum years, it was much more common for slaveholders to buy yards of cloth than to purchase ready-made clothing. Sometimes this cloth was distributed to the slaves, who then had to cut and sew their own clothing, either as part of their regular work or in their spare time. Other slaveholders designated a group of slaves, usually elderly and heavily pregnant women, to construct all of the plantation laborers' clothing.

Group of slaves on J. J. Smith's plantation, Beaufort, South Carolina, 1862. (Library of Congress.)

123

Sunday Best

Julia Larken, a former Georgia slave, remembered Sunday church as a time for wearing one's best clothing:

Dey would git up 'way 'fore dawn on meetin' day, so as to git dar on time. Us wouldn't wear our shoes on dem long walks, but jus' went barfoots 'til us got nearly to de meetin' house. I jus' kin 'member dat, for chillun warn't 'lowed to try to walk dat fur a piece, but us could git up early in de mornin' and see de grown folks start off. Dey was dressed in deir best Sunday Clothing go-to-meetin' clothes and deir shoes, all shined up, was tied together and hung over deir shoulders to keep 'em from gittin' dust on 'em. Men folks had on plain homespun shirts and jeans pants. De jeans what deir pants was made out of was homespun too. Some of de 'omans wore homespun dresses, but most of 'em had a calico dress what was saved special for Sunday meetin' wear. 'Omans wore two or three petticoats all ruffled and starched 'til one of dem underskirts would stand by itself. Dey went barfoots wid deir shoes hung over deir shoulders, jus' lak de mens, and evvy 'oman pinned up her dress and evvy one of her petticoats but one to keep 'em from gittin' muddy. Dresses and underskirts was made long enough to touch de ground dem days. Dey allus went off singin', and us chillun would be wishin' for de time when us would be old enough to wear long dresses wid starched petticoats and go to meetin'.

Source: George P. Rawick, ed. *The American Slave: Georgia Narratives*, Vol. 13. Westport, CT: Greenwood Press, 1972.

Many field women were weavers, spinners, and knitters or had rudimentary sewing skills. Enslaved women often worked a double shift for which they labored in the fields in the day and made clothing or other textiles at night. This night work could include anything from spinning a certain amount of yarn or weaving a certain length of cloth to sewing up a number of shirts. Whether planting cotton or flax and raising sheep for wool, these women were involved in the production of their own clothing from the very beginning stages of the raw materials.

Children of both genders as young as three and four often were employed in carding, spinning, and throwing the shuttle of a loom for the weaver. Women worked as weavers and sewers and sometimes as spinners. Inclement weather often meant a day of textile manufacturing for the enslaved women and children of the plantation rather than a day of rest.

Slaveholders who retained large numbers of slaves or who were artisans in the dressmaking or tailoring trades were most likely to possess slaves with these special skill sets. These skilled slaves usually were employed in making fashionable clothing for the slaveholder's family rather than the utilitarian clothing worn by fellow slaves. And these enslaved women sometimes were able to use these skills to either purchase their own freedom or to support themselves when they fled slavery. Elizabeth Keckly (ca. 1818–1907), who bought her freedom and that of her son using her dressmaking skills, became a well-known dressmaker for many of Washington, D.C.'s elite, including Mary Anna Randolph Custis (1808–1873), Varina Davis (1826–1906), and, most famously, Mary Todd Lincoln (1818–1882). Another well-known enslaved seamstress was Harriet Jacobs (1813–1897), who was taught to sew by her original owner in North Carolina and then used those skills to sustain herself while she hid for seven years from an oppressive master.

Rural Slave Dress

In the 17th and 18th centuries, slaves on the North American mainland were given clothing as they needed it or when a plantation owner saw fit. By the 19th century, a distribution timetable had been established for large plantations. Almost all wealthy slaveholders distributed slave clothing in December and many also gave additional lighter garments in May or June. Slaveholders who had only a few slaves followed the more informal system of distributing clothing as they deemed necessary. Most accounts show that enslaved people had one or two changes of clothing. Men received shirts and pants; women got dresses. Other items received on a more discretionary basis included jackets, caps, wrappers, and handkerchiefs.

Slaves wore a variety of clothing styles made from several different materials. Most summer clothing was made from cheap **linen**, often referred to as oznaberg. "Plains," an inexpensive woolen material, usually was used for winter clothing. Other materials included flax (linen), jeans, and various mixtures of fibers. Linsey-woolsey was a commonly used mixture for summer and winter clothing. It was a sturdy, rough fabric that combined a linen warp and a wool weft. These fabrics usually were undyed.

Sometimes slaves dyed their own clothing with natural dyes found in the surrounding woods or with **indigo** if they had access to it. Dyeing fabrics in early America was a laborious and time-consuming task. It involved the gathering of natural dyestuffs such as roots, tree barks, and nuts from the surrounding area, boiling or soaking the yarn or cloth in large pots of water while maintaining the heat of a large fire, rinsing the wet and heavy fiber, and then waiting for it to dry. In some cases, time was given to the slaves to dye cloth before it was made into clothing as part of the finishing process. In other instances, enslaved people took time from their free hours to dye their clothing themselves.

Urban and House Slave Dress

Slaves who worked in the slaveholder's house and urban slaves usually had better-quality clothing than fieldworkers, who were most often dressed in the same styles and types of clothing. They often looked more similar to each other in appearance than did house slaves, who were dressed in clothing that reflected their duties as cooks, nursemaids, scullery maids, housemaids, or personal (body) servants. **Livery**, or uniforms worn by male servants, was supplied for those enslaved men who had visible duties as footmen and doormen. It usually was made from expensive fabrics such as wool broadcloth trimmed with silk and lace but not commonly worn after the 1830s. Slaveholders could display their wealth on the bodies of their slaves. Visitors to a rural plantation or more commonly to an urban townhouse might judge the wealth and therefore the worth of the slaveholder by the appearance of his enslaved servants.

Children's Dress

Like white children of the time, slave children were dressed in unisex clothing, although in much cheaper materials than their white counterparts. Girls' clothing was often called a "slip," while boys wore a shirt-tail that was a one-piece dress or long shirt that went below the knees. Most children, unless they worked in the house or lived in the city, went without shoes, hats, or coats at all times of the year. **Blankets** were distributed in lieu of outerwear in the colder months. Since children did not work as full hands, many planters thought it wasteful spending to provide them with the wardrobe of a working field hand. They thought that extra garments were unnecessary as most children spent the colder months huddled inside or close around a fire.

Clothing was an important marker for the transition from child to adult for enslaved individuals. In the 18th and early 19th centuries, boys received breeches, or short pants, between the ages of 5 and 10. By the early 19th century, this transition from boyhood to adult life was marked by the wearing of long pants. The period of boyhood seems to have been prolonged for black men, as many of those interviewed by the Works Progress Administration's Federal Writers' Project between 1936 and 1938 indicated they were fully grown and working in the fields before they received any kind of pants. Girls usually received long dresses to signify womanhood between the ages of 10 and 13. Female transitions into adulthood often were linked with the start of a girl's menstrual cycle and her ability to bear children. On many plantations, female slaves wore the clothing of adults earlier than boys. This practice was linked to the slaveholder's desire to reap as much profit as possible from slave bodies. Male slaves became most desirable in their late teens and early 20s when they were at peak physical strength. Female slave bodies increased in value dramatically as soon as they were able to bear children and increase the holder's enslaved population.

Shoes

In the 17th and 18th centuries, those enslaved men and women who wore **shoes** were given styles similar to those worn by indentured white servants. By the 19th century, specific shoe styles for the enslaved were manufactured in New England and shipped to the South. Former slaves interviewed by the Federal Writers' Project who wore shoes most commonly describe them as brogans. These shoes had wooden soles, leather uppers, and metal pieces on the sole. Other types of footwear included heavy lace-up boots with a wood and metal sole similar to brogans and softer soled shoes often referred to as moccasins. Descriptions of slaves wearing moccasin footwear are more prevalent in the western states of the Old South, particularly Alabama, Mississippi, and Texas, where slaves had a greater chance of interacting with Native Americans.

Like cloth, shoes could be purchased from a local merchant who ordered them from Europe or the North, but many slaves had locally made footwear. Large plantations often had an adult male slave who worked as a shoemaker. Other planters hired local shoemakers, enslaved and free, to make the shoes for their slaves. In other instances, planters enlisted the special skills of enslaved blacksmiths and carpenters familiar with the wood and leather components of shoemaking.

Shoes of the lower and working classes changed little in material, style, or technology during the 18th and early 19th centuries. Commercially produced shoes came in a variety of sizes and were made on straight lasts and therefore not specific to the right or left foot. The leather was usually a rough, thick rawhide that had to be treated with grease or fat to soften it enough to be worn. Many accounts given by slaves mention the discomfort of these shoes. Whether store-bought or homemade, shoes were not a cheap commodity and hundreds of slaves went barefoot for most of their lives. Often slaves who did have shoes noted they were too uncomfortable to wear, creating blisters, bunions, and other physical discomforts just as debilitating as wearing no shoes at all.

Headgear

Slaves wore a variety of different coverings on their heads. During the day, some enslaved women wore brightly colored **headwraps** that, depending on the choice of fabric, color, and even how they were wrapped, expressed the wearer's individuality. However, it is difficult to determine the extent to which slave women continued an African-associated tradition of wearing tied cloth on their heads, as many slaveholders required women to wear the same types of caps and hats worn by white servants. Men wore caps and hats of varying styles and also wrapped kerchiefs or pieces of fabric on their heads. Male slaves who worked as supervisors were often given higher quality shoes and hats to separate them from those lower in the perceived social order.

Dressing Up

Apparel was especially important to the enslaved. They took extra care to look nice when going to Sunday services or other special social events. They devoted their free time to completing the extra work required to make a garment as well as earning expendable income to acquire nicer clothing. Slaves often spent Saturdays washing themselves and their clothing to appear in their best at church. Many accounts describe slaves going barefoot during the week and on the walk to church, but stopping to put on their shoes before getting too close to the church. Sunday services were a time to worship but also a time to see slaves from neighboring plantations. By dressing up, slaves were able to assert themselves as members of the fashionable world, as well as express their individuality.

A practice unique to New Orleans and, to a lesser extent, Charleston was the so-called fancy trade, in which extremely light-skinned female slaves were sold specifically as concubines for wealthy white Southern men. Many lived as mistresses in the urban dwellings of men who also had a wife and children on a rural plantation. Some women or their children eventually were freed by their owners and, in rare cases, white men married their concubines. Fine clothing was an aspect critical to the success of the slave traders who sold and the men who owned fancy girls. These women were not dressed as prostitutes, but as fashionably showy ladies. On the **auction blocks** they wore clothing that was in the latest fashion and had jewelry and baubles. This style of dress continued after they were purchased as concubines. Much like enslaved house servants, these women's bodies were places for slaveholders to signify their social power by displaying their wealth. While dressing up meant a degree of freedom and an avenue of individual expression for most slaves, for these women, fine clothing was only another form of exploitation.

Enslaved people owned a variety of finery from gold pocket watches and earrings to fur hats and silk dresses. Even though on a lower level, women's calico dresses and men's leather coats were still above the quality of most everyday slave clothing. When the cage crinoline, or hoopskirt, became popular after the 1830s, enslaved women would sometimes buy hoops, receive cast-offs from white women, or make them out of natural materials such as grapevines. The finer clothing acquired by slaves was saved for special occasions such as weddings, dances, or barbeques. Because they often functioned as markers of important life events, these items were well taken care of and more likely to have survived through generations of use.

See also Churches and Praise Houses; Linen Textiles; Spinning Houses; Wool Textiles.

FURTHER READING

Baumgarten, Linda. "'Clothes for the People': Slave Clothing in Early Virginia." *Journal of Early Southern Decorative Arts* 14, no. 2 (November 1988): 26–70.

Baumgarten, Linda. "Plains, Plaid and Cotton: Woolens for Slave Clothing." *Ars Textrina* 15 (July 1991): 203–221.

Foster, Helen Bradley. *"New Raiments of Self": African American Clothing in the Antebellum South*. New York: Berg, 1997.

Hunt, Patricia K. "Fabric Production in the 19th-Century African American Slave Community." *Ars Textrina* 15 (July 1991): 83–92.

Starke, Barbara M. "Nineteenth-Century African-American Dress." In *Dress in American Culture*, edited by Patricia A. Cunningham and Susan Voso Lab, 66–79. Bowling Green, OH: Bowling Green State University Popular Press, 1993.

White, Shane, and Graham White. *Stylin': African American Expressive Culture from Its Beginnings to the Zoot Suit*. Ithaca, NY: Cornell University Press, 1998.

KATIE KNOWLES

COFFINS AND CASKETS. Coffins and caskets, the receptacles that house and transport the dead during the funeral ritual and then are placed in the **grave**, also are a form of material communication because they allow mortuary symbols to be associated with the dead. Coffins are anthropomorphic. They follow the general contour of the body, usually made in an elongated hexagonal form. An elongated trapezoidal shape ("taper-to-foot" coffin) is occasionally seen in American slave cemeteries. This form may result from contact with French or Spanish societies, particularly those from the Caribbean.

Caskets deemphasize their human contents by assuming less anthropomorphic shapes. Most tend to be rectangular. In nonslave societies, this shape provided a means of adding more symbols to the dead; among slave communities, however, the casket was a simple appliance to make, requiring little skill and a minimum of materials.

The use of burial cases in West Africa can be documented as early as the 18th century, and some slaves may have seen them used before they were enslaved. In the Americas, burial in a wooden receptacle was an established mortuary tradition. Slaves often were afforded burial only in a shroud or a wooden box, although coffins seemed to be the norm. On rare occasions, commercially made coffins were provided. Slaves and slaveholders rarely stocked coffins, so they tended to be made quickly from readily available materials. While large-scale slaveholders were able to hire carpenters or woodwrights to build coffins, small-scale slaveholders or the slaves themselves sometimes were responsible for building them. This tradition of noncommercially produced coffins continued after emancipation in many free communities.

Construction typically began with string used to determine the deceased's dimensions. The types of wood used to manufacture coffins varied widely, but coffins typically were made from what was available locally. Archaeologists have recorded pine, poplar, elm, maple, cedar, and other softwoods as the most common types, but panels and occasionally entire coffins made of oak, ash, chestnut, cypress, walnut, and other hardwoods have been documented. Whenever possible, sides, tops, and bases were manufactured from single planks; joining was kept to a minimum. To create a seamless bend around the shoulder of the coffin, the long side panels were soaked, scored vertically on the interior side (referred to as "kerfing" or "breaksiding"), and bent around the outer margin of the base. Vertical side panels were fastened to the base with **nails,** or an adhesive such as tar or pitch was added to secure the upper portions together. After the body was placed in the coffin, the lid was secured using nails or screws. Some coffins may have had fabric liners. Burial cases typically were unadorned and many were left with rough finishes. Some may have been painted or had stained or rubbed finishes. Functional hardware, usually that used for furniture, was occasionally added. In exceptional cases, brass tacks were affixed in the shape of African or Christian symbols. Coffins, therefore, could be a vehicle for the slaves to express ideas about themselves and their world.

See also Crosses.

FURTHER READING

Jamison, Ross W. "Material Culture and Social Death: African-American Burial Practices," *Historical Archaeology* 29, no. 4 (1995): 39–58.

HUGH B. MATTERNES

COFFLES. The term "coffle" refers to a group of slaves on the march, usually under the supervision of a slave trader. The word derives from *qâfilah*, Arabic for caravan. An iron shackle, when the chain is long enough to secure several slaves together, is also called a coffle.

In the American South, slave coffles are associated with the rise of the early 19th-century intrastate slave trade. As the cultivation of **tobacco** declined precipitously in the Upper South and large enslaved populations were no longer needed for plantation labor, the enslaved were sold to slave traders or speculators and marched in groups into the Deep South—sometimes in chains, over great distances—to be purchased by cotton or sugar planters. Hired out to the Washington Navy Yard in the 1820s, Charles Ball witnessed "large numbers of people of my colour chained together in long trains, and driven off towards the south" on the streets of the nation's capital. In fact, these coffles, which were a regular feature on Washington's

A slave trader leads a coffle of slaves from Virginia to Tennessee. From *Sketchbook of Landscapes in the State of Virginia* by Lewis Miller, Virginia, 1853–1867, watercolor and ink on paper. (Abby Aldrich Rockefeller Folk Art Museum, The Colonial Williamsburg Foundation. Gift of Dr. and Mrs. Richard M. Kain in memory of George Hay Kain.)

To Sale in a Coffle

Ben Simpson and his family endured a terrible walk to Texas in a slave coffle that resulted in his mother's death:

> He [the master] got in trouble there in Georgia and got him two good-stepping hosses and the covered wagon. Then he chains all he slaves round the necks and fastens the chains to the hosses and makes them walk all the way to Texas. My mother and my sister had to walk. Emma was my sister. Somewhere on the road it went to snowin' and massa wouldn't let us wrap anything round our feet. We had to sleep on the ground, too, in all that snow.
>
> Massa have a great, long whip platted out of rawhide and when one the niggers fall behind or give out, he hit him with that whip. It take the hide every time he hit a nigger. Mother, she give out on the way, 'bout the line of Texas. Her feet got raw and bleedin' and her legs swoll plumb out of shape. Then massa, he jus' take out he gun and shot her, and whilst she lay dyin' he kicks her two, three times and say, "Damn a nigger what can't stand nothin.' " Boss, you know that man, he wouldn't bury mother, jus' leave her layin' where he shot her at. You know, then there wasn't no law 'gainst killin' nigger slaves.

Source: George P. Rawick, ed. *The American Slave: Texas Narratives*, Vol. 5, Parts 3 & 4. Westport, CT: Greenwood Press, 1972.

Foster Weathersby from Mississippi told of how his parents were separated and marched away just a few months after his birth:

> At times, hearts was made sad from separations caused from sellin' slaves. I can see de tragic sight, yet, of my people, chained together by deir han's in pairs, lined up in a long row, wid men leadin' 'em, and men at de end of de line takin' 'em to de auction-block. Large sums would be paid for some of 'em. Husbands was sol' and took from deir wives, wives sol' and took from deir chillun, de sons and daughters sol' away from home. My mother was sol' and took from my father when I was jes a few months old. I never seed him tw'ell I was six. I had to be tol' who he was. He saw my mother, for the first time in six years, in de fiel's where we was a-working; dey didn't know how to ack or what to say; dey seemed kinda let down lak. You see, he had married ag'in an' my mother had, too.

Source: George P. Rawick, ed. *The American Slave: Mississippi Narratives*, Supp. Ser. 1, Vol. 10, Part 5. Westport, CT: Greenwood Press, 1978.

streets, provoked antebellum abolitionists to begin the fight for a ban on the slave trade in the District of Columbia. Later Ball found himself part of a coffle in which the male slaves were fitted with padlocked slave collars and handcuffed to each other. He recalled, "A Chain of iron, about a hundred feet in length, was passed through the clasp of each padlock, except at the two ends, where the clasps of the padlocks passed through a link of the chain." The man Ball was attached to trembled and "wept like an infant" when the blacksmith fastened his chains in preparation for their march. In Ball's coffle, several slaves died as a result of the long walk and their bodies were summarily discarded along the road.

Leg shackles made of iron, steel, and copper were used to prevent slaves from running away. Great Britain or America, 1750–1820. (The Colonial Williamsburg Foundation. Acquisition funded by an anonymous donor.)

FURTHER READING

Ball, Charles. *Slavery in the United States: A Narrative of the Life and Adventures of Charles Ball, a Black Man, Who Lived Forty Years in Maryland, South Carolina and Georgia.* New York: John S. Taylor, 1837. Also at Documenting the American South Collection, http://docsouth.unc.edu/neh/ballslavery/ball.html.
International Slavery Museum. At www.liverpoolmuseums.org.uk/ism/.
Tadman, Michael. *Speculators and Slaves: Masters, Traders, and Slaves in the Old South.* Madison: University of Wisconsin Press, 1989.

KYM S. RICE

COINS AND CURRENCY. Well into the 19th century, the money in daily use throughout America included an array of coins and currency from all over the world. In addition to coins minted on this continent, British shillings, Spanish dollars, German *thalers*, French *ecus,* and Bolivian *reales* were all in circulation. Many enslaved men and women were familiar with these coins because they used them while carrying out errands for their owners or while engaged in other work required by their masters. Still others were familiar with them because they received coins and currency from their masters and their guests as tips or gifts, as payment for goods they sold in the **markets**, as wages when they were hired out and were allowed to keep some of that money, or as cash stolen from their owners.

One anomaly of slavery was that even though slaves were regarded as property and bought and sold like livestock, they were also active participants in their local market economies. Slaveholders recorded in detail—in diaries, letters, and account books—the payments made to slaves for their crops, their goods, and their labor. And with the money the slaves earned, the slaves went to local merchants, fellow slaves, free blacks, poor whites, and other masters to purchase goods for themselves and their families.

Making Money

On Susan MacIntosh's Georgia plantation, slaves sold their own butter, eggs, and brooms and used the money to buy fabric, clothes, and shoes:

> Marse Billy let the slaves raise chickens, and cows, and have cotton patches too. They would sell butter, eggs, chickens, brooms, made out of wheat straw and such like. They took the money and bought calico, muslin and good shoes, pants, coats and other nice things for their Sunday clothes.

Source: George P. Rawick, ed. "*The American Slave: Georgia Narratives*, Vol. 13. Westport, CT: Greenwood Press, 1972.

Fannie Fulcher recalled that the Georgia slaveholder provided work clothes, but slaves worked for cash to buy everything else:

> Dey give 'um evy-day work clothes . . . but dey bought de res' themselves. Some raise corn, punkins, squashes, potatoes, all sich things like dat in dey patches; sell 'em to different stores. Jus' like persons wanted ground clear up, they git big torches for light, clean up new ground at night, dat money belong to them. I year my mother and father say de slaves make baskets and quilts and things and sell 'em for they-selves.

Source: George P. Rawick, ed. *The American Slave: Georgia Narratives*, Supp. Ser. 1, Vol. 3, Part 1. Westport, CT: Greenwood Press, 1978.

Laura Thornton, a former Arkansas slave, talked about her father being paid for his work:

> Slaves had money in slave time. My daddy bought a horse. He made a crop every year. He made his bale of cotton. He made corn to feed his horse with. He belonged to his white folks but he had his house and lot right next to theirs. They would give him time you know. He didn't have to work in the heat of the day. He made his crop and bought his whiskey. The white folks fed 'im. He had no expenses 'cept tending to his crop. He didn't have to give Tom Eford anything he made. He just worked his crop in his extra time. Many folks too lazy to git theirselves somethin' when they have the chance to do it. But my daddy wasn't that kind. His old master gave him the ground and he made it give him the money.

Source: George P. Rawick, ed. *The American Slave: Arkansas Narratives*, Vol. 10, Parts 5 & 6. Westport, CT: Greenwood Press, 1972.

Throughout the 18th and 19th centuries, enslaved men and women sold food items—primarily **chickens** and vegetables—to their masters and in the local markets. Francis Taylor, an Orange County, Virginia, planter wrote in his diary in May 1795, that his "Negroes [were] planting for themselves," and he also purchased such items as carp, oysters, cabbages, and potatoes for his own table from his slaves. Joseph Ball, writing in 1744 from London to his nephew, Joseph Chinn, the manager of his plantations in Virginia, recommended that he "keep the keys of the folks' [slaves'] Corn-house or else they will sell it, and starve themselves." In 1759, a slave named Jemmy ran away from Middletown, Pennsylvania, and his owner advertised that "he understands making of Corn **Baskets**, and it is supposed he will go about to sell them."

Enslaved men and women also received tips for doing extra work for their owners or doing work for others. In 1768, in a letter to his cousin, John Hatley Norton in Virginia, John Frere of London asked Norton to send any plant or animal fossils that might be found in the area. Frere wrote "if such Things are to be found, the Negroes I suppose for a small Gratuity wou'd bring them to you." In 19th-century Upson County, Georgia, enslaved midwives earned up to three dollars per delivery, and enslaved men made and sold charcoal.

Runaway slave advertisements attest to the fact that slaves who ran away often took cash with them to finance their escape. John James, who lived in Stafford County, Virginia, advertised in the June 22, 1779, issue of the *Maryland Journal and Baltimore Advertiser* for his enslaved man, Robin, who took £200 with him when he ran away. James thought that Robin would purchase new **clothing** with some of the money.

With the money, enslaved men and women purchased goods of every type available to them. In 1737, "Negro Jack" bought **cloth**, scissors, thread, hose, and penknives from Thomas Partridge, a Virginia storekeeper. In Bedford County, Virginia, Richard Stith's slave, Sukey, was able to purchase a **mirror** and some **ribbon** with money she received for selling "**cotton** in the seed." Charles Ball, writing about his life as a slave in Maryland, noted, "A part [of the slaves' own money] is disbursed in payment for **sugar**, molasses, and sometimes a few pounds of coffee, for the use of the family; another part is laid out for clothes for winter; and no inconsiderable portion of his pittance is squandered away by the misguided slave for **tobacco**, and an occasional bottle of rum."

As much as some slaveholders accepted that their enslaved workers earned money for themselves by selling goods of all kinds to individuals other than their masters, some slaveholders strongly advised against it, pointing out that if slaves had money and knew what it could buy, they would steal items to sell. One South Carolina overseer noted in 1836 that "Negroes should in no instance be permitted to trade, except with their masters. By permitting them to leave the plantation with the view of selling and buying, much is lost by the owner than he is generally aware of." About 20 years later, a small Alabama planter wrote, "I never allow them to have money unless they can give a satisfactory account of the way in which they obtained it." The fear of theft and misuse of money was ever-present in the minds of these masters.

But despite these fears, it is clear that enslaved men and women had access to a wide range of goods, that they wanted to have these goods, and that they were able to pay for these goods themselves.

See also Barter Goods; Corn; Credit Accounts; Gardens; Liquor; Locks and Keys.

FURTHER READING

Ball, Charles. "Fifty Years in Chains, or, The Life of an American Slave." Documenting the American South. At http://docsouth.unc.edu/fpn/ball/ball.html.

Breeden, James O., ed. *Advice among Masters: The Ideal in Slave Management in the Old South.* Westport, CT: Greenwood Press, 1980.

"Coins and Currency in Colonial America." Colonial Williamsburg. At www.history.org/history/museums/coinExhibit/.

Fithian, Philip Vickers. *Journal & Letters of Philip Vickers Fithian, 1773–1774: A Plantation Tutor of the Old Dominion.* Williamsburg, VA: Colonial Williamsburg, 1957.

Heath, Barbara J. "Slavery and Consumerism: A Case Study from Colonial Virginia." *African-American Archaeology: Newsletter of the African-American Archaeology Network* 19 (early winter 1997). Also at the African Diaspora Archaeology Network, www.diaspora.uiuc.edu/A-AANewsletter/newsletter19.html.

Katz-Hyman, Martha. " 'In the Middle of This Poverty Some Cups and a Teapot': The Furnishing of Slave Quarters at Colonial Williamsburg." In *The American Home: Material Culture, Domestic Space, and Family Life,* edited by Eleanor McD. Thompson, 197–216. Winterthur, DE: Henry Francis Du Pont Winterthur Museum, 1998.

Martin, Ann Smart. *Buying Into the World of Goods: Early Consumers in Backcountry Virginia.* Baltimore, MD: Johns Hopkins University Press, 2008.

Paterson, David E. "Slavery, Slaves, and Cash in a Georgia Village, 1825–1865." *Journal of Southern History* 75, no. 4 (November 2009): 879–930.

MARTHA B. KATZ-HYMAN

COLLARDS. The collard green (*Brassica oleracea acephala*) is a nonheading member of the cabbage family eaten as a leafy vegetable. Although the cool-weather vegetable originated in Eurasia, and its American name comes from a corruption of an Anglo-Saxon term "colewort," meaning "cabbage plants," it became most closely associated with slaves in the South. Collards found favor with enslaved Africans because of their similarity to wild and cultivated greens that were staples of their traditional diet. In some markets in West Africa, dozens of varieties of these greens are offered for sale, destined for pots of **stew** or as a base for sauces. Collards may have been introduced to West and Central

---

Favorite Foods

Ezra Adams, an ex-slave from South Carolina, recalled collard greens and other food:

If you wants to know what I thinks is de best vittles, I's gwine to be obliged to omit (admit) dat it is cabbage sprouts in de spring, and it is collard greens after frost has struck them. After de best vittles, dere come some more what is mighty tasty, and they is hoghead and chittlings wid 'tatoes and turnips. Did you see dat? Here I is talkin' 'bout de joys of de appetite and water drapping from my mouth. I sho' must be gittin' hongry. I lak to eat.

Source: George P. Rawick, ed. *The American Slave: South Carolina Narratives,* Vol. 2. Westport, CT: Greenwood Press, 1972.

Africa by the Portuguese, who valued them for use in *caldo verde*, a soup of greens flavored with preserved pork. Full of vitamin C and fiber, collards form a culinary link between the American South, West and Central Africa, and the Portuguese world, including Brazil, where enslaved blacks also made collards key in their food traditions. In 1709, John Lawson noted "coleworts" as one of the common "salads" of the Carolinas. On August 17, 1781, Capt. William Feltman saw collards growing in the cabin gardens of an enslaved community in Hanover County, Virginia, noting, "The Negroes here raise great quantities of snaps and collerds [sic] they have no cabbages here." The variety he saw most likely resembled "Green Glaze," a large branching, waxy-leafed heirloom sold by the Landreth Seed Company in Philadelphia in 1820. Because vegetables typically were not used for rations, the growing of leafy greens such as collards and other vegetables like turnip greens, kale, and rape were essential to a more balanced and nutritionally complete diet. Collards were typically grown in fields as livestock fodder, as was done by 18th-century Virginia planter Landon Carter, and called "cow-collards." This added to their common availability in most of the lower South. Collards were most valued for the by-product known as "pot-liquor," a rich stock produced by boiling them with salt meat that was soaked up with bland-tasting **hoecake** or ashcake. John Patterson Green, who wrote about his slave times in his native North Carolina, observed that

> To the inhabitants of the country districts of the South, the collard is a very great blessing: because when boiled in a pot with a piece of fat meat and balls of corn-meal dough, having the size and appearance of ordinary white turnips, called dumplings, it makes palatable a diet which would otherwise be all but intolerable.

Easily cultivated, nutritious and tasty, the collard was a key staple in many enslaved communities.

See also Pigs and Pork; Pot Likker.

FURTHER READING

Carter, Landon. *The Diary of Colonel Landon Carter of Sabine Hall, 1752–1778*, edited by Jack P. Greene. 2 vols. Charlottesville: Published for the Virginia Historical Society by the University Press of Virginia, 1965.

Feltman, William. *The Journal of Lt. William Feltman 1781–82*. New York: New York Times, 1969.

Green, John Patterson. *Recollections of the Inhabitants, Localities, Superstitions, and KuKlux Outrages of the Carolinas. By a "Carpet-Bagger" Who Was Born and Lived There.* Cleveland, 1880.

Greene, Wesley. "Brassicas." Colonial Williamsburg. At www.history.org/history/cwland/resrch3.cfm.

Weaver, William Woys. *Heirloom Vegetable Gardening*. New York: Henry Holt and Company, 1997.

MICHAEL W. TWITTY

COLONOWARE. "Colonoware" (or colono ware) is an overarching term that encompasses diverse, localized **pottery** that was produced by enslaved Africans in the United States, Native Americans, and possibly enslaved Native Americans. Colonoware from these traditions generally is a low-fired pottery produced either through lump-forming or coil-building, but never through wheel-throwing. Colonoware was used in rural and urban slave contexts, in Native households and in planters' **kitchens**, and it was sold in **markets**. Colonoware was made predominantly in the late 17th to early 19th

Colonoware chamber pot and bowl. (The Colonial Williamsburg Foundation.)

century and appears to have not been produced after the Civil War. Much of the colonoware is burnished or semiburnished bowls and jars, but decorative modes and forms mimicking refined European ceramics are also known. Colonoware was apparently used for many functions, including cooking, eating, cleansing, healing, and rituals. In the United States, there were two main pockets of colonoware manufacture and use by enslaved Africans: coastal South Carolina and eastern Virginia and Maryland. Similar pottery was made by African Caribbeans in the Greater and Lesser Antilles.

The following examples of people and groups who made colonoware underline the temporal, spatial, and ethnic complexity of the many manifestations lumped together as colonoware. As early as the 1540s, Guale and Yemassee Indian women in coastal Georgia and the Sea Islands were making low-fired pots in imitation of Spanish forms, for exchange with Spanish missionaries. In the 1680s, a Pamunkey woman coil-built a few pots in imitation of European forms and traded them to local, enslaved Africans in eastern Virginia. In the 1850s, an enslaved potter produced burnished, footed bowls and footless bowls for the 20 households of her community near Hilton Head, South Carolina. In the 1780s, a Catawba potter and her family produced thousands of low-fired, burnished pots for sale to slaves and planters of the South Carolina Low Country.

When first recognized, colonoware was considered to have been an Indian product made for exchange with the occupants of early plantations. In South Carolina, the correlation between colonoware and occupation sites of enslaved Africans was observed later, suggesting that slaves produced colonoware. Indeed, more than 75 percent of all shards (broken pieces of pottery) found in certain South Carolina slave communities is colonoware. It has thus been suggested that both Indians and enslaved Africans produced colonoware. Colonoware also was found in planters' houses, so colonoware might not have been limited to the enslaved and Indians. Colonoware has been viewed as the product of creolization resulting from the interaction of Indians and enslaved Africans. However, colonoware produced by the Catawba, the Pamunkey, and other Indian groups does not seem to show influence from the enslaved Africans. Indeed, these Indians maintained their technological traditions that extended back to the prehistoric period and simply altered the vessel forms and decoration to mimic European wares. Nothing stands out in 18th-century colonoware in South Carolina or Virginia and Maryland as reflecting input from an African-derived tradition. When enslaved African Americans began making their own colonoware, their product was often a coarse imitation of the trade ware produced by Native Americans. As would be expected of potters unfamiliar with the local clays, the colonoware produced by slaves seems to have had a greater percentage of pots lost in firing than seen in Native-made colonoware.

At least some of the colonoware produced by enslaved Africans was uniquely incorporated into their ritual and belief system, but the basic idea of producing low-fired, hand-formed imitations of European vessels seems to have come from the Native Americans and not the Africans. This interpretation—the Native inspiration for colonoware—is bolstered by recent research at historic Catawba town sites by the University of North Carolina–Chapel Hill. This interpretation has not yet been examined extensively in the literature, and many archaeologists still prefer to see colonoware as a product of creolization.

Colonoware was formed by hand, either through coil construction or through the shaping and thinning of a single lump of clay. The quality of the workmanship varies from pots with thin, even walls and well-executed burnishing to vessels with thicker, uneven walls and irregular semiburnishing. Burnishing refers to the rubbing of a leather-dry pot with a smooth pebble, a shard of bottle glass, a spoon, a piece of bone or antler, or a section of river cane to produce a compacted, less porous, and shinier vessel surface. The vague consistency in surface treatment misled early researchers to think all colonoware was part of a shared tradition. When a broader, global perspective is taken, it becomes obvious that semiburnished to burnished pots are common in low-fired traditions worldwide. The compaction of the surface makes a pot less porous and easier to clean. Burnishing helps to even the vessel walls, while the act of burnishing or semiburnishing changes the aesthetics of a pot. The broad occurrence of burnishing in low-fired traditions worldwide may be related to the simple tools required to successfully burnish a pot.

It is likely that most pots were fired in surface hearths, much like a camp fire, and reached only 600°C to 800°C. Colonoware often has fire clouds and different surface colors on the interior and exterior surfaces. These traits suggest certain pots were fired mouth-down, thereby restricting air flow, and that most were fired using wood for fuel. No evidence indicates kiln-fired colonoware, even among slave communities occupied in the production of bricks in kilns.

Pieces destined for sale by their makers may have been better made than those made informally for immediate household use. The overriding consistency is that colonoware was never produced on a pottery wheel. Although a few enslaved Africans produced wheel-thrown stoneware, for example, Dave of the Edgefield District of South Carolina, that stoneware closely resembled the stoneware made by white potters, which was glazed and fired in a kiln.

The production and use of colonoware by enslaved African Americans appeared to be predominantly an 18th-century phenomenon. Since 1990, work at several 19th-century slave villages has demonstrated the continuation of colonoware manufacture and use up to the Civil War in certain communities. Recent research in South Carolina and Virginia has started to address possible reasons for the perceived abandonment of colonoware-making after the Civil War. The reasons are far from clear, but one suggestion that fits the present data is that by the 1860s, colonoware had become a negative marker of slavery, and once emancipation came, the last colonoware potters were inspired to discontinue its manufacture and use.

The sheer amount of colonoware in certain domestic middens (refuse deposits) suggests that colonoware was used in the preparation and consumption of **food** and possibly beverages. It has been estimated that there might have been more than 1 million colonoware pots broken in slave communities of the South Carolina Low Country. Certain researchers have suggested that in its earliest periods of use colonoware was a response to either lack of capital or poor supply regimes. This view argues that the slaves manufactured pottery, or obtained it through trade with the Native Americans, to make up for the shortfalls in the dishes provided by the planters. Colonoware is also found in planter kitchen contexts, and the archival record suggests a preference for the use of low-fired pots in the preparation of certain African-derived meals, especially **rice**-based dishes. Beyond these utilitarian tasks, at least a portion of the slave-made pottery had deeper meaning. The jars found in South Carolina are similar to those used in certain West African countries in cleansing and curing activities. The very act of continuing to produce or purchase a non-European ware suggests that colonoware was possibly a manifestation of resistance, a tool for maintaining a separate, non-European identity. In South Carolina, a number of pots have been found with incised or etched designs reminiscent of the BaKongo **cosmogram**. It has been posited that pots were used in religious rituals, possibly focusing on riverside activities. Evidence indicates that in South Carolina there were generalized trends in the uses of colonoware, with cooking jars disappearing by the turn of the 19th century, but small footed and footless bowls continuing up to the Civil War. Colonoware use may have become increasingly personal and ritual, possibly in response to an increasing role of a creolized Christianity among slave communities. To date, the known slave communities that continued to make colonoware up to the Civil War are all located in the heartland of Gullah culture, where a distinct set of cultural behaviors and African-derived words continue to be seen in the 21st century.

The evidence is clear that certain Native groups created colonoware for their own use and for exchange with slaves and European American planters. As early as the Spanish Mission period, Guale and Yemassee Indians were making low-fired pottery that imitated European forms. Perhaps the most prolific Native producers were members of the Catawba confederacy. Recent archaeological research shows that the Catawba were mass-producing and marketing colonoware to Low Country plantations by 1759. The archival record suggests that the Catawba produced much colonoware in their communities in upstate South Carolina, and that they moved seasonally to clay sources near the Low Country plantations to produce pots for use in slave communities and planters' homes.

As a general rule, colonoware was a minor feature (by shard or vessel count) in slave assemblages in Virginia and Maryland, even though it dominated slave site collections from coastal South Carolina. There have been attempts to link the quality of burnishing and vessel thinness to a specific class of producers (e.g., Native American trade ware is generally finer than slave-made ware), but these distinctions do not always hold up when the colonoware produced in a single slave community is examined. Colonoware was produced by Native Americans of various tribes, by slaves directly imported from diverse areas of western Africa, and by slaves who were moved to the Southeastern United States via the Caribbean. There was not a one-to-one correlation with Africans and slaves; many slaves were Native Americans. Undoubtedly, interaction and intermarriage occurred between people originally belonging to many African and Native American cultures. Even for those people from cultures with well-developed pottery traditions, the existence of an Africa Diaspora meant huge changes to the contexts for making, teaching, sharing, and using pottery.

Only limited research has been done on the nature of pottery production within slave communities. It is assumed that women were the potters, based on the pan-African generalization that women made pottery by hand and men made only wheel-thrown pottery. Women probably produced the colonoware of the Catawba, the Pamunkey, and other

Native American groups. Ethnography and oral history among the Catawba and other groups indicates that females were the potters, but males could assist in the gathering of clay and fuel and in the firing. In a preliminary investigation of pottery-making by black slaves in three 19th-century communities in coastal South Carolina, possible technological and stylistic indicators of individual potters were examined. It was concluded that for each of the three slave communities, all within five miles of each other, there was probably a single potter working at any one time, and that potter provided colonoware to all houses of the community but did not trade her product outside the community.

Archaeological excavations in urban contexts of Charleston, South Carolina, provided data possibly supporting another mechanism of colonoware dispersal. Two varieties of colonoware were recovered from early 18th-century contexts predating the known start date for Catawba production of colonoware. One variety was thick, clunky, and barely semiburnished, and the other variety was thinner, more uniform, and well burnished. Bolstering their argument with the evidence of apparent canoe-loads of colonoware being lost in local rivers, the researchers suggested that the former variety was made by slaves for slave use, and the latter was made by slaves for sale or **barter** in the markets of Charleston and Beaufort. None of the canoe assemblages has yet been subjected to detailed archaeological analysis, and recent research suggests that colonoware made by the Yemassee and Apalachee Indians was reaching Charleston in the early 18th century. Further research will be necessary to determine to what degree enslaved African Americans were producing colonoware for market. The informal market was known to have been an important source of cash income and bartered items for the slaves of the Southeast and Caribbean. It is reasonable to infer that colonoware was among the foodstuffs and crafts exchanged at such markets.

Colonoware research in recent years has profited from the recognition of the complexity of the traditions. Archaeologists have begun to recognize the need to carefully describe and interpret each local manifestation of the pottery. The discipline of African American archaeology has productively advanced beyond simplistic rules—for example, colonoware is an Africanism, or colonoware at a site means the occupants were enslaved blacks. It is now recognized that the production of colonoware by Native Americans and blacks had direct implications for the status of the potters. Analysts have recognized that colonoware moved through a number of functional, ritual, and economic realms. The study of this hand-formed, low-fired pottery still has much to offer to interpretations of gender relationships, African American religion and ritual, colonization, foodways, and the economies of barter and market. Researchers are just beginning to link Indian production trajectories with tribes' broader social histories. It remains puzzling why various slave communities stopped making or using colonoware, and why certain areas and communities adopted colonoware, while adjacent areas generally did not.

FURTHER READING

Ferguson, Leland. *Uncommon Ground: Archaeology and Early African America, 1650–1800.* Washington, DC: Smithsonian Institution Press, 1992.

Galke, Laura J. "Colonowhen, Colonowho, Colonowhere, Colonowhy: Exploring the Meaning Behind the Use of Colonoware Ceramics in Nineteenth-Century Manassas, Virginia." *International Journal of Historical Archaeology* 13(3): 303–326.

Kelly, K. G., and N. L. Norman. "Medium Vessels and the Longue Dureé." In *African Re-Genesis: Confronting Social Issues in the Diaspora,* edited by J. B. Haviser and K. C. MacDonald, 223–234. New York: UCL Press, 2006.

CHRISTOPHER T. ESPENSHADE

CONJURE BAGS. A conjure bag is a power object, such as a **charm**, amulet, talisman, or ritual container, used to convey protection to the wearer or to exert control over those who come into contact with it. Conjure bags were worn on the body or strategically placed in and around dwellings as a part of the loosely defined system known as "conjure" or "root-work," through which enslaved individuals sought to empower themselves spiritually and control their circumstances and surroundings through magic, mystical intention, and metaphysical lore. The tradition is thoroughly West and Central African in origin with some influences from the Native American and European cultures with which enslaved people came into contact, but it developed and grew beyond its original trappings to fit the lives and circumstances of American slavery and plantation life. Conjure bags contained multiple ingredients related to healing, the powers of the **grave**, herbs, bones, and other aspects sacred to the owner or maker. They were simultaneously a form of identity display and a hidden form of spiritual practice and resistance.

Although conjure bags, also known as "mojo bags," "diddy bags," *gris-gris, paquet Kongo,* and *wanga,* are associated with New World religious beliefs from the Caribbean and South America, the tradition was just as alive and well in mainland North America because of the consistent and diverse approaches to making ritual objects throughout West and Central Africa. Along the 3,500-mile coast from which enslaved Africans were drawn, almost every culture had some form of spiritual container used for protection or as a tool of mystical intent. Thousands of power objects were used for ritual work, and entire markets and sacred spaces were given over for the procurement of objects that would be tied or enclosed in these sacred vessels, given the name **fetishes** by early Portuguese slave traders. The word "fetish," from the Portuguese, *feitiço,* affirms the Latin origin of the word in the sense of being a human-made object associated with primitive polytheism rather than a religious artifact used for focus and intention, such as the ritual objects the Portuguese themselves used in their services and the adoration of the Catholic saints.

Across West and Central Africa, each community had its particular approach to the making and use of sacred bags. Most Mande people had a charm to protect them and keep them well. The Mande and their neighbors are particularly well known for clothing covered in sacred bags, some of which may contain scripture from the **Koran**, owing to the presence of Islam in Senegambia. Sacred bag charms may be worn suspended from the neck, around the wrist or ankle, or sewn onto **clothing**. Mande speakers were responsible for the origin of the Louisiana term *gris-gris,* used in the Lower Mississippi Valley for similar charms, and their role in Louisiana Vodun (voodoo). Clippings of body **hair**, feathers, fingernails, animal parts, ashes, **shells**, charcoal, salt, seeds, and **herbs** often are placed in the charm by a ritual expert specially charged with the responsibility of making such *gris-gris* for the community. Although a power object need not be made by a specific ritual expert, this craft usually was reserved for those who had been initiated into a secret society or priestly class deemed

Conjuring Spell

As former Texas slave Wash Wilson explained, various remedies could counter a conjuring spell:

Iffen you knows someone workin' a conjure trick 'gainst you, jes' take some powdered brick and scrub de steps real good. Dat'll kill any conjure spell, sho'. De bes' watchdog you can get for de hoodoo is a frizzly chicken. Iffen you got one dem on de place, you can rest in peace, 'cause it scratches up every trick lay down 'gainst its owner. Iffen you see dat frizzly chicken scratchin' round de place, it a sho' sign you been conjured. A frizzly chicken come out he shell backwards, and day why he de devil's own. De old folks allus told me to make a cross inside my shoe every mornin' 'fore leavin' de house, den ain't no conjurer gwine git he conjure 'gainst you foots. Iffen you wear you under clothes wrong side out, you can't be conjured. 'Nother way am to put saltpetre in de soles you shoes. Iffen you wears a li'l piece de "peace plant" in you pocket or you shoe, dat powerful strong 'gainst conjure. A piece of de Betsy bug's heart with some silver money am good. But iffen you can't git none dese, jes' take a piece newspaper and cut it de size of you shoe sole and sprinkle nine grains red pepper on it. Dere ain't no hoodoo gwine ever harm you den, 'cause he'd have to stop and count every letter on dat newspaper and by dat time, you gwine be 'way from dere.

Iffen you want to find de conjure tricks what done been sot for you, jes' kill you a fat chicken and sprinkle some its blood in de conjure doctor's left palm. Den take you forefinger and hit dat blood till it spatter, and it gwine spatter in de direction where dat trick am hid. Den when you find de trick, sprinkle a li'l quicksilver over a piece of paper and put de paper on de fire, and dat trick gwine be laid forever.

Source: George P. Rawick, ed. *The American Slave: Texas Narratives*, Vol. 5, Parts 3 & 4. Westport, CT: Greenwood Press, 1972.

qualified for imbuing the vessel with spiritual power. All of these elements were brought intact to enslaved communities in North America.

Despite the diversity of religious beliefs and localized approaches, sacred bags gave a sense of consistency and pan-ethnic identity to enslaved people. Among the Fon, one of the groups central to the belief system known as Vodun, sacred bags were known as *ka*. The bags, worn hanging from the neck or arms or legs, were typically of white or black **cotton**. Other objects such as wood or powdered objects might be put into cloths of other colors and were tied in specific ways. Among the Yoruba the bags were known as *apo*, meaning a sacred pouch. The ethnic group most associated with the creation of this tradition is the BaKongo of Central Africa. The *feitiço* the Portuguese encountered there were central to the BaKongo belief system and were known as *minkisi*.

For the BaKongo, the minkisi were not merely containers for objects associated with healing and spiritual power but they were spiritual abodes, and they often were identified with specific spiritual powers and entities. They were tied in specific ways, and often the colors red and white were used along with specific objects because of linguistic puns to attract, embody, and direct specific activities in the world of the living. Minkisi were especially identified with the powers of the grave and the active use of the ancestral spirits to effect change in favor of the bearer. Tying, wrapping, binding, and enclosing the selection of sacred objects, and the feeding and appeasement of the forces contained within, formed the basis of the ritual work that bound the Kongo *nkisi* to the *apo* of the Yoruba and the *gris-gris* of the Mande.

In early North America, most enslaved Africans lived and died strangers to Christianity. In the Lower Mississippi Valley, Florida, and other parts of the French and Spanish colonies, carryovers from Afro-Caribbean societies reinforced the syncretic practices found in Catholic societies. All of these enslaved societies developed a general approach to the spiritual world based on their ancestral pasts in West and Central Africa but centered on their newfound American realities. The conjure bag, often found dangling from the necks of men, women, and children; pierced **coins** worn on a string; and consecrated bottles containing sacred objects carried or hung from trees were forms of semivisible yet invisible forms of spiritual protection in a world defined by illness, oppression, rape, violence, and the instability of familial and personal connections. Sometimes these conjure bags were ignored and dismissed as superstition by whites, and other times they were actively and violently rooted out as missionaries and slaveholders sought to curb what they saw as "Voodooism," and "devil worship." More likely, the whites understood that conjure bags, ritual bottles, herbalism, and knowledge of poisons could be used as a means of resistance.

According to Josh Hadnot, a formerly enslaved man, "Dey was conjure men and women in slavery days. Dey make out like dey kin do t'ings to keep to keep de marster from whippin' you. One of them gib a ole lady a bag of san' and told her dat keep Marster from whippin' her." Famed abolitionist Frederick Douglass testified to the similar practices of Sandy, a conjure man on the plantation on the Eastern Shore of Maryland where they both were enslaved. Chloe West from the South Carolina Low Country reported hiring a conjure man to remove a conjure bag from her property that had been placed there to hex her. He dug for it and removed it and reported that it contained goofer dust, or graveyard dirt. The practice of requiring a ritual expert to dig and touch the charm and to remove it—and the fact that it contained soil from a cemetery—demonstrates clear links with the tradition's origins. In Louisiana, where the making of *gris-gris* and *wanga* (a word of Kimbundu origin from Angolan) became legendary, journalist Lafcadio Hearn (1850–1904) noted that "fetishes—consisting of bones, hair, feathers, rags, or some fantastic combination of these and other trifling objects—[are put] into a pillow used by the party whom it is desired to injure." New Orleans was full of love charms wrapped in red flannel, empowered by specific ritual language used while tying and binding the intentions of the user within. In Missouri, enslaved blacks carried around a knotted conjure bag known as a "luck ball."

In 19th-century Kentucky, William Webb (1836–unknown), an itinerant slave minister, used the conjure tradition and its deep-rootedness in the community to bring other enslaved people to Christianity:

I asked them what they thought the bags of roots were for. One said it was to conjure old master; another said he thought it was to draw master down. I could talk with him then. I told them those roots were to make them faithful when they were calling on the Supreme Being, and to keep your mind at work all the time.

As slavery drew to a close, and through the remainder of the 19th century and into the early 20th century, black men and women were known to carry around "asafetida bags," leather pouches containing that herb for protection against illness. Clearly across geographic borders and across three centuries, the wearing and use of conjure bags bound generations across time and members of the African Diaspora across the ocean and seas. They cut through their oppression and pain by faith in an enchanted world where, on some level, they would be able to exert invisible control over their circumstances and daily realities.

See also Bottle Trees; Shrines and Spiritual Caches.

FURTHER READING

Douglass, Frederick. *Life and Times of Frederick Douglass: His Early Life as a Slave, His Escape from Bondage, and His Complete History to the Present Time.* Hartford, CT: Park Publishing Company, 1881.

Doumbia, Adama, and Naomi Doumbia. *The Way of the Elders: West African Spirituality and Tradition.* St. Paul, MN: Llewellyn Publications, 2004.

Herskovits, Melville J. *Dahomey: An Ancient West African Kingdom.* Volume II. Evanston, IL: Northwestern University Press, 1967.

Mellon, James. *Bullwhip Days: The Slaves Remember.* New York: Avon Books, 1990.

Thompson, Robert Farris. *Flash of the Spirit: African and Afro-American Art and Philosophy.* New York: Random House, 1984.

Young, Jason. *Rituals of Resistance: African Atlantic Religion in Kongo and the Lowcountry South in the Era of Slavery.* Baton Rouge: Louisiana State University Press, 2007.

MICHAEL W. TWITTY

CONTRABAND CAMPS. Contraband camps were temporary settlements organized to shelter refugee slaves behind Union lines during the Civil War. These camps became common through many parts of the wartime South, but the conditions and treatment that former slaves experienced as contrabands varied widely in each state and even among camps. Although their size ranged from less than 100 to several thousand inhabitants, established camps often housed 500 to 2,000 residents; however, the populations were highly mobile and dramatic fluctuations occurred weekly. Slaves often arrived with few possessions; many camps either provided clothing as part of aid rations or produced it independently, using contract seamstresses who usually were contrabands. Some camps were organized largely by freed people who built their own shelters, repurposed military barracks, or reused army tents. Other camps were supervised carefully by army officials and were not only places of shelter but also became centers for education and employment for freed slaves, such as the Freedman's Colony on Roanoke Island, North Carolina; Camp Shiloh and Camp Dixie near Memphis, Tennessee; and the Corinth Contraband Camp in Corinth, Mississippi.

Group of "contrabands" at Foller's house, Cumberland Landing, Virginia, 1862. (Library of Congress.)

The seizure of the property of an opposing military force was a well-established practice when the principle was first applied to slaves in 1861. Although the term for this property—"contraband"—was considered offensive by most freedmen and freedwomen because it is a generic term for confiscated assets, the word regularly was used in wartime official records and by historians to refer to former slaves. In 1861, slaves sought freedom by fleeing to Fort Monroe in Hampton, Virginia, which was then under the control of Union Gen. Benjamin Butler (1818–1893). Confederate loyalists and politicians insisted that slaves were legal property and continued to advocate for wartime enforcement of the 1850 Fugitive Slave Act, which required the return of slaves to their owners. On the night of May 24, 1861, Frank Baker, Sheppard Mallory, and James Townsend fled their Confederate master to the fort and appealed directly to the Union general for their freedom. Gen. Butler reasoned that any property, including slaves, could be confiscated under the contraband practice and refused to return the refugees. This action initiated the legal basis for breaking any ownership rights if a slave had been forced to work for Confederate soldiers or their supporters. Butler's policy essentially supplied an early step toward emancipation.

News spread rapidly in 1861 and 1862 that freedom from Confederate masters could be obtained by reaching Union Army lines. Travel on foot often was the only means to secure freedom for thousands of former slaves and they set out in every direction to find the closest Union Army stronghold. Eventually, the 1863 **Emancipation Proclamation** ensured much broader manumission, but slavery remained legal in loyal Union border states like Kentucky and Missouri as well as the portions of the Confederacy then under the control of Union forces. As a result, contraband camps remained places of relative safety for self-liberated men and women throughout the war.

Contraband camps were established throughout the South, with major centers established along the Virginia and Carolina coast, the Mississippi Valley, southern Louisiana, and Washington, D.C. People arrived at contraband camps tired and disoriented from days or weeks of travel. Some who had reached Union encampments risked their lives to cross Confederate lines to tell friends and families of the opportunity. Waves of refugees arrived with few possessions desperately hoping for a new life, and the migration continued throughout the war. The refugees occasionally brought livestock that typically became property of the army. Refugees often came in family or plantation groups that facilitated the quick development of communities within these settlements.

Most contraband camp residents were housed in crowded barracks or tents as they struggled to adapt to new living conditions. Fabric military tents of the period provided immediate shelter while former slaves, sometimes guided by Union Army officials, constructed more permanent buildings made of logs, wood planks, or salvaged building materials. These buildings often were on a scale similar to slave housing.

Sometimes the camps occupied captured or abandoned plantations and their former **slave quarters**. Makeshift camps often began wherever Union control remained for a few months. If territory was lost and the Union Army retreated, freedmen and freedwomen moved with them. Camps, especially those in the Mississippi Valley, were used as recruitment centers for black military regiments, and the families of these soldiers often followed the unit to each duty station.

The most physically able of freedmen and freedwomen found employment in the Union Army, while the disabled, sick, and orphaned were dependent on the support supplied through contraband camps. The Union Army employed freedmen in ways that were strikingly similar to, and doubtless uncomfortably reminiscent of, their previous experiences in slavery or working for the Confederacy. For example, they served as entrenchment diggers, laundry workers, personal servants, and carpenters, and they filled a wide variety of other positions. Within the camps, former slaves worked in sawmills and clothing factories and did agricultural fieldwork. Many Union officials were dedicated to facilitating self-sufficiency among blacks emerging from slavery, even if their efforts were misguided by paternalism and latent racism.

Images and stories of refugee slaves captured the interest of newspapers throughout the nation, and numerous examples appeared in publications like *Frank Leslie's Illustrated Journal* and *Harper's Weekly*. The popular press fueled the Northern public's interest in the conditions of contraband camps and the people who lived within them. Sometimes, stories relating the great need for basic necessities or incidences of horrible treatment created enough outrage among the reading public to force changes within the camps. Numerous aid societies throughout the North and Midwest sent clothing, **books**, and other goods to support blacks' transition from slavery to freedom. When the Union Army forced families to abandon camps and refused to assist the refugees gathering around installations, reports in papers and letters fueled public anger that helped to reverse those decisions.

Several government agencies supervised efforts to manage the former slave population, including the Bureau of Negro Affairs, established within the War Department in 1863. The continued influx of refugees ensured the expansion of densely populated camps. As hostilities continued in 1863 and 1864, Congress passed laws and guidelines for the establishment of Freedmen's Home Colonies and Freedmen's Labor Colonies. Both of these settlement types were highly organized and more permanent than contraband camps. In Freedmen's Home Colonies, government superintendents representing the Bureau of Negro Affairs were responsible for providing shelter and other necessities for colony inhabitants. Freedmen's Labor Colonies had similar housing and aid requirements but also gave supervisors the ability to seize abandoned land for cultivation by freedmen and freedwomen.

As the Civil War came to a close, the Bureau of Refugees, Freedmen, and Abandoned Lands (widely known as the Freedmen's Bureau), created in 1865 as a replacement for the Bureau of Negro Affairs, was left in charge of the welfare of freedmen and freedwomen. The laws that influenced bureau policy had a profound impact on former slaves' eventual housing and settlement patterns after the war. In Circular Order 13, a legal order issued July 28, 1865, freedmen were granted access to abandoned lands controlled by the Freedmen's Bureau. This decision became the source of the infamous "forty acres and a **mule**" promise. Under this decree, lands abandoned by Confederate supporters were redistributed to freed slaves. Even before this order was issued, many former contraband camp families already had taken over these farms and continued land cultivation. However, the shifting political tide initiated by President Andrew Johnson's Reconstruction policies overturned the earlier order with Circular Order 15, which stipulated that abandoned land should be returned to those Confederates who were officially pardoned by the United States. Nevertheless, settlements that had begun as contraband camps often persisted as black centers and remained significant throughout Reconstruction.

FURTHER READING

Berlin, Ira, et al. *Freedom: A Documentary History of Emancipation 1861–1867. Selected from the Holdings of the National Archives of the United States. Series I, Volume III. The Wartime Genesis of Free Labor: The Lower South.* Cambridge: Cambridge University Press, 1990.
Berlin, Ira, et al. *Freedom: A Documentary History of Emancipation 1861–1867. Selected from the Holdings of the National Archives of the United States. Series I, Volume II. The Wartime Genesis of Free Labor: The Upper South.* Cambridge: Cambridge University Press, 1993.
Click, Patricia C. *Time Full of Trial: The Roanoke Island Freedmen's Colony, 1862–1867.* Chapel Hill: University of North Carolina Press, 2001.
Engs, Robert. *Freedom's First Generation: Black Hampton, Virginia, 1816–1890.* Philadelphia: University of Pennsylvania Press, 1979.
The Roanoke Island Freedmen's Colony. At www.roanokefreedmenscolony.com/index.html.

LAURA RUSSELL PURVIS

COOKING AND COOKS. In the 18th and 19th centuries, enslaved cooks were among the most important of domestic house servants. Their culinary skills and knowledge of elite dining styles enhanced a planter household's status. Training to cook came from many sources. On plantations and farms, black women cooks learned the required European style of cookery from mistresses as well as through apprenticeship to other kitchen slaves. In cities along the Atlantic coast, slave cooks were trained in taverns, hotels, and large gentry establishments. In those settings, cooks were most often men. George Washington traveled with his chef, Hercules, from Mount Vernon to Philadelphia and other urban headquarters where Washington lived during the American Revolution. Hercules eventually was able to take advantage of these urban settings to successfully run away. French slave masters fleeing the Haitian Revolution largely settled in cities such as Charleston, Savannah, and especially New Orleans and brought their black chefs with them. The regional influence of these cooks trained in the French culinary style added depth to an already complex American cuisine.

In wave after wave of forced migration to the Americas from the 16th to the 19th centuries, African men and women brought with them knowledge of culinary customs from their many societies. Farmers who already grew as many as five varieties of native African **rice** welcomed Asian rice when it migrated westward across the African continent. In both the interior and the coastal deltas of the Niger River, culinary traditions included millet, rice, **fish**, and many vegetables. The vast stretches of tropical forest had many types of cultivated vegetables and wild greens, African **yams** (*Dioscorea cayenensis*), plantains and cooking bananas (*Musa paraisiaca*), and small poultry. Cattle, goats, camels, and horses were protein sources for meat and dairy products for populations within the Sahel. Traditional African crops, such as ground nut (*Voandzeia subterranea*), **okra** (*Abelmoschus esculentus*), eggplant (*Solanum melongena*), kola nut (*Cola acuminata*), and varieties of edible **gourds** were cultivated broadly.

"The Cook," wood engraving by David Hunter Strother, published in *Harper's New Monthly Magazine*, January 1856. (Library of Congress.)

By the mid-16th century, Spanish and Portuguese slavers had begun to introduce New World **food**stuffs into disparate African cultures spread across the almost immeasurable terrain of the continent. The new foods included **corn** (*Zea maize*), sweet potato (*Imopaea batata*), chilies (*Capsicum annum*), tomato (*Lycopersicon esculentum*), common beans (*Phaseolus vulgaris*), **peanuts** (*Arachis hypogaea*), and cassava (*Mangifera utilissima*). African women began to accept these crops into their gardens and fields and diets. Enslaved African cooks often arrived in America from cultures long familiar with foods they would be expected to cook in white kitchens. Once in America they learned new culinary combinations and new styles of dining practiced by the master class.

For most people at that time, apprenticeship was the most common way to learn a life's occupation. Picking a good apprentice for the **kitchen** would have involved picking a child as a scullion to carry firewood, haul ashes, rotate a spit, take out the garbage, and do other simple chores. If the child showed interest and competency in the kitchen, the child would be given more chores specifically focused on food, such as kneading bread, chopping vegetables, and stirring the pots. Attributes that made a good cook's apprentice were a willingness to obey orders and to be neat and precise. As scullions and apprentices improved at their kitchen skills, a cook would welcome the assistance of a worker who was creative and enjoyed the work, especially in a kitchen expected to serve many elite guests on a regular basis. In 1784, Thomas Jefferson took his young slave, James Hemings, to Paris for the express purpose of having the young man learn to cook in the French manner. Upon his return to America, Hemings taught

French cookery to his younger brother, Peter Hemings, who continued to cook at Monticello until 1809. Two more slaves from Monticello were also apprenticed to a French chef. Edith Hern Fossett and Frances Gillette Hern each spent more than six years at the president's house under the culinary tutelage of Jefferson's French chef, Honoré Julian. The two women created excellent complex meals for the president and from 1809 to Jefferson's death in 1826 were the head cooks at Monticello.

It was not unusual on rural plantations for the cooks from several households to be brought together to make elaborate wedding feasts that might last days and involve more than a hundred guests. At one such feast in 1785 in Tidewater Virginia, the cooks prepared not only a midday dinner for the hundred in attendance but a supper at midnight after the dancing. At 10:00 the next morning the assembled party breakfasted on tea, coffee, chocolate, cold ham, fowls, hashed mutton, and other dishes. During that event, the large group of cooks, scullions, and dining room attendants would have had little sleep. Politicians routinely hired groups of male cooks to tend huge barbeque suppers for their potential voters. In 1835, for a Washington, D.C., dinner for 12, the cook prepared a bouli (boiled beef in broth), boiled fish, canvasback ducks, and pheasants for the main meat dishes, accompanied on the side by a small ham, a small turkey, partridges, mutton chops, sweetbreads, a macaroni pie, and an oyster pie. The menu included four vegetable dishes along with several kinds of puddings and sweet pies for the dessert course. This meal was prepared with the efforts of the house's cook, a local French chef, and the black caterer who kept it all organized.

In the homes of less affluent planters, where food was plainer, the cook still needed the help of others to get daily meals to the table. It was a time when every culinary process was done by hand. Water was hauled from wells; firewood had to be cut and stacked; poultry, game, and livestock all had to be butchered, salted, and cured, and stored on site; and plantation **gardens** and fields supplied freshly picked vegetables.

Cooks walked a fine line regarding daily negotiations with mistresses over provisions and expectations. Imported menu ingredients such as nutmeg and cinnamon, French brandy and wines, lemons, black pepper, vanilla, Parmesan cheese, and olives came from afar and were kept under **lock and key** by slaveholders. In plantation storage rooms across the South, barrels of molasses, cones of **sugar**, and bags of coffee beans and tins of tea were doled out to cooks for each day's menu.

A significant part of a white mistress's duties was to transmit her knowledge of Anglo-European cookery, or individual family recipes, to her slave cook. For dinner each day in a gentry household, the cook prepared several meat dishes, usually beef, ham, and poultry. The meat in the first course was accompanied by breads and vegetable dishes, perhaps stuffed cabbages, seasonal vegetables with sauces, and root vegetables prepared in myriad ways. The second course would consist of an assortment of desserts and pastries, nuts, and dried or candied fruits. Wine and then coffee and tea signaled the end of the meal. The appearance of iced cakes with almond paste, jellies and sweet pies, candied flowers, and whipped cream on the dessert menu were indicators of a cook's skills. After the meal, the cook's duties involved storing the remaining foods to be used for a later supper meal or for the next day, usually under the supervision of the mistress. Even in the simplest kitchen in the most remote, newly cultivated western plantation, where elite dining customs were modified to meat, cornbread, and stewed vegetables, a slave cook had to answer for all the ingredients assigned for a meal.

In urban taverns, boarding houses, and the homes of the very wealthy, kitchen slaves may have been given the leftovers as part of their diet.

Cookery styles changed over time and region, and individual cooks also evolved their own different styles and specialties. A skilled cook had to know how to create a stuffed calf's head with forcemeat balls, a common fancy presentation in the late 18th century, or souse, which was a chopped, well-seasoned, jellied mixture of the **pig** offal from the fall butchering. Dining fashions and menu choices varied in different regions of the South; rice dishes abounded along the Southeast coastal states, while **fish**, shrimp, and **gumbos** were popular along the Gulf Coast as well as hot sauces made from chilies to serve at the side. Oysters prepared many ways had to be included in the repertory of experienced cooks no matter where they lived. Black cooks learned to preserve whole fruits, to make jams and jellies, and to make fruit wines.

The slave cooks in the plantation Big House were part of the larger enslaved community in which they lived. Listed right along with the field hands in the plantation's records, rural cooks also received standard rations of cornmeal and salt pork, and they, too, had to create a diet for their families of simple food combinations of garden vegetables, small game, home-raised **chicken** and eggs, and fish. Archaeological studies of **faunal remains** in slave quarters across the Chesapeake Tidewater detail finds of foot bones of hogs, fish bones, and well-boiled and chopped bones of small game. Corn pone, small cakes made from ground cornmeal, water, and salt, could be cooked on a griddle, on the hot bricks of the hearth, on smoothed wooden slabs, or on the broad blade of a **hoe** over a small fire while working in the field.

In South Carolina, rice was more common than corn in the slave diet. Slave cooks in the Big House specialized in highly regarded dishes, such as golden fried rice cakes and sweet rice puddings. When cooking for their families in the quarters, however, people often served rice of several varieties grown only in their provision gardens and unknown to whites. Along the Gulf Coast, slaves had more opportunity to become introduced to Native American foodways, such as the filé for the gumbo, fishing for crayfish, and new varieties of dry beans and squashes. The cooks introduced foods such as gumbo, okra, or peanut soup into the menus of the white family and passed on to her scullions and other kitchen assistants the best of her culinary skills.

One **cast iron pot** or kettle was the standard allotment for each enslaved family; thus, one-pot meals based on cornmeal and other ingredients were the norm. In the plantation kitchen, the tools were much more elaborate. In 1796, as he left with his emancipation paper in hand, James Hemings wrote a one-page inventory of the many kitchen utensils at Monticello: no less than 85 objects appear, and the cooks were expected to know the uses of each. A plantation kitchen hearth often contained a bake oven for the daily breakfast breads and the wheat rolls for dinner. There were many iron pots, there were tin reflector roasters, and the hearth was outfitted with spits and cranes for moving large pots on and off the flames. Bread was mixed and risen in large wooden bowls; egg custards and other multi-ingredient dishes were mixed in pottery mixing bowls. For precise temperature control, tin-lined copper pans were used on specially designed stew-hole stoves found in the finest kitchens. A cook's occupation demanded an eclectic list of skills: grating and pounding sugar from large solid cones to produce different finenesses, plucking and eviscerating poultry, and understanding a balanced menu of complementary dishes to be served at each multicourse dinner. Another responsibility was for the cook to train younger apprentices and guide other kitchen staff in their duties.

The importance of a skilled cook to a planter's household and reputation was reflected by the high purchase prices realized for competent slave cooks during the antebellum era. After emancipation, black cooks made every effort to use their culinary skills to make a living for themselves and their families. Three formerly enslaved cooks left written records of their experience as culinary professionals: Malinda Russell (in Virginia, Kentucky, and Michigan), Abby Fisher (in South Carolina and California), and Rufus Estes (in Tennessee and Chicago).

The earliest of these books is that of Russell, who learned to cook from her freed grandmother, and an enslaved woman named Fanny Steward in Virginia. Russell went on to become a well-respected baker of pastries and cakes. She lost everything she owned when roaming gangs of whites chased her out of Tennessee in 1864. She relocated to Paw Paw, Michigan, where she wrote and published her cookbook in the hope that sales would allow her to continue to support her invalid son. Her book details her techniques for making cordials, jams, cakes, pies, and main dishes.

At both the Sacramento State Fair of 1879 and the San Francisco Mechanics' Institute Fair of 1880, in California, ex-slave Abby Fisher won awards for her pickles and jams. Unable to read or write, Fisher dictated her recipes to helpful friends in the Women's Co-operative Printing Office. Born in 1832, Fisher's experiences as a cook began on a South Carolina plantation. The rice recipes in her book reflect that early culinary influence. After a stay in Alabama where she married and began her family, Fisher finally was able to make her way to California. In San Francisco, she was listed in the 1880 directory as "Mrs. Abby Fisher & Co., 569 Howard St., pickles, preserves, brandies, fruits, etc."

One of the most prestigious jobs available for black men after slavery was that of porter on Pullman cars on the railroads that were beginning to span the nation in the late 19th century. Rufus Estes became one of those men. He was born in 1857 in Tennessee. By the age of 30 he was an accomplished butler and houseman, ready to join the ranks of Pullman porters. He rapidly advanced to the position of chef on privately owned rail cars kept by wealthy industrial barons. The 600 recipes in his self-published book, *Good Things to Eat as Suggested by Rufus*, reflect the highest level of dining service combined with fine food.

These three cookbooks are invaluable windows into the skills and knowledge of a black cook, whether enslaved or free, man or woman.

FURTHER READING

Bower, Anne L., ed. *African American Foodways: Explorations of History and Culture*. Urbana: University of Illinois Press, 2009.

Estes, Rufus. *Rufus Estes' Good Things to Eat: The First Cookbook by an African American Chef*. 1911. Reprint, Mineola, NY: Dover Publications, 2004.

Fisher, Abby. *What Mrs. Fisher Knows about Old Southern Cooking: Soups, Pickles, Preserves, Etc: with Historical Notes*. Edited by Karen Hess. 1881. Reprint, Bedford, MA: Applewood Press, 1995.

Russell, Malinda. *A Domestic Cookbook: Containing a Careful Selection of Useful Receipts for the Kitchen.* Edited by the Longone Center for American Culinary Research. 1866. Reprint, Ann Arbor, MI: William L. Clements Library, 2007.

Wright, Louis B., and Marion Tinling, eds. *Quebec to Carolina in 1785–1786. Being the Travel Diary and Observations of Robert Hunter Jr., a Young Merchant of London.* San Marino, CA: Huntington Library, 1943.

Leni A. Sorensen

COOPERAGE. "Cooperage" refers to containers, usually round, made from individual vertical pieces of wood called staves and held together by the tension of hoops driven from the narrower toward the wider part of the container until they are tight. Those containers were domestic items that were part of the daily life of every individual, slave or free, such as buckets, tubs, and butter churns. Cooperage also includes casks, or barrel-shaped containers, which in one size or another served as the shipping containers for a wide variety of commodities. Slaves were involved heavily in both the manufacture and the movement of cooperage, particularly in the American South and the Caribbean. Almost all of the commodities produced and exported from those areas, with the notable exception of **cotton**, were shipped primarily in casks.

"Portrait of Enslaved Girl" by Mary Anna Randolph Custis, Arlington, Virginia, 1830. Watercolor, pencil, and ink on wove paper. Enslaved coopers made tubs that they sometimes sold or bartered for other goods. (The Colonial Williamsburg Foundation.)

In a society in which slaves formed such a large part of the labor force, many business owners engaged in shipping goods found it logical to have slaves trained as coopers to manufacture the casks that they required, rather than hiring free coopers to do the same work. The methods by which they arranged that training varied. The ideal arrangement, insofar as it usually produced well-skilled craftsmen, was to apprentice out a slave child in much the same way a free child might be apprenticed to learn a trade. At about the age of 14, the child would be placed with a skilled cooper to learn the art, skill, and mystery of the trade. In the case of slaves bound out as apprentices, the term of the apprenticeship might be only three or four years, as opposed to the seven or so usually served by free individuals, although some enslaved apprentices served for much longer.

Whether the tradesman taking on the slave apprentice was paid to do so depended entirely on the arrangements with the slaveholder. In other cases, slaveholders might simply hire a skilled tradesman to work on

151

their property for a certain length of time to teach a slave the trade. At times, such as when the slaveholder decided not to keep paying for the free tradesman after several months, slaves received only the bare minimum of training. The result was a system in which the skill of slave coopers varied widely.

No matter how long they had been trained, or what type of cooperage they were asked to produce, a slave cooper would have learned the same basic techniques. The manufacture of any piece of cooperage involves the same basic processes, although the level of precision required in the shaping of the component parts may vary. The cooper generally would begin with blank stock: rectangular boards cut to the length required for the container to be made, roughly uniform in thickness, but varying in width. Each stave had to be shaped in proportion to the overall shape of the finished container, and all of the necessary shapes were judged by eye. To produce a cask (a barrel-shaped container), the staves would be cut so they were widest at the middle, tapering off toward each end. The staves were carved in such a way that they were rounded on the outside and the inside, and beveled on the edges so that they would fit properly together to form the circular shape of the container.

Once a sufficient number of staves had been shaped, they were assembled, or raised, inside a construction hoop equal in diameter to the desired dimension of the narrow end of the container. In the case of a cask, because the staves were widest at the middle, this resulted in a unit appearing to have all the joints closed at the top but with the bottom ends of the staves splayed out. With the staves standing in this first hoop, another hoop, called the "sizing hoop" and representing the diameter of the widest point of the cask, would be dropped over and then driven tight. This hoop would rest at the midway point of the staves. The cask was then heated over a small controlled fire of wood shavings contained in a small metal basket. The heat made the wood pliable enough that it could be bent without breaking, at which point the hoop sitting at the middle of the cask was driven down to the ground, which had the effect of beginning to draw the staves at the open end of the cask inward. The container was then turned over and a series of gradually smaller and smaller rings driven back toward the middle of the cask until the staves were drawn closed and the cask had achieved its final shape.

With the walls of the container completed, the ends of the staves were leveled off and grooves cut into each end of the container with a specialized tool called a "croze." Those grooves would receive the heads, or ends, of the cask, which usually were made up of several pieces of wood doweled together and then shaped as a single piece, cut into the proper circular shape and beveled on the edge to fit tightly into the groove. The heads were inserted one at a time by removing the hoops nearest the end of the cask to allow the staves to separate just a bit as the head was slid into place. Finally, with the heads inserted, the cask was finished by replacing the construction hoops, into which the container had been built, with permanent hoops made to fit the finished container. Those permanent hoops also would be made by the cooper. The hoops could be made out of metal, usually iron, or wood, with the advantage of the metal being its durability, while the wooden hoops made for a cheaper container.

If the cask was being made to contain bulky goods, such as **tobacco** or potatoes, the quality of this work did not have to be terribly high. Indeed, people in the tobacco trade in 18th-century Virginia often commented on the rough construction of tobacco hogsheads in which gaps between the staves often were wide enough to slide one's hand through sideways. If, on the other hand, the container was intended to hold liquids, the quality of the joints had to be high indeed.

The level of production expected of, and achieved by, slave coopers could be quite high. Thomas Jefferson expected the slave coopers working at his grist mill at Shadwell, near Charlottesville, Virginia, to produce an average of five flour barrels a day, each with a capacity of about 200 pounds of flour. Much larger casks—such as tobacco hogsheads, which stood four feet tall, were about three feet in diameter at their widest point, and held an average of 1,100 pounds of tobacco—would represent less than one day's work to produce. Whether slave coopers worked as efficiently as possible depended in part on what kinds of incentives they were given to be productive. Jefferson offered pay to his slave tradesmen if they achieved certain production rates, for instance. Other slaveholders offered skilled slaves the opportunity to hire themselves out for profit—if they had time left over after completing their appointed tasks. Slaveholders operating in such a fashion usually could expect to see better results than those who offered no incentives at all or who threatened punishment if goals were not met.

The weight of goods handled in these containers explains the prevalence of casks as the shipping containers for all manner of goods. Moving half a ton of tobacco from the plantation to the docks in a bale or a box would have required a significant number of laborers. Placed into a cask, that same half-ton could be moved with relative ease by a single person rolling it down the road. As laborers on the plantation, or at the grist mill, or in any other business, slaves would be responsible for filling the casks with the goods to be shipped. Other slaves were assigned the task of transporting the casks to their immediate destination. In seaports it was slaves who often formed the bulk of the labor force on the docks and who saw to the loading and unloading of casks full of goods from the ships that either would take the goods overseas or had just arrived with goods newly imported.

See also Corn; Wheat.

FURTHER READING

Kilby, Kenneth. *The Cooper and His Trade*. London: J. Baker, 1971.
Kulikoff, Allan. *Tobacco and Slaves: The Development of Southern Cultures in the Chesapeake, 1680–1800*. Chapel Hill: University of North Carolina Press, 1986.
Morgan, Phillip D. *Slave Counterpoint: Black Culture in the Eighteenth-Century Chesapeake and Lowcountry*. Chapel Hill: University of North Carolina Press, 1998.

JONATHAN A. HALLMAN

CORN. Corn, a plant commonly referred to as "maize" or "Indian corn," served as the primary **food** source from the early years of American slavery through Emancipation. Corn production was introduced to the Europeans and Africans by Native Americans and, along with beans and squash, was one of the most important crops to Native Americans. Corn's versatility ensured its future as one of the most important crops in American agriculture. Corn, during this time period, became such an essential part of life that it represented work, entertainment, and food in the lives of enslaved people.

Corn was a crop that could be grown in large fields and in small **gardens**. It matured within three months of being planted, but it was labor intensive and required enslaved persons' constant attention. Land had to be cleared of trees to create fields to plant it. Holes were poked into the ground and seeds were carefully planted and covered over. Hills were created around the plant to support it as it grew. During its cultivation, enslaved persons, generally children or elderly adults, were charged with protecting the harvest from weeds, insects, birds, and wild and domestic animals. Once the corn reached optimal stage, it would be harvested at one of two times: while it was young, for immediate consumption, or left to mature longer for use at a later time. Upon the completion of the harvest, the field was cleared in preparation for the next growing season.

As a source of food, corn was consumed in a variety of ways. Corn that was picked while it was still young and tender was usually roasted and eaten straight off the cob. Due to its layered and durable husk, mature corn was flexible in scheduling its harvesting. Corn left to mature was cut down and stored in its husk in **corn cribs**. It generally would stay there until the other crops were harvested or until there was time to shuck the corn.

Shucking of corn was an important part of the corn harvesting process. It also served as an important time in the lives of enslaved people. "Shucking" or husking frolic was one of the few times a year enslaved persons could gather and enjoy each other's company while working. This event took place once a year, but numerous planters would host this event at their various plantations or farms. The shucking gatherings were generally held in the evening, thus not conflicting with any workday tasks. Each planter would host a shucking gathering; the planter in some cases would invite other planters and their enslaved workers to attend the event. Corn-shucking gatherings provided an opportunity for the community to come together in

"Planting Corn. Old Driver. House Negro Digging Corn Holes." Drawing by William Berryman, ca. 1808, Jamaica. (Library of Congress.)

Shucking Corn

James V. Deane, a former Maryland slave, described the celebration that accompanied corn shucking:

> At corn shucking all the slaves from other plantations would come to the barn, the fiddler would sit on top of the highest barrel of corn, and play all kinds of songs, a barrel of cider, jug of whiskey, one man to dish out a drink of liquor each hour, cider when wanted. We had supper at twelve, roast pig for everybody, apple sauce, hominy, and corn bread. We went back to shucking. The carts from other farms would be there to haul it to the corn crib, dance would start after the corn was stored, we danced until daybreak.

Source: George P. Rawick, ed. *The American Slave: Kansas, Kentucky, Maryland, Ohio, Virginia, Tennessee Narratives*, Vol. 16. Westport, CT: Greenwood Press, 1972.

---

fellowship. While the enslaved people were engaged in the festivities, the planters would partake in their own forms of entertainment. (**See also** opening essay "Dance and Music.")

Corn, still in the husk, would be placed in a large pile and the enslaved persons would come and shuck the corn. The activity involved working competitively, while singing, drinking corn whiskey, and feasting. During these gatherings, songs would be sung about corn to a rhythm that coincided with the motion one's body would make while shucking corn. Most of the songs were "call and response": one person would sing the first line and the group would respond with another line of the song. "Shuck That Corn before You Eat" and "Ain't You Gwine to the Shuckin' of the Corn" are just two examples of songs that would be sung on these occasions.

In addition to singing, some planters would create competitions for the attendees. The planter would take one group of people and have them compete against another to see which group could shuck the fastest, and the winner would receive a prize. Although the celebration was entertainment, the shucking was a hard job and particularly hard on one's hands. A shucking peg, a sharpened piece of hardwood, was often used to aid in the husk removal.

Mature corn was hard and could be kept long periods of time post shucking, stored in aerated corn cribs before it was shelled and ground. Shelling was the process of removing the corn kernels from the cob. The sheller would use a piece of iron or corn cob. Around the 1840s, a hand-cranked device was created to shell the corn, thus freeing up time for other tasks.

The sustainability of mature corn made it the primary form in which corn was consumed. The corn kernels were placed into a stone or wood mortar and were ground by hand with a pestle. To make **hominy** (coarse ground flour), a hominy block was used, which consisted of a hollowed stump and a wooded plunger, which was used to pound the corn into the flour. If the plantation was large or located next to a large plantation, the corn was taken to a mill to be ground. The mill was powered by water or animals, and the power generated would drive the millstones that ground the corn kernels into a fine meal. In most cases, it would be the job of an enslaved boy to take the corn to the mill for grinding.

Corn was among the most commonly consumed crops in the South. An enslaved person was given an estimated food **ration** of one peck of corn or cornmeal, along with some form of meat. The cornmeal was used to make numerous dishes: corn bread, pudding, pone, porridge, hominy grits, **hoecakes**, and mush. Mush and grits (coarsely ground hulled corn), made by adding water and then **cooking**, were among the most common ways to eat the cornmeal. To flavor the various dishes, meat and vegetables, when available, were added.

Although corn's primary function was as a food source, it also served many other functions. It served as the principal feed for animals and fodder for larger livestock. Fermented corn was used to produce hard drinks, such as beer and whiskey. In the early 1800s, people were consuming an estimated five gallons of whiskey a year. The whiskey also was used as a home remedy for various ailments, such as fever or hives. Corn cobs were used as kindling and fuel for fires. Some people fashioned the cobs into fishing hooks and smoking pipe bowls. The corn husks often were used by enslaved persons as fillings for **pallets** or mattresses or used to weave rugs for their quarters. Husks also were used as padding for horse collars to protect the animal. And though enslaved children did not always have the time or opportunity to play, there are a few references to **dolls** being made out of corn cobs and dressed in corn husk clothing.

By the mid-1800s, corn production had increased to the point that the Midwest was referred to as the "Corn Belt." Corn was one of the only crops that was cultivated in every state of the Union, and it occupied the largest surface area of all agricultural crops. Corn was so much a part of the lives of enslaved persons that almost every aspect of their lives was touched by corn.

FURTHER READING

Abrahams, Roger. *Singing the Master: The Emergence of African-American Culture in the Plantation South.* New York: Penguin, 1992.

Blassingame, John W. *The Slave Community: Plantation Life in the Antebellum South.* New York: Oxford University Press, 1972.

Burns, William E. *Science and Technology in Colonial America.* Westport, CT: Greenwood Press, 2005.

Halpern, Rick, and Enrico Dal Lago, eds. *Slavery and Emancipation.* Oxford: Blackwell Publishers, 2002.

Morgan, Philip. *Slave Counterpoint: Black Culture in the Eighteenth-Century Chesapeake and Lowcountry.* Chapel Hill: University of North Carolina Press, 1998.

Warman, Arturo. *Corn Capitalism.* Chapel Hill: University of North Carolina Press, 2003.

ALEXANDRA JONES

CORN CRIBS. For most of the antebellum period **corn** was the dominant food crop on Southern farms and plantations, and a basic staple of the diet of most slaves. Typically, the corn crib was the place where both slaves and masters stored the corn they ate. European settlers and their slaves borrowed the structure's basic design from the

Native Americans and later modified it for their own purposes. Thus, in the Antebellum South, the corn crib became the central granary on almost all of the farms and plantations where slaves labored.

The typical corn crib walls were constructed with logs or slatted boards (called "cribbing") with sufficient space between the wooden pieces to allow air to circulate through the corn. This prevented any accumulation of moisture that could lead to mold, rot, or bacterial growth. The corn crib also had a roof to protect the corn from the rain, and the floor of the structure normally was raised off the ground to keep the corn away from groundwater and to prevent rodent infestation. On the inside were one or more narrow receptacles, or "pens," into which the corn was placed. Some corn cribs included apertures in the walls of the structure that allowed workers to dump the corn into pens inside the corn crib. Antebellum Southerners constructed many different types of corn cribs, the designs of which depended on the type of plantation or farm it serviced. A large plantation might have a corn crib resembling a small barn, with room for many storage pens inside, while smaller plantations or farms usually had single- or double-pen corn cribs. Some corn cribs were square box-like structures. Others were constructed in a "keystone" design, with a narrow base and walls that flared out near the top.

In addition to its practical function as a storage facility for food, the corn crib also played a central role in the social lives of slaves. The "corn shucking" was one of the most popular events on Southern farms and plantations. This event usually took place at the end of a harvest when slaves had large quantities of corn to shuck (remove the husks). The participants piled the corn they had harvested in large mounds near the corn crib, sometimes one or two stories high depending on the size of the harvest. The slaves would gather together, often inviting friends or relatives from neighboring farms or plantations, to shuck corn, socialize, and share news or gossip. At these events, music and dancing typically accompanied the hard work of shucking corn (*see also* opening essay "Dance and Music"). Masters usually encouraged this practice by offering rewards or incentives to shuck as much corn as quickly as possible. For example, a master might offer some **liquor**, or a small cash reward to the slave who shucked the most corn, or to the first slave who found a red ear of corn. After the festivities and shucking concluded, the participants stored the corn in the corn crib.

FURTHER READING

Genovese, Eugene D. *Roll, Jordan, Roll: The World the Slaves Made*. New York: Pantheon Books, 1974.

Roe, Keith E. *Corn Cribs in History, Folk Life, and Architecture*. Ames: Iowa State University Press, 1988.

Vlach, John Michael. *Back of the Big House: The Architecture of Plantation Slavery*. Chapel Hill: University of North Carolina, 1993.

MATT HERNANDO

COSMOGRAMS. When **slave ships** first landed in North American ports, their chattel passengers, though perhaps carrying few if any material possessions, brought memories, cultural traditions, and religious worldviews with them. The elements of religious material culture that survived illustrate both the innovation and tradition in American religious slave life. Although sometimes merged with Christian beliefs, some African traditions remained fairly distinct. Many African slaves brought to 18th-century America were either BaKongo or Yoruba. Both West African groups adapted their beliefs and practices in their new surroundings. Many African influences seen in early black material culture and religious beliefs are mainly from the Yoruba or BaKongo traditions.

The BaKongo cosmogram, the visual depiction of their cosmology, is a clear element of their religion that continued in American slave life. Represented as a **cross** with a circle bisecting the arms, the cosmogram signifies the cosmos and the relationship that follows between the human world and afterlife. In the BaKongo religion, people are born on the right side of the cross at due east. As one's life progresses, one moves toward the west and reaches north at the apex of life. Death comes in the west, and the soul moves across the ocean Kalunga and is reborn in Mpemda, the land of the dead. After living in Mpemda and moving back toward the east, the soul is reincarnated back in the world of the living. The arms of the cross represent the mountain of the earth, for the living, and mountain of Mpemda, for the dead. When alive, a person and the soul climb the mountain going westward, and this process is mirrored in Mpemda. Known as the *yowa*, meaning "four moments of the sun," the cosmogram indicates the continuity of human life. The overlaying circle represents the path of souls, and the arms of the cross symbolize the intersection between the two worlds. The cosmogram shows both the close relationship and the fluid threshold between the world of the living and world of the dead.

In its ability to visually depict the intricate relationship between the world of the living and the world of spirits, any material manifestations of the cosmogram open a pathway for communication between the two worlds. When calling upon spirits or deities, be they ancestors, African deities, Christian figures, or syncretized deities, practitioners must forge a link between themselves and the supernatural. With its ability to open a crossroads, the cosmogram successfully performs this function.

Scholars find evidence of the use of the BaKongo cosmogram in American slave life. Slave narratives recorded by the Works Progress Administration's Federal Writers' Project in the 1930s reveal instances of religious gardening practices among slaves in the Chesapeake region and elsewhere in the South. **Gardens** provided slaves with a source of extra income and food but also could be a religious resource if designed in a cosmogram pattern. By transforming their gardens into a physical and religious crossroads, these slaves invited spirits to inhabit the space, a practice especially significant for a conjurer or root-worker. Conjure falls under a number of categories, including religion, magic, and **medicine**. Using herbology, conjurers could bestow blessings or curses.

Detail of tobacco pipe with incised cosmogram excavated at the Rich Neck plantation site, Williamsburg, Virginia. (The Colonial Williamsburg Foundation.)

The cosmogram also graces elements of material culture first introduced to slaves by Europeans. Cosmograms adorn the handle of a pocketknife found at Somerset plantation in Creswell, North Carolina, and several pewter spoons uncovered at two plantations in Maryland. Archaeological excavations in Virginia unearthed pipes and spoons emblazoned with the cosmogram. These slaves altered practical instruments from the culture of their slaveholders and imparted their religious significance onto the tools. This suggests the continuation of a religious worldview among enslaved people where the sacred and profane interpenetrate one another.

Many **colonoware pottery** bowls have been unearthed in South Carolina that bear evidence of the BaKongo cosmogram on their bottoms. "Colonoware" is a term used by many archaeologists to describe unglazed earthenware pottery made over a low fire that was produced in a style similar to that of Native Americans. The inclusion of the cosmogram on bowls likely began in the mid-17th century, peaked in the 18th century, and began to languish in the early 19th century. While initially thought to be a maker's mark, contextual research about the region points to religious significance. Excavations in South Carolina found a high number of such colonoware bowls, which corresponds with the high number of BaKongo slaves who arrived in the Carolinas. In fact, scholars conclude that BaKongo culture remained stronger in South Carolina than in any other part of the United States. Excavations in and around national parks in the Carolina Low Country discovered many bowls marked with the cosmogram, often found in rivers adjacent to former **slave quarters**. In general, their primary use was utilitarian, but the cosmogram suggests that the bowls possessed religious and ritual properties as well. Their presence in rivers connects directly to the symbolism of the cosmogram itself. It has been argued that the bowls were not left in the river as trash, but, rather, slaves intentionally placed them in the water. For the BaKango, the ocean Kalunga separates the land of the living from Mpemda, and in crossing Kalunga's waters, one travels to the other world. Kalunga not only separates the worlds but also subsequently links the two. The river in which the bowls were found possibly played a role uniting the worlds and creating a crossroads for enslaved Africans.

These bowls might have held minkisi, which is the plural form of nkisi, a BaKongo power object or **charm** that possesses medicine and a spirit with the capability to do either benevolent or malevolent deeds. A nkisi, by possessing a spirit and the power to heal or harm, is thought to represent the cosmos in miniature. Clay pots and bowls historically have been typical holders for minkisi. Therefore, slaves likely used the bowls in medicinal healing and various practices related to conjuring.

Farther south and west, at the Levi Jordan plantation, in Brazoria, Texas, slave quarter excavations expanded on the use of the BaKongo cosmogram in slave life. A cosmogram was uncovered between the floor of a slave cabin and the ground below. The cosmogram would properly consecrate the space and prepare it for religious ritual by establishing a connection between the space of the cabin and the world of the spirits. Concealed under the floor, the religious significance of the cosmogram also becomes a source of resistance and empowerment. Hidden from view of slaveholders, ritual practices involving the cosmogram allowed slaves to communicate with spirits unknown to and out of reach of their masters. These spirits connected with the crossroads and therefore their powers were accessible only to the Jordan slaves. Also tucked within the floorboards were various conjurer kits for medicinal work and a nkisi. By using these tools within the space outlined by the cosmogram, the practitioner could call on the supernatural world of the spirits for assistance in the human world.

Similarly, excavations at the Brice House in Annapolis, Maryland, uncovered cosmograms beneath the floors, doorways, and hearths. Unlike other plantations where cosmograms typically were confined to the slave quarters, Brice House provides an example of domestic slaves presumably incorporating their religious worldview into the slaveholder's home. As a threshold, doorways are inherent crossroads, and as a source of fire, hearths are links to spirits and other deities associated with fire. At Brice House, slaves creatively constructed cosmograms from European resources, which suggests that the cosmogram's materials were less important than its function once it was created.

Although a dominant example and the most cited academically, the BaKongo cosmogram is not the only visual depiction of the cosmos in slave life. After the Haitian Revolution in the late 18th century, many French landowners fled to southern Louisiana and New Orleans and brought their slaves and their slaves' Vodun practices with them. Haitian Vodun is a diasporic religion that syncretizes the Dahomean (Yoruba) religion of West Africa and Roman Catholicism. Vodun practitioners create elaborate veve ground paintings out of colored powder to worship and summon their deities. Cruciforms representing the cosmos abound in veve patterns. Often a post is placed in the middle of the veve to represent the physical crossroads connection between the worlds. Like the BaKongo cosmogram, typically these veve ground paintings illustrate the realm of the gods and the realm of humans. In particular, reverence to deity Eshu or Legba remained strong during slavery in Louisiana. Vodunists must invoke Eshu at the commencement of any ritual, for he is the deity of the crossroads and opens the means of communication between the human and supernatural worlds.

See also Conjure Bags; Shrines and Spirit Caches; Subfloor Pits.

FURTHER READING

Brown. Kenneth L. "Material Culture and Community Structure: The Slave and Tenant Community at Levi Jordan's Plantation, 1848–1892." In *Working toward Freedom: Slave Society and Domestic Economy in the American South*, edited by Larry E. Hudson Jr., 95–118. Rochester, NY: University of Rochester Press, 1995.

Ferguson, Leland. *Uncommon Ground: The Archaeology of African America, 1650–1800*. Washington, DC: Smithsonian Institution Press, 1992.

Samford, Patricia. "The Archaeology of African-American Slavery and Material Culture." *The William and Mary Quarterly* 53, no. 1 (January 1996): 87–114.

Samford, Patricia. *Subfloor Pits and the Archaeology of Slavery in Colonial Virginia*. Tuscaloosa: University of Alabama Press, 2007.

Thompson, Robert Farris. *Flash of the Spirit: African and Afro-American Art and Philosophy*. New York: Random House, 1984.

EMILY S. CLARK

COTTON AND COTTON PLANTATIONS. Since the founding of Jamestown in 1607, European settlers experimented with the growing of cotton. Several species of this vegetable fiber are connected with the genus *Gossypium*, but only a few significant types were grown in North America. *G. brasilianum* is the long staple variety that Low

Country planters in South Carolina and Georgia cultivated with great financial success for the first time by the late 18th century. G. *hersutium* and G. *herbaceum*, or short staple cotton, were grown for domestic consumption on small farms in the colonial era but never in enough quantities to make them cash crops until the invention of the saw cotton gin by Eli Whitney in 1793. Sometime just before or after this invention, the two short staple varieties were cross-cultivated to produce a variety commonly called "green seed" cotton, the short staple variety that made the South the leading producers of cotton in the world by the first quarter of the 19th century. Until 1820, South Carolina was the leader in cotton production as short staple plantations quickly sprang up throughout the piedmont region of the state. Although long staple varieties were the more valuable, the geographic region for its cultivation remained limited to the Low Country of South Carolina and Georgia. But as short staple cotton production was introduced into piedmont regions of South Carolina after 1794, it soon spread across the South. It is estimated that in 1820 the black population of the Alabama–Mississippi region was just 75,000; some 20 years later, it had dramatically expanded to half a million. Fueled by cotton, this expansion extended into Louisiana and Texas and, to a lesser degree, to Arkansas and to Tennessee's western counties.

The vast increase in the slave workforce during this period continued up to the Civil War era. By 1850, 3.2 million enslaved people lived in the South. Of this number more than one-half, or 1.8 million, worked on cotton plantations alone, producing 2.4 million bales annually. Although most cotton farmers owned fewer than 20 enslaved workers, the plantations that actually produced the bulk of the South's cotton were substantial in size and possessed 20 or more enslaved workers. In 1860, more than 5.3 million total bales of cotton were produced, and more than half (3.5 million) was harvested in just four states: Mississippi, Alabama, Louisiana, and Georgia. These states also had the largest number of slaveholders with 20 or more enslaved workers.

Within these four states, most of the cotton produced came from plantation workforces that ranged from 100 to more than 1,000 enslaved workers. To operate productively, these plantations developed efficient organizations based on a hierarchical system. At the top of the hierarchy was the plantation owner, who hired a white overseer to carry out his plans. Along with instructions on how to cultivate and harvest the cotton crop, many planters gave strict guidelines to their managers on how to direct the slave workforce, including their work schedule, weekly food **rations**, and punishment for idleness or poor work. Regardless of how detailed such instructions might be, every planter's bottom line was to maximize the cotton harvest to gain the best market price. The humanity of enslaved workers rarely concerned the owner or his overseer. Consequently

Blacks preparing cotton for the gin on Smith's plantation, Port Royal Island, South Carolina, 1862. (Library of Congress.)

161

Picking Cotton

Lewis Evans worked on a South Carolina cotton plantation:

Maj. Bell had ten families when I got dere. Put me to hoein' in de field and dat fall I picked cotton. Next year us didn't have cotton planters. I was took for one of de ones to plant de cotton seed by drappin' de seed in de drill. I had a bag 'round my neck, full of seeds, from which I'd take handfuls and sow them 'long in de row. Us had a horse-gin and screwpit, to git de cotton fit for de market in Charleston. Used four mules to gin de cotton and one mule to pack it in a bale. Had rope ties and all kinds of bagging. Seems to me I 'members seein' old flour sacks doubled for to put de cotton bales in, in de screwpress.

Source: George P. Rawick, ed. *The American Slave: South Carolina Narratives*, Vol. 2. West-port, CT: Greenwood Press, 1972.

Henry Wright remembered that slaves had to pick 200 pounds or more of cotton a day during peak harvest in Georgia:

At the sounding of the horn they had to get up and feed the stock. Shortly after the horn was blown a bell was rung and at this signal they all started for the fields to begin work for the day. They were in the field long before the sun was up. Their working hours were described as being from "sun to sun." When the time came to pick the cotton each slave was required to pick at least 200 lbs. of cotton per day. For this purpose each was given a bag and a large basket. The bag was hung around the neck and the basket was placed at the end of the row. At the close of the day the overseer met all hands at the scales with the lamp, the slate and the whip. If any slave failed to pick the required 200 lbs. he was soundly whipped by the overseer. Sometimes they were able to escape this whipping by giving illness as an excuse. Another form of strategy adopted by the slaves was to dampen the cotton or conceal stones in the baskets, either of which would make the cotton weigh more.

Source: George P. Rawick, ed. *The American Slave: Georgia Narratives*, Vol. 13. Westport, CT: Greenwood Press, 1972.

overseers usually were not troubled by any poor working conditions that affected their slave workers. If overseers could attain or surpass their employers' production goals, they often received a financial reward at the end of the harvest season. Base salaries for the season usually started at $200 but could reach as high as $1,000 if production goals were exceeded. But to earn a higher salary, overseers often overworked the slaves on a daily basis, while providing only minimal amounts of **food** per week as well as inadequate rest, especially during the harvest season. Enslaved workers were considered chattel, without legal rights, so slaveholders and their overseers usually administered punishment indiscriminately to induce the slave workforce to produce more. Although the treatment of slaves varied from plantation to plantation, the master and his overseer had few external legal limitations to how they dealt with their enslaved workforce.

No matter what the individual circumstances on any given cotton plantation, enslaved workers worked long and hard. From the slaves' perspective their work was not only difficult but also fraught with danger. Each worker had minimum daily requirements and work quotas to achieve through most of the year. Before the cotton seed could be planted, the fields had to be plowed into beds, or ridges, with a plow. In most regions of the cotton South, an ox or **mule** was used for this. Both enslaved women and men were employed in this work, tasked with the responsibility to care for the animals both in the fields and when the animals returned to the stables at the end of the day. Each cotton bed was six feet wide, and once the ridges were complete, the slave workers (often women) planted the seed into the top of the ridge. Generally this work was carried out in March and April with teams of three workers assigned to a row. If the rains were sufficient, the seeds usually sprouted in a week. Within several days, the first hoeing of the rows was undertaken to cut out the grass and other weeds, often referred to as "scraping cotton." Four hoeing cycles usually occurred during the summer to keep down the weeds and ensure the cotton plants produced as many bolls (seedpods) as possible. During this approximately four month work phase, the slave workforce was supervised by overseers or their **slave drivers**. Slave drivers were hand-picked slaves whom the overseers thought the most loyal to them. They kept a close watch on the work in each row with a **whip** in hand. If a worker seemed to be too slow, idle, or not doing the work as instructed, the whip was quickly used on the unfortunate worker. By the end of August, the cotton plants were mature enough to begin the harvest. But each plant was picked more than once because cotton bolls matured at different rates on every plant. When the cotton plant's bolls had opened, then the cotton was ready to be picked. Unopened bolls had not matured enough, and so the harvest often continued into December. Then, each enslaved worker turned his attention to harvesting, or picking, cotton. Every picker had a sack with a strap that went around the neck. The mouth of the sack reached the worker's chest and the bottom went to the ground. A large **basket** was placed at the end of each row, into which the contents of each sack were to be deposited so that the workers did not have to stop their work in the fields. When new workers were assigned to picking, their progress was followed closely and at the end of the day their cotton harvest was weighed. Once their daily quota was measured, individual workers were expected to reach or exceed this amount on subsequent days. When workers failed, the overseer or his driver used the whip to administer lashes; these varied depending on the whim of the overseer. Although a day's work varied somewhat on every plantation, it was expected to be 200 pounds per worker. By reaching or exceeding the day's harvest goal, a slave picker avoided punishment for the day.

To maximize the harvest, workers often had to be in the fields before sunup and continued to work well after dark. Lunch was brought to the workers in the field by slaves assigned to that task. It usually consisted of cold bacon and, perhaps, **corn** bread. When the day's work ended in the field, slaves took their cotton baskets to be weighed each evening. Once the seeded cotton was weighed, workers who had not achieved their daily quota received punishment. Then the cotton was placed in the cotton house to tramp it down to be stored like hay. When the cotton was wet or damp, it was placed on platforms, two feet off the ground, to dry out the fiber before storing. That completed, workers still had more work to perform that included feeding the livestock, cutting firewood, and other assigned duties connected to the plantation. Finally, permission was given for the slaves to return to their quarters to prepare a meal and perform other personal chores before going to sleep.

Food allowances on cotton plantations were basic, often consisting of an allotment of corn and bacon that was distributed to each hand every Sunday, consisting of three and a half pounds of bacon and enough corn to make a peck of meal. On some plantations, the food allowance was dispensed on Wednesday or Saturday evenings. While this varied from one plantation to another, other basics such as coffee, tea, **sugar**, and even molasses usually were considered luxuries that the slaveholder gave only at special occasions, such as Christmas and weddings. The long days in the field made it difficult for slave households to prepare proper meals even if they had other food to supplement their assigned rations. Many slaveholders allowed their workforce to cultivate small **garden** plots to complement their meager food allowance. Such gardens often consisted of sweet potatoes, corn, and squash. In addition, slaves often hunted wild game such as squirrels, possum, and rabbits. Because slaves usually were not permitted by law to possess **firearms**, they used **animal traps**, spears, or bows and arrows. Such activities were limited to nights or Sundays, the one day off that most slaveholders gave their workforce.

With such long days spent in the fields, the enslaved workforce was under constant pressure to keep up the steady work rate regardless of weather conditions or concerns for health and safety. Such harsh working conditions made it almost inevitable that masters and their slave workforce were constantly at odds, even though many antebellum apologists for the slave system tried to insist that slaves were submissive and accepted their chattel status. Numerous accounts from the period indicate that slaves tried both psychological and physical means to sabotage the work they were forced to do and, where possible, subvert the cotton plantation system. Slaveholders and slave narratives reported enslaved workers setting fire to plantation barns, stealing food such as corn and hogs, taking tools, and selling portions of the cotton crop on the black market. Others broke the tools and slowed down their output. Such clandestine actions were easier to hide from the master, who often had difficulty finding and punishing the culprits. Although more dangerous, slaves ran away when they could no longer accept the harsh conditions on their plantation. Sometimes they tried to escape the South and gain their freedom, but such a strategy rarely succeeded due to the long distances involved and unfamiliarity with the geography and people. More often, slaves who escaped the fields would hide away in the nearby woods or swamps to rest. They were sustained by visits from slaves who remained on the plantation who gave them food at night. Such was the case on the Louisiana plantation where slave Solomon Northup was confined for more than 10 years in the 1840s. One slave, who already had been punished for visiting a neighboring plantation without permission, decided to run away. After several weeks the slave master failed to track him down, but then the escapee suddenly reappeared at the plantation. After trying to find his way through the swamps without success, he remained at large until he was discovered and recaptured by a white man who returned him to his master. Once back, he was immediately punished with a severe flogging. Despite the punishment that awaited any recaptured slave, this did not deter many attempts.

Along with running away, there were other examples of outright rebellion on cotton plantations. Slave rebellions and conspiracies to carry them out were uncommon, but such actions happened more frequently than slaveholders wanted to admit. Although the Nat Turner rebellion of 1831 that took place in Southampton County, Virginia, is the most noted and bloody of any that occurred during the cotton era, it took place in the heart of **tobacco**-growing country. In the cotton areas of the Deep South, nothing quite so bloody occurred, but several conspiracies and actual rebellions are documented. The Denmark Vesey conspiracy of 1822 in Charleston, South Carolina, may have been the most thoroughly planned insurrection, although it was suppressed just days before it was unleashed. Organized by Vesey, a free black who had purchased his freedom years before, conspirators plotted for several years. They accumulated hundreds of weapons and secured them in various hiding places in the city. But the plot was leaked to white authorities before it could be implemented. Soon 139 freemen and slaves were arrested, of whom 47 were found guilty and either executed or transported out of the state to the Caribbean. A decade later, several slaves in Monroe County, Georgia, were hanged or severely whipped for complicity in another conspiracy. Isolated slave uprisings occurred in Alabama, Louisiana, and Mississippi through the end of the 1850s, but all were ruthlessly suppressed by white leaders with executions or transportation out of the country for all those convicted.

Clear evidence of the harsh working environments at cotton plantations is partially revealed in correspondence, travelers' accounts, and the agricultural magazines of the period. Even on plantations where slaves were fed and clothed sufficiently, a South Carolina planter complained that many large slaveholders tended to require their slave workforce to continue their duties well into the night and even on Sundays. Another planter recommended to other slaveholders that one's slave workforce had to be instructed that if they failed to perform their duties adequately the workers "will be punished for it." In nearly every case, this meant several lashes by a whip on the bare back.

Many planters did not just rely on physical punishment to keep their enslaved workers doing the jobs that they required. Some planters periodically provided special food allowances and feasts to their workforce. During the Christmas season, most planters gave their slaves a large feast and sometimes distributed new sets of clothes to them for the New Year. Even on the harshest plantations, some owners recognized the season as a time to provide extra food and entertainment. Solomon Northup described how he and his fellow slaves enjoyed a huge feast that neighboring planters hosted for their workers. The Christmas feast was hosted by different plantations each year. From 300 to 500 slaves assembled at the host plantation in their best clothes and at the dinner's conclusion a dance was held that lasted into the following morning. This combination of alternating punishment with rewards was a hallmark of the American slave system.

See also Work Routines.

FURTHER READING

Franklin, John Hope. *From Slavery to Freedom: A History of Negro Americans*. 3rd ed. New York: Alfred A. Knopf, 1967.

Gray, Lewis C. *History of Agriculture in the Southern United States to 1860*. Vol. 2. Gloucester, MA: Peter Smith, 1958.

Jones, Norrece T. *Born a Child of Freedom, Yet a Slave: Mechanisms of Control and Strategies of Resistance in Antebellum South Carolina*. Hanover, NH: Wesleyan University Press, 1990.

Lakwete, Angela. *Inventing the Cotton Gin: Machine and Myth in Antebellum America*. Baltimore, MD: Johns Hopkins University Press, 2003.

Northup, Solomon. *Twelve Years a Slave*. 1853. Edited by Sue Eakin and Joseph Logsdon. Reprint, Baton Rouge: Louisiana State University Press, 1968.

Oakes, James. *The Ruling Race: A History of American Slaveholders*. New York: Vintage Books, 1983.

Olmsted, Frederick Law. *The Cotton Kingdom: A Traveler's Observations on Cotton and Slavery in the American Slave South*. 1860. Edited by Arthur M. Schlesinger. New York: Alfred A. Knopf, 1953.

FRITZ HAMER

COURTHOUSES. Courthouses in colonial America and the antebellum United States ranged from simple log structures to massive Greek revival edifices of brick, stone, and marble. There was no uniformity in appearance either on the inside or the outside. Some courthouses consisted of merely a room or two, while others contained two or more courtrooms, private chambers for judges, and a variety of related offices. Courthouses were always a work in progress. In 1689, for example, the magistrates of Norfolk County in Virginia decided to replace the existing courthouse with one made of brick measuring 35 by 20 feet. They abandoned the plan, however, when they were convinced by the protests of county residents that it would be "too burthensome to the inhabitants." Courthouses changed as the community grew in population, as its stability increased, and as the prosperity of the area rose. Slave artisans often participated in the construction of the courthouse as they did in other public buildings, and slaves continued to maintain them after they were completed.

At the heart of the courthouse, of course, was the courtroom. By the second quarter of the 18th century, Virginia courthouses adapted the style of English provincial civic architecture. They contained a courtroom ranging from 20 to 24 feet in width and from 25 to 40 feet in length. A bar across the width of the room separated the elevated platforms of the magistrates and the jury together with seating for litigants and their representatives, from the public spectators. Jury rooms flanked the courtroom's base, forming a "T." As a flourish, a covered arcade provided a place for people to gather in bad weather as well as an open space where lawyers and their clients could formulate strategy before court.

Yet, simple or grand in appearance, the courthouse stood as the symbolic representation of the law's majesty and the public face of the community. Candidates on the campaign trail spoke from its steps. Local militia units drilled before it on the courthouse square. Merchants and auctioneers posted notices of coming sales. Slaves from the town and the surrounding farms and plantations, as bystanders on the fringe, saw it all. The courthouse and its surroundings was a place of celebration and dread.

When slaves confronted the courthouse, they experienced both emotions—although more often they experienced dread. They and their masters might enter the courthouse to register a deed of manumission and freedom. Slaves might attend their owners as silent observers when a contract was certified transferring ownership from one master to another or hiring out a slave or slaves to perform a specific task or to serve a temporary master for a specific length of time. Masters might even bring slave children to the courthouse to record their ages for tax purposes.

Finally and most dreaded, slaves might appear within the courthouse walls as defendants in a case that lay beyond the ability of a master to punish. Slave codes were long and elaborate. Slaves could be found guilty for a deed, a word, or a look. According to a 1690 South Carolina law, a slave could be severely whipped for striking a white person, and in 1712, a magistrate was authorized to sentence a slave to 40 lashes for assisting a runaway or robbing a **chicken** coop.

Although neither slaves nor free blacks could testify in cases involving white men and women, they could be called as witnesses in cases dealing with others of African descent. Most colonies and states did not allow blacks to be sworn in on a **Bible**; testimony was recorded and left to the judge and a jury, most often composed of slaveholders, to evaluate. In Mississippi's 1857 Slave Code, the court was required to inform any slave, mulatto, or free Negro:

> You are brought here as a witness, and, by the direction of the law, I am to tell you before you give your evidence, that you must tell the truth, the whole truth, and nothing but the truth; and if it be found hereafter, that you tell a lie, and give false testimony in this matter, you must, for so doing have both your ears nailed to the pillory, and cut off, and receive thirty-nine lashes on your bare back, well laid on, at the common whipping-post.

For offenses more serious than petty crimes or misdemeanors—such as murder, rape or attempted rape of a white woman, deadly assault, arson, or attempted servile insurrection—slaves were tried in circuit courts rather than by local magistrates. There, they or their masters acting for them were granted most of the procedural rights and rights of a free person. Because the law saw slaves as both property and "persons," such protections were given both as a means of assuring masters of the court's due deliberation in issues involving their property and as recognition of, as one Tennessee superior court justice put it, a "slave's high-born nature." So, an accused slave's lawyer was allowed to challenge jurors, request a change of venue, and use other technical measures to defend his client. In the case of *Celia (a slave) v. Missouri* (1855), for example, Celia's lawyer attempted to have the court instruct the jury of the legal rules applicable to the facts. He argued that his client had murdered her master because of his sexual exploitation. Although this request was denied, other procedural requests were increasingly granted in the last decades of the antebellum period.

For those like Celia who were convicted of a capital or other serious crime, the carrying out of justice was often conducted on the courthouse grounds. The gallows, whipping post, and stocks were often located on the courthouse's square. The last sight of the condemned, therefore, would be of the courthouse.

See also Freedom Papers; Legal Documents; Runaway Slave Advertisements.

FURTHER READING

Finkleman, Paul. *Slavery and the Law*. New York: Rowman & Littlefield, 1997.

Lounsbury, Carl. "The Structure of Justice: The Courthouses of Colonial Virginia." In *Perspectives in Vernacular Architecture, III*, edited by Thomas Carter and Bernard L. Herman, 214–226. Columbia: University of Missouri Press, 1989.

Morris, Thomas D. *Southern Slavery and the Law, 1619–1860*. Chapel Hill: University of North Carolina Press, 1996.

MARTIN HARDEMAN

CREDIT ACCOUNTS. Throughout the colonial period, until at least the middle of the 19th century, American merchants, tradespeople, and shopkeepers conducted much of their business via credit accounts. Credit accounts were used because of the scarcity of hard currency. For the enslaved, credit accounts afforded them the opportunity to purchase goods for themselves and their families that otherwise would have been impossible to acquire.

Most merchants in the 18th century used a variation of double-entry bookkeeping, in which every transaction, whether a payment or a purchase, was entered twice: once as a credit and once as a debit. Customers came to a store, chose the items they wished to purchase, and the storekeeper or merchant would in turn enter a description of the goods and their value into a "waste book," which was a record of each day's transactions as they happened. These brief notes were then copied into the journal, where prices and item descriptions were written out more thoroughly and clearly and then, finally, these journal transactions were transferred into the account ledgers, with one page used for each person or company with which the storekeeper had any business. Some storekeepers and merchants kept day books instead of waste books; the difference between the two was that information was more carefully kept in day books than in waste books and therefore the need for a separate journal might be eliminated, as the transactions would go directly from the day book to the ledger. In the same way, tradespeople performed work for their customers and then entered the description of the work and its value in their ledgers. Customers could pay either in cash or sometimes in **barter**, in which case the customer would give the tradespeople agricultural products or other goods in payment. Accounts were settled on a periodic basis; some customers paid off their purchases little by little, while others only paid off their account yearly, with the amount the customer paid entered on the facing page of the ledger page for that particular account.

For the enslaved, who themselves were bought and sold and whose names and prices were entered in these same ledgers, the possibility of acquiring goods may have seemed out of reach. On the contrary, many enslaved men and women were active participants in their local economies, selling a variety of agricultural products that they raised themselves, or selling small items of furniture such as stools or chairs that they made after their regular tasks were completed, thus acquiring cash. In addition, the custom of giving slaves cash tips for small favors or tasks or as presents on

Slaves in the Marketplace

Travelers to slaveholding regions remarked on how slaves were active participants in the marketplace. For example, Julian Niemcewicz, an aide to Polish general Tadeusz Kosciuszko, visited George Washington at Mount Vernon in 1798. He visited one of Washington's outlying farm quarters, looked inside one of the slave quarter houses, and wrote in his diary,

> A very small garden planted with vegetables was close by [the quarter], with 5 or 6 hens, each one leading ten to fifteen chickens. It is the only comfort that is permitted them [the slaves]; for they may not keep either ducks, geese, or pigs. They sell the poultry in Alexandria and procure for themselves a few amenities.

Source: Julian Ursyn Niemcewicz, *Under Their Vine and Fig Tree: Travels through America 1797–1799, 1805.* Translated and edited by Metchie J.E. Budka, 100–101. Reprint, Elizabeth, NJ: Grassmann Publishing Co., 1965.

Christmas meant that those enslaved men and women who would not have had other access to cash had the means to purchase goods as well.

These transactions would have been recorded in a merchant's cash book with the simple notation of what was purchased and its amount, with no notation of the purchaser's name, so it is almost impossible to know which of those purchases were made by enslaved people. Many storekeepers were willing to keep credit accounts with slaves. William Johnston, Francis Jerdone's predecessor as the eastern Virginia agent for Buchanan & Hamilton of London (ca. 1736), kept an account of goods he sold to slaves in exchange for peas. These men and women bought fabric, including lace and silk, **liquor**, hats, eating utensils, and even cheese in exchange for their produce. Jack, a slave who worked the estate of Mr. Linton near Colchester, Virginia, earned credit of more than £100 from Glassford & Company between 1759 and 1769 for doing all kinds of work, including mending bridges, building furniture, and selling poultry. With that credit Jack purchased, among other things, rum, fabric, a wine glass, and a plane iron. Almost 80 years later, William Cobb, a merchant in Thomaston, Georgia, recorded credit transactions with 80 people who could be identified as slaves. They purchased **tobacco**, fabric of all kinds, shoes, padlocks, handkerchiefs, and even a Barlow knife.

FURTHER READING

Baxter, W. T. "Accounting in Colonial America." In *Studies in the History of Accounting,* edited by A. C. Littleton and B. S. Yamey, 272–287. Homewood, IL: Richard D. Irwin, 1956.

Forret, Jeff. "Slaves, Poor Whites and the Underground Economy of the Rural Carolinas." *The Journal of Southern History* 70, no. 4 (November 2004): 783–824.

Gill, B. Harold, Jr. "The Retail Business in Colonial America." Unpublished draft research report, Colonial Williamsburg Foundation, 1988.

Martin, Ann Smart. *Buying into the World of Goods: Early Consumers in Backcountry Virginia.* Baltimore, MD: Johns Hopkins University Press, 2008.

Morgan, Philip D. *Slave Counterpoint: Black Culture in the Eighteenth-Century Chesapeake & Low Country.* Chapel Hill: University of North Carolina Press, 1998.

Paterson, David E. "Slavery, Slaves and Cash in a Georgia Village, 1825–1865. *Journal of Southern History* 75, no. 4 (November 2009): 879–930.

"Slave Lifeways at Mount Vernon: An Archaeological Perspective." George Washington's Mount Vernon Estate & Gardens. At www.mountvernon.org/learn/collections/index.cfm/pid/243/.

MARTHA B. KATZ-HYMAN

CROSSES. Enslaved Africans brought their own traditions and worldviews to the Americas. They were influenced by the religious practices of their owners, most of whom were Christian. As it developed in America, slave religion encompassed elements from both African religions and Christianity. Through their religious belief and practice, slaves could maintain both creativity and agency.

The symbol of the cross possessed both Christian and African significance in the slave world. In many African traditions, the cross is a visual marker of the crossroads, and the crossroads signifies the intersection of the sacred and secular worlds. It provides the ideal location to interact with spirits. Enslaved Africans brought their belief in the power of the crossroads with them to the Americas, and some integrated the sign of the crossroads with Christianity. For them, the cross could represent Christian belief, African belief, or a rich mixture of both. For example, slaves from the BaKongo tradition, who were the second-largest African group brought to the United States, saw parallels between Jesus' role as mediator between humans and God as symbolized by the cross and the crossroads' significance as the site of contact between humans and spirits. In both instances, the cross represented the means of communication with the sacred. Even if not at a physical crossroads, a slave could establish a junction with the sacred world through material representations of the cross.

The cross was especially common in various Hoodoo or **conjure** practices. Conjure is simultaneously religion, magic, and **medicine**. Slaves did not view conjure as opposed to Christianity but rather as another source of religious power. Using herbology, conjurers could bestow blessings and curses. Archaeologists discovered a Hoodoo ritual site under the floorboards of an 18th-century slave dwelling in New York with a cross at its center. Drawing a cross upon the ground consecrated the space as a plane that connected the world of the dead, ancestors, and spirits with the human world. The cross is prevalent in other aspects of Hoodoo, and a cross possessed various meanings depending on the context of its use. Slaves used cross marks for both protective, benevolent means and destructive, malevolent means. Cross **charms** and medallions were sources of good luck and protection. Slaves also inscribed cross marks on graves to keep the spirit contained. They also integrated the natural world into their religious material culture. The leaves of various plants, such as the peace plant, which have a cross-shaped pattern, possessed a sacred and powerful property when used in conjure protection prayers.

The cross and the crossroads remained dominant images in slave life. As a symbol that could be associated with both Jesus of Christianity and particular African cosmologies, the cross signified the transcendent nature of the sacred. **Marbles** with inscribed crosses found at Hermitage plantation near Nashville, Tennessee, suggest that informal teaching methods in cosmology could remain hidden from slave masters. When used in play, the crosses on the marbles possessed the power to imbue good or bad luck onto the slave children who played with them. As a symbol, the cross offered slaves an effective visual technique for teaching children religious beliefs.

See also Cosmograms; Herbs; Subfloor Pits.

FURTHER READING

Chireau, Yvonne. *Black Magic: Religion and the African American Conjuring Tradition.* Los Angeles: University of California Press, 2006.

Raboteau, Albert J. *Slave Religion: The "Invisible Institution" in the Antebellum South.* New York: Oxford University Press, 2004.

Ruppel, Timothy, Jessica Neuwirth, Mark P. Leone, and Gladys-Marie Fry. "Hidden in View: African Spiritual Spaces in North American Landscapes." *Antiquity* 77, no. 296 (2003): 321–335.

Russell, Aaron L. "Material Culture and African-American Spirituality at the Hermitage." *Historical Archaeology* 31, no. 2 (1997): 63–80.

EMILY S. CLARK

D

DAIRIES. Dairies on plantations tended to be small buildings dedicated to milk processing. Dairy products had been an important part of English diets, so colonists transported that culture. By 1662, the Coles family in Maryland had 12 milk cows as well as six wooden tubs to cool milk, 15 pans to raise the cream, a churn and butter pots for butter making and a cheese tub. Women processed the milk. African female slaves worked with their mistresses to process milk from cows, even though dairy products had not been common in their countries of origin. They may have more regularly processed goat's milk. The first African in South Carolina, in 1670, drank two glasses of milk a day. Yet Southern colonists complained that many staples of their English diet, including cheese, proved difficult to recreate in the hot southern climate. By the Revolutionary War, slaves in the North were most likely to work with milk processing and spend time in and around a dairy.

Dairying played a relatively limited role in Southern agriculture through the Civil War. Compilations of data from the U.S. agricultural censuses for 1850 and 1860 indicate that Southerners produced only about one-third of the butter that Northerners did. Livestock generally, and dairying specifically, accounted for only about 5 percent of the output of large southern plantations. Furthermore, dairy products did not play a critical role in southern diets or in southern agricultural processing. Therefore, dairies were exceptions rather than the rule across the South. Only the wealthiest planters or businessmen invested in such buildings. On large plantations, field slaves might not benefit from the products of the dairy, but the lives of other slaves on large plantations revolved around the dairy, particularly those assigned to work with dairy cattle, to skim cream or process the raw product into a consumable commodity. Slave cooks also worked at the dairy, gathering milk, cream, uncured cheese, butter, or cured cheese to serve to residents on the plantation. Slaves also might be responsible for selling dairy products to customers beyond the plantation.

The few dairies documented on plantations were relatively small buildings, often 14 feet square, and constructed to maintain as cool an interior as possible during long hot southern summers. Louvers for ventilation and overhanging eaves and porches for shade regulated the interior temperature. Some planters insulated the buildings; others built one section of the building into the ground, like a root cellar, to reach

Mississippi Dairy

On the Mississippi plantation where David Weathersby was enslaved, the service buildings included a dairy:

> My ole Marse wuz a big plantation owner. I spec' he had mos' a thousand acres an' when de war ended he freed round a hundred an' twenty five slaves. De house he lived in wuz big an' fine, his house, servant house, barns, milk houses an' all civered a quarter uv an' acre. Dat milk house wuz built o' brick in de side yard under some trees an' wuz kept full o' creamy milk an' loads o' butter. Back in dem days dey had no way a keepin' milk an' butter cold so dey couldn't keep hit in de warm house an' dots why it wuz kept in dairys outside. Yo' know everything back in dem days had to be in de rough.

Source: George P. Rawick, ed. *The American Slave: Mississippi Narratives*, Supp. Ser. 1, Vol. 10, Part 5. Westport, CT: Greenwood Press, 1978.

cooler air. More plantations and small farms may have constructed **spring houses** and stored milk and dairy products there.

The dairy often had a stone floor that helped maintain a cooler temperature. Low to the floor, shelving held the pans used to cool the milk and allow the cream to rise. Slaves poured milk into the shallow milk pans, often made of earthenware. After the cream rose to the top, slaves skimmed the cream from the pans and collected it and

Old milk house, Ionia, Virginia. (Library of Congress.)

stored it in the cream pots until they had enough to churn a batch into butter. During the hot summer, slaves churned in the dairy because excessive heat created watery butter. Buttermilk that remained from the churning could be consumed by plantation residents either raw or in baked goods; skim milk often became pig food. Uncured cheese could be made simply by letting the milk warm naturally on a slow fire or in the sun until curds formed. The drained curds could be consumed without additional processing. Whole milk usually was processed into both cured and uncured cheese. Salted butter stored in tubs or stoneware crocks and cheeses were stored in the dairy until consumed or sold.

Slaves had to maintain a clean environment in the dairy. Equipment had to be scalded, and large copper cauldrons often were used for this purpose because the milk pails, pans, tubs, cream pots, and churns used in processing were large. Slaves interviewed during the 1930s as part of the Federal Writers' Project remembered that some dairies had workrooms with hearths or stoves to heat water to clean buckets, strainers, cheese cloth, and other utensils because the dairy products would sour if processing equipment was not clean. Introducing heat into the vicinity of a dairy could work against the goal the building performed, to maintain a temperature of around 50°F to ensure the best dairy product. Regardless, planters often had workrooms in dairies, and dairies were built next to smokehouses, if not contiguous. Thomas Jefferson had two smokehouses built on each end of a room used as a dairy in 1790.

Many factors could affect the slave work cycle associated with a dairy. Dual-purpose breeds, particularly Durham or Devon cattle, proved good choices on plantations because they produced milk and good beef as well as hardy calves that could be trained as oxen. Some evidence of Ayrshire cattle, a dairy breed, existed in the antebellum South. Cattle, regardless of breed, calved once a year and they gave the most milk at that time. In northern climates, calving occurred in the spring when temperatures moderated and new stock could take advantage of new grass. In more moderate southern locations, cattle could calve at any time, and this could keep a southern dairy in operation year-round. Cows give milk in decreasing quantities until "dried off" so they can prepare to calve. Drying off coincided with decreased fodder during the winter. In the antebellum South, the open-range system allowed stock to roam. This meant that all cattle had to forage, and it could be difficult to manage feed for a dairy cow to maintain her production under such circumstances. Wealthy planters already inclined toward scientific agricultural methods may have enclosed a permanent pasture for their best dairy cattle, and this could have ensured an active dairy year-round.

Businessmen in towns or cities might have operated commercial dairies, and employed slaves to do the work, but this required contracting with farmers and planters to provide enough whole milk to meet demand. Most Southerners likely kept a milk cow, even in town, thus making commercial dairies less critical to southern urban environments.

FURTHER READING

Carr, Lois Green, Russell R. Menard, and Lorena S. Walsh. *Robert Cole's World: Agriculture and Society in Early Maryland.* Chapel Hill: University of North Carolina Press, 1991.

Edelson, S. Max. *Plantation Enterprise in South Carolina.* Cambridge, MA: Harvard University Press, 2006.

Fogel, Robert William. "American Slavery: A Flexible, Highly Developed Form of Capitalism." In *Society and Culture in the Slave South*, edited by J. William Harris, 77–99. London: Routledge, 1992.

Gray, Lewis C. *History of Agriculture in the Southern United States to 1860*. Reprint, Gloucester, MA: Peter Smith, 1958.

Hilliard, Sam Bowers. *Hog Meat and Hoe Cake: Food Supply in the Old South, 1840–1860*. Carbondale: Southern Illinois University Press, 1972.

Vlach, John Michael. *Back of the Big House: The Architecture of Plantation Slavery*. Chapel Hill: University of North Carolina Press, 1993.

DEBRA A. REID

DEPENDENCIES. Dependencies, or outbuildings, were separate structures usually located away from the main house on farms, plantations, and city dwellings. Together with an adjacent service yard, they formed a network that supported both the enslaved and the white members of large extended households. **Food** preparation and preservation, refrigeration, laundry, **cloth** production, storage, skilled trades, livestock care, and other essential activities took place in dependencies. Slaves resided in other outbuildings called **slave quarters**. Many of them lived out their lives within a community of dependencies.

Dependencies in the United States were direct descendants of similar clusters of work buildings found on landed estates and farms in Europe. Early colonists simply built what they knew when setting up their agricultural operations in the New World. At first, these dependencies reflected the distinct regions of 17th-century England and Ireland from which colonists emigrated. In 18th-century Louisiana, dependencies resembled those found in France. Eventually, the architectural style used for Southern dependencies associated with slaveholding was "Americanized" to cope with the climate, use the building materials at hand, and reflect individual slaveholder's needs. Outbuildings were universal on farms, plantations, and urban dwellings throughout the tenure of slavery in the United States. Some vestiges remain in the 21st century throughout the United States in the form of detached garages and backyard storage sheds.

The vast majority of dependencies were small brick or wood buildings with gable ends and shingled roofs. Wooden dependencies resembled log cabins. Most had one room only and were 400 square feet or less in size. Two-room and two-story outbuildings existed, but room dimensions remained the same. Eventually, a few wealthy planters and farmers built larger dependencies, mainly stables and barns, as a testament to their prosperity.

Inside, dependencies were unfinished. Plastered walls were unusual. Dirt floors were commonplace. Some dependencies, such as **dairies** or storage areas, did have brick and wood floors, depending on their function. With the exception of free-standing **kitchens**, outbuildings had no windows or heat source unless their function required sunlight, a fireplace, and a chimney. Almost all, except those in poor repair, had doors. These could easily be put under lock and key to secure the goods inside.

Owners routinely built, renovated, demolished, and moved outbuildings around their property as their needs and fortunes changed. Some colonial settlers built small

Dependencies on a Texas Plantation

Wash Wilson described the Texas plantation he grew up on:

On Marse Bill's place every quarters had its barn and mule, but Marse and he wife, Miss Deborah, lived in de quality quarters. Round dem was de blacksmith shop and smokehouse and spinnin' house and Marse Bill have a li'l house jus' for he office. De cookhouse was a two-room house side de big house with a covered passage to de dinin' room. De milk house was de back part de cook house.

In de smokehouse was hams and sides of hawg meat and barrels of syrup and sugar and lard, and bushels of onions, and de 'tater room was allus full. Dey dug a big place and put poles and pieces of cane and lumber cross, like a top, and put dirt and leaves and banked de dirt round de 'tater room. Dey'd have a place to crawl in, but dey kep' it tight and dem 'taters dey kep' most all winter.

Dey was hayricks and chicken roosties and big lye hoppers where us put all de fireplace ashes. Come de rain and de water run through dat hopper into de trough under it, and dat make lye water. De women put old meat skins and bones and fat in de big, iron pot in de yard and put in some lye water and bile soap. Den dey cut it when it git cold and put it on de smokehouse shelves to dry. Dat sho' fine soap.

Mammy worked in de kitchen mostly and spin by candlelight. Dey used a bottle lamp. Dat a rag or piece of big string, stuck in de snuff bottle full of tallow or grease. Later on in de years, dey used coal oil in de bottles. Sometimes dey wrap a rag round and round and put it in a pan of grease, and light dat for de lamp. Dey used pine torches, too.

De black folks' quarters was log cabins, with stick and dirt chimneys. Dey had dere own garden round each cabin and some chickens, but dere wasn't no cows like in Louisiana. Dere was lots of possums in de bottoms and us go coon and possum huntin'. I likes cornbread and greens, cook with de hawg jowls or strip bacon. Dat's what I's raised on. Us mad lots of lye hominy dem days. Marse Bill, he gwine feed everybody good on his place. Den us had ash cake, make of cornmeal. Us didn't buy much till long time after de War.

Us had poles stuck in de corner and tied de third pole cross, to make de bed. Dey called "Georgia Hosses." Us filled ticks with corn shucks or crab grass and moss. Dey wasn't no cotton beds for de niggers, 'cause dey wasn't no gins for de long time and de cotton pick from de seed by hand and dat slow work. De white folks had cotton beds and feather beds and wool beds.

Source: George P. Rawick, ed. *The American Slave: Texas Narratives*, Vol. 5, Parts 3 & 4. Westport, CT: Greenwood Press, 1972.

outbuildings as their initial home places on newly acquired land. As their fortunes improved, they constructed more substantial houses, and their original residences became dependencies, most likely kitchens. If a settler eventually built a newer kitchen, closer to the main house, the same building might become a slave quarters.

The evolution of dependencies and their functions at individual sites varied over time and place. Typically, individual dependencies fell into four fluid categories of use: agricultural, domestic, craft, and slave dwellings. A fifth area, the yard, was an outside service area that essentially functioned as a dependency. Slaves swept it bare of most vegetation to create a smooth dirt floor. Dependencies often surrounded the yard; large, messy tasks spilled over into it. Many other activities routinely took place in the open air year-round. Occasionally, slaveholding establishments had **yards** designed by plantation architects; many others evolved organically with development of the property. Most were open and located near the **master's house**; some were surrounded by wood plank or brick walls.

Agricultural outbuildings provided storage for agricultural and food products, care for livestock, and sites for some food preservation activities. Their functions often straddled the domestic and agricultural spheres of farm and plantation life. Barns, stables, chicken houses, pig houses, dairies, **corn cribs**, and smokehouses were examples of these dependencies.

Barns were used to store agricultural products, tools, and equipment and to shelter livestock. In much of the slaveholding South, they were indistinguishable from other outbuildings. Some had small lofts for hay; planters used others to cure **tobacco** or store **cotton** after harvest.

Stables sheltered **horses**, their feed, and tack. On farms and small plantations, they looked like standard dependencies. On more prosperous plantations, stables were customized structures where planters and their sons kept prize mounts. Slave men and boys cared for horses in plantation stables. In urban settings, stables often included loft living space for those enslaved workers.

Corn cribs held the **corn** crop after harvest. Often farmers and planters removed strips of clapboard from building walls to allow air to circulate inside. In some regions, corn cribs took on a different form. Some were raised up on sills or stilts to prevent rats from plundering the corn; elsewhere walls slanted outward from the structure's foundation for the same reason. The corn crop inside became livestock feed.

Chicken houses or coops were small sheds with a door. Some had a triangular shape and sat up on stilts. Inside, hens laid eggs in small compartments called nesting boxes. Slaves collected the eggs and delivered them to the plantation kitchen and, often, their own quarters. **Chickens** spent nights locked up in the coop to prevent their theft and to keep them away from predators.

Pig houses, open sheds built of scrap materials, offered **pigs** a place to get out of the sun or to nurse their young. On wealthier farms and plantations, pig houses were well built and the centerpiece of a fenced pig pen. More frequently pigs ran loose around plantation properties and surrounding woods. Slaves rounded them up and brought them into the pig pen in time for the annual winter butchering.

Dairies were small outbuildings with overhanging eaves, louvers, or other means of ventilation. They were open inside with shelves along the walls. Slave women, who kept cows nearby, milked them outside in the yard. They brought their buckets inside, poured the milk into shallow dishes resembling large pie pans and set them on the shelves. There the milk sat undisturbed in relatively cooler temperatures until cream rose to its surface. Slave women collected the cream and took it to the plantation kitchen.

Smokehouses held cured pork and other meats. They had widely spaced wall clap-boards for ventilation, dirt floors, high sills or foundations, shelves built along the walls, and solid doors that could easily be put under **lock and key**. Slaves hung newly slaughtered and salted meat on large metal hooks suspended from the walls or rafters. They placed bacon and other flat pieces on the long shelves inside. Then a slow fire was lighted on the dirt floor, and the door was closed. Smoke from the fire enveloped the meat and cured it over an extended period. The cured meat remained in the smokehouse until farm or plantation residents were ready to prepare and eat it.

Domestic dependencies supported the everyday needs of slave and white popula-tions living on farms and plantations. These included food preservation, food prepara-tion, refrigeration, and water supply. The kitchen, laundry, **spring house**, ice house, and well house were examples of these outbuildings.

Kitchens, where slave cooks prepared and preserved foods, were the most impor-tant domestic dependencies. Although they differed in size from one property to another and were not always in separate buildings, their exteriors looked like stand-ard outbuildings with chimneys. Inside, kitchens were open spaces with fireplaces. Many 18th-century kitchens had built-in dressers and shelves; others had an assort-ment of tables, dressers, barrels, chairs or benches, and utensils. Basic food items from the dairy, henhouse, smokehouse, spring house, and barns, along with water from the well and ice from the ice house, flowed into the kitchens. Meals for the owner's family and guests went out to the master's house and other locations. On larger plantations, the kitchen also prepared and delivered noontime meals for the field hands.

Laundries or wash houses existed on larger holdings, sometimes in a separate out-building, sometimes in a room adjacent to the kitchen. Inside, like kitchens, they were open spaces with a fireplace, chimney, and minimal furnishings. Most had tables and contained laundry tools like irons. A few had built-in tubs for washing. At most locations, the cleaning of the everyday clothes and household linens took place in large cauldrons of boiling water in the yard or at a nearby creek. Slave laundresses washed the finer linens and did the ironing in the wash house.

Well houses had many forms, ranging from low walls to full-fledged wood or brick outbuilding structures. They surrounded wells, deep holes, or shafts dug or drilled into the earth that provided access to water on farms and plantations. Larger establish-ments had a series of wells to service the master's house, yard, slave quarter, and other areas. The location of an individual well house on the plantation determined the quality of its design and construction.

Spring houses, dependencies built over or near natural springs, provided refrigera-tion for food products. Each had two sections: a pool of cool spring water, either natu-rally occurring or man-made, lined with rock or stone, and an outbuilding structure built to cover the pool. Jugs of milk and cream, butter crocks, and other containers of food, stood in the cool waters and did not spoil. Shelves, built into the outbuilding portion above the pool of spring water, held fruit and other food. The natural spring determined the location of the spring house on the farm or plantation property.

Ice houses were large man-made pits, 10 to 12 feet deep, covered and enclosed by a dependency structure. Ice pits ranged from primitive holes in the ground to brick-lined vaults. Ice houses ranged from poorly constructed sheds to architecturally designed brick structures. Each winter, slave men harvested thick ice from ponds on or rivers running through their master's property. They placed it in the ice pit. If ice was not available, planters and farmers purchased it from suppliers in colder climates or went without. Insulated by sawdust, straw, or other materials, this plantation ice supply lasted most of the year. Owners refrigerated food items in the ice house.

Most slave dwellings, called quarters, were single-room dependencies with a window, door, fireplace, and chimney. Over time, slave quarters evolved into a distinct architectural form with regional characteristics. Usually one family occupied each dwelling. In double pen (two room) or two rooms over two-story quarters, the one family to one room ratio remained. Slaves made furniture and housewares or scavenged them from other parts of the plantation for their home.

Craft dependencies sustained cloth production and skilled trade activities on large plantations. Wealthy planters, with the resources to support contingents of skilled slave artisans and the onsite or neighboring populations requiring their services, supported a wide variety of crafts at their establishments. The **spinning house**, loom house, blacksmith forge, and carpenter's shop are a few examples of these.

Spinning houses were simple dependencies, where slave women spun yarn for future weaving or knitting. These buildings were open spaces full of spinning wheels for producing cotton, wool, hemp, and flax yarns. They may have had fireplaces and chimneys and required windows for light.

Loom or weaving houses held looms for the production of cloth. The dimensions of the individual loom determined the size of these outbuildings and consumed their interior space. They may have had fireplaces and chimneys and required windows for light. Some plantations combined spinning and weaving operations under one roof.

Forges, where slave blacksmiths produced iron and other metal implements for agricultural and domestic use, took many forms. Some were in open sheds; others in stone buildings. The blacksmith furnished the forge interior with the specialized tools and fixtures of his trade: the fire, anvil, bellows, and an assortment of hammers, chisels, tongs, and other items.

Carpenter shops were dependencies where tradesmen produced and repaired agricultural and domestic items made from wood. These shops had windows for light and open interiors. Work tables and woodworking tools filled the inside space. Here carpenters produced everything from kitchen spoons to plough handles.

Dependencies existed to provide a plantation or farm with a level of self-sufficiency. The more goods and services produced by the slaves who worked in them to meet the needs of the establishment meant that the slaveholder paid less to import goods and services into his operation. The number of dependencies at each slaveholding establishment varied widely in urban and rural areas. With goods and services more readily available, smaller city dwellings may have had only a storage shed, whereas larger homes featured detached kitchens, stables, slave quarters, and several outbuildings for storage. In the countryside, farms and smaller plantations had a basic set of dependencies such as barn, kitchen, corn crib, and smokehouse. Larger plantations sometimes had dozens of dependencies covering many more specialized functions.

The presence of multiple dependencies on a large plantation or farm allowed skilled slaves to establish a level of self-sufficiency and independence that created communities of their own. Dependencies that were grouped together around the yard resembled a small village. Skilled slaves, who were neither house servants nor field hands, worked and lived there. They had only intermittent contact with the fields or the master's house. In the absence of this contact and influence, they created a world with its own culture, society, activities, and rituals. Much from this culture ultimately spilled over into post–Civil War African American life.

See also Blacksmith Shops; Cooks and Cooking; Double-Pen House; Laundries; Lofts; Two Rooms over Two Rooms Houses.

FURTHER READING

Baron, Robert C., ed. *The Garden and Farm Books of Thomas Jefferson*. Golden, CO: Fulcrum, 1987.

Berlin, Ira, Marc Favreau, and Steven E. Miller, eds. *Remembering Slavery: African Americans Talk about Their Personal Experiences of Slavery and Emancipation*. New York: New Press, 1998.

Dalzell, Bert F., Jr., and Lee Baldwin Dalzell. *George Washington's Mount Vernon: At Home in Revolutionary America*. New York: Oxford University Press, 1998.

Hanson, Susan Atherton. "Home Sweet Home: Industrialization's Impact on Rural Households, 1865–1920." PhD dissertation, University of Maryland, 1986.

Kimball, Marie. *Jefferson, the Road to Glory 1743 to 1776*. New York: Coward-McCann, 1943.

Phillips, Ulrich B. *Life and Labor in the Old South*. 3rd ed. Boston: Little, Brown and Company, 1963.

Spruill, Julia Cherry. *Women's Life and Work in the Southern Colonies*. 2nd ed. New York: W.W. Norton and Company, 1972.

Vetare, Margaret L. *Philipsburg Manor/Upper Mills*. Tarrytown, NY: Historic Hudson Valley Press, 2004.

Vlach, John Michael. *Back of the Big House: The Architecture of Plantation Slavery*. Chapel Hill: University of North Carolina Press, 1993.

SUSAN ATHERTON HANSON

DOGS. Many slaves had dogs. Dogs were useful for companionship, protection, and assistance in hunting, especially when a gun was lacking. Some slaves may have even raised them for sale. The 1800–1810 ledger for John Hook's Franklin County, Virginia, store indicates that he purchased dogs from local slaves.

Faithful Dog

When Charles Ball escaped from plantation slavery in Georgia in the early 19th century, he left his hunting dog Trueman behind, tied to a tree. The dog had been with Ball for four years, had saved his life from a panther attack on one occasion, and been a true companion, but Ball could not risk the dog barking and revealing him. As Ball abandoned Trueman, he observed sadly "Thou laidest thyself down at my feet when the world had united to oppress me."

Source: Charles Ball, "Slavery in the United States. A Narrative of the Life and Adventures of Charles Ball, a Black Man, Who Lived Forty Years in Maryland, South Carolina, and Georgia, as a Slave under Various Masters, and Was One Year in the Navy with Commodore Barney, during the Late War." Documenting the American South. At http://docsouth.unc.edu/neh/ballslavery/ball.html.

"Scenes of Slave Life," probably Mid-Atlantic or New England, 1820–1835, ink and watercolor on wove paper. Left corner: a white man firing a gun at an enslaved man who is being chased by bloodhounds. (Abby Aldrich Rockefeller Folk Art Museum, The Colonial Williamsburg Foundation.)

Slaveholders had dogs, too. They used them to guard the plantation livestock, accompany them on hunting expeditions, and police the slaves. On occasions that were recalled by different ex-slaves when interviewed in the 1930s, slaveholders employed specially trained bloodhounds to track runaway slaves. These dogs, trained to be vicious, inflicted injury, even death, on would-be escapees, and slaves had good reason to fear them.

For the most part, owners looked the other way over the issue of dogs in the **slave quarters**. They apparently recognized the role that dogs played in hunting game and wild animals that supplemented the enslaved community's diet. Yet, an underlying suspicion also existed among them that slave dogs assisted their owners in evading nighttime patrols or helped them to steal from plantation storehouses by standing guard and offering a warning bark if someone approached. For this reason, George Washington ordered that all the dogs kept by slaves at Mount Vernon and his other farms be killed immediately because he assumed that they "aid them in their night robberies." Other slaveholders, including Thomas Jefferson, portrayed slaves' dogs as menaces and blamed them for killing their sheep. Jefferson wrote his Monticello overseer in 1808 that "to secure wool enough, the negroes dogs must all be killed. Do not spare a single one." However, Jefferson's own dogs, who also might have found sheep a tasty temptation, were spared. In South Carolina, distrust of slaves owning dogs gathered strength during the antebellum period. In 1859, after more than a decade of heated debate during which slaves' dogs were blamed outright for killing sheep and other livestock and implicated less directly for contributing to problems with enforcing slave behavior, South Carolina passed a law prohibiting all slaves from owning dogs.

FURTHER READING

Campbell, John. " 'My Constant Companion': Slaves and their Dogs in the Antebellum South." In *Working Toward Freedom: Slave Society and Domestic Economy in the American South*, edited by Larry E. Hudson Jr., 53–76. Rochester, NY: University of Rochester Press, 1995.

"Dogs," Thomas Jefferson Encyclopedia. At http://wiki.monticello.org/mediawiki/index.php/dogs.

Heath, Barbara J. "Slavery and Consumerism: A Case Study from Colonial Virginia." *African-American Archaeology: Newsletter of the African-American Archaeology Network* 19 (Winter 1997). The African Diaspora Archaeology Network. At www.diaspora.uiuc.edu/A-AANewsletter/newsletter19.html.

KYM S. RICE

DOGTROT HOUSES. Dogtrot houses, with two rooms or pens of equal size with an open breezeway or passage (called a "dogtrot") separating the rooms, are often associated with poor white Southern culture. This association emerged during the early 20th century as fictional accounts of Southern life in general and photographic depictions of Appalachia specifically linked the vernacular form to impoverished Southern mountain culture. The form appeared in Pennsylvania at least by the late 1780s, but likely existed in the Middle Atlantic colonies before that. The post-Revolutionary appearance coincided with the demise of slavery as an institution in the North. Yet, the house type existed across the South, on flatland as well as hillsides, and served as home to slave and free alike.

Dogtrot house. Zeno Chestang House, Mobile, Alabama. (Library of Congress.)

The dogtrot house was affordable to build. Builders used logs or frame construction in early dogtrots. Later in the 19th century, builders took advantage of dimension-sawn lumber and either balloon-frame or box-frame construction.

A single-span roof covered the two pens and breezeway, and the large open area on the second story served as additional sleeping and storage space, accessible either from each pen (or room) or from a stairway in the breezeway. The residents used the breezeway as additional living and working space during the hot southern summers. A porch across the front and sometimes back of the structure afforded some protection from the elements for the open interior.

The basic floor plan was similar to the **two rooms over two rooms house** built by middling farmers and planters across the South. Residents entered the structure through the breezeway, and entered each pen through doors that opened onto the breezeway. Owners could add a **kitchen** and other shed appendages off the back of the structure. Prosperous planters built dogtrots as slave housing, too, but these differed from yeoman and planter houses because the doors from the separate pens opened directly onto the front porch or yard. The two families that lived in the duplex could share the common hall as a workspace. James Thornton, the planter who owned Thornhill in Greene County, Alabama, housed 150 slaves in dogtrot houses by the early 1830s.

See also Slave Housing; Slave Quarters.

FURTHER READING

Ferris, William. "The Dogtrot: A Mythic Image in Southern Culture." *Southern Quarterly* 25, no. 1 (1986): 72–85.

Glassie, Henry. *Pattern in the Material Folk Culture of the Eastern United States.* Philadelphia: University of Pennsylvania Press, 1969.

Hulan, Richard H. "The Dogtrot House and Its Pennsylvania Associations." *Pennsylvania Folklife* 26, no. 5 (1977): 25–32.

Jordan, Terry G., and Matti Kaups. "Folk Architecture in Cultural and Ecological Context." *Geographical Review* 77, no. 1 (1987): 52–75.

Kniffen, Fred B. "Louisiana House Types." *Annals of the Association of American Geographers* 26, no. 4 (1936): 179–193.

Kniffen, Fred B. "The Physiognomy of Rural Louisiana." *Louisiana History* 4, no. 4 (1963): 291–299.

Vlach, John Michael. "'Snug Li'l House with Flue and Oven': Nineteenth-Century Reforms in Plantation Slave Housing." In *Gender, Class and Shelter: Perspectives in Vernacular Architecture*, edited by Elizabeth Collins Cromley and Carter L. Hudgins, 118–129. Knoxville: University of Tennessee Press, 1995.

DEBRA A. REID

DOLLS. Dolls come in a variety of forms and are created from materials such as wood, cloth, porcelain, bisque, celluloid, wax, and rubber. As playthings, religious icons, fashion emissaries, collector's objects, and objects of cultural expression, dolls have a complex and far-ranging history. As cultural artifacts, dolls and doll play offer unique perspective not only about children's lives under slavery but also about the values, rules, and practices of slavery in American society.

Dolls in Europe and North America

Archaeological evidence suggests that the doll may be the oldest known toy. Miniature human figures have been unearthed from burial sites around the world, dating from as early as 2000–3000 BCE. The earliest dolls were fashioned out of organic materials like bone, clay, rags, wood, and ivory. They were placed in graves of children as well as adults, possibly for purposes of entertaining the dead or to serve the departed in the afterlife. In many ancient cultures, dolls were used for ceremonial and ritualistic purposes, as talismans to ward off illness or to facilitate healing, and perhaps as objects of amusement and play.

From the Renaissance through the 19th century, Europeans dominated the manufactured doll market. In the late 14th century, fashion dolls resembling mature women, dressed in the latest French styles, began circulating between the courts of Europe. In the 17th and 18th centuries, fashion designers used these dolls to showcase their designs throughout Europe and North America. For more than four centuries, dolls served as conduits of fashion and consumption; not until the turn of the 18th century did engravings and fashion magazines begin to replace the three-dimensional doll as the chief purveyors of European fashion trends.

"Scipio" doll in livery carved by David Catheal, America, ca. 1812. (The Colonial Williamsburg Foundation. Acquired with funds from Mr. and Mrs. Robert S. Wilson.)

When adults were finished with their fashion dolls, they very likely passed them on to children to use as playthings. More commonly, however, young girls in early America would have played with dolls created out of leftover materials of various kinds—**cloth**, wood, **corn**, nuts, and even **tobacco** leaves—found around the home. Homemade dolls, particularly "rag dolls" made from scraps of fabric, discarded clothing, and sack cloth were consistently the most popular dolls among children of all backgrounds. Although they varied regionally and culturally, rag dolls typically had flat heads with stitched or painted faces and hair made of yarn, fur, or human hair.

Early Black Dolls in America

Rag dolls—black, brown, and white—were made by free women and by slave women in early America. Of the various rag dolls produced during slavery, the Topsy Turvy or Upside Down doll is the most complex and controversial. Topsy Turvy dolls feature a black doll, often represented as "mammy," on one end and a white doll on the other. The dolls are joined at the waist, rendering it impossible for both to be seen at once;

Girls and Dolls

Susan Matthews, enslaved in Georgia, cherished a doll that her master made for her:

> But I did have a doll to play with. It wuz a rag doll an my mistis made it for me. I wuz jes crazy 'bout that doll and I learned how to sew making clothes fer it. I'd make clothes fer it an wash an iron 'em, and it wasn't long 'fo I knowed how to sew real good, an I been sewing ever since.

Source: George P. Rawick, ed. *The American Slave: Georgia Narratives*, Vol. 13. Westport, CT: Greenwood Press, 1972.

In Texas, Emma Taylor got in terrible trouble for playing with the master's child's doll:

> De worstest whippin' I ever got was for playin' with a doll what belonged to one marse's chillen. I 'members it yet and I ain't never seed a doll purty as dat doll was to me. It was make out a corncob with arms and legs what moved and a real head, with eyes and hair and mouth painted on. It had a dress out of silk cloth, jist like one my missus weared when she went to meetin'. Dat li'l gal done leave de doll under de tree, but missus found me playin' with it and whipped me hard.

Source: George P. Rawick, ed. *The American Slave: Texas Narratives*, Vol. 5, Parts 3 & 4. Westport, CT: Greenwood Press, 1972.

---

when one doll is exposed, the other lies hidden beneath a skirt. It is generally agreed that Topsy Turvy dolls originated in the plantation South, but scholars and doll enthusiasts continue to speculate about their original purpose and how children would have used them. The dolls likely were produced for slave children and perhaps as "maid dolls" for white children. The issue of how children played with these dolls remains hotly debated. Some have imagined that slave children were barred from playing with white dolls and thus slave mothers fashioned dolls that could quickly and surreptitiously be transformed from white to black. By contrast, others have speculated that slave children were permitted to display only white dolls in front of their masters and mistresses. Still others have argued that the Topsy Turvy doll allowed slave girls to imitate the domestic practices of their mothers and other female relatives charged with caring for white babies and children.

Black women's association with domestic service was most starkly embodied by the black mamma or "mammy" doll, readily identified by her exaggerated smile, head scarf, apron, and occasional presence of a white baby. In the antebellum period, these dolls were made of cloth and also out of household materials like bottles and nursing nipples. From slavery through the Jim Crow era, the mammy caricature supported the Southern myth of the loyal and contented slave. "Mammy" is an enduring racial stereotype that found its greatest expression in the iconic Aunt Jemima, whose ubiquitous image remains highly collectible.

Pre– and post–Civil War, Harriet Beecher Stowe's 1852 novel *Uncle Tom's Cabin* spawned commercial tie-ins of every conceivable sort, including dolls. "Tomitudes"—Staffordshire figurines of Uncle Tom and Little Eva—first produced in the 1850s, reinforced a sentimentalized portrait of slavery and its victims. In the 1860s, McLoughlin Brothers in New York produced Eva and Topsy paper dolls, complete with a range of noninterchangeable outfits for both girls. Later versions expanded the cast of characters to include Tom, Eliza, and Chloe. Uncle Tom's Cabin rag dolls, including Topsy Turvy dolls featuring Eva and Topsy, proliferated from the 1850s through the 20th century.

For their part, abolitionists in Great Britain and the United States used dolls to raise public awareness about slavery and to generate empathy for slaves. Philadelphia Quakers sent black dolls, both male and female dressed in traditional Quaker clothing, to Friends in Britain, perhaps as testimony to free blacks' piety and respectability. The Boston Antislavery Bazaar sold Scottish fashion dolls holding paper declarations such as "Sell me as they do women and children in your country. It will be no sin in my case." Aimed at adults as well as children, these abolitionist dolls drew a hard line between buying "things" and buying people. Dolls were human replicas, not human beings.

Dolls, Doll Play, and Slavery

Under slavery, race, gender, and class hierarchies were reinforced through the objects and rituals of play. Through play, children acquire social, emotional, cognitive, and physical skills that prepare them for adulthood. During slavery, doll play offered girls—slave and free—domestic apprenticeship that often mirrored the gendered and racial realities of adult women; however, historians also have uncovered ample evidence of children using dolls to engage in subversive forms of play.

Mudpies and Dolls

The Works Progress Administration's Federal Writers' Project **slave narratives** offer numerous descriptions of doll play in the antebellum South. In his 90th year, Al Rosboro of Winnsboro, South Carolina, who had been a slave on the plantation of Billie Brice, recalled playing with the daughter of his master:

> One of de gals marry a Robertson, I can't 'member her name, tho' I help her to make mud pies many a day and put them on de chicken coop, in de sun, to dry. Her had two dolls; deir names was Dorcas and Priscilla. When de pies got dry, she'd take them under de big oak tree, fetch out de dolls and talk a whole lot of child mother talk 'bout de pies, to de Dorcas and Priscilla rag dolls. It was big fun for her tho' and I can hear her laugh right now lak she did when she mince 'round over them dolls and pies.

Source: George P. Rawick, ed. *The American Slave: South Carolina Narratives*, Vol. 3. Westport, CT: Greenwood Press, 1972.

Doll play was an activity that brought children of differing social standing together. It could foster interracial bonds but it could also serve to remind slave children of the disparities between themselves and their white playmates.

On some plantations, black children were prohibited from playing with white children, but most children were not subjected to such strict segregation. In fact, historians have shown that it was common in the South for young children, slave and free, black and white, to engage in common play and leisure activities. This integrated play could foster positive relationships; however, it could also reinforce the material inequality between slave and free children. There was a stark contrast in the quality and aesthetic appeal of dolls and other toys owned by slave children and those owned by the children of their masters. The slave child might have a bundle of rags tied together while the white child had a porcelain doll. Archaeologists excavating slave quarters have found physical evidence that in addition to homemade dolls, some slave children also owned manufactured European dolls. Some slaveowners gave slave children dolls as gifts, bribes, and rewards. In other cases, mistresses encouraged slave children to learn how to sew by making dolls and doll clothing. The needlework skills that girls acquired making doll clothes would later be applied to more general household production.

See also Caricatures; Nurseries and Nursemaids.

FURTHER READING

Boehn, Max von. *Dolls and Puppets*. Newton, MA: C. T. Branford Company, 1956.

Formanek-Brunell, Miriam. *Made to Play House: Dolls and the Commercialization of American Girlhood, 1830–1930*. Baltimore, MD: Johns Hopkins University Press, 1998.

Fraser, Antonia. *A History of Toys*. New York: Delacorte, 1966.

King, Wilma. *Stolen Childhood: Slave Youth in 19th Century America*. Bloomington: Indiana University Press, 1998.

Mitchell, Michele. "The Colored Doll Is a Live One! Material Culture, Black Consciousness, and Cultivation of Intraracial Desire." In *Righteous Propagation: African Americans and the Politics of Racial Destiny after Reconstruction*. Chapel Hill: The University of North Carolina Press, 2004, 173–197.

Peers, Juliette. *The Fashion Doll: From Bebe Jumeau to Barbie*. Paris: Berg Publishers, 2004.

Rondon, Nayda. *Black Dolls: Proud, Bold & Beautiful*. New York: Reverie Publishing, 2004.

"Uncle Tomitudes," Uncle Tom's Cabin and American Culture. At http://utc.iath.virginia.edu/tomituds/tohp.html.

Wallace-Sanders, Kimberly Gisele. *Mammy: A Century of Race, Gender, and Southern Memory*. Ann Arbor: University of Michigan Press, 2008.

ALICE TAYLOR

DORMITORIES. Dormitories were buildings used for the communal housing of a number of often-unrelated individuals. Dormitories, also called "quarters" or "barracks," were primarily a feature of American slave life in the late 17th and 18th centuries, generally on plantations that were at an early stage of their development, when there tended to be more men than women, or when there were a sizeable number of newly imported slaves from Africa. Over the course of the 18th century, the use of dormitories declined as sex ratios became more balanced, enabling enslaved people to form families, which were more likely to be housed in cabins. By the middle of the century, dormitories had largely given way to other forms of **slave housing** in both the Chesapeake and the Carolina Low Country, but they continued to be used into the 19th century. A dormitory known as the "long quarter" at Wye Plantation in Maryland was the boyhood home of abolitionist Frederick Douglass (ca. 1818–1895).

Communal quarters, whether of brick or frame construction, tended to be larger and more substantially built than individual cabins. In 1731, what was described as a particularly large quarter in New Kent County, Virginia, measured 16 by 20 feet (320 square feet), the same size as two quarters built in the 1760s by Robert W. Carter. Kingsmill Plantation near Williamsburg, Virginia, featured two brick structures, each 45 feet by 22 feet (990 square feet), used as the **kitchen**, pantry, scullery, offices, and housing for slaves; the plantation also had two communal quarters, 40 feet by 18 feet (720 square feet), and 28 feet by 20 feet (560 square feet). A 1798 listing of communal quarters in St. Mary's County, Maryland, recorded that these structures typically ranged in size from 20 feet by 16 feet to 50 by 16 feet (800 square feet). The number of slaves living in dormitories might also vary widely. At a plantation owned by Philip Ludwell Lee in Tidewater Virginia, 8 to 24 slaves lived communally in structures with only one to two rooms. Dormitories, similar to those used in the Caribbean, could also be found in Charleston, South Carolina, where as many as 50 slaves might live in crowded communal **slave quarters** behind the slaveholder's home.

One of the most interesting surviving examples of what may be a communal quarter or dormitory dating to the early 19th century can be seen at Keswick Plantation in Powhatan County, Virginia. It is a round brick structure about 36 feet in diameter, sporting a conical roof. In the center is a round fireplace with three separate hearths. Two interior features that did not survive were a plaster and lath ceiling, as well as a gallery or ledge that went around the wall at the top of the windows, about 3 feet under the ceiling. Some historians have surmised that the highly unusual shape of this building can be traced back to traditional house styles in Africa, but others argue that this is highly unlikely, as most of the enslaved Africans brought to Virginia were from areas where buildings tended to be square or rectangular.

An intermediate stage between communal quarters and cabins for individual families involved partitioning the quarters, so that families could have their own apartments. One example of this housing method is the building at George Washington's Mount Vernon, which was known as the "Quarters [or House] for Families." Whether it may have started as a dormitory space and evolved into a partitioned space for families is not known. A two-story frame building, constructed on a brick foundation, with a chimney on each end and glazed windows, it appears to have been the principal slave dwelling on the estate for about 30 years. Located on the service lane north of the mansion, it was first depicted in a map drawn by English visitor Samuel Vaughan in 1787 and later appeared in a 1792 painting that has been attributed to Edward Savage. Although the building was torn down in the 1790s, much of the current knowledge about the material life of the Mount Vernon slaves was learned as a result of archaeological investigations in a small section of its cellar in the 1980s.

Perhaps the best known example of a communal slave quarters can be found in a slightly later building in the greenhouse complex at Mount Vernon. Contrary to the trend in slave housing, which saw an increase in privacy as more and more people lived in cabins with their families, after the Revolution, Washington had one farm that was very much like those on earlier plantations. By this period, Mount Vernon consisted of 8,000 acres divided into five farms. Large-scale agricultural production took place on the four outlying farms, while the Mansion House Farm was home to Washington, his pleasure grounds, and most of his skilled workers, both hired and enslaved. Among those slaves were house servants, postilions and grooms, carpenters, blacksmiths, gardeners, carters, cooks, knitters, shoemakers, and ditchers. The majority of them were men, whose wives and children lived and worked on the outlying farms. Because the men typically went home on their time off, which was Saturday evening through Sunday night, Washington needed a way to house them during the week and seems to have turned to a communal model he knew well from his days in the military.

In the years between his return from the Revolution and his inauguration as president, Washington built a greenhouse where he could raise tropical plants. A solid two-story brick structure, the side of the greenhouse that faced the formal garden featured large glazed windows, while the other side held a stove room, used for stoking the fire to heat plants in cold weather, and a shop used by the shoemaker. By the spring of 1792, wings were being added to both ends of the greenhouse, providing four large rectangular rooms, each 33 feet 9 inches by 17 feet 9 inches, having a total living space of about 600 square feet. Each of the rooms had a fireplace on one of its shorter walls, brick floors, and the luxury of glazed windows. At that time, the farm manager wrote that he thought the new quarter would adequately house all the slaves Washington might wish or need on the Mansion House Farm, about 80 people. Knowing that, at this time, other slaves at the Mansion House Farm were living in family cabins, or over the outbuildings where they worked, the four rooms in the new quarter would have been more than adequate to house about half that number: skilled workers with families elsewhere and people who were single. The inhabitants moved in late in 1792 or early the following year. Slaves would continue to make their homes in the Greenhouse complex until December of 1835, when a tremendous fire destroyed the roughly 40-year-old structure. It was rebuilt in the 1950s using what little physical and documentary evidence had survived.

Probably the most striking feature of these reconstructed quarters was the arrangement of bunks on the east and south sides of the room, creating a barracks-like atmosphere similar to military housing. Examples of 18th-century military uses of bunks can be seen today at Fort Frederick, a French and Indian War fortress in Maryland, as well as at Valley Forge, and the Old Barracks at Trenton, New Jersey. The wooden huts at Valley Forge, at 14 feet by 16 feet (224 square feet), would have housed 12 men in two-level bunks, each wide enough to hold two people. Similarly, each of the 20 rooms for soldiers at the Trenton barracks provided living space for 12 men, who would have slept two to the bunk. In these situations, the planks typically were covered with straw, over which the men would place their straw-filled mattresses. The straw, which could be supplemented with rushes or leaves, needed to be aired out periodically and replaced on a regular basis to inhibit vermin.

FURTHER READING

"History: Valley Forge: Setting Up Camp," National Park Service. At www.nps.gov/history/ logcabin /html/vf2.html.

Morgan, Philip D. *Slave Counterpoint: Black Culture in the Eighteenth-Century Chesapeake and Lowcountry.* Chapel Hill: University of North Carolina Press, 1998.

Old Barracks Museum. At www.barracks.org.

Sobel, Mechal. *The World They Made Together: Black and White Values in Eighteenth-Century Virginia.* Princeton, NJ: Princeton University Press, 1987.

Vlach, John Michael. "Plantation Landscapes of the Antebellum South." In *Before Freedom Came: African-American Life in the Antebellum South,* edited by Edward D. C. Campbell Jr. with Kym S. Rice, 20–49. Richmond and Charlottesville, VA: The Museum of the Confederacy and University Press of Virginia, 1992.

Vlach, John Michael. *Back of the Big House: The Architecture of Plantation Slavery.* Chapel Hill: University of North Carolina Press, 1993.

Wilford, John Noble. "An Abolitionist Leads the Way in Unearthing of Slaves' Past." *New York Times,* September 5, 2006. At www.nytimes.com/2006/09/05/science/05doug.html.

MARY V. THOMPSON

DOUBLE-PEN HOUSES. Enslaved people lived in buildings that were as varied architecturally as the places where they worked. A common vernacular form found throughout the rural South, the double-pen house was built and occupied by both whites and blacks from the 18th through the 20th centuries. Scholars believe that the basic double pen was originally built from pine in the southeastern United States. In the late 18th century, immigrants going west along the Red and Mississippi rivers to Louisiana, Mississippi, and Texas copied the form, which they considered a "big dwelling." The structures were also prevalent in the Ozarks, particularly in Kentucky.

Double-pen slave cabin, built in 1843 from Eastern red cedar logs, from Gen. Andrew Jackson's plantation, The Hermitage. (Library of Congress.)

Generally, the double-pen house was regarded as an improvement over another favorite housing construct, the single pen, which was a modest one-room domestic structure that often was a core to which other rooms were added. By one estimate, the double-pen form or its variation was the most common type of housing built for the enslaved.

In its basic form, the double pen was composed of two single rooms, frequently separated by a hallway, or "dogtrot," and covered with a roof. This simple building rested on foundation piers and usually contained just one chimney with a fireplace between the two pens. Although they were sometimes smaller, the rooms typically measured about 16 by 16 feet. A double-pen variation features gable-ended exterior chimneys. The double pen was usually built of log with deep eaves, a small porch extending across the breadth of the house, and each room had a front door. Houses with more rooms usually had add-ons built at the rear of the house, typically only to one of the pens.

Although in the antebellum period, slaveholders debated the number of slave families who should occupy a single building, the double pen usually sheltered at least two slave families. Sometimes the building was two stories, with an upstairs **loft** space for an additional family. Simple and quick to construct, these were basic, utilitarian buildings that allowed few comforts. They had limited light or air circulation and were usually neither dry nor warm. Although the log walls frequently were filled in with mud, clay, or other materials including rags, holes remained. Former Texas slave John White remembered, "The cold winds in the winter go through the cracks between the logs like the walls was somewhere else, and I shivers with the misery all the time."

See also Dogtrot House; Slave Housing; Slave Quarters.

FURTHER READING

Atkins, Shauna. "House Types Found in Region 2, Red River Valley and the Neutral Strip," Louisiana Regional Folklife Program. At www.nsula.edu/regionalfolklife/StokesCollection/varchPaper.html#footnote.

Vlach, John Michael. *Back of the Big House: The Architecture of Plantation Slavery*. Chapel Hill: University of North Carolina Press, 1993.

Wright, Martin. "The Antecedents of the Double-Pen House Type." *Annals of the Association of American Geographers* 48, no. 2 (June 1958): 109–117.

FRED LINDSEY

DOVECOTES. Among the more specialized outbuildings found within the plantation landscape was the dovecote or pigeonaire, where pigeons and doves nested and were raised as **food**. Recipes for squab (young pigeon or dove) and pigeon are found in 18th- and 19th-century recipe books. The birds were cared for by slaves, who probably tended to other poultry and small farm animals. Their droppings were considered a source of good fertilizer for **gardens**, and the feathers were used for bedding. Enslaved workers were responsible for feeding, cleaning, collecting eggs, sweeping up, and otherwise removing the manure and plucking the feathers after the birds were killed.

Although not widespread, dovecotes nevertheless were found throughout the South. They take different architectural forms, and some elaborate brick examples are found in Virginia and Louisiana. The structures typically were wooden, so that they could be seasonally whitewashed, included holes for bird entry and exit, and were raised up above the ground on legs. This allowed air to circulate through the birds' quarters on top, protected them from predators, and provided enslaved workers greater ease in cleaning. Because of concerns among slaveholders about noise, they were sometimes set at the edge of plantation outbuilding complexes. The George Wythe House at Colonial Williamsburg in Virginia includes a large reproduction dovecote among its outbuildings. Magnolia Mound Plantation in Baton Rouge, Louisiana, has an example of a dovecote (ca. 1825) moved there from a plantation in Sunshine, Louisiana.

FURTHER READING

Olmert, Michael. *Kitchens, Smokehouses and Privies: Outbuildings and the Architecture of Daily Life in the Eighteenth-Century Middle Atlantic.* Ithaca, NY: Cornell University Press, 2009.

Vlach, John Michael. *Back of the Big House: The Architecture of Plantation Slavery.* Chapel Hill: University of North Carolina Press, 1993.

KYM S. RICE

Dovecote at Hill Plantation, Wilkes County, Georgia. (Library of Congress.)

DRUMS. African American music is multiethnic in the racial, cultural, and regional senses. Slaves from various African ethnic groups were brought to the Americas, and once enslaved in the Western Hemisphere, Europeans largely forced them to abandon their separate cultural identities and cast them into an amalgamated group that knew no cultural distinctions. Few African traits were allowed to flourish openly, but those that survived did so in the essential, rather than the traditional, sense. Instead of speaking their traditional languages, the English the slaves spoke absorbed the rhythm and nuance of the African tongue. Elements of ritual dance combined with recreational and secular dance, and slaves played Western instruments with the potency and vigor of the African style. The Africans had no choice but to use the systems afforded by their European captors. Accordingly, they synthesized, as opposed to syncretized, a culture.

Analyzing the drum's connection to slavery necessarily requires an expanded view of the instrument, which invites a broader understanding of a cultural aesthetic that overrides genres of instrumentation and defined disciplines. Slave masters took the drums away from slaves, but they could not stop the beat because Africans clapped their hands and stomped their feet; they put their hands in the air and slapped their knees, thighs, chest, heels, and mouths.

Drums signaled the 1739 Stono Uprising in South Carolina, which meant the end of the drum for Africans in the United States because that event heightened plantation owners' fears that "wild Negroes" would revolt—beating drums, dancing, and killing whites. Enticed by a desire to be free and by the open invitation of Florida's Spanish forces in a black-controlled area known as Fort Mose, the Africans acted. Nearly 100 Angolans and a few creolized Africans planned and executed the revolt they hoped would lead them to Florida. Some of them died and others were caught, but a few tasted freedom. But things would never be the same for black music as European domination, particularly by the British, meant that drum, dancing, and worship would be tightly controlled from that point on. The drum and many types of signal horns were banned.

Blacks consistently continued a vital drum culture that lives in languages (like Gullah), shouting, dancing, body percussion, hand clapping, juba (a dance of African origin), steppin', tambourine, call and response, work songs, and preaching. In Florida and Georgia's Maroon encampments, composed of fugitive black slaves, and on Sea Island plantations, Africans and their descendants hid drums and played them. At Congo Square in New Orleans, Louisiana, authorities "allowed" drums on certain occasions, and Florida's Seminole Indian camps offered another unique opportunity for musical synthesis as African and indigenous (primarily Creek) forms combined.

Concepts of pitch variation and polyrhythm are important in analyzing the development and evolution of drum culture in the United States, as these factors undergird the range of African-derived drum forms. Various practices like foot stomping, pitched hand claps, stamping the stick, tambourines, and bones are African derived. The unique characteristic of this form of African-derived "drumming" draws its essential duality from tonal semantics, that is, using subtle and overt intonation shifts to change meaning or feeling. That is essentially how pitch variation works. Drums are not merely rhythm or sound effects as in Western music; they are the music. Pitch changes and manipulations allow musicians to create a range of sounds or moods equal to or greater than those of any tuned instrument.

Polyrhythm concerns the deliberate layering of those pitches into interlocking or contrasting rhythmic shapes, and rhythms are the superstructures of orchestrated patterns that move and breathe in relation to one another. Playing in unison is generally used as an effect rather than as the music's substance. Clearly, then, the thumping of pestle in mortar, the clump of multiple axes on a tree, and the flailing of rice chaff were the plantation's drums music, especially when accompanied by rhythmic chanting and singing.

Both on plantations and in Maroon camps, drums were a form of praise, worship, and community. Even when banned, practices like the shout sprang forth, again making drums the center of the community. The shout, a circular shuffling movement supported by a "stampin' stick," hand claps, tambourine, and call and response was a culmination of all essential African American forms of drumming in lieu of the physical drum. The form developed in response to the absence of drums in Christian worship, and African Americans invigorated Christian worship with it.

Drums connected African Americans to their ancestors. Worship was exhaustive, lively, and sparked with possessions by the Holy Spirit and trances. Sea Islanders' worship services often were considered vulgar, barbaric, and "too African." Their style, whether intentional or not, evoked the drum's true spirit in a new context. The shout brought together the best and most characteristic African American percussion styles. From call-and-response vocalizations to rhythmic movements, it underscored the

African personality's innovative capacity and adaptability. Other forms of expression, including juba, buck dancing, and tap, owe much to the shout, either spiritually or literally, as they continue the idea of the frontline drum in a polytonal and polyrhythmic sense.

See also opening essay "Dance and Music."

FURTHER READING

Hartigan, Royal J. "Blood Drum Spirit: Drum Languages of West Africa, African-America, Native America, Central Java, and South India." PhD dissertation, History Department, Wesleyan University, 1986.

Jones, Bessie, and Bess Lomax Hawes. *Step It Down: Games, Plays, Songs, and Stories from the Afro-American Heritage*. Athens: University of Georgia Press, 1987.

DAVID PLEASANT

E

EMANCIPATION PROCLAMATION. On January 1, 1863, Abraham Lincoln (1809–1865), the 16th president of the United States, issued the Emancipation Proclamation. In this document, Lincoln declared that all slaves in states or portions of states in rebellion against the United States were free. He promised that the executive branch of the government would recognize and help maintain the freedom of the former enslaved men, women, and children. Although Lincoln stated that the Emancipation Proclamation was a "fit and necessary war measure for suppressing said rebellion," the announcement of this proclamation changed the purpose of the American Civil War. After January 1, 1863, the struggle between North and South became both a fight to preserve the Union and a battle with a moral purpose—to end slavery in the country.

Lincoln's Early Thoughts about Emancipation and Slavery

In early 1849, near the end of his first and only term in Congress, Abraham Lincoln, a representative from Illinois, took a public position against slavery when he introduced a bill to emancipate slaves in the District of Columbia. The legislation detailed a program of gradual emancipation in the nation's capital. Congress did not approve the measure because of opposition from Southerners who believed that Northerners did not have a right to interfere with slavery. At the end of his term, Lincoln returned to Illinois and resumed his law practice.

As a private citizen, Lincoln condemned the 1854 Kansas-Nebraska Act because it allowed for the expansion of slavery into U.S. territories. This legislation enabled the residents of the Kansas and Nebraska territories to decide whether they wanted their state to be a "free state" or a "slave state." The bill nullified the 1820 Missouri Compromise that stated slavery would not exist above the 36 degree 30 minute line in the Louisiana Territory.

Lincoln's stand against the Kansas-Nebraska Act caught the attention of members of the new Republican Party. In 1856, Lincoln became a member of this political party, and two years later, in 1858, Lincoln was the Republican nominee in the Illinois Senate race. In his acceptance speech, Lincoln stated "A house divided against itself cannot stand."

Answered Prayers

Long before the Emancipation Proclamation began the legal process of ending slavery, enslaved individuals yearned for freedom. A former Arkansas slave, Tom Robinson, remembered his mother's prayers:

> I can just barely remember my mother. I was not 11 when they sold me away from her. I can just barely remember her.
>
> But I do remember how she used to take us children and kneel down in front of the fireplace and pray. She'd pray that the time would come when everybody could worship the Lord under their own vine and fig tree—all of them free. It's come to me lots of times since. There she was a'praying, and on other plantations women was a'praying. All over the country the same prayer was being prayed. Guess the Lord done heard the prayer and answered it.

Source: George P. Rawick, ed. *The American Slave: Arkansas Narratives*, Vol. 10, Parts 5 & 6. Westport, CT: Greenwood Press, 1972.

As Robert Falls from Tennessee recalled, when freedom finally arrived, it was a special moment:

> I remember so well, how the roads was full of folks walking and walking along when the niggers were freed. Didnt know where they was going. Just going to see about something else somewhere else. Meet a body in the road and they ask, "Where you going?" "Dont know." "What you going to do?" "Dont know." And then sometimes we would meet a white man and he would say, "How you like to come work on my farm?" And we say, "I don't know." And then maybe he say, "If you come work for me on my farm, when the crops is in I give you five bushels of corn, five gallons of molasses, some ham-meat, and all your clothes and vittals whils you works for me." Alright! That's what I do. And then something begins to work up here, (touching his forehead with his fingers) I begins to think and to know things. And I knowed then I could make a living for my own self, and I never had to be a slave no more.

Source: George P. Rawick, ed. *The American Slave: Kansas, Kentucky, Maryland, Ohio, Virginia, and Tennessee Narratives*, Vol. 16. Westport, CT: Greenwood Press, 1972.

Lincoln continued to speak about slavery in the summer and early fall of 1858 in a series of seven debates with Stephen A. Douglas (1813–1861), the Democratic candidate in the state's Senate race. As the candidates debated before audiences throughout Illinois, Lincoln gained a reputation for his stand on slavery. He told people that although he wanted to prevent the spread of slavery in the territories, he did not want to end

"Emancipation." Engraving ca. 1865. Artist Thomas Nast's celebration of the emancipation of Southern slaves with the end of the Civil War. Nast envisions a somewhat optimistic picture of the future of free blacks in the United States. The central scene shows the interior of a freedman's home with the family gathered around a "Union" wood stove. The father bounces his small child on his knee while his wife and others look on. On the wall near the mantel hang a banjo and a picture of Abraham Lincoln. Below this scene is an oval portrait of Lincoln and above it Thomas Crawford's statue of "Freedom." On either side of the central picture are scenes contrasting black life in the South under the Confederacy (left) with visions of the freedman's life after the war (right). At top left, fugitive slaves are hunted down in a coastal swamp. Below, a black man is sold, apart from his wife and children, on a public auction block. At bottom, a black woman is flogged and a male slave branded. Above, two hags, one holding the three-headed hellhound Cerberus, preside over these scenes, and flee from the gleaming apparition of Freedom. In contrast, on the right, a woman with an olive branch and scales of justice stands triumphant. Here, a freedman's cottage can be seen in a peaceful landscape. Below, a black mother sends her children off to "Public School." At bottom, a free black receives his pay from a cashier. Two smaller scenes flank Lincoln's portrait. In one, a mounted overseer flogs a black field slave (left); in the other, a foreman politely greets black fieldworkers picking cotton. (Library of Congress.)

slavery in the South. Lincoln's statement that the institution of slavery was "a moral, a social, and a political wrong" distinguished him from Douglas.

Although Lincoln lost a close race to Douglas in 1858, he gained a national reputation as a moderate on the question of slavery because he opposed the expansion of this institution. Lincoln also favored colonization, sending freed slaves or free blacks to Africa, because he believed that blacks were not the equals of whites. In 1860, Lincoln supported the Republican Party platform because it stated that neither Congress nor a territorial legislature had the authority to extend slavery in any of the country's territories. At the 1860 Republican Convention, Lincoln became the party's candidate for president and on November 6, 1860, he was elected president.

Lincoln, Emancipation, and the Beginning of the Civil War

The news of Lincoln's election was met with a variety of reactions in the country. Southerners disliked his opposition to the expansion of slavery and feared that he would try to free their enslaved laborers. Many northern Democrats hoped that the new president would not emancipate the country's slaves because they did not want to see blacks become free. Laboring whites also worried that blacks, if freed, would move to the North and compete for jobs. Greater competition for jobs would lead to lower wages and higher unemployment. On the opposite end of the political spectrum, radical Republicans and abolitionists—white and black—welcomed the news of Lincoln's victory and began to pressure the new president to free the country's slaves.

On March 4, 1861—the day of his inauguration—Lincoln knew that he faced a challenge to his authority as president. Between January 13, 1860, and February 1, 1861, South Carolina, Mississippi, Florida, Alabama, Georgia, Louisiana, and Texas seceded from the Union. In his inaugural address, Lincoln tried to reassure Southerners when he said, "I have no purpose directly or indirectly to interfere with the institution of slavery in the States where it exists." Lincoln took a firm position against secession and told residents of the Southern states that they did not have the right to leave the Union.

After the April 12, 1861, attack on Fort Sumter and the beginning of the Civil War, Virginia, Arkansas, North Carolina, and Tennessee left the Union. Lincoln worked to keep the border states of Delaware, Maryland, Kentucky, and Missouri loyal to the United States. The president informed residents of these states that the North entered the conflict to preserve the Union, not to free the slaves. Lincoln also directed these words to Northerners who did not want to fight a war to free black men, women, and children.

In spite of Lincoln's public stand, the concerns about slavery and emancipation remained a prominent part of the war. To keep the border states from seceding, on September 2, 1861, the president nullified the freedom that Gen. John C. Fremont (1813–1890) gave to slaves in Missouri. The following year, Lincoln retracted the freedom that Gen. David Hunter (1802–1886) had promised to enslaved laborers in Georgia, Florida, and South Carolina.

Emancipation also remained an issue because Lincoln began to formulate plans about the best way to end slavery in the country. Lincoln moved slowly and carefully because he knew that he had to retain the loyalty of slave owners who lived in the border states. In December 1861, the president drafted a plan in which Delaware's slave owners would receive financial compensation for any slaves they freed. A second proposal included the possibility that the federal government would help cover the costs of compensation. News of opposition to both plans prevented the introduction of the bills in the Delaware legislature.

Lincoln and the Emancipation Proclamation

In 1862, President Lincoln began to view emancipation as a key part of his plan to win the war. He knew that he needed to bolster morale in the North, find additional men to fight, and prevent the South from gaining diplomatic recognition from European countries. A plan to emancipate slaves would appeal to the country's abolitionists, who in turn would help blacks to join the Union Army. The offer of freedom to Southern blacks would give the North a second cause for fighting the war. Lincoln knew that European countries, including England, would not support the South and its effort to preserve slavery.

On April 16, 1862, Lincoln signed a bill that abolished slavery in Washington, D.C. The legislation continued two provisions designed to gain support of members of Congress. First, slaveholders received compensation for each slave who became free. Second, former slaves could receive money to help pay for their voluntary immigration to either Haiti or Liberia. Two months later, on June 19, 1862, Lincoln signed legislation that prohibited slavery in U.S. territories. This plan did not include compensation for slaveholders in the territories.

Next, Lincoln turned to a bolder plan. On July 13, 1862, the president discussed a draft of the preliminary Emancipation Proclamation with two members of his cabinet, Secretary of State William H. Seward (1801–1872) and Secretary of the Navy Gideon Welles (1802–1878). Nine days later, on July 22, Lincoln read the plan to his entire cabinet. Lincoln proposed the emancipation of slaves held in areas in rebellion against the Union. After listening to the president, Seward urged him to wait for a Union victory before he announced the proclamation.

On September 22, 1862—five days after the Union victory at the Battle of Antietam—Lincoln issued a preliminary Emancipation Proclamation. The president began this decree with a reminder that the goal of the war was to restore the rebellious states to the Union. He offered financial compensation to Southerners who resided in states that rejoined the United States and voluntarily adopted a plan for either immediate or gradual emancipation of their slaves. Lincoln also noted that the federal government would work to colonize blacks who consented to move to another country on the North American continent or elsewhere. Next, Lincoln announced his intention to free all people held as slaves in rebellious states on January 1, 1863.

The reaction to Lincoln's promise to free slaves on the first day of 1863 was overwhelmingly negative, even in the North. Many Northerners now believed that the purpose of the war was to free slaves, not to preserve the Union. Even many abolitionists disliked the preliminary Emancipation Proclamation because it did not free slaves held by bondage in the border states. Abolitionists realized that no slaves would be freed if the Confederate States ended their rebellion by the end of 1862. Some abolitionists worried that Lincoln would bow to public pressure and decide not to issue the final Emancipation Proclamation.

Lincoln followed through on the promise he made in the preliminary document because none of the Confederate states rejoined the Union and no Confederate slaveholders therefore received compensation for their slaves. On December 31, 1862, and early on January 1, 1863, the president made final revisions to the Emancipation Proclamation. That evening, telegraph operators in the Department of War sent out the text of the document over the wires.

The president began the Emancipation Proclamation with a reminder that he promised freedom on January 1, 1863, to slaves held in rebellious states. Lincoln also stated that he issued the document based on his authority as commander in chief of the army and navy. The president reiterated his belief that his decision to emancipate slaves was a wartime measure that would end the rebellion.

Next, Lincoln listed the states in rebellion against the Union: Arkansas, Texas, Mississippi, Alabama, Florida, Georgia, South Carolina, and North Carolina. Enslaved men, women, and children in these areas became free on January 1, 1863. In addition, slaves in portions of Louisiana and Virginia also received their freedom. Slaves in Union-controlled areas of Louisiana and Virginia as well as the border states remained the property of their owners.

The president asked the emancipated slaves to refrain from violence, unless in self-defense, and to find jobs. More important, the Emancipation Proclamation paved the way for the introduction of African American soldiers into the U.S. military. Lincoln noted that the former slaves would be welcomed in the Union Army and Navy. In conclusion, Lincoln stated he believed the Emancipation Proclamation was an act of justice and a measure acceptable under the provisions of the U.S. Constitution because it was a military necessity. Lincoln also invoked "the considerate judgment of mankind, and the gracious favor of Almighty God."

Reaction to the Emancipation Proclamation

After hearing the news of the Emancipation Proclamation, Northern blacks and whites went to churches and meeting halls to celebrate the news. For abolitionists—black and white—it was a time to celebrate what they had worked for more than 30 years to achieve.

Although many abolitionists disliked the fact that President Lincoln issued the Emancipation Proclamation as a wartime measure, it was clear that this decree helped the Union's cause in the Civil War. As news of the Emancipation Proclamation spread, reactions overseas and in the United States reflected the role this document played as a wartime measure. Although many British industrialists purchased Southern cotton for their mills and even expressed sympathy for the Confederacy, England did not recognize the Confederate States of America as a separate country. To acknowledge the independence of the Confederacy would have required England to support slavery, an institution that it already had abolished.

After the Emancipation Proclamation, the Union Army accepted black soldiers from both the North and the South. In May 1863, the War Department established the Bureau of Colored Troops. The 54th Massachusetts Colored Regiment, led by Robert Gould Shaw, was the first all-black regiment (although the officers were white). In 1864, the members of this regiment as well as other groups of black soldiers received pay equal to that of white soldiers. By April 1865, more than 185,000 former slaves had fought against the Confederacy.

Extending the Promise of the Emancipation Proclamation

Many abolitionists saw the Emancipation Proclamation as just a first step in the struggle to end slavery in the United States because it did not end enslavement in Delaware, Maryland, Kentucky, Missouri, and the areas occupied by Union forces. Lincoln's actions in 1864 and 1865 indicate that he also believed that the wartime promise of freedom had to become an act of justice guaranteed to all slaves. In 1864, the president suggested that the Republican Party should include a call for a constitutional amendment to end slavery.

The Republicans debated Lincoln's request and devoted a section of the 1864 party platform to a discussion of slavery. The third plank in the platform stated that slavery was the cause of the rebellion and that justice and national safety required the end of slavery. The party advocated a constitutional amendment to end slavery forever. The fifth statement was an endorsement of Lincoln's decision to issue the Emancipation Proclamation and to allow former slaves to serve as Union soldiers.

After Lincoln's November 8, 1864, reelection, Congress turned to work on a constitutional amendment to abolish slavery. On January 31, 1865, Congress approved the Thirteenth Amendment. Lincoln signed the amendment the following day, and it was sent to the states for approval. The president did not live to see the December 18, 1865, ratification of the Thirteenth Amendment. Six months later, in June 1866, Congress passed the Fourteenth Amendment to the Constitution. This measure prohibited states from denying citizens the "equal protection of the laws," required states to allow black men to vote or risk a reduction in representation in Congress, and prohibited some former Confederates from holding state or national office. The Fourteenth Amendment became part of the Constitution on July 1868. Seven months later, in February 1869, Congress approved the Fifteenth Amendment, a measure that declared that citizens could not be denied the rights of citizenship because of their race, color, or previous condition of servitude. The states ratified this amendment in March 1870. By the late 19th century, however, many former Confederate states ignored the U.S. Constitution and relied instead on discriminatory Jim Crow state constitutions. They used violence, intimidation, poll taxes, and grandfather clauses to deny basic rights to black men. These limits on freedom existed for African Americans until the 1960s and the passage of the Civil Rights Acts.

FURTHER READING

"Africans in America; Judgement Day; Resource Bank; The Civil War and Emancipation," PBS. At www.pbs.org/wgbh/aia/part4/4p2967.html.

"Featured Documents: The Emancipation Proclamation," National Archives and Records Administration. At www.archives.gov/exhibits/featured_documents/emancipation_proclamation/.

Franklin, John Hope. *The Emancipation Proclamation*. Wheeling, IL: Harlan Davidson, 1995.

Franklin, John Hope, and Alfred A. Moss Jr. *From Slavery to Freedom: A History of African Americans*. 8th ed. New York: Alfred A. Knopf, 2003.

Klingaman, William K. *Abraham Lincoln and the Road to Emancipation, 1861–1865*. New York: Viking, 2001.

"Primary Documents in American History: Emancipation Proclamation," Library of Congress. At www.loc.gov/rr/program/bib/ourdocs/EmanProc.html.

JULIE RICHTER

F

FAUNAL REMAINS. Faunal remains are bones, teeth, claws, hooves, scales, and **shells** from nonhuman animals that are found on archaeological sites. These remains are analyzed by zooarchaeologists, who use type collections of faunal remains to identify the fauna by species, element, age, sex, processing method, cut of meat, and amount of edible meat. The goal is to determine the relative importance and the exploitation level by humans over time of animal resources as **food**, tools, or other cultural functions. The study of faunal remains recovered from slave contexts has focused primarily on diet and nutrition, but research has provided insights into social stratification, for example, status, ethnicity, gender, and racism, and the genesis of "soul food." In addition, faunal remains were used by slaves for nondietary functions such as needles, **buttons**, jewelry, musical instruments, **medicine**, protective **charms**, and decoration on **graves**. Information on slave diet has been documented in plantation diaries and journals, the Works Progress Administration's (WPA) Federal Writers' Project oral interviews with former slaves conducted in the 1930s, and through archaeological investigations. The archaeological investigations have focused on Southern **slave quarters**, uncovering a more diverse diet than what has been documented in the written records.

Historical documents, like planters' diaries or account books, often outline food **rations** given to enslaved African Americans, such as cornmeal, beans, molasses, and pork that was salted or smoked. Most allotments were either raised on the same farms and plantations or were purchased by the master from local markets. Some historians have used planters' diaries to argue that enslaved African Americans' diets and health were extremely poor, lacking adequate caloric and nutrient intake and resulting in severe health problems. This would have included higher rates of infant mortality and malnutrition. Overall, the quality and quantity of food consumed by slaves varied greatly by region, urban versus rural context, size of farm or plantation, age, gender, and job duties, status within the agrarian economy and within the slave community, and the master's or overseer's personality and generosity. For example, slaves who worked in the Big House **kitchen** or in urban areas are thought to have had greater access to food than field hands on large plantations.

The planters' diaries and account books only record what the plantation owner provided as rations. They do not describe the quality of food, how it was distributed to

---

Hunting

As Reuben Fox, a former Mississippi slave, attested, hunting wild game provided an important supplement to the diet of the enslaved:

> The biggest fun what the men had on the place was going hunting. Game wasn't scarce like it is now, and they could keep the kitchen supplied with everything such as coons, possums, squirrels, and rabbits. Once I went hunting and killed a rabbit just as he was comming out of a hole in the grave yard. Everybody what ate a piece of that rabbit got sick. When ever I wanted to make two bets, all I had to do was catch me a nice big terrapin. The white folks loved terrapin soup, and they would always buy them from me. All of us was allowed to keep any money we made.

Source: George P. Rawick, ed. *The American Slave: Mississippi Narratives*, Supp. Ser. 1, Vol. 7, Part 2. Westport, CT: Greenwood Press, 1978.

---

each slave, or how the slaves supplemented these allotments with additional resources. The WPA interviews and a small number of autobiographies offer a slave's perspective of their diet. These testimonies highlight pork as the most common meat, including pork by-products, such as grease or lard, that were added to vegetables and bread. Other rationed meats included beef, mutton, goat, and poultry such as **chicken**. Goat was often requested by some slaves because it was part of their traditional foodways in West Africa. After **pigs**, chickens were next in importance for both their meat and eggs. Beef and mutton constituted only a small portion, if any, of the daily rations. In some instances, little or no meat was given as part of the food allotments, and when it was provided, it often was tainted or included the lowest quality cuts of meat or offal, for example, organs, feet, heads, and intestines. In coastal regions, meat allotments were replaced by **fish**.

The WPA oral interviews, along with archaeological research, have shown that a slave's diet was not limited to the planter's rations, but included more diverse foods, including domestic animals or produce raised by enslaved African Americans in adjacent animal pens or **gardens** and wild resources gathered or hunted in nearby fields and forests. Many masters encouraged their slaves to obtain or raise their own food because this reduced the amount that they would need to spend on rations. Pigs and chickens were the most common animals owned and raised by slaves. Surplus produce and eggs were sold by slaves in the local markets for foodstuffs or material goods that were not provided by their masters, and they also were traded to their owners in exchange for **clothing** or even cash. Occasionally, the money generated could be saved to buy freedom for themselves or a family member.

Slaves had access to guns as part of their work, for example, to scare or shoot crows from the fields, or to hunt wild game for their owners. While doing either of these tasks, they sometimes could obtain other animals for their personal use. Archaeological evidence supports this with both ammunition and gun parts recovered from slave

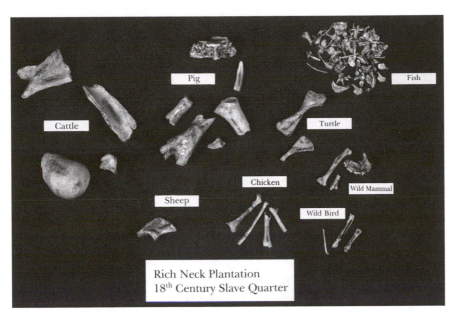

Faunal remains from the Rich Neck plantation site, Williamsburg, Virginia. (The Colonial Williamsburg Foundation.)

quarters along with a wide array of wild species, including deer, turkey, raccoons, opossum, rabbit, and turtles. In some localities, fish and other aquatic resources such as mussels were also a major element in the slave diet. Fishing with a line, net, or trap and foraging for mussels, oysters, or crabs were performed as part of their work assignments or were conducted during free time on Sundays or late in the day.

A final method used to supplement the slaves' rations was stealing. The WPA interviews document the common occurrence of unauthorized killing of pigs, chickens, and calves by enslaved African Americans from the same plantation. As part of the master's "property," some slaves justified their action as just redistributing their master's assets. Others saw it as a form of payment for their work and service or a necessity to survive an inadequate diet.

Comparative archaeological studies of selected Southeastern plantations have addressed the diversity in diet and the cuts of meat between planter, overseer, free white artisans, and the enslaved. General dietary patterns have been identified and marked differences have been linked to status levels or ethnic identity. Investigations at the Nina Plantation in Pointe Coupee Parish in central Louisiana provide evidence for how economics and ethnicity affected the diet of pre-emancipation and post-emancipation African Americans. Differences were best represented by the changing proportions of meat cuts and species of animals. In particular, distinct ethnic foodway patterns were identified between the French planters and antebellum African-American residents. French planters had access to high- and low-quality cuts of beef and ate little pork. In contrast, antebellum African Americans at Nina Plantation consumed little beef but had access to all varieties of pork cuts.

At Cannon's Point Plantation in coastal Georgia, a distinct difference in the percentage of wild species and cuts between the enslaved and planter households has been documented from archaeological remains. Wild game represented nearly 50 percent of the slave's protein, which was nearly double the planter's diet. For domestic livestock, meat processing and specific elements were distinctly different. The enslaved and overseer's faunal remains normally were processed with cleavers for "one-pot" or communal meals, such as **stews** and **gumbo**, and the cuts of meat were of lesser nutritional value. In contrast, the planter's household had sawn bones for individual cuts of high-quality meat. Linked to this processing difference, the enslaved households also had a statistically higher frequency of bowls than flatware when compared with the planter assemblage, which had more plates than bowls. The butchering method and vessel form differences suggest that stews and gumbos were more frequently eaten by the enslaved. These foodways patterns were not universal, however.

On farms and plantations with small slave populations, there may have been little to no difference in the domestic cuts of meat consumed by the planter family and the slaves, but the slaves continued to have a greater diversity of wild species. Over time, archaeological evidence suggests a general shift in the slave diet from a heavy reliance on wild resources during the colonial period to an increased importance of domestic species by emancipation. This shift was probably the result of improved access to domesticated foods or more limitations and control by slave owners over their bondpeople's freedom to hunt and gather their own food.

Food was caught within the dominance and resistance relationship between master and slave. Slave owners would use rations as motivation to promote obedience and a hard work ethic or to punish misbehavior or noncompliance. In reaction to enslavement and racism, African American slave **cooks**, predominantly women, used their imagination and resourcefulness to create new recipes and dishes, forming a traditional foodways pattern now called "soul food." The term "soul food" was coined in the 1960s and is used in the 21st century to describe African American cooking traditions that extend back to the days of enslavement and formed through a creolization of African, European, and Native American foodways. This food tradition fulfilled nutritional needs of the body as well as sociocultural and psychological needs of the soul, creating personal and community identity in the face of oppression.

The "food" of soul food consists of preparation styles and diet that were developed during slavery. Pork and chicken are the most common soul food meats, including cuts that are typically the most economical. From the pig, these inexpensive elements consist of ears, feet, heads, intestines, and backs, and from the chickens, the wings, necks, backs, feet, heart, and liver. Pork grease was important in cooking the soul food staples of chicken, fish, and potatoes as well as vegetables like **collards** or turnip greens. Wild game are a vital element on the soul food menu and include deer, duck, fish, goose, guinea hen, opossum, rabbit, raccoon, squirrel, turkey, and turtle. The importance of pork in the slave diet is best supported by archaeological research, which has uncovered high frequencies and types of pork cuts yet little beef or mutton, when compared with the planter's diet. In particular, the most common pork cuts have been head and feet, which correspond to today's soul food preparation and cooking traditions.

Nondietary use of faunal remains has been a secondary research topic for most scholars. After consumption, leftover bones and shell were sometimes altered or transformed into tools and jewelry or used in medicine and religious practices. Slaves created tools for their own use or for market production as part of their work tasks, with bone button manufacture as the most common. At the Levi Jordan Plantation in eastern Texas, excavations focused on a row of slave and tenant dwellings documenting a bone and shell carver's workshop in one of these households. This interpretation was based on the recovery of several tools, including pocket knives, files, chisels, and saws, for carving shells and bone, a large cache of both freshwater and marine shells, more than 25 shell buttons, a carved shell cameo, and worked bone fragments such as bone-handled utensils. Adjoining cabins may have included finished bone tools from this carver, including a pendant made from a cock spur and a fly whisk.

The WPA oral interviews have recorded that animal bones or their by-products also were used as medicine. For example, whooping cough was treated with a hog mandible mixed with horse milk, or blood from a land turtle was placed in a cup and then dipped with a **sugar** cube. Flu was treated with a tea made from cow or hog hoofs. Other faunal remains were not consumed, but worn to treat an illness or as amulets/charms to prevent sickness. A mole's feet were tied around a baby's neck to reduce pain during teething, and a rabbit's foot was strung around the neck to keep chills and fever away.

The use of animal bones as charms is connected to ideological beliefs about the afterlife and spirits. In the Chesapeake Bay region, archaeologists have found caches of artifacts in domestic or work contexts of enslaved African Americans. These artifact bundles included a wide assortment of objects, including faunal remains, and were typically placed in the wall or floor near an entrance to protect the slaves from harm and evil spirits. They also could be used in Hoodoo to create a "fixing," or a conjure, to harm someone. In this case, the bundle was placed below the floor near the intended's bed or beneath stairs that they would regularly climb. Again at the Levi Jordan Plantation, another slave and tenant household contained material evidence of a healer or religious leader who may have used Hoodoo rituals. This interpretation was based on a possible conjurer's kit that consisted of faunal remains and various objects, including iron kettle bases, chalk, small **dolls**, and many **nails**, spikes, and knife blades. The faunal remains were represented by bird skulls, an animal paw, marine shells, and four worked pieces that may have been oracle bones. Based on ethnographic evidence from West Africa and the Caribbean, these objects were likely part of a religious ceremony or used in healing practices.

Shells such as those from mussels or conch were also used in African American **cemeteries**. In particular, shells often were placed on or in the grave to help the deceased in their journey into the afterlife. Shells were used because of their link to water, which is the location of the underworld in many West African cultures. The shells made the spirits at ease and prevented them from coming back to haunt the living. Evidence of shell use has been recorded in graves from the African Burial Ground in New York City and the practice of shells placed on the graves still occurs in the 21st century on West African and African American graves, primarily in the Deep South.

See also Beds; Cast Iron Pots; Conjure Bags; Corn; Fetishes; Firearms; Fishing Poles; Food and Foodways; Nets and Seines; Punkah; Sewing Items and Needlework.

FURTHER READING

Bower, Anne, ed. *African American Foodways: Explorations of History and Culture*. Urbana: University of Illinois Press, 2008.

Eisnach, Dwight, and Herbert C. Covey. *What the Slaves Ate: Recollections of African American Foods and Foodways from the Slave Narratives.* Santa Barbara, CA: Greenwood Press, 2009.

Franklin, Maria. "The Archaeological Dimensions of Soul Food: Interpreting Race, Culture, and Afro-Virginian Identity." In *Race and the Archaeology of Identity,* edited by Charles E. Orser Jr., 88–107. Salt Lake: University of Utah Press, 2001.

Heath, Barbara. "'Your Humble Servant': Free Artisans in the Monticello Community." In *"I, Too, Am America:" Archaeological Studies of African-American Life,* edited by Theresa A. Singleton, 193–217. Charlottesville: University Press of Virginia, 1999.

Hess, Karen. *Carolina Rice Kitchen: The African Connection.* Columbia: University of South Carolina Press, 1999.

McKee, Larry W. "Food Supply and Plantation Social Order: An Archaeological Perspective." In *"I, Too, Am America:" Archaeological Studies of African-American Life,* edited by Theresa A. Singleton, 218–239. Charlottesville: University Press of Virginia, 1999.

Opie, Frederick Douglass. *Hog and Hominy: Soul Food from Africa to America.* New York: Columbia University Press, 2008.

Otto, John S. *Cannon's Point Plantation, 1794–1860: Living Conditions and Status Patterns in the Old South.* New York: Academic Press, 1984.

Reitz, Elizabeth J., Tyson Gibbs, and Ted A. Rathbun. "Archaeological Evidence for Subsistence on Coastal Plantations." In *The Archaeology of Slavery and Plantation Life,* edited by Theresa A. Singleton, 163–191. New York: Academic Press, 1985.

Scott, Elizabeth M. "Food and Social Relations at Nina Plantation." *American Anthropologist* 103 (2001): 671–691.

Whitehead, Tony. "In Search of Soul Food and Meaning: Culture, Food, and Health." In *African American in the South: Issues of Race, Class, and Gender,* edited by H. A. Baer and Y. Jones, 94–110. Athens: University of Georgia Press, 1992.

Williams-Forson, Psyche A. *Building Houses Out of Chicken Legs: Black Women, Food, and Power.* Chapel Hill: University of North Carolina Press, 2006.

Yentsch, Anne Elizabeth. *A Chesapeake Family and Their Slaves: A Study in Historical Archaeology.* Cambridge: Cambridge University Press, 1994.

TIMOTHY E. BAUMANN

FENCES. African American slaves designed and constructed a variety of fences that formed an integral part of the landscape. The enslaved built fences on their owners' land to corral animals, to divide property, and to provide boundaries within a single property, such as around groups of **dependencies**. Internal boundaries kept the animals in their pens and out of the **gardens** and separated the house and the **yards**. Fences designated the more private house space, where only certain slaves were permitted. Slaves sometimes built small wooden fences near their homes for vegetable gardens and to raise **chickens**. In the Upland South, the Bluegrass region of Kentucky and the Central Basin of Tennessee, slaves also constructed low stone walls, colloquially called "rock fences."

One type of wooden fence consisted of vertical posts, evenly spaced, with saplings or vines woven between them. Archaeological evidence shows that sometimes these fences were built by the slaves in a circle instead of a rectangle. The most common type of fence for slaves to build was the paling fence, held together with **nails** and created with mostly vertical pieces of wood. Slaves also built fences with vertical posts and mostly horizontal planks. Those constructed for the owner often used new wood and nails, while those made for the slaves' use consisted of salvaged planks and reused nails. Although the enslaved kept vegetables and poultry within fences on their owners' land, they sometimes could use those resources as they wished. If they produced more than they were able to eat or share, the slaves were sometimes permitted to sell the excess either to their owners, those living nearby, or at **markets**. The extent of ownership that the enslaved had over these resources and the profits they made varied throughout the regions and changed over time. These fences and what they contained allowed slaves to exercise some control over material goods and therefore some aspects of their lives. On occasion, slaves even purchased freedom with money made through sales of vegetables and chickens.

Rock fences that the enslaved built in the Upper South consist of two types: plantation and turnpike. Slaves constructed these fences with the limestone abundant in the region. Plantation fences had double walls held together with tie-rocks and were topped with a cap course or diagonal coping. Turnpike fences typically lined either side of a roadway. The two types look similar, but turnpike fences used smaller exterior stones and had fill between the two walls. Rock fences served as property boundaries or contained livestock. This Irish and Scottish style of masonry was passed on to African Americans by itinerant white craftsmen hired to build these fences. Stonemasons frequently supervised enslaved people who did the majority of the work. After emancipation, some African Americans earned their living as stonemasons, continuing to build and maintain these rock fences.

FURTHER READING

Gibbs, Patricia A. "'Little Spots Allow'd Them': Slave Garden Plots and Poultry Yards," Colonial Williamsburg Foundation Research Publication. At http://research.history.org/Historical_Research/Research_Themes/ThemeEnslave/SlaveGardens.cfm.
Murray-Wooley, Carolyn, and Karl Raitz. *Rock Fences of the Bluegrass*. Lexington: University Press of Kentucky, 1992.

KRISTEN BALDWIN DEATHRIDGE

FERRIES. Ferries played an important part in the transportation network that developed during the colonial period and continued to operate into the 21st century. Ferries provided the local connection to the larger Atlantic world network within which many of the early colonies operated and developed. They later served as an important element in the transportation network that developed across the United States.

Slaves played a dual role in the history of ferries in the United States. On one hand, they operated the ferries, first as slaves and later as freedmen; on the other hand, laws under slavery and later during segregation restricted their use of ferries. Operating a ferry was a skilled position that brought esteem to the individual, yet ferries also provided opportunities for slaves to escape. During the Jim Crow era, African Americans continued to work on ferries, but when they rode as passengers, they did so in separate sections of the boats. Segregation did not dissuade African Americans from using ferries to connect their worlds to wider ones, however.

In most of the United States before the Civil War, slaves worked as ferrymen, but their travel on ferries slowly became more controlled by their white owners, who feared the freedom ferries offered. In fact, slaves operated and managed most of the ferries in the South Carolina Low County, and they integrated their own experiences and traditions to make the ferries work. By 1701, African slaves operated various forms of boats along the Savannah River to transport skins from the Native American tribes upriver to trading posts in Savannah. One can assume that the slaves and Native Americans exchanged knowledge of trade routes as well as how to navigate the region's rivers. Also, the Africans used their boatbuilding expertise to adapt colonial **boats** for the needs of trade and travel. Slaves proved to be good pilots for boats that carried goods from plantations to the **markets** in Charleston, Beaufort, and Georgetown, South Carolina.

Africans continued to adapt the river flats and other plantation watercraft to reflect their maritime traditions. For example, many scholars contend that the introduction of the African-derived pirogue (or periagua) provided the first step in the evolution of the ferryboat in the lower colonies. Historical records indicate that both Africans and Native Americans favored the pirogue for early river travel. As both skilled and unskilled laborers, enslaved Africans were critical in the construction of ferries and other boats.

With the expansion of the English colonies and the rise of cash crops in the Southern colonies, planters relied more and more on enslaved Africans for both skilled and unskilled labor, including in the maritime realm. For example, during the 1720s and 1730s, many ethnic Congo-Angolan slaves were members of boat crews. Because they already had learned boating skills in their home country, they translated those skills to the rivers of the Low Country. A skilled boatman was accorded a higher status than other skilled and unskilled positions on the plantation.

In addition to their work in ferry construction, ferry owners routinely used slaves as ferrymen in many British American and Caribbean colonies. For example, the British used slaves on ferries that crossed the "wide estuaries" of their Caribbean colonies. Philadelphia's large slaveholders included the ferry operator who ran ferries between Philadelphia and Burlington, New Jersey; historical records indicate that he used his slaves to operate his ferries. In South Carolina, the earliest ferry charters suggest that slaves staffed several Low Country ferries. Others state that the owner could operate the ferry with slaves or servants.

Work as ferry operators or even as deck hands represented a level of freedom for slaves. For example, ferry tenders were exempt from working on road projects. If a direct white overseer was not present, and this often was the case, the slaves were responsible for collecting the ferriage and ensuring that the ferryboat and equipment were in working order. Because ferries operated 24 hours a day, these slaves most likely lived at or near the ferry site, away from the larger slave community on the main plantation. This added freedom might have included a garden space at the ferry.

In addition to these tangible aspects of freedom, some enslaved ferrymen undoubtedly gained direct contact with travelers from outside their normal social realm. They might meet famous politicians, religious leaders, or ordinary citizens from other colonies who used the ferry. Like enslaved individuals who worked in town as skilled artisans, slaves who operated ferries gained opportunities that most field slaves lacked.

Officials and slaveholders understood that ferries offered an avenue for unsupervised slave mobility. In 1740, the South Carolina Commons House of Assembly passed a "Bill for the better ordering and governing of Negroes and other Slaves in this Province," also known as the Negro Act, which instituted more restrictive controls on slaves. The resulting ferry charters forbade slaves from operating ferries without direct white supervision, which ensured that slaves stayed "in their place" and did not use the ferry for their own means. If a ferry operator carried over any slaves without **passes** or tickets, he was subject to a penalty. White government officials hoped to create checkpoints at ferry crossings where they could apprehend runaway slaves, indentured servants, or deserting seamen. Again, in 1801, the South Carolina General Assembly passed legislation that forbade the transportation of slaves on ferries without the written permission of their owners. That same year, the General Assembly required all ferry keepers to swear an oath to prevent slaves from entering the state. These laws further isolated the slave community from travel and outside interaction, and increasingly made ferries a "white-only" space.

Many other slave states passed laws to control slaves' travel on ferries. In 1831, the Kentucky State Assembly forbade ferry operators along the Ohio River from transporting slaves without the written consent of their owners. To ensure that ferry operators followed the law, the operators had to post a $3,000 bond and pay a $200 fine for every violation. In Mississippi, the General Assembly outlawed slaves from crossing at ferries and toll bridges without the permission of their owners. In 1839, the Virginia legislature established a special penalty against ferrymen who allowed slaves to cross the rivers that bordered the state. These laws, which attempted to exert greater control on slave travel, were part of an antebellum legal system that curtailed African American mobility at every possible avenue.

The operation of Coosaw Island Ferry, Port Royal, South Carolina, illustrates the duality of ferry history for African Americans. Laws restricted blacks' use of the ferries before the Civil War. During the Jim Crow era, African Americans continued to work on ferries but had to ride in separate sections of the boats. In spite of the segregation, ferries in the Progressive Era opened travel to the Sea Islands, integrating the previously isolated Gullah culture into the larger state. Then, in the 1950s, African Americans developed a ferry service as a means to bring social mobility to their communities.

See also Canoes.

FURTHER READING

Cecelski, David S. *The Waterman's Song: Slavery and Freedom in Maritime North Carolina.* Chapel Hill: University of North Carolina Press, 2001.

Fleetwood, Rusty. *Tidecraft: An Introductory Look at the Boats of Lower South Carolina, Georgia, and Northeastern Florida: 1650–1950.* Savannah, GA: Coastal Heritage Society, 1982.

Salo, Edward. "Crossing the Rivers of the State: The Role of the Ferry in the Development of South Carolina, Circa 1680–1920s." PhD diss., Middle Tennessee State University, 2009.

Salo, Edward. "They Can Run the Boat, but Not Ride: Slavery, Segregation and Ferries." *African Diaspora Archaeology Newsletter* (March 2009).

Wood, Peter H. *Black Majority: Negroes in Colonial South Carolina from 1670 through the Stono Rebellion.* New York: Alfred A. Knopf, 1974.

EDWARD SALO

FETISHES. The term *fetish* derives from the Latin term *facticius* meaning artificial, or untrue. As early as the 17th century, Western Europeans used the term to describe supernatural items crafted to protect their wearer or inflict harm. Soon thereafter,

Europeans used versions of this term to describe unfamiliar religious items encountered in the burgeoning Atlantic World. In their accounts of West and Central Africa, the French used explanatory words such as *fétiche*, while the Portuguese used the term *feitiço*, to describe the items used by indigenous people to celebrate life, to protect against cosmological uncertainty, and to channel malevolent forces. Although some religious devotees in West or Central Africa use derivations of "fetish" to this day, the term does little to provide cultural or historical context. At the broadest level, fetish is more closely associated with the Vodun religious tradition with concentrations of devotees in the coastal areas of modern Togo, Bénin, and Nigeria. In the African Diaspora, versions of the term were used in French-, Portuguese-, and to a much lesser degree English-speaking areas to describe mostly portable religious items. Therefore, it is possible to find accounts in which practitioners use versions of the term for items involved in the religious traditions of Candomblé in Brazil, Santeria in Cuba, Vodun in Haiti, and so forth. In modern parlance, the term is used in a manner fitting with the original Latin, thus associating the religious item it defines with less advanced, or in the most pejorative cases, false religious practices. Given the derogatory associations and western origins of *fetish*, whenever possible it is preferable to use locally specific terms for the material culture of the African Diaspora and trace those terms outward from the African continent. One such example of a class of items with such exacting historical and cultural context is the nkisi of West Central Africa.

The BaKongo people use nkisi, or minkisi in the plural, to concentrate cosmological forces, attract the attention of ancestral figures, heal illness, and gain insights into the future. The materiality of minkisi is composite; ritual specialists are engaged to combine wooden statues, iron **nails**, **shells**, blood, and so forth into objects that bridge the divide between earthly and spiritual planes. In terms of physicality, they often take the form of anthropomorphic figurines or *minkisi minkondi*, cloth pouches, or ceramic containers. In turn, these receptacles often contain natural substances, which ritual specialists use in healing rites and ritual processes that generates ancestral power. Minkisi and the substances they contain resist simple definition or description, particularly given that ritual specialists incorporate everyday items into the sacred amalgamations that are minkisi. Nonetheless, the combination of sacred and the profane objects serves as a metaphor for the multiple social fields and personal histories connected by minkisi.

These practices and histories often are associated with the deceased; some argue that the dead embodied in minkisi are lower order figures that fall below ancestors, ghosts, and local spirits in the hierarchy of the dead. Origin accounts for nkisi are numerous and conflicting but often revolve around an unusual birth, which is a common metaphor used throughout West and Central Africa for the balance between the cosmos and earthly planes being out of balance with energies from one spilling into the other. In one version of the origin account of nkisi, Musau (a Kongo woman) gave birth to a human being alongside a leopard, a snake called Muziki, and a lump of chalk. Thereafter, children associated with exceptional births, alongside others invested with cosmological energies, created nkisi as **medicine**, protective items, and objects for channeling cosmological energies. At times these ritual specialists add chalk to the ritual mix to reference this origin account.

In the social world in which minkisi are created, a triangular relationship often exists between the artisan who creates a nkisi and charges it with cosmological energies, the client who commissions the piece, and the object itself. At times, the relationship between artisan and craft is difficult to separate, with little distinction being given between the minkisi and those who manipulate and animate it. Specialists who use minkisi and share their healing power with such objects are experts designated banganga, or nganga in the singular. Banganga use minkisi in the creation and containment of ingestible medicines and salves that are applied directly to the body. Occasionally, the objects containing these sacred medicines are considered to have medicinal qualities in their own right. Given this quality, nkisi objects are described as exerting agency over social situations. One account of the healing process suggests that the nkisi "strikes" the sick and once they are subdued "drags" them through the illness. After a client is healed, the client is expected to honor the nkisi with a gift paid directly to the religious specialist. In turn, the religious specialists are reliant on the nkisi, who are considered to direct clients to their practice. Thus, the composite ideal extends to the social relationships embodied in the nkisi figures. Such social bonds are described as being reinvigorated, as the statue is used through daily acts of veneration and supplication and in terms of the sick, through the continued well-being of a treated patient.

In this system of sacred reciprocity, some sacrifices are given directly to the minkisi. Through reoccurring and frequent worship, minkisi accumulate grain, local oils, flour, meat, sweet sodas, hard alcohol, and water. These offerings are presented to the minkisi and form an exterior patina; its efficacy can be referenced by thick layers and multiple surfaces that materialize the cycling of request, successful outcome, and material reward and payment request. In terms of more public minkisi, these layers of patina are substantial as people gravitate to those minkisi that are considered effective. Alongside these sacrifices, the form of the nkisi works to activate the various element of its composition. Once together, the nkisi serves a defined purpose and taps into specific social domains to collect its powers. Thus specific nkisi are created to articulate with specific regions of the broad BaKongo cosmos. Accordingly, following the logic of assembly outlined, the aesthetics of minkisi are both composite and work to evoke certain deities, or qualities of deities. For example, ritual specialists work to check hot situations that can cause political reconfiguration, rapid economic loss, and social disjunction with cosmological elements representing the balance of the cool. Ritual specialists conversely create and prescribe minkisi with elements of the hot when political action is desired or when profits stagnate. At times, elements of the hot and the cold are combined to create objects that reference a life in balance or a world in harmony. As such, minkisi make concrete the opposition and concordance of life and the fickleness of fate.

Positioned at the thresholds of transcendence and becoming, BaKongo consider minkisi to be in a constant state of motion by delivering messages, directing implorations, and channeling malevolence. They further consider a cosmos in motion with a given society as necessary for cultural reproduction and societal prosperity. In terms of social action, BaKongo charge minkisi with maintaining this fine balance and monitoring the points of transition between the realms of existence. Indeed, BaKongo use minkisi to mediate with displeased ancestors, to keep malevolent deities at bay, or to direct such unwanted attention elsewhere. As powerful guardians of liminal spaces, minkisi often are found throughout domestic spaces in and around the house compound, along paths traversing untamed areas, and in and around agricultural fields where people work on a daily basis. Perhaps it would be more precise to describe these objects as heavily implicated in socializing these spaces.

BaKongo often describe minkisi as providing cosmological foundation points to anchor structures to socialized and relatively safe landscapes, which are considered to be constantly buffeted by malevolent cosmological forces. Some minkisi are located aboveground in freestanding structures that are immediately apparent to passersby and easily identifiable by children who play nearby. These public sacred spaces are points of veneration used daily by devotees, who worship in ceremonies presided over by a ritual specialist and attended by specialized singers or in acts of solitary supplication. The location of other nkisi is known only by those ritual specialists, or heads-of-household who placed them in secret locations. As points of access into the socialized space of the household and points of negotiation with ancestral figures, minkisi are susceptible to people attempting to bring malevolence to their enemies or rivals. The more personal the space monitored and protected by a minkisi, the higher the stakes for keeping its location concealed. BaKongo suggest that misplaced or purloined minkisi hold the potential for the collapse of families or the ruin of an individual. Devotees often are described as sharing subjective and intimate moments of their life with minkisi that in turn serve as long-term life companions and confidants. As items that inhabit such close and subjective spaces, it can be argued the minkisi are closely associated with the maintenance of preferred emotional states.

Just as it is impossible to remove the minkisi from the social world from which they derive animation, it is also difficult to describe these items in isolation. They work in concert, and in the true plural sense of the term minkisi, to provide networks of protection and worship. However, BaKongo consider these networks to be at times fickle and occasionally in a state of flux that causes long-term disruption. Nonetheless, the networks of effective, ineffective, forgotten, and abandoned minkisi can be found in an array of spaces from the homes of kings to the houses of commoners. Minkisi are ensconced at various scales of settlement: bracing individual rooms; overlooking points of physical access to, and exits from, the house compound; monitoring village boundaries; and marking the houses of political elites. The ubiquity of their placement throughout the landscape makes them a part of the bustle of daily of life, as well as making them ever-present in realms of existence often partitioned—in historical and anthropological accounts of the region—from religion. For the BaKongo, such a separation of sacred and profane would be anathema; it would represent a cessation of the state of constant motion embodied by minkisi.

It is difficult to chart the deep historical trajectory of minkisi, as very early oral and documentary sources are sparse for the region. Yet from the accounts of late 15th-century Portuguese explorers and interlopers, there are descriptions of items sharing formal and social qualities to those described. Historical documents are more numerous for the 16th and 17th centuries, and accordingly accounts of minkisi emerge from European accounts of the BaKongo Kingdom. Many of these documents were written by missionaries, who wished to convert the BaKongo to Christianity and curtail the use of minkisi. During this period, the BaKongo Kingdom was heavily involved in the trans-Atlantic trade in captives bound for New World enslavement. The importance of the BaKongo region as a point of exchange for people would build from the mid-17th through early 19th centuries. From 1619 to 1866, an estimated 5.6 million people embarked from West Central Africa, bound for enslavement in the Americas. Although recent historical research suggests that these captives were stripped of most of their material possessions before boarding **boats** for the Americas, elements of BaKongo culture and the history of the region were more difficult for slavers and traders to remove at Luanda Beach.

In terms of modern material culture studies, researchers make forceful connections between the BaKongo region and diasporic religious spaces in locales ranging from Havana to the Bronx to Los Angeles. Similar connections have been made at archaeological sites where objects similar in formal execution and accumulative quality to West Central African minkisi have been recovered at numerous sites inhabited by enslaved Africans in the 17th through 19th centuries. For example, researchers investigating the archaeology of the Charles Carroll house in Annapolis, Maryland, recovered caches of quartz crystals, glass **beads**, pierced **coins**, and ceramic shards decorated with "x" marks. The deposits, associated with a structure occupied between 1721 and 1821, were placed under floorboards in spaces where enslaved individuals worked and lived.

Research linking "x" marks on artifacts and BaKongo cosmographic markings is well known and of long standing in the archaeology of the African Diaspora. Early work was focused on the **rice**-growing Low Country area of South Carolina, where researchers associated x-incised marks found on hand-built low-fired local earthenware ceramics recovered from settings near rivers with nearby communities of enslaved Africans and other blacks. There is much debate over the nature of the incised marks, as well as the contexts from which the ceramic vessels were recovered. However, x-incised items have been recovered from other archaeological contexts associated with enslaved and emancipated individuals. Researchers also associate the x layout with the way in which minkisi are deposited in the ground. In Brazoria, Texas, researchers working at the **slave quarters** at the Levi Jordan plantation recovered four caches of artifacts located at the perimeter of the house in each of the cardinal directions. The caches contained iron kettles, burned iron nails, ash, silver coins, iron wedge fragments, and **shells**, and in composite, the four caches are associated with the dikenga cosmographic marker, often used in concert with minkisi, and even incorporated into minkisi.

Yet the broad range of minkisi forms and composite elements presents numerous challenges to the effort of predicting patterns in related material culture in the Americas. Moreover, the same aesthetic of accumulation that is at the heart of minkisi has been associated with Vodun practitioners in the Bight of Benin region. Therefore, it is necessary to carefully demonstrate the historical entanglements linking African Diaspora religious items with the world of motion embodied in minkisi.

See also Subfloor Pits.

FURTHER READING

Blier, Suzanne. *African Vodun: Art, Psychology, and Power.* Chicago: University of Chicago Press, 1996.

Fennell, Christopher C. "Group Identity, Individual Creativity, and Symbolic Generation in a BaKongo Diaspora." *International Journal of Historical Archaeology* 7, no. 1 (March 2003): 1–31.

Fennell, Christopher C. *Crossroads and Cosmologies: Diasporas and Ethnogenesis in the New World*. Gainesville: University of Florida Press, 2007.

Ferguson, Leland. *Uncommon Ground: Archaeology and Early African America*. Washington, DC: Smithsonian University Press, 1992.

Galke, Laura J. "Did the Gods of Africa Die? A Re-Examination of a Carroll House Crystal Assemblage." *North American Archaeologist* 21, no. 1 (2000): 19–33.

Handler, Jerome S. "The Middle Passage and the Material Culture of Captive Africans." *Slavery and Abolition* 30 (2009): 1–26.

Hill, Shannen. "'Minkisi'" Do Not Die: BaKongo Cosmology in the Christian Rituals of Simon Kimbangu and Simon Mpadi." In *Undressing Religion: Commitment and Conversion from a Cross-Cultural Perspective*, edited by Linda B. Arthur, 25–43. New York: Oxford University Press, 2000.

Isaki, Nsemi. "Sacred Medicines (*Min'kisi*)." In *An Anthology of Kongo Religion: Primary Texts from Lower Zaire*, edited by John M. Janzen and Wyatt MacGaffey, 34–38. Lawrence: University of Kansas Publications in Anthropology, 1974.

Joseph, J. W. "One More Look into the Water: Colonoware in South Carolina Rivers and Charleston's Market Economy." *The African Diaspora Archaeology Network Newsletter* (June 2007). At http://www.diaspora.uiuc.edu/news0607/news0607.html#2.

Leone, Mark, and Gladys-Marie Frye. "Conjuring in the Big House Kitchen: An Interpretation of African American Belief Systems." *Journal of American Folklore* 112 (Summer 1999): 372–403.

MacGaffey, Wyatt. *Religion and Society in Central Africa: The BaKongo of Lower Zaire*. Chicago: University of Chicago Press, 1986.

MacGaffey, Wyatt. "Complexity, Astonishment and Power: The Visual Vocabulary of Kongo Minkisi." *Journal of Southern African Studies* 14, no. 2 (1988): 188–203.

MacGaffey, Wyatt. *Art and Healing of the Bakongo Commented by Themselves: Minkisi from the Laman Collection*. Stockholm: Folkens Museum Etnografiska, 1991.

Norman, N. L. "Powerful Pots, Humbling Holes, and Regional Ritual Processes: Towards an Archaeology of Huedan Vodun." *African Archaeological Review* 26, no. 3 (2009): 187–218.

Thompson, Robert Ferris. *Face of the Gods: Art and Altars of Africa and the African Americas*. New York: Museum for African Art, 1993.

Young, Jason R. *Rituals of Resistance: African Atlantic Religion in Kongo and the Lowcountry South in the Era of Slavery*. Baton Rouge: Louisiana State University Press, 2007.

NEIL L. NORMAN

FIDDLES. Dancing was a central social activity in the Americas commencing with the earliest European colonists, and the musical accompaniment for that dancing was provided by the violin or fiddle. The mastery of the fiddle by slaves was well under way by 1690 when a slave fiddler provided accompaniment at a dance for white people in Virginia. The role of the musician was the only role available to blacks, who were excluded from performing as the dance master or a caller, both common roles at social dances from the 17th through the 19th centuries. Sometimes the fiddle was played together with the quills, which were pan pipes or homemade fifes made from reeds, or the **banjo**. English traveler Nicholas Cresswell witnessed two black slaves playing the fiddle and the banjo together at a Georgia barbeque in 1774.

African antecedents exist for the fiddle in various parts of the continent, such as the West African instrument called the *goge*, but most African bowed chordophones are single-string instruments and normally are not used for dance accompaniment.

Inspiration to Play the Fiddle

Andy Brice first saw his former master play the fiddle in South Carolina:

One day I see Marse Thomas a twistin' de ears on a fiddle and rosinin' de bow. Then he pull dat bow 'cross de belly of dat fiddle. Sumpin' bust loose in me and sing all thru my head and tingle in my fingers. I make up my mind, right then and dere, to save and buy me a fiddle. I got one dat Christmas, bless God! I learn and been playin' de fiddle ever since. I pat one foot while I playin'. I kept on playin' and pattin' dat foot for thirty years. I lose dat foot in a smash up wid a highway accident but I play de old tunes on dat fiddle at night, dat foot seem to be dere at de end of dat leg (indicating) and pats just de same. Sometime I ketch myself lookin' down to see if it have come back and jined itself up to dat leg, from de very charm of de music I makin' wid de fiddle and de bow.

Source: George P. Rawick, ed. *The American Slave: South Carolina Narratives*, Vol. 2. Westport, CT: Greenwood Press, 1972.

Previously enslaved blacks interviewed in the 1930s from the Deep South did describe the use of homemade one-string **gourd** fiddles, played with a stick bow strung with horsehair, at dances. In Texas, Harre Quarls remembered, "I made a fiddle out of a gourd 'fore freedom and larns to play it."

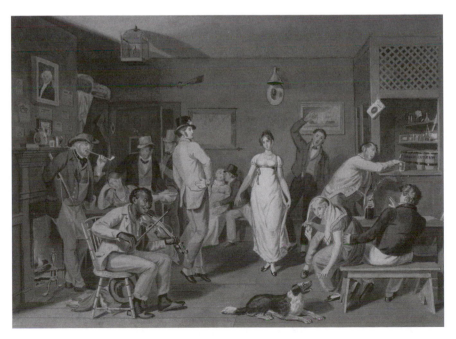

"Barroom Dancing," by John Lewis Krimmel. Dance in a country tavern shows people drinking and dancing while a black man plays the fiddle. Watercolor ca. 1820. (Library of Congress.)

Runaway slave advertisements in colonial newspapers beginning in the 1700s made reference to the skills and reputations of slaves as violinists, fiddlers, and even fiddle makers. It was not unusual for slaveholders to send a promising slave fiddler to New Orleans or another major urban center to be trained in the proper repertoire. Andrew Jackson attended a dance in celebration of his victory during the War of 1812 with a New Orleans–trained fiddler. A slave's ability to provide skilled dance accompaniment increased his value in the marketplace as well as provided increased prestige to the slave owner. Slave owners found value in having a fiddler to provide music for slave recreation as well. One slaveholder kept his fiddler supplied with strings and required him to play a dance every Saturday night.

The ability of slaves to adapt to the European instrument and master the European dance repertoire provided them with a unique access to both money and privilege. In her diary, Mary Chesnut, a South Carolina author, referred to William, a coachman who played fiddle for all her parties and was paid five dollars a night. Solomon Northup, a free black from New York State, was kidnapped and sold into slavery in Louisiana partly because of his value as a skilled violinist. Northup found his musical skills excused him from labor in the fields, provided him with "pipes and **tobacco**, and extra pairs of **shoes**," and spread his reputation throughout the area.

In most cases, the slave fiddler developed at least two completely different repertoires, one for accompaniments at white dances and another for accompaniment at slave dances, often called "frolics" or "sukey jumps." This dichotomy of a separate white and black repertoire was maintained well into the 20th century and can be seen in the recorded output of African American fiddlers Jim Booker (b. 1872–d. unknown) and John Lusk (b. 1886–d. unknown). Booker, from Kentucky, learned to play fiddler from his father, a former slave. He recorded with both the white rural group, Taylor's Kentucky Boys, performing such standard white fiddle tunes as "Grey Eagle," "Soldier's Joy," and "Forked Deer," and his own black string band, the Booker Orchestra, recording tunes from the black repertoire such as "Salty Dog" and "Camp Nelson Blues." Tennessee fiddler Lusk, whose enslaved grandfather was sent to New Orleans for training as a fiddler, led a square dance band in Central Tennessee that regularly played for both whites and blacks, but had tunes that were primarily for a black audience.

Importantly, both Booker and Lusk not only mastered the white repertoire, but were highly popular performers in the white community. The profound changes to technique and approach in rural Euro-American dance music caused by innovative slave fiddlers became such a deeply ingrained part of the culture itself that the music transcended concerns over the race of the musicians in even highly segregated circumstances. Characterized by the hoedown that blends African and European musical elements, historians describe American fiddle music as a uniquely American form that synthesizes black and white musical traditions.

FURTHER READING

Epstein, Dena J. *Sinful Tunes and Spirituals: Black Folk Music to the Civil War*. Champaign: University of Illinois Press, 1977.

Minton, John. "West African Fiddles in Deep East Texas." In *Juneteenth Texas: Essays in African American Folklore*, edited by Francis Edward Abernathy, 291–312. Denton: University of North Texas Press, 1996.

Southern, Eileen. *The Music of Black Americans: A History.* New York: W.W. Norton and Company, 1983.

Wolfe, Charles. *Notes to Altamount: Black Stringband Music from the Library of Congress.* Rounder Records, 1989.

JARED SNYDER

FIREARMS. Firearms are handheld weapons that propel a projectile, usually a lead bullet, at a target by means of a controlled gunpowder explosion. As technical innovations improved the effectiveness of firearms, Americans relied on these weapons to supply themselves with **food** and to provide security against hostile threats on the frontier. Prompted by white fears of armed slave rebellion in the 18th and 19th centuries, many states passed laws that prohibited the use of firearms by slaves or free blacks.

Evolution of the Musket

North American firearms have a lineage reaching back to the Middle Ages. The earliest European firearms appeared in the 14th century and were crude metal tubes packed with gunpowder and a solid projectile fired by placing a lighted match at the weapon's touchhole. The arquebus, as this firearm was called, required a wood or metal stand to aim and shoot. Though primitive and inefficient by later standards, the military arquebus had a faster rate of fire than a crossbow and could penetrate steel armor at short ranges. By the end of the 16th century, gunsmiths introduced technical improvements like the trigger, the stock, the wheel lock, and the flintlock and adapted these innovations to a lighter firearm called the musket. The musket was a long-barreled, muzzle-loaded, shoulder-fired weapon. The musket had been in use in China since the 14th century and in the Ottoman Empire since the 15th century, and by the 17th century, muskets were the standard firearms in Europe and its colonies.

Most early North American muskets were military designs imported from England, Belgium, the Netherlands, and Germany, but by the 18th century, a significant number of weapons were being produced by American gunsmiths. Smoothbore flintlock muskets, and to a lesser extent, pistols, were the most common firearms encountered by slaves and free blacks in colonial America and the early United States. North American gunsmiths adapted popular flintlock designs from European models. Imported weapons like the British Army's Land Pattern Musket, more commonly known as the "Brown Bess," were commonly used during the Revolutionary War era.

Use and Composition

A flintlock mechanism relied on a locking spring-loaded lever called a "hammer," with a clamp securing a piece of flint in its jaws. To fire a musket, the shooter loaded the weapon by first loading a charge of gunpowder along with a wad, which was a bit of crumpled paper or cloth, and a lead ball into the barrel, and then pushing the charge down with a ramrod. Next, the shooter primed the musket by pouring powder in the pan, a small compartment at the base of the barrel. Then the hammer was pulled back, or cocked, which locked it into place. Cocking the hammer was a two-step motion that prevented the musket from accidentally firing, an occurrence known as "going off half-cocked." Once fully cocked, the shooter aimed by bringing the musket to the shoulder and sighting along the length of the barrel. The hammer was released by pulling the trigger. This caused the flint to strike a hinged metal piece called a "frizzen," and the resulting spark ignited the powder in the pan and burned through a tiny hole connecting it to the barrel. This explosion ignited the main powder charge, rapidly expelling the ball from the barrel. The flintlock firing process led to a slight delay between the moment of pulling the trigger and the actual discharge of the weapon, and stray sparks could lead to misfires, resulting in "a flash in the pan" or a premature discharge.

Early musket barrels were usually up to 60 inches long, with greater lengths increasing accuracy and efficiency at the price of added weight and unwieldiness. Lighter muskets, mostly of British manufacture, began to appear in North America in the mid-18th century. These weapons had barrels up to around 50 inches in length, and fired a projectile between 0.60 and 0.70 caliber, which was the measurement of the inside diameter of a firearm. Stocks, the main body of a firearm, to which the barrel is attached, often were constructed of polished cherry, walnut, or maple. American firearms tended to incorporate a variety of parts and fittings culled from different firearms or custom-built to fit an individual weapon. Many of these weapons had brass furniture, which were mountings, such as the trigger; ornate stocks; and large iron screw locks that allowed for easy disassembly and repair. Firearms were extremely valuable to their owners, both as items of craftsmanship and as practical tools, and muskets figure prominently in colonial wills as family heirlooms.

Development of the Rifle

In the 19th century, several technical developments greatly increased the range and accuracy of firearms. Rifling, or a grooved bore that caused a projectile to spiral when fired, increased the effective range of muskets to 500 yards or more and made firearms extremely accurate in skilled hands. The advent of aerodynamic gas-expanding bullets, such as the conical minié and Burton bullets, further increased the range, accuracy, and muzzle velocity of these weapons. Rifled muskets, however, were costly to manufacture and difficult to maintain and were not as common as smoothbore muskets until the mid-19th century. The longrifle, also known as the Kentucky or Pennsylvania rifle, was an exception and appeared as early as the 18th century. The longrifle was a flintlock-rifled musket with an extremely long barrel, some more than 60 inches in length, and it could be deadly accurate in the right hands. Longrifles were difficult to manufacture, however, and were not widely available. Rifles were not in common use until the 1850s and 1860s, when mass-produced military firearms like the American Springfield Model 1861 and British Pattern 1853 Enfield saw widespread use by both Union and Confederate forces. Percussion cap firing systems replaced flintlocks, increasing the reliability of firearms. Percussion caps were small copper or brass capsules coated with fulminate of mercury. Caps were placed on a metal nipple mounted on the base of a musket's barrel and, when struck by the hammer, caused an instantaneous explosion that ignited the charge. More efficient and dependable than flintlocks, percussion caps could be manufactured in vast numbers.

Restrictions on Slave Ownership of Firearms

Slaves and free blacks, like whites, used firearms to provide themselves with food and protection. Americans could supply themselves with shot and powder without too much difficulty, and many came to rely on their muskets for survival. In fact, many colonial and state militia laws assumed residents would be armed and required all able-bodied adult males to present themselves for military service in case of emergency. By the 18th century, however, many colonies and states had passed laws restricting slaves and free blacks from serving in militias and from possessing or using weapons, including firearms. In the 1750s in Louisiana, for example, the French Code Noir prohibited blacks from carrying weapons and authorized punishment up to and including death for violations. When the United States took possession of the Louisiana Territory, American authorities affirmed the Code Noir's restrictions and, as elsewhere, moved to restrict blacks' use of firearms. Maryland and Georgia went further, prohibiting blacks from owning knives, canes, or even **dogs** for fear that these items could be used as weapons. Tennessee amended its constitution to explicitly prohibit free blacks from owning firearms. These actions resulted in part from white fears triggered by armed slave rebellions in the 18th and early 19th centuries. The Stono Rebellion of 1739, for example, resulted in dozens of deaths and inspired additional rebellions in Georgia and South Carolina. In 1775, Virginia's royal governor, Lord Dunmore (1732–1809), proclaimed that he would emancipate and arm slaves who escaped from their masters and enlist in the British Army, triggering fears of racial violence and disorder among Virginia's slave-holding class. The Haitian Revolution of the 1790s involved armed rebellion by the slave population against their French masters, and white Americans in slave states were horrified as the revolt escalated into a full-fledged race war. Slave rebellions in Virginia organized by Gabriel Prosser (1800) and Nat Turner (1831), along with increasing sectional tensions, further reinforced many white Americans' fears of armed blacks and racial violence and led them to prohibit slave use of firearms. Yet, at least in 18th-century Virginia, despite laws to the contrary, slaves were given guns by their masters to hunt for food or to kill predators.

See also Military Equipment.

FURTHER READING

Brown, Christopher Leslie, and Philip D. Morgan, eds. *Arming Slaves: From Classical Times to the Modern Age*. New Haven, CT: Yale University Press, 2006.

Chase, Kenneth. *Firearms: A Global History to 1700*. Cambridge: Cambridge University Press, 2008.

Dubois, Laurent. *Avengers of the New World: The Story of the Haitian Revolution*. Cambridge, MA: Belknap Press of Harvard University Press, 2005.

Morgan, Philip D. *Slave Counterpoint: Black Culture in the Eighteenth-Century Chesapeake and Lowcountry*. Chapel Hill: University of North Carolina Press, 1998.

Parker, Geoffrey. *The Military Revolution: Military Innovation and the Rise of the West, 1500–1800*. Cambridge: Cambridge University Press, 1988.

Usner, Daniel H., Jr. *Indians, Settlers, & Slaves in a Frontier Exchange Economy: The Lower Mississippi Valley Before 1783*. Chapel Hill: University of North Carolina Press, 1992.

Wood, Peter. *Black Majority: Negroes in Colonial South Carolina from 1670 through the Stono Rebellion*. New York: Knopf, 1974.

Worman, Charles G. *Firearms in American History: A Guide for Writers, Curators, and General Readers*. Yardley, PA: Westholme Publishing, 2007.

ANDREW S. BLEDSOE

FISH AND SHELLFISH. One of the most important sources of **food** for many enslaved communities were fish, shellfish, and aquatic reptiles caught on the coasts, rivers, bays, swamps, and creeks coursing through or abutting plantations or small slaveholding farms. Sometimes this catch served as part of the daily or seasonal ration system. Other times it represented food acquired during much-needed leisure time. Enslaved blacks not only caught seafood for their own use, but also often sold the excess as a means of participating in local economies or in a **barter** system with their masters and other members of the planter class. Enslaved blacks drew on a wealth of fishing knowledge brought with them from West and Central Africa. They became well known for their skill, particularly on the coast from Massachusetts to northern Florida, and along the lower Mississippi River valley. From **nets** and net-casting methods brought from Sierra Leone to **basket** traps from Central Africa and hook and line techniques from the Niger River, a substantial amount of maritime knowledge was transferred by enslaved Africans and passed on to their descendants. With fishing came the introduction of styles of fishing vessels familiar to creeks, rivers, swamps, and bays that would influence boat building along the waterways of the eastern seaboard and Gulf Coast.

The most important fish in the life of enslaved people were anadromous species that lived in saltier waters but bred in fresh water and returned each spring and summer to their native rivers and tidal creeks. Of these the one most crucial to the enslaved person's livelihood were several species of herring caught by the thousands and then gutted and preserved in barrels of brine for use as **rations**. Most common in the Chesapeake and Carolina Tidewater, but available to enslaved people across the eastern seaboard, salt herring were a dietary staple found into the Blue Ridge. Those planters who did not have their own fisheries ordered the herring from others like George Washington, who operated a massive fishery on the Potomac River staffed by his enslaved workforce. Charles Ball, a master fisherman from Maryland who was sold into South Carolina in the early 19th century, described a fishery like that at Mount Vernon. Ball was the "driver" of a weir that supplied shad, the next most important fish after herring in the plantation diet. Ball convinced his owner to let him leave the fieldwork by displaying "cat(fish), perch, mullets, and especially two large pikes, that

---

Catching Fish

James Bolton caught fish with poles and basket traps in Georgia:

> Long Crick runned thoo' our plantation an' the river woan' no fur piece off. We sho' did ketch the fishes, mos'ly cats, an' perch, an heaps an' heaps er suckers. We cotch our fishes mos'en genully with hook an' line, but the cyarpenters on our plantation knowed how to make basket traps that sho' nuff did lay in the fishes.

Source: George P. Rawick, ed. *The American Slave: Georgia Narratives*, Supp. Ser.1, Vol. 3, Part 1. Westport, CT: Greenwood Press, 1978.

had been caught to-day and assured them that upon such fare as this, men must needs get fat." Such fisheries processing shad, herring, menhaden, eels, and other so-called trash fish became especially important in the late 18th to mid-19th centuries along the coast of North Carolina as slaveholders specialized in provisioning plantation communities with dried, salted, or brined fish.

Fishing for income might be a way out of fieldwork, but it was highly regulated as a means of controlling enslaved blacks. In many parts of the South, the first group of enslaved blacks brought from Africa introduced fish poisoning, a method that was used by some southeastern Native American groups as well. Portions of a river or creek would be dammed and powerful neurotoxins were allowed to float in the water until all the fish in that portion of the creek floated belly up, stunned, but safe for human consumption. As early as the 18th century, several colonies took measures to include in their laws that regulated slave behavior the regulation that enslaved people were not to poison creeks. Slave codes in Maryland restricted the ability of enslaved and free black fisherman to compete in the fishing industry there, limiting which fish, oysters, and clams they could catch, sell, and market. In Virginia, some locales did not allow enslaved blacks to sell their catch door-to-door, with authorities especially suspect of the lingering African tradition of selling fermented (European travelers just called it "stinking") fish even during times of epidemics of cholera and other diseases.

Regardless of the fact that fishing provided better nutrition and a richer diet, some plantation owners were adamant that their workforce would not be allowed free access to the property's resources. In a famous scene in the escape narrative of abolitionist Frederick Douglass (ca. 1818–1875), a starving black man diving for oysters was shot dead in the water after being accused of poaching another slaveholder's oyster beds. Some planters took the middle ground and required a portion of the catch or made enslaved people request a pass to go fishing on the property. Despite these measures, enslaved blacks supplied much of the fish in Southern locales and became legendary for their "catch and fish" tales.

Judging from the archaeological record, migratory fish like shad, herring, striped bass, and eels were not the only varieties available to enslaved communities. Archaeologists at Mount Vernon have noted that larger species such as sturgeon, often reserved for the planter and his family, were absent from the record, while smaller fish such as perch, catfish, pickerel, gar, and bluegill sunfish were more common. A Polish visitor to Mount Vernon during the late 18th century recalled that blacks preferred the muddier-tasting bullhead catfish, while whites were sold the white catfish, a denizen of cleaner, flowing waters. Such preferences are probably underscored by the fact that fish that lived and lurked in murky water were more likely to be caught by a trap set by an enslaved worker who simply did not have the time or permission to catch species found in more open waters. On plantations near saltier waters, blue crabs, clams, oysters, sharks, mullet, sea turtles, stingrays, gafftopsail catfish, mussels, and occasionally marine mammals familiar to slaves from West Africa, like manatees, entered the diet. In some regions, varieties of diamondback terrapin, a member of the turtle family, were an important addition to the diet along with oysters and the like. In Maryland, so many terrapin were used in the rations at one point in the 18th century that enslaved people were said to go on a legendary strike. Frederick Douglass recalled a plantation larder that provided sunfish and perch from the farm's millpond and "[t]he teeming riches of the Chesapeake Bay, its rock perch, drums, crocus, trout, oysters, crabs, and terrapin were drawn hither to adorn the glittering table."

Fish and shellfish were relished as a source of protein by enslaved communities. Because of their African heritage, preserved fish—salted, dried, or smoked—were important additions to otherwise meatless dishes and were valued for their distinctive flavor. Many enslaved people in the Chesapeake, Tidewater, and Carolina Low Country reported receiving three to four salted herring or an occasional shad per week as long as supplies lasted. Such preserved fish were soaked, hung to dry, and quickly fried in a pan to be eaten with the meager ash or **hoecake** that was their daily bread. Other times, a bit of preserved fish was soaked, drained, and added to a pot of leafy greens, field peas, and the similar produce from their **gardens**. An accumulation of lard or bacon grease permitted an occasional fish fry, social occasions that permitted enslaved people to mingle with one another, and in the case of Virginia slave Gabriel Prosser (1776–1800), in 1800 to foment rebellion. Such fried fish as catfish, perch, sucker, and chub were dredged in cornmeal and inevitably eaten with whatever salt was available and a condiment made from hot pepper. Another substantial Sunday meal might be the one noted by a formerly enslaved North Carolinian who described "catfish stewed with onions" as a popular dish. When Charles Ball ran his master's fishery, he and his men ate large broiled shad each day as their ration. Often times, a simple way to cook such a fish with limited utensils was to wrap it in leaves, tie it tight, and roast it in the ashes of the fire. Fish, crabs, and oysters were used in many of the African-influenced dishes of the Low Country, Louisiana, and the Gulf Coast and formed the main proteins of **gumbos**, **okra** soups, and even groundnut (**peanut**) and **sesame**-based soups.

See also Canoes; Fishing Poles.

FURTHER READING

Ball, Charles. "Slavery in the United States: A Narrative of the Life and Adventures of Charles Ball, a Black Man, Who Lived Forty Years in Maryland, South Carolina and Georgia, as a Slave under Various Masters, and Was One Year in the Navy with Commodore Barney, During the Late War," North American Slave Narratives, Documenting the American South. At http://docsouth.unc.edu/neh/ballslavery/ball.html.

Cecelski, David S. *The Waterman's Song: Slavery and Freedom in Maritime North Carolina.* Chapel Hill: University of North Carolina Press, 2001.

Douglass, Frederick. *Life and Times of Frederick Douglass: His Early Life as a Slave, His Escape from Bondage, and His Complete History to the Present Time.* Reprint, 2nd ed. New York: Bedford/St. Martin's, 2002.

Morgan, Philip D. *Slave Counterpoint: Black Culture in the Eighteenth-Century Chesapeake and Lowcountry.* Chapel Hill: University of North Carolina Press, 1998.

Pogue, Dennis. "Slave Lifeways at Mount Vernon: An Archaeological Perspective." In *Slavery at the Home of George Washington,* edited by Philip J. Schwarz, 111–135. Mount Vernon, VA: Mount Vernon's Ladies Association, 2001.

Roosenburg, Willem M. *Final Report: Chesapeake Diamondback Terrapin Investigations for the Period 1987, 1988, and 1989.* CRC Publication Number 133. Solomons, MD: Chesapeake Research Consortium, 1990.

Singleton, Theresa A. "The Archaeology of Slave Life." In *Before Freedom Came: African-American Life in the Antebellum South,* edited by Edward D. C. Campbell with Kym S. Rice, 155–175. Charlottesville: University Press of Virginia, 1991.

Vlach, John Michael. *The Afro-American Tradition in Decorative Arts.* Athens: University of Georgia Press, 1990.

Wood, Peter. *Black Majority: Negroes in Colonial South Carolina from 1670 Through the Stono Rebellion*. New York: Norton, 1974.

MICHAEL W. TWITTY

FISHING POLES. Fishing poles are long slender rods of wood, cane, or other material, with a line and hook at one end, for use in catching **fish**. Fishing poles would have been used by both adult slaves—primarily men—and children, partly as a way of adding to a rather meager and often monotonous diet of **rations**, but also as a pleasant way to spend the few hours when they did not have to work for others. Slaves in the Carolina Low Country were described fishing with a pole equipped with a line and wooden hook, perhaps much like they or their ancestors had known in Africa. In other cases, hooks might have been fashioned from already existing objects, such as needles or pins. Manufactured fishhooks could have been acquired by slaves with access to money or may also have been issued by a slave owner. Slaves are known to have made fishing lines out of strong grasses.

Many former slaves interviewed by the Federal Writers' Project in the late 1930s recalled fishing and explained the various reasons for this activity. One elderly man, Gus Johnson, remembered going fishing when the weekly rations ran short. Another, John Sneed, mentioned fishing as an activity similar to trapping small game and gathering wild greens, by which slaves could provide **food** for themselves, rather than simply being dependent on what was doled out by their masters. According to others, these activities took place during their time off: typically in the evenings or on Sundays, but occasionally if they happened to be off on a Saturday afternoon. A particularly difficult slave owner might forbid his people to hunt or fish on their own time; others, perhaps for religious reasons, would ban the practice on Sunday. In an unusual case, Hannah Crasson recalled that, as a child in North Carolina before the Civil War, she would go fishing in the evenings with her mistress.

In 18th-century Virginia, it was not unusual for a slave with particularly good skills to fish for a plantation owner's family table. Landon Carter (1710–1778), the owner of a plantation called Sabine Hall, complained in September of 1775 that his slaves had been so sick that there was no one well enough to fish for his family. The slave entrusted with supplying fish to George Washington's table was an elderly man named Jack, who had been born in Africa. Early in the morning Jack would go out on the Potomac River in a light **canoe**, keeping the small vessel in place by tying it to a stake, and catch fish, one of Washington's favorite foods, by using a pole, line, and hook. He—and his catch—were expected back at the kitchen, in plenty of time for the cook to have the fish prepared by three in the afternoon, when dinner was served.

FURTHER READING

Carter, Landon. *The Diary of Colonel Landon Carter of Sabine Hall, 1752–1778*, edited by Jack P. Greene. 2 vols. Charlottesville: Published for the Virginia Historical Society by the University Press of Virginia, 1965.

Custis, George Washington Parke. *Recollections and Private Memoirs of Washington, By His Adopted Son, George Washington Parke Custis, With a Memoir of the Author, By His Daughter;*

And Illustrative and Explanatory Notes, By Benson J. Lossing. 1860. Reprint, Bridgewater, VA: American Foundation Publications, 1999.

"Fly Fishing Tackle," Shelton, CT, Colonial Crafts/Early American Trades. At http://sheltonct.newenglandsite.com/history-crafts.shtml.

Howell, Donna Wyant, comp. *I Was a Slave: True Life Stories Dictated by Former American Slaves in the 1930s*. Book 1: *Descriptions of Plantation Life*. Rev. ed. Washington, DC: American Legacy Books, 2004.

Hurmence, Belinda, ed. *My Folks Don't Want Me to Talk about Slavery: Twenty-one Oral Histories of Former North Carolina Slaves*. Winston-Salem, NC: John F. Blair, 1984.

Larson, Todd E. A. *The History of the Fish Hook in America: An Illustrated Overview of the Origins, Development, and Manufacture of the American Fish Hook*. Vol. 1: *From Forge to Machine*. Cincinnati, OH: Whitefish Press, 2007.

Morgan, Philip D. *Slave Counterpoint: Black Culture in the Eighteenth-Century Chesapeake and Lowcountry*. Chapel Hill: University of North Carolina Press, 1998.

MARY V. THOMPSON

FLUTES. The flute provides a good example of how African musical traditions were brought to the West Indies and Americas and came to have a significant impact on the formation of new musical styles. Flute music played a central role in the musical traditions of many societies indigenous to the western and central regions of Africa, from where so many were taken into captivity for the Atlantic slave trade. Some flutes might have been taken on slave vessels, but otherwise slaves easily could make them from reed cane, tree limbs, and bamboo. As in Africa, flute playing figured in a full complement of religious and secular purposes, and it was also clearly played for entertainment and self-expression.

The African flute shares the basic characteristic of all flutes: it is a cylindrical tube or cone. Generally made of cane, wood, bamboo, plant stem, bone, **gourd**, or metal, there were and are many varieties of African flutes, including one-tone flutes; straight flutes, open on both sides; long transverse side-blown flutes, sometimes with up to five finger holes; and end-blown flutes either with or without finger-holes and notched mouthpieces.

Enslaved Africans adapted their knowledge of flute making to the resources available to them in the Caribbean, South America, and North America. Slaves in Jamaica and Surinam found the wood of the trumpet tree amenable to flute making. Jamaican plantation slaves played a flute that became known as the "Koramanti flute." About one yard in length and with three finger-holes, it had a distinctly beautiful sound, even to European ears. William Beckford (d. 1799) describes it in his narrative, *A Descriptive Account of the Island of Jamaica* (1790): "I have frequently heard these flutes played in parts; and I think the sounds they produce are the most affecting, as they are the most melancholy that I ever remember to have heard. The high notes are uncommonly wild, but yet are sweet; and the lower tones are deep, majestic, and impressive."

Slaves in America also learned to play the European-style transverse flute. In the Caribbean, exposure to European-style fife and drum corps music influenced the tradition of flute and percussion bands, and in the antebellum South, many accounts include positive references to the flute playing in black dance bands that played for slaves and masters.

As Afro-Caribbean, Afro-Latin, and Afro-American styles developed and as European-style music and instruments became more familiar and widespread to slave musicians, the flute, like the violin, provided opportunity for cultural transmission and acculturation. While not quite as ubiquitous as the **drum**, the flute plays a central role in all these genres and in many styles of jazz and pop more generally.

See also Fiddles.

FURTHER READING

Abrahams, Roger D., and John F. Szwed, eds. *After Africa: Extracts from British Travel Accounts and Journals of the Seventeenth, Eighteenth, and Nineteenth Centuries concerning the Slaves, Their Manners, and Customs in the British West Indies.* New Haven, CT: Yale University Press, 1983.

Roberts, John Storm. *Black Music of Two Worlds: African, Caribbean, Latin, and African-American Traditions.* 2nd rev. ed. New York: Schirmer Books, 1998.

LINDA E. MERIANS

"Plantation Melodies." Lithograph by J. H. Bufford and Company, Boston, ca. 1847. (Library of Congress.)

FOOD AND FOODWAYS. The foods created by African Americans in slavery represent a mixture of influences from Africa, the Caribbean, Europe, and Native America. In turn, the foodways developed by enslaved adults directly affected the foods consumed by their children and the ideas about diet and food preparation that these children carried with them throughout their lives. Over time, however, these foods' influences might evolve and change depending on that child's location and relocation. Many factors affected eating patterns: the availability of familiar foods, a new climate, and movements and migrations across time and space, which resulted in a variety of African American eating patterns. These patterns combined several different regional influences, personal preferences, and changes over time. As the slave trade changed between the 17th and the 19th centuries, so African American foodways evolved as well.

Before enslavement, the acquisition of food was a ritualistic part of community life for many West Africans. Everyone participated in preparing the daily meal, from getting the food to cooking it. During the Middle Passage, in which Africans were taken from their homelands and sold into slavery in exchange for money or goods, many captured people experienced starvation, vitamin deficiencies, and even death. Given the trauma of this experience, including having very little to eat except small portions of grains or African yam, goobers (**peanuts**), plantains, or limes, they were malnourished if they lived to disembark. Some slave traders consistently used indigenous African crops, including peppers, herbs, spices, and medicinal plants, to treat illnesses and to sustain their captives during the voyage. Once African people arrived at their destination, they would again have to adjust to new surroundings, including the foods available to them.

The foods of the newly enslaved Africans were highly regulated, carefully watched, and minimally dispersed. This reality meant finding new ways of acquiring enough food to survive. New surroundings, new ingredients, and new utensils with which to cook and eat also meant that African traditions would have to be incorporated with those of the Native Americans and Europeans around them. Africans adopted the customs and traditions of their land and learned to prepare dishes using foods like **corn, collards**, deer, opossum, and potatoes. Considerable archaeological evidence has been found to indicate that slaves preferred hollow containers like bowls and cups. This, coupled with evidence of small, cut animal bones, which generally suggests poor cuts of meat, and the West African preference for liquid-based meals such as soups and **stews**, indicates a continuation of African culinary traditions. What emerged over time were contributions to the culinary lexicon of the Americas that in the 21st century continue to have a lasting impact on the food preferences and diets of all Americans.

Ashcakes and Butter

In Mississippi, Sarah Thomas's mother baked ashcakes:

> I used to hear my mother say how dey baked bread in dem times. I don' know wether any one else has ever tole you 'bout it, specially dis kin' of bread—Ash Cake. Dey would make a big fire wid oak wood, let it burn down to coals and ashes, and when dey made up dere bread wid meal and salt and water dey rake de ashes back and pour in de stiff batter, and kivver it up wid ashes and coals while dey was hot. Dat baked it quick and when it wuz done dey tek it out of de ashes, and wash it off wid clean water, and I tells you It wuz good eatin.'

Foster Weathersby learned to churn butter in Mississippi:

> My first wuk as a slave-child was when I was a little chap. Dey made me churn out in de back yard under de big trees. De churn was big an' tall, an' hel' gallons of milk. I had to churn, and churn, and den churn some mo'; dey just never would, look lack, let me stop; dey made me walk 'roun' and 'roun' dat churn. I jes natu'ally growed to lak dat job.

Source: George P. Rawick, ed. *The American Slave: Mississippi Narratives*, Supp. Ser. 1, Vol. 10, Part 5. Westport, CT: Greenwood Press, 1978.

The significance of this culinary influence reveals itself when the myth of all Africans and their descendants having eaten the same food is ignored. The reality of different systems of slavery makes this belief both unrealistic and impossible. Slavery varied from time period to time period and from place to place, directly affecting the economics of a plantation or farm. While archaeologically recovered **faunal remains**, along with planter's letters and diaries, reveal that, by and large, slaves, depended on a core group of foodstuffs for their survival, the variability of these foods was as extensive as the range of their availability. Plantation diets varied greatly, even though they were sparse, and much depended on the provisions given to the enslaved population by a plantation owner. According to **slave narratives**, planters' journals and letters, and travelers' diaries, most slaves were allotted a small portion of meal, molasses, low cuts of pork, and sometimes coffee. Meals and their components depended on the rations provided by slaveholders, **work routines** that may or may not have left time to cultivate **gardens**, hunt, or fish, and weather conditions in specific geographic locations. For example, in the Carolina Low Country, some enslaved Africans arrived with the knowledge of how to plant and process **rice**. Undoubtedly, rice was often part of the diet consumed by the enslaved in the Low Country whether it was given to them or they managed to pilfer enough for their own consumption. The French influence in Louisiana is mirrored in archaeologically recovered faunal remains that reveal consumption of various amounts of beef and pork by Africans and their descendants over an extended period of time. If rivers, lakes, and streams were nearby, freshwater **fish** such as catfish, bass, carp, and perch could augment **rations**. Many slaves in the Mid-Atlantic supplemented their rations by hunting wild game such as deer, squirrel, rabbit, opossum, turkey, capon, and other fowl and also raised **chickens** that they both ate themselves and sold to their masters and in local **markets**. This, in turn, sometimes meant that eggs could be added to their diet. Wild berries, greens like pokeweed, and nuts round out the foods that could be located in the woods and other surrounding areas.

In addition to differences in geographic locations, differences in work and nonwork time affected the amount of time that enslaved people had to acquire additional food. Some planters allowed their slaves to cultivate their own **gardens** and raise livestock, which provided vegetables and chicken. Still other enslaved people were given permission to hunt or took it upon themselves to hunt in nearby woods to supplement their diets. These activities were limited, however, because many plantation owners thought these tasks took time away from work. Whether enslaved African Americans were able to undertake these activities, however, depended on whether their owners tolerated or even allowed them. In addition, work routines used in different parts of the country governed how much personal time slaves had to tend to a garden or hunt. For example, the work done on the rice and **cotton** farms of Georgia was organized using the task labor system in which slaves were assigned specific tasks. Once these tasks were completed, enslaved laborers could use whatever time remained in the day for their own purposes. In these locations as well as on plantations and farms where enslaved workers were not required to work on Sundays and holidays, food acquisition—hunting, fishing, gardening, tending livestock, and foraging— occupied some of that time. Travelers' accounts and slave narratives from the 18th and 19th centuries documented the existence of these practices. Slaves who worked in the houses of their owners sometimes were afforded treats like tea, coffee, molasses, and brown sugar, but even these foods were primarily holiday treats.

Several other forms of food acquisition were used by African women and men both enslaved and free: hawking, bartering, and trading as well as theft. Once their assigned work was completed, and if the owner agreed, enslaved people could participate in commercial activity. Hucksters and hawkers bought and sold barnyard fowl, eggs, honey, berries, melons, shrimp, oysters, and other goods they acquired to sell or that they made. Some sold goods they made like wooden stools, ceramic pots, or sweetgrass **baskets**. Oftentimes, they would sell or barter these goods to their owners. In some rare instances, these enslaved men and women saved enough money to purchase their own freedom or that of their family. This tradition of selling food continued through and after the Civil War. One of the best-documented cases of such practices is found in Gordonsville, Virginia, among a group of women who called themselves "Waiter Carriers." One magazine observer described their occupation in this way:

> Upon the arrival of our special train we were surrounded with a swarm of old and young negroes of both sexes, carrying large servers upon their heads, containing pies, cakes, chickens, boiled eggs, strawberries with cream, ripe cherries, oranges, tea and coffee, biscuits, sandwiches, fried ham and eggs, and other edibles, which they offered for sale.

Like their predecessors who bought their freedom, generations of these food vendors used their earnings to build houses for their families, open restaurants, and feed community members who were without food.

Slave owners often thought that their enslaved workers stole provisions and then sold those provisions in local markets. This idea was most prevalent in instances in which the market activities of slaves and free blacks affected the profits of white merchants. Laws regulating how, when, and what foodstuffs could be sold by blacks were regularly enacted because it was presumed that these goods were acquired illegally. However, these laws were sporadically enforced and often ignored. When livestock like chickens, fowl, pigs, sheep, turkeys, or geese were missing, it was easy to accuse blacks of stealing because these animals tended to roam free and were difficult to find when they wandered. African Americans did, in fact, steal out of hunger. They took foods like corn, cabbage, and potatoes from gardens, livestock from coops and pens or wandering about, and corn and rice from troughs. As abolitionist Frederick Douglass (ca. 1818–1895) noted in his narrative, some slaves stole simply because they thought it was their right to do so. But others stole food because of hunger: it was part and parcel of the imperative to survive.

But the accusation of theft was a tool of control used not only against slaves but also against free blacks and fugitives. Newspapers and other sources often spoke with contempt of poor free blacks, in particular indicating that they "rely upon their ingenuity in rascality" and are "lazy" and therefore steal. Even the Waiter Carriers were accused of stealing the recipe for their famous fried chicken from other vendors, thus denying their own creativity and talents.

But African Americans have always exercised inventiveness as it relates to food, far beyond the simple idea of cooking and consuming pork scraps. Black men and women, both slave and free, found ways to make money by catering and serving food in dining establishments as well as on street corners. They ran restaurants, cafes, boardinghouses, oyster houses, lodges, and inns. In Virginia, George Washington's enslaved cook, Hercules, cooked for Washington both at Mount Vernon and, after he was elected president, in Philadelphia. Thomas Jefferson (1743–1826) brought James Hemings (1765–1801), brother of Sally Hemings (ca. 1773–1835), to France in 1784, where he was apprenticed to learn cooking. Upon their return to the United States in 1791, Hemings continued to cook for Jefferson in Philadelphia and then, finally, at Monticello. In the 18th century, Samuel Fraunces (ca. 1722–1795), a West Indian nicknamed "Black Sam," was the owner and operator of Fraunces Tavern in New York City, a famous haunt of George Washington, and he later worked in Washington's Philadelphia household. This century also bore witness to further selling and hawking of street food—cooked rice, cakes, candies, oysters—by women and men from Savannah to Baltimore. Black butchers, pastry chefs (who also made tarts, fruitcakes, puddings, and candy), and greengrocers were making a living in the world of commercial food.

As early as 1827, African American authors began documenting their roles in the world of hospitality when Robert Roberts published *The House Servant's Directory*. Roberts was butler at Gore Place, the home of Massachusetts Governor Christopher Gore (1758–1827), from 1825–1827. The receipts included in his book, as well as the advice he gives to house servants, reflect the upper-class household in which he worked and of the community in which he lived. Likewise, in 1848, Tunis Campbell (1812–1891), who became one of Georgia's most influential 19th-century African American politicians after the Civil War, published *Hotel Keepers, Head Waiters, and Housekeepers' Guide*, a reflection of his early experiences as hotel waiter and steward in New York and Boston. In 1866, Malinda Russell published what is considered the first cookbook published by an African American, *Domestic Cook Book: Containing a Careful Selection of Useful Receipts for the Kitchen*. Fifteen years later, in 1881, Abby Fisher (ca. 1832–unknown), who was born in North Carolina but who lived in San Francisco, published *What Mrs. Fisher Knows about Old Southern Cooking*, becoming the second African American woman to publish a recipe book.

Oral histories and other sources describe the mistreatment, malnourishment, and hunger that, until very recently, plagued African Americans. Families—enslaved and free—had to survive with meager rations and food supplies. Some enslaved individuals even remembered eating in groups, with several people consuming greens and grains from a trough. At the same time, African American food and foodways history overall illustrates tenacity, ingenuity, and creativity in the ways that foods were stretched, augmented, made tasty and sustaining, and filled with ritual, proper accoutrement, and dignity. Free and escaped blacks lived across the United States throughout the Midwest, West, and New England. This suggests that African American foodways may be more complex because of this national culinary mix. Yet regardless of their origin, African American foods and foodways form a central part of American cuisine, their ingredients and preparation venerable and revered.

See also Cooking and Cooks; Faunal Remains; Pigs and Pork; Pottery.

FURTHER READING

Franklin, Maria. "The Archaeological Dimensions of Soul Food: Interpreting Race, Culture and Afro-Virginian Identity." In *Race and the Archaeology of Identity*, Charles Orser Jr., 88–107. Salt Lake City: University of Utah Press, 2001.

"George Washington's Mount Vernon Estate and Gardens. Slave Lifeways at Mount Vernon: An Archaeological Perspective," Mount Vernon. At www.mountvernon.org/index.cfm/fuseaction/print/pid/243/sti/3/sis/36/.

Hall, Robert L. "Food Crops, Medicinal Plants, and the Atlantic Slave Trade." In *African American Foodways: Exploration of History and Culture*, edited by Anne L. Bower, 17–44. Urbana: University of Illinois Press, 2007.

Harris, Jessica B. *Iron Pots and Wooden Spoons: Africa's Gift to New World Cooking*. New York: Athenaeum, 1989.

Lichtenstein, Alex. "'That Disposition to Theft, With Which They Have Been Branded': Moral Economy, Slave Management, and the Law." *Journal of Social History* 21 (1989): 413–440.

Markell, Ann. "Patterns of Change in Plantation Life in Pointe Coupee Parish, Louisiana: The Americanization of Nina Plantation, 1820–1890." New Orleans: R. Christopher Goodwin and Associates, 1996.

Moore, Stacy Gibbons. "'Established and Well Cultivated': Afro-American Foodways in Early Virginia." *Virginia Cavalcade* 39 (1989): 70–83.

Opie, Frederick Douglass. *Hog and Hominy: Soul Food from Africa to America*. New York: Columbia University Press, 2008.

Wilkins, Sharron. "The President's Kitchen: African American Cooks in the White House." *American Visions* 10, no. 1 (February–March 1995): 56–59.

Williams-Forson, Psyche. *Building Houses Out of Chicken Legs: Black Women, Food, and Power*. Chapel Hill: University of North Carolina Press, 2006, 13–113.

Yentsch, Anne. "Excavating the South's African American Food History." In *African American Foodways: Exploration of History and Culture*, edited by Anne L. Bower, 59–100. Urbana: University of Illinois Press, 2007.

Zafar, Rafia. "Recipes for Respect: Black Hospitality Entrepreneurs before World War I." In *African American Foodways: Exploration of History and Culture*, edited by Anne L. Bower, 139–152. Urbana: University of Illinois Press, 2007.

PSYCHE WILLIAMS-FORSON

FREEDOM PAPERS. Before 1868, when slavery had ended in every state and region in the United States, free people of color were required by law to carry official documents, freedom papers, that verified their free status. Freedom papers were also referred to as "freeman's papers" and "free papers." Issued at the time of manumission, the papers declared freedom for a particular individual as described and were almost always notarized by whatever legal body was in charge, usually the courts. Manumission was granted to individuals and to kinship groups. If, for example, a freeing agent manumitted a family, then the court record typically would list the names of all the freed family members, while each individual of the group received his or her own freedom papers.

The papers served as identification papers for free persons of color that clearly stated and certified that the person was free and not enslaved. Upon manumission, the free person was required to carry his or her freedom papers at all times. The document included the date of manumission; the name of the enslaved's original or last slaveholder; the freedman's name and frequently a brief physical description; a statement of liberty; and the signature of a court representative and possibly the freeing agent, commonly the enslaved's most recent master. Free African Americans were well advised to carry their freedom papers on their person at all times: possession of the document meant the difference between liberty and reenslavement. A free white person could demand to be shown a person's freedom papers as a challenge to the movements or actions of a person of color.

Former slave and noted abolitionist Frederick Douglass (ca. 1818–1895) famously described Maryland's custom and issuance of freedom papers. He explained that free persons of color were required to regularly renew their papers, a process that involved a fee for having the state write the document. The document included the name, age, color, height, and a physical description of the person's shape or unique scars or markings. Douglass acknowledged that the physical descriptions were general enough on freedom papers that multiple people could manage to use a document, as he did, to escape slavery by impersonating the true owner of a particular document. The successful fugitive was responsible for seeing that the document was returned to its rightful owner by mail or by other arrangements. Failing to return the document could imperil the life of the benefactor. The lives of the fugitive and his benefactor were in great danger if the document was discovered to be in the hands of the wrong person.

Other kinds of official documents were produced to certify that men, women, and children were free. For example, birth certificates of children born to slaves could be written for a newborn child by the slaveholder stating that the child was to become free at a future date or was free when the mother was manumitted or some other arrangement that enabled the newborn to prove free status at a later date. This kind of document could be used to obtain state-issued freedom papers later in life. In some instances, enslaved individuals in the Upper South used this type of evidence as support in "freedom suits," where they sued their owners for their freedom in court. Some wills of slaveholders included instructions to manumit particular individuals or groups. The wills often specified when an individual would be manumitted and the conditions for each manumission. Some wills also included instructions about how to finance the manumissions. Others spelled out monetary or material inheritances that were to be made to specific newly manumitted individuals or groups. A "Petition for Freedom" was a formal request from an enslaved individual to a slaveholder via the courts, to recognize that the enslaved individual wanted to receive notice of freedom based on a purchase price, a formal agreement, or other legal arrangements.

FURTHER READING

Douglass, Frederick. *Narrative of the Life of Frederick Douglass: An American Slave, Written by Himself*. 2nd ed. Edited by David Blight. Boston: Bedford/St. Martin's, 2002.
Schafer, Judith Kelleher. *Becoming Free, Remaining Free: Manumission and Enslavement in New Orleans, 1846–1862*. Baton Rouge: Louisiana State University Press, 2003.

JULIA ROSE

FREE PRODUCE. Some abolitionists urged that consumers boycott goods made by slave labor and instead give preference to "free produce," that is, goods made by free labor. Initially championed primarily by anti-slavery Quaker women in the 1820s and 1830s, the

Free Produce movement generated voluntary associations, free produce stores, and efforts to buy, grow, or make substitutes for key slave-grown commodities such as **cotton, sugar**, coffee, and **rice**. Although not successful in diminishing the profitability of slave labor, free produce advocates had some impact in compelling Americans to confront the moral ambiguities of benefiting from slavery by purchasing products of slave labor.

Perhaps the first free produce advocate was John Woolman (1720–1772), a mid-18th-century Quaker from New Jersey. During the 1750s and 1760s, Woolman walked across the Mid-Atlantic colonies, trying to persuade slaveholders to free their chattel. On these trips, Woolman neither slept nor ate in households maintained by slave labor, as a way of maintaining his moral purity. Sixty years later, the Quaker reformer, Elias Hicks (1748–1830), advanced an economic argument that abstention from slave produce would deal a blow to the vitality of slavery. In 1824, Elizabeth Heyrick (1769–1831), a British Quaker, contended that consumers' abstinence from slave-grown sugar would lead to the liberation of West Indian slaves. Heyrick drew her inspiration from British abolitionists' efforts to boycott slave-made sugar in the 1790s campaigns against the slave trade. Heyrick's American readers could find encouragement in the American colonists' successful boycotts of British goods during the Revolutionary-era nonimportation campaigns.

By the late 1820s, support for these views led to the creation of free produce stores.

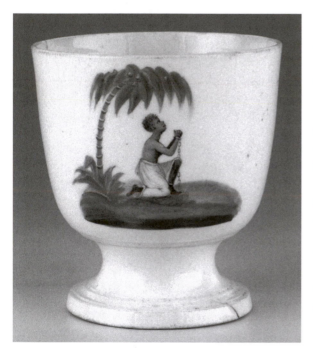

Sugar bowl encouraging the use of sugar made by free labor in the East Indies. England, 1825–1830, porcelain, bone china, enameled and gilded. (The Colonial Williamsburg Foundation. Gift funded by Phyllis M. Carstens; Joan N. Woodhouse; Ann Winter Odette; John F. Orman Jr.; Mrs. Joyce Longworth, Ms. Joan M. Ploetz; Mr. and Mrs. John C. Austin; Mr. and Mrs. Robert Prioleau; Mr. and Mrs. John R. Maness; Mr. and Mrs. Dwight P. Black; Mr. and Mrs. Thomas G. Potterfield.)

Benjamin Lundy (1789–1839), publisher of *The Genius of Universal Emancipation* in Baltimore, noted the opening of a free produce store in that slave state in 1828. The longest-operating free produce store was run by Lydia White, a Philadelphia Quaker, from 1830 to 1847. In all, more than 50 such stores sold free labor–produced goods in more than 20 free state locations, as well as Baltimore, Maryland, and Wilmington, Delaware.

In the 1830s, promoters of free produce formed voluntary associations, often in tandem with the spread of the movement for the immediate abolition of slavery. Philadelphia Quaker women, including Lucretia Mott (1793–1880) and Mary Grew (1813–1896), founded the Female Association for the Promoting the Manufacture and Use of Free Cotton in 1829, aided by Mott's husband, then a cotton commission merchant. Free people of color founded companion organizations in the next two years. The Philadelphia Female Antislavery Society, organized in 1836, urged its members to prefer free produce over its slave-made competition. Support for free produce thus formed an important component of women's entry into organized activity in support of abolition in the 1830s.

But free produce stores faced significant difficulties in obtaining key commodities that had not been grown or harvested by slaves. Importing sugar from Mexico, Java, or Malaya (Malaysia) avoided slave labor, but led to higher priced and often lower quality goods. Efforts to obtain free labor–grown cotton and coffee encountered similar problems. In short, purchasers of free produce had to acknowledge that they paid higher prices than for slave-made commodities.

Attempts to produce substitutes for slave-grown cane sugar, such as by growing sugar beets or tapping maple trees for syrup, failed to attract substantial numbers of customers. Sugarless candies simply did not taste as good to most consumers. Higher prices for purchasing free produce also dissuaded many from participating in the movement. This was especially true for free people of color, who typically had little discretionary income. Frances Ellen Watkins Harper (1825–1911), a prominent black abolition lecturer who supported free produce purchasing, admitted that her lecture fees made it easier for her to opt for free produce than her poorer black counterparts, but she also conceded that free produce cotton was coarser than its competition.

Some abolitionists saw the free produce movement as an impractical distraction. William Lloyd Garrison (1805–1879), editor of *The Liberator*, a major abolitionist newspaper, contended that slaveholders were not moved primarily by economic calculus, but rather by the desire to dominate other humans by holding them as slaves; hence, boycotting slave-made goods was unlikely to weaken slavery. Garrison also claimed that the free produce movement's focus on maintaining the moral purity of nonconsumers of slavery was largely irrelevant. For Garrison, boycotting slave goods achieved nothing of value for the slave and thus nothing of value for the abolition movement.

Most white abolitionists shared Garrison's skepticism, and by the 1840s the free produce movement was in retreat. The World Antislavery Convention of 1840, held in London, rejected a call for its supporters to endorse free produce, and other antislavery bodies followed suit. But black opponents of slavery had views of their own.

In the 1850s, black abolitionists began to evince interest in black immigration to the West Indies and Africa. Discouraged by slaveholders' domination of national politics in the United States, some leaders reconsidered their longstanding opposition to schemes to "colonize" American free people of color to foreign countries. Samuel Ringgold Ward (1817–ca. 1866) promoted the idea of black immigration to Jamaica, and Martin Delany (1812–1885) traveled to West Africa to look into the possibility of black-led colonization movements. Both Ward and Delany claimed that successful colonization could lead to the free black production of sugar and cotton that would undersell and undermine slave-grown products. The onset of the Civil War swept away Ward and Delany's plans, and slavery came to an end without a direct impact from the free produce movement.

FURTHER READING

Bacon, Margaret Hope. "By Moral Force Alone: The Antislavery Women and Nonresistance." In *The Abolitionist Sisterhood: Women's Political Culture in Antebellum America*, edited by Jean Fagin Yellin and John C. Van Horne, 275–298. Ithaca, NY: Cornell University Press, 1994.

Faulkner, Carol. "The Root of the Evil: Free Produce and Radial Antislavery, 1820–1860." *Journal of the Early Republic* 27 (2007): 377–405.

Gellman, David N. *Emancipating New York: The Politics of Slavery and Freedom, 1777–1827.* Baton Rouge: Louisiana State University Press, 2006.

Nuremberger, Ruth. *The Free Produce Movement.* Durham, NC: Duke University Press, 1942.

T. STEPHEN WHITMAN

FRENCH HORNS. Africans became familiar with the French horn, a brass wind instrument, through European contact; in Africa, wind instruments consisted exclusively of woodwinds. Numerous African-born and Creole slaves became proficient on the French horn, along with the violin, **flute**, clarinet, and a variety of other Western instruments. The French horn was a popular instrument in 17th- and 18th-century Europe, and horn-playing African slaves could be found scattered throughout the British colonies, from North America to India. Spanish, Portuguese, and Dutch colonizers and slaveholders also possessed French horn–playing black slaves. It was, however, an unusual accomplishment even among musically trained slaves.

Slaves took pleasure in their ability to express themselves musically on their adopted instruments, adapting African musical traditions, borrowing from European folk music and Anglo-American patterns, and inventing new musical forms. Musical expression was intrinsic to central and western African peoples' cultures, and slaves who could play instruments preserved ties to their roots. Knowledge of how to play a Western musical instrument allowed them to traverse the cultural landscape between the land of their captors and their African heritage, connecting both worlds. Musically trained slaves also turned their masters' appreciation, and the higher valuation consequently placed upon them, to their advantage, gaining privileges and indulgences denied to other slaves.

Runaway slaves valued their instruments sufficiently to frequently take them along when they escaped, despite the physical encumbrance and the danger of carrying something that might identify them. In their autobiographical **slave narratives**, musically trained slaves spoke of their music as providing profound consolation during times of hardship; Olaudah Equiano, who learned to play the French horn while living in London, was perhaps the most famous.

Extremely wealthy, aristocratic slaveholders enhanced their prestige by displaying exotic-looking musically trained black slaves as part of their retinue. The Seventh Earl of Barrymore's stag hunt included a train of four black French horn players. Likewise, a slave named Cato, said to be the best French horn player in England at the time, belonged first to Sir Robert Walpole, and later to the Earl of Chesterfield, who in 1738 gave him to the Prince and Princess of Wales. Conspicuous markers of their owners' wealth and status, such slaves usually were exempt from menial labor, but not necessarily from harsh treatment. The number of advertisements found in English and American newspapers listing runaway slaves who could play the French horn suggests that they were by no means happy with their lot, however much better off they were than less accomplished slaves.

See also Fiddles.

FURTHER READING

Caponi-Tabery, Gena, ed. *Signifyin(g), Sanctifyin' & Slam Dunking; A Reader in African American Expressive Culture.* Amherst: University of Massachusetts Press, 1999.

Fryer, Peter. *Staying Power: The History of Black People in Britain*. London: Pluto Press, 1984.

Gates, Henry Louis, Jr., ed. *The Classic Slave Narratives*. New York: Penguin, 2002.

Morgan, Philip D. *Slave Counterpoint: Black Culture in the Eighteenth-Century Chesapeake and Lowcountry*. Chapel Hill: University of North Carolina Press, 1998.

HILLARY MURTHA

FURNISHINGS. Furnishings are vital to understanding the material world of American slaves. These basic, everyday artifacts shaped, defined, and reflected the lives of the men and women who made and used them. Although many examples of slave housing have survived into the 21st century to enrich understanding of the domestic life of American slaves, few examples of the furnishings used in those spaces remain to complete the picture. Oral histories, archaeological remains, narrative descriptions, travelers' diaries, and rare photographs, paintings, and drawings of enslaved blacks from the 18th and 19th centuries provide an important glimpse into the past.

Slave furnishings varied considerably depending on their context. A cook working in the sophisticated urban setting of Williamsburg, Virginia, in the 1760s lived in different surroundings than an enslaved mine worker for hire in Richmond in the 1820s, or a fieldworker on a large plantation in Georgia in the 1850s. Some generalizations can be made, however. Furnishings used by the enslaved were rarely high style or numerous in quantity. Furniture and other household items often were handmade by the slaves. Other times, they were purchased used or handed down from the Big House. Basic furnishings commonly provided for or acquired by enslaved people included **beds** and bedding, seating furniture, tables, eating and sometimes **cooking**

Drawing of interior of Spotsylvania County, Virginia, cabin with three black women and four children, by Edwin Forbes, ca. 1864. (Library of Congress.)

Inside the Slave Cabin

In South Carolina, George Fleming recalled the contents of his cabin, which included a mirror:

All de things we had in de house was home-made, but we sho had good beds. Dey made wid boards, and 'stead of slats, ropes was stretched twixt de sides real tight by slipping dem through holes and making knots in de ends. Over dese we laid bags; den feather or straw ticks. We had plenty kivvers to keep us warm. We had shelves and hooks to put our clothes on. We had benches and tables made wid smooth boards. Missus Harriet, dat Marse Sam's wife, she give us a looking-glass so we could see how to fix up.

Source: George P. Rawick, ed. *The American Slave: North Carolina and South Carolina Narratives*, Supp. Ser. 1, Vol. 11. Westport, CT: Greenwood Press, 1978.

---

utensils, storage containers, lighting and temperature control devices, and other utilitarian gear such as buckets and **brooms**. Furnishings frequently included small personal and luxury items, purchased by slaves with money earned through a variety of sources, salvaged from the waste stream, handmade after working hours, or carefully preserved gifts from family members.

Early Slave Furnishings

Most slaves in the 17th century lived in small households, whether urban or rural, consisting of a free landholder, his family, and a handful of enslaved and indentured servants. In New York City, some slaves owned by the Dutch East India Company lived independently, but this was not the norm elsewhere in the colonies.

Most 17th-century plantation houses were small by modern standards, with one or two rooms on the first floor and a half story or loft above. Urban houses were not much larger. In such cramped quarters, there was little differentiation between slave furnishings and those used by the rest of the household. Enslaved men and women might have a straw pallet of their own on which to sleep, but most seating furniture, tables, cooking utensils, and accessories would have been used in common by all members of the household.

In larger households, some differentiation of space, and therefore of objects, may have been possible, although few specifics survive to document it. Most likely, enslaved individuals simply received the oldest, least fashionable, and most basic furnishings available for their use.

Slave Furnishings in the Colonial Period and Early Republic

As the slave system became entrenched and the number of slaves in the colonies increased, slave living areas became more and more differentiated from those of white servants and free people. Therefore, it is possible to identify specific furnishings used primarily or exclusively by slaves. Detailed descriptions, however, are few and far between. A 1711 inventory of Bacon's Castle in Surry, Virginia, for example, describes "Negroes Bedding & a parcell Lumber" without giving details about what might have been considered "bedding," or what was contained in the parcel of "lumber," which was an 18th-century term meaning "stuff" or sometimes "junk."

One of the best descriptions of the furnishings found in an 18th-century **slave quarter** comes from George Washington's plantation, Mount Vernon. Julian Niemcewicz (1758–1841), a Polish statesman, who visited there in 1798, penned the following record of the conditions endured by Washington's enslaved agricultural workers:

> We entered one of the huts of the Blacks, for one cannot call them by the name of houses. They are more miserable than the most miserable of the cottages of our peasants. The husband and wife sleep on a mean pallet, the children on the ground; a very bad fireplace, some utensils for cooking, but in the middle of this poverty some cups and a teapot.

Niemcewicz also viewed a small garden, where Washington's slaves grew vegetables and raised hens to sell to "procure for themselves a few amenities." The cups and teapots he described may have been broken or outmoded objects from Washington's table, or they may have been among the "amenities" purchased by the slaves themselves with the proceeds from their **gardens** or the sale of their hens—a common practice among 18th-century slaves in Virginia.

Although Niemcewicz' description dates to the end of the 18th century, it could accurately describe conditions throughout North America for much of the 18th and early 19th centuries. James Williams, who was born in 1805 and whose fugitive slave narrative was published in 1838, described the contents of his lodgings while enslaved in Alabama: "The furniture consisted of a table, a few stools, and dishes made of wood, and an iron pot, and some other cooking utensils."

One rare visual depiction of furniture in a known slave context is a four-legged stool that is visible in a well-known watercolor depicting slaves dancing and playing music in the plantation **yard**, now in the collection of the Colonial Williamsburg Foundation. Another type of furniture found in some slave quarters was wooden boxes, sometimes with iron or leather hinges, clasps, and even **locks**. Landon Carter (1710–1778), a wealthy Virginia plantation owner, noted in his diary on September 21, 1770, that he sent "Billy Beale to search all their [his slaves'] holes and boxes." These hiding places would have provided a private space for storing personal objects away from the prying eyes of slaveholders, overseers, and fellow slaves.

A variety of smaller utilitarian and luxury items could also be found in 18th- and early 19th-century slave quarters. Williams mentions "dishes made of wood, an iron pot, and some other cooking utensils," which may have included skillets, fire pokers, and forks and spoons of wood, iron, and pewter. Buckets, brooms, and **baskets** all would have been needed for cleaning, cooking, and food storage. Archaeological evidence indicates that slaves used a variety of ceramics and glassware in their quarters. These included glass bottles and ceramic jugs for drinking and storing liquids, which were also visible in "The Old Plantation" watercolor (ca.1800, owned by the Colonial Williamsburg Foundation), utilitarian **colonoware** ceramics made by the slaves or acquired from Native Americans, and more typical European-style stoneware, red-ware, and occasionally even fine creamware or porcelain, such as the "cups and a tea-pot" mentioned by Niemcewicz. Finally, personal items including pipes, children's toys, and articles of adornment such as **beads, buttons,** and buckles also were present in slave quarters.

The furnishings allocated to an enslaved person varied based on status in the plantation community. Field slaves had access to the smallest quantity of material goods but in exchange had more autonomy and control of their nonworking hours. Domestic servants were on call 24 hours a day to tend to their owners' whims, but the proximity often led to special treatment, including the provision of better living quarters, food, and clothing. For example, in 1754, wealthy Virginia landowner Joseph Ball (d. 1760), who was then living in London, provided his favored slave, Aaron Jameson (who he had sent back to his plantation, "Morattico"), with one of his old bedsteads as well as a selection of bedding and cooking gear that far exceeded the single blanket and minimal pots and utensils typically given to field slaves.

By the early 19th century, urban slavery had become increasingly differentiated from plantation slavery. In cities such as Richmond, Virginia, slaves were often rented out by their owners, either to other private individuals for use as household servants or to serve as industrial laborers in **mines** and factories. This "hiring out" arrangement provided enslaved workers with additional autonomy and privacy, and many lived independently during the period of their hire. Some were even permitted to earn wages to put toward purchasing material goods or their own freedom. Although little is specifically known about the furnishings of urban hired slaves, they were probably similar to those of free blacks and poor whites during the same period, including basic, unfashionable bedsteads, seating furniture, and tables, as well as simple cooking utensils and household accessories similar to those aforementioned.

Slave Furnishings in the Antebellum South

The most detailed picture of slave furnishings emerges from the antebellum period. A wide variety of sources survive, the most vivid being the words of the slaves themselves from the Works Progress Administration (WPA) Federal Writers' Project interviews during the 1930s. By the 19th century, most enslaved workers on large plantations lived in small freestanding slave quarter buildings, each ideally accommodating a single-family unit. Slaves without family ties were sometimes quartered with other families and sometimes housed together in **dormitories** or communal cabins. These quarters were used for sleeping, craft production, recreation, and sometimes cooking and eating. In good weather, activity spilled out into the plantation yard, and in bad weather, it was centered around individual fireplaces.

The system for acquiring furnishings seems to have varied from plantation to plantation. Some furnishings, such as **blankets** and sometimes beds and cooking equipment, were routinely provided by slaveholders, but most were produced or purchased by the slaves themselves. Occasionally plantations boasted skilled carpenters and blacksmiths. Specific forms and materials varied from plantation to plantation based on what was locally available and popular.

The main piece of furniture mentioned in most descriptions of mid-19th-century slave quarters is a bedstead. By the 1850s, most adult slaves were sleeping in raised bedsteads. Often the bedstead was a form known as the "Georgia bed," which was built into the corner of the room and used two cabin walls for support. Other ex-slaves described freestanding bedsteads with roped bottoms. The bedsteads would be covered with a pallet or tick made of rough fabric stuffed with straw, **cotton, corn** husks, or whatever surplus material was handy. Children and single adults slept in surplus bedsteads, trundle beds, **pallets** on the floor or in **lofts**, or boards propped in front of the fire.

Typical seating furniture described by former slaves consisted of benches and stools rather than chairs. Several styles of benches and stools were used, including four-legged stools in which the legs were pegged into a plank seat and longer board benches consisting of three boards nailed together. Occasionally ex-slaves described chairs, probably ladder-backed, with caned or hide-bottom seats, but these appear to have been the exception rather than the rule. Presumably this was because benches and stools were easier and faster to make than chairs, while serving the exact same purpose, and spare production time was limited. Where seating was at a premium, boxes, stumps, stoops, and beds could all be used as makeshift seats.

Another common feature of 1850s slave cabins was a table. Tables were nailed together from simple unfinished wooden planks, sometimes rubbed with sand to create a smooth finish. Some had two legs and the wall was used as support.

Some slaves also created storage furniture for their houses. This included boxes and chests, possibly for storing extra bedding, clothing, and personal items, as well as makeshift shelving and cupboards for food storage. Cupboards often consisted of boxes or crates to which a few shelves had been added. Sometimes these cupboards were secured to keep children out when the adults were in the fields.

On some plantations, a single cook prepared food for all or a portion of the enslaved workers. In these cases, food was eaten communally in the kitchen or yard. More typically, however, enslaved women prepared food for their own families over individual quarter fireplaces. Thus, many quarters were also furnished with basic cooking and eating implements. Much of a plantation slave's diet consisted of one-pot meals cooked in a large iron pot over the open fire. This was supplemented by corn cakes that could be baked on a footed iron skillet called a "spider," directly in the ashes, or sometimes on the back of a hoe, giving them the name "**hoecakes**." Simple iron implements and wooden spoons would have been necessary to cook these basic food items. When not in use, these often hung from **nails** on the wall. **Rations** typically were distributed weekly and ceramic crocks, fabric bags, wooden boxes, and hollowed-out **gourds** were used to store food within the quarters.

Wooden spoons, forks, and plates are frequently mentioned in ex-slave narratives. These were often handmade on the plantation and could be replaced as needed. Tin plates, pans, and cups were used at some plantations, as were iron forks and knives and shell spoons. Occasionally, high-style ceramics and glass have been found in archaeological excavations of slave quarters, although they rarely are mentioned in ex-slave interviews.

Other small furnishing items used by enslaved men and women included gardening tools for tending small vegetable and herb gardens, water buckets, and brooms. Slaves might make woven baskets, brushes, and straw hats for their own use or for sale. For lighting they used grease lamps, pine knots, wooden torches, and occasionally homemade tallow candles. Households with children might include simple toys like **marbles** or a riding stick.

Although most furnishings in antebellum slave quarters were strictly utilitarian in purpose, many enslaved men and women actively sought to improve and even beautify their living quarters. Many ex-slaves recall that their mothers kept the dirt floors carefully swept, and that they slept not only under coarse blankets, but also carefully made **quilts** of scrap **cloth** and cut-up garments. Slaves created furniture, eating utensils, and household objects to make their lives more comfortable. Many former slaves also recalled handmade or purchased instruments including **banjos** and **fiddles** that provided entertainment for the entire plantation community.

See also Blacksmith Shops; Cast Iron Pots.

FURTHER READING

"Born in Slavery: Slave Narratives from the Federal Writers' Project, 1936–1938," American Memory, Library of Congress. At http://memory.loc.gov/ammem/snhtml/.

Campbell, Edward D. C., Jr., with Kym S. Rice, eds. *Before Freedom Came: African American Life in the Antebellum South*. Richmond, VA: Museum of the Confederacy, 1991.

Carter, Landon. *The Diary of Colonel Landon Carter of Sabine Hall, 1752–1778*, edited by Jack P. Greene. 2 vols. Charlottesville: Published for the Virginia Historical Society by the University Press of Virginia, 1965.

"First Person Narratives of the American South," Documenting the American South. At http://docsouth.unc.edu/fpn/.

Heath, Barbara J. *Hidden Lives: The Archaeology of Slave Life at Thomas Jefferson's Poplar Forest*. Charlottesville: University Press of Virginia, 1999.

McDaniel, George W. *Hearth & Home: Preserving a People's Culture*. Philadelphia: Temple University Press, 1982.

Taylor, Yuval, ed. *I Was Born a Slave: An Anthology of Classic Slave Narratives*. 2 vols. Chicago: Lawrence Hill Books, 1999.

"The African-American Experience in Ohio 1850–1920, Works Progress Administration, Ex-Slave Narratives, 1937–1938," The Ohio Historical Society. At http://dbs.ohiohistory.org/africanam/mss/gr7999.cfm.

Vlach, John Michael. *Back of the Big House: The Architecture of Plantation Slavery*. Chapel Hill: University of North Carolina Press, 1993.

Wilson, Jackie Napolean. *Hidden Witness: African-American Images from the Dawn of Photography to the Civil War*. New York: St. Martin's, 1999.

CATHERINE E. DEAN

G

GARDENS. West and Central Africans came from largely agrarian societies where the cultivation of small gardens was essential to domestic subsistence as well as to market economies centered in the trade and **barter** of produce, foodstuffs, and medicinal and culinary **herbs**. In early America these garden-ways melded with European and Native American traditions and became the basis for gardening in enslaved communities from small farmsteads and urban settings in New England and the Mid-Atlantic to the plantation landscapes of the South. Before the settling of mainland British North America, however, the cultivation of gardens in the West Indies set a precedent for patterns followed in the hearth areas of the coastal Mid-Atlantic, the greater Chesapeake, the Low Country, and the Lower Mississippi Valley. These traditions spread from these core areas into the Southern backcountry and westward to Texas as slavery expanded. Not all enslaved Africans and their descendants were permitted to cultivate plots for themselves and their families, but many benefited in some way from the nutritional, financial, and sociocultural consequences to which the garden patch gave rise.

African Roots and Creole Transformations

The types of compound gardens cultivated in West and Central Africa were the basis for the gardens known in the Caribbean and mainland North America. Unlike their Enlightenment-era colonial masters, West and Central Africans did not see the garden as a geometrically defined space where the natural world was dominated or shaped by humanity, but rather as a space where humanity and nature worked in harmony. To outsiders, African gardens were a primitively enclosed tangle of plants interspersed with weeds and rubbish. European chroniclers from the era of the slave trade often used the phrase "without cultivation" to suggest that Africans lacked industry and a strong work ethic in the pursuit of subsistence. It was actually a low-impact gardening culture where edible and medicinal "weeds" were encouraged and exploited, and where compost heaps became new grounds for gardens because of their fertile soil.

Among the useful practices that enslaved African Americans would inherit was the custom of intercropping companion plants. Intercropping made intensive use of

---

Garden Patch

Pet Franks and her family sold extra produce from their garden patch in Mississippi:

All de niggers on de Tatum place had dey own patches where dey could plant what ever dey wanted to and dey could work dey patch on Satdays. When dey could sell anything from dey patch de mistress would let dem keep de money dey got for it and when de boats went down to Mobile we could send down for anything we wanted to buy. One time I had $10.00 saved up and I bought lots of pretties with it.

Source: George P. Rawick, ed. *The American Slave: Mississippi Narratives*, Supp. Ser. 1, Vol. 7, Part 2. Westport, CT: Greenwood Press, 1978.

Mary Childs worked in the "patch" at night with her father in Georgia:

I went to the patch many nights with my father. I'd hold the kindling light while he worked the patch. He'd know I was sleepy when the light began to fall down. He'd holler at me: "If you don't wake up, I'll knock you in the head with this hoe."

Source: George P. Rawick, ed. *The American Slave: Georgia Narratives*, Supp. Ser.1, Vol. 3, Part 1. Westport, CT: Greenwood Press, 1978.

---

garden space, reduced insect infestation, and conserved precious water resources. For example, the Igbo grew **yams** and **corn** together. Other combinations were cassava, eddo, beans, and **gourds** or millet and ground nuts. Shifting cultivation and rotation was traditional to Fon culture; they cultivated plants that would grow upright as well as low-lying plants side by side. In Senegambia, Wolof women planted a plot behind their houses consisting of tomatoes, red peppers, **okra**, eggplant, and **sesame**. Like the Fon they interplanted cowpeas with sorghum, allowing the peas to climb the stalk. Echoing descriptions of similar traditions found in 19th-century Virginia, **tobacco** often was planted under the eaves of the houses.

In the West Indies, seeds brought to grow crops familiar to the enslaved population quickly took root alongside those grown by the Caribbean's indigenous peoples. Several cultural patterns emerged that would endure and later be transplanted to North America. First, the monoculture of **sugar** and other plantation crops made necessary a supplementary **food** supply to augment rations of salty proteins and starches poor in nutritional value. Second, the gardens transformed peripheral areas of the plantation into spaces where continuity with generalized African ways of shaping the landscape could be maintained and crops could be cultivated in the precious spare or leisure time afforded the enslaved population. Last, the provision grounds encouraged economic activity between slaveholders and their workforce, between blacks, and between whites and blacks at marketplace where surplus crops were sold. The result is that the gardens inspired in enslaved people a sense of ownership, reduced nutritional stress, reinforced West and Central African foodways, and created supplementary economic opportunities and a **market** presence for enslaved producers.

In the greater Chesapeake, the cultivation of gardens was almost an agreed-on privilege extended to enslaved communities. Allowing for huck ("to sell," from the word "huckster") or truck (from the word "truck" meaning "food" or "grub") patches meant that part of the responsibility of supplementing the diet was placed squarely in the hands of the enslaved. In tobacco-growing regions, tobacco was cultivated to the exclusion of other crops to the point at which lower-class and middling planters in Virginia were legally required to plant some sort of kitchen garden to provide for their household dietary needs. Because of the nature of tobacco's monoculture, these gardens not only supplied vegetables for the enslaved families but also for the tables of whites from the elite to the poorer classes. The gang system, which employed groups of enslaved workers under an overseer or foreman, limited the number of hours in a day in which workers could cultivate their own small patch, often located at the back of a dwelling. In daylight, gardening was done by children or elders; at night, men and women cultivated under the full moon, or by pine torch or lantern. If at all possible, much of the garden work was done on Sundays or half-Saturdays if personal time was allowed. In the Carolina-Georgia Low Country where **rice** prevailed, the task system required that each person work on a set parcel known as a task and if the work was completed, ideally, they had some time in the workday to tend to their own affairs, including gardening. Much like those in the West Indies, Low Country gardens might be located on less desirable land and often were considerably larger than those cultivated in the Chesapeake. Like their Chesapeake counterparts, enslaved people sold garden produce and herbs in the marketplaces of Charleston and Savannah and relied heavily on these gardens to vary and improve a meager diet based on broken rice and preserved **fish** or meat. Systems similar to the Caribbean, the Chesapeake, and Low Country could be found in the early Lower Mississippi Valley where influences from each of these areas as well as the cultivation of tobacco and rice determined the nature of slave gardens. Much like the urban centers of other regions, New Orleans and Natchez, Mississippi, served as sites where produce grown by enslaved hands made it into the market economy.

Form and Function

There are descriptions of enslaved people's garden plots from as early as the 18th century. Former slave Charles Ball (ca. 1781–unknown) noted, "On every plantation, with which I ever had any acquaintance, the people are allowed to make patches, as they are called—that is, gardens, in some remote and unprofitable part of the estate, generally in the woods, in which they plant corn, potatoes, pumpkins, melons, &c. for themselves." Philip Vickers Fithian (1747–1776) described the **fence**-making process in 1774 in Virginia's Northern Neck: "The Negroes make a fence, then drive into the ground chestnut stakes about two feet apart in a straight row and twist in the boughs of savin (red cedar), which grows in great plenty here." Near Lynchburg, Virginia, just after the Civil War, John Dennett (1838–1874) described African American gardens as "a fence of palings, or of pickets interwoven with brushwood, encloses a small patch of garden ground, planted with cabbages, string-beans and tomatoes, . . . near by is a bush or two of red peppers, much used by these people in medicine and cookery."

The garden patches probably were not as aesthetically vacant as these descriptions suggest. Many of the symbols of a developing Afro-Creole spiritual world built from a variety of African, European, and Native American beliefs and customs probably would have adorned the spaces. Power objects (**charms**), **conjure bags**, strips of cloth, feathers tied in bunches, **shells**, bottles, special rocks, or earth—would have been placed carefully in gardens to attract fertility, growth, and plentitude and to serve as a warnings to would-be thieves to keep their distance. Gourds were used as a means to arrest spiritual forces before they entered the garden or home.

The form of the garden patches varied. More than likely, slaves' gardens throughout most of the South were similar to those described by Rev. Charles Colcock Jones Jr. (1831–1893), who wrote that the garden of an elderly man on his Georgia Sea Island plantation included arrowroot, long **collards**, sugarcane, tanniers (an edible starchy root found in the tropics, also known as cocoyam), ground nuts, benne, gourds, and **watermelons** grown "in commingled luxuriance." In keeping with descriptions by whites of slave quarters as dirty, disheveled and disorganized, gardens among the enslaved were not likely the geometric, linear forms known to the gentry. The commingled luxuriance described by Reverend Jones was a reflection of an African aesthetic that worked with the contours of nature and the local environment rather than against it or in efforts to control or manipulate it. Fireplace ashes, chicken manure, bones, and other compost materials kept the plots fertile. Inevitably visitors to plantations would have seen these materials scattered about the soil.

Archaeological research provides concrete evidence for what enslaved people may have grown in their gardens. To date, the archaeological record attests to the fact that beans, corn, cowpeas, watermelons, squash, pumpkins, **peanuts**, sweet potatoes, sunflowers, sorghum, gourds, and millet were among the crops. These remains do not tell the whole story, however, because many of the cultivated vegetables would have been varieties of greens and tubers that would have decayed quickly. In 1732, William Hugh Grove noted the companion cultivation of cowpeas, sweet potatoes, and cymling (white pattypan squash) in plots. Peter Kalm (ca. 1716–1779) noted **okra** in the gardens of Philadelphia in the late 1740s, and William Feltman described "snaps and collards," in the gardens of Hanover County, Virginia, in the 1780s. In the Low Country, sugarcane, benne or sesame seed, "Negro pepper," yams, okra, and cowpeas were recorded. Thomas Jefferson (1743–1826) not only testified to okra, tomatoes, peanuts, and red pepper being commonly grown in Virginia but also lived on a plantation where his own enslaved workers supplied themselves and the Jefferson household with two dozen fruits and vegetables, including cucumbers, beets, greens, muskmelons, onions, lettuce, cabbage, and both Irish and sweet potatoes. Both Jefferson and George Washington (1732–1799) noted the introduction of the green-striped cushaw pumpkin, then known as the sweet potato pumpkin, to the plantations of the South via Jamaica in the late 18th century and remarked that it was "highly esteemed" among enslaved African Americans. Between the late 18th and early 19th centuries, migrants from Haitian, Jamaican, and other Caribbean black communities introduced new varieties of okra, peppers, tomatoes, and pumpkins that spread among African American gardeners in the United States.

Recent interest in food history and heirloom vegetables has shed even greater light on the subject, allowing scholars to further contextualize the varieties of crops grown. In Maryland the "**fish** pepper" was grown to season seafood dishes, while in Philadelphia the "pepperpot" pepper gave heat to that city's famed stew. In Georgia, the "rattlesnake" watermelon flourished; in Virginia "green glaze" collards grew; North Carolina slave gardens had the "seven top" turnip green; and chayote or mirliton, a vegetable central to the Afro-Caribbean heritage, grew in Louisiana. Culinary and medicinal herbs grown in these patches included sage, parsley, mint, basil, thyme, pennyroyal, and balm.

Gardens and Power

Gardens were material markers of social and cultural power in the world of slavery. They were contested spaces where the African Diaspora asserted itself and yet slaveholders still had some say over what might be cultivated. Thomas Jefferson directed his son-in-law at his Poplar Forest estate to curtail the cultivation of tobacco among enslaved workers because there was no way of knowing in the end what was his enslaved workers' product versus his own. Some slaveholders saw the garden as a traditional right; others saw it as a privilege to be withdrawn as a means of control. In the westward expansion of slavery, the industrial nature of the cotton kingdom limited garden cultivation. On some plantations from Mississippi to Texas, a large plantation garden might be cultivated for the entire enslaved community, tended by those deemed too old for intensive fieldwork, which obviated the need for individual plots. On other plantations, gardens were less elaborate than those along the southeastern seaboard with enslaved people planting simple crops—leafy greens, sweet potatoes, and legumes—that demanded little cultivation. Consequently, these became the most common garden staples grown across the slave states.

These gardens allowed enslaved people to participate in the local economy. At Jefferson's Monticello, extensive records demonstrate the sale of hops, fruit, and vegetables to the main house from 43 enslaved persons. This was fairly common in the Chesapeake region. Other slaveholding families, including the Randolphs and Washingtons, document similar transactions in their records. In Baltimore, the cultivation of huck or truck patches translated into enslaved blacks having precedence in the marketplace of what was then a major metropolis. The marketplace provided a place for enslaved blacks to congregate, exchange knowledge about the wider world, make money, and establish networks away from the plantations and farms. The garden culture promoted the marketplace in which the "tumultuous" public culture of sing-song sales, religious meetings and storytelling, **cooking**, joking, and dancing lived alongside commercial exchanges. In the Virginia Piedmont, William Tatham described "potatoes, garden-stuff, pumpkins, melons, a few particular fruit trees, peas, hops, flax and cotton," being "confirmed by custom to slaves." These crops were sold to passersby or brought to market and often were bartered for goods at local stores that kept records of enslaved people exchanging their produce for luxury items and even gunpowder, **Bibles**, and door **locks**, which tested the bounds of slavery's reach.

Gardens and Folklife

As sources of food, the gardens helped maintain a link with the mainly vegetarian diet of West and Central Africa. The **ration**-based diet of most enslaved African Americans was poor, and garden produce provided necessary variety and nutrition. Through these gardens, foods introduced to the American diet partly through the agency of enslaved Africans, such as peanuts, tomatoes, red pepper, eggplant, rice, okra, sesame, millet, sorghum, cowpeas, garden huckleberry, watermelons, sweet potatoes, leafy greens, and tanniers, all became part of the Southern diet. This fostered the continuation of dishes common to West and Central Africa and the Afro-Caribbean. The semicultivation or maintenance of native fruit trees and bushes—apple, peach, persimmon, cherry, honey locust, blackberry, and raspberry—further strengthened the connections between African and American landscapes. The presence of culinary and medicinal herbs, along with archaeological evidence suggesting the use of lamb's quarter or goosefoot, purslane, and dock for greens and **medicine**, suggests the community's agency in healing itself and managing its health. The gourd vines that grew up and over the fences and roofs of slave cabins provided the raw material for a host of domestic utensils and musical instruments, including water dippers, spoons, bowls, and gourd **banjos**, **fiddles**, **drums**, rattles, and **thumb pianos**.

See also Bottle Trees; Fetishes.

FURTHER READING

Ball, Charles. *Slavery in the United States: A Narrative of the Life and Adventures of Charles Ball.* New York: John S. Taylor, 1837. Documenting the American South. At http://docsouth.unc.edu/neh/ballslavery/menu.html.

Benoit, Catherine. "Gardens in the African Diaspora: Forging a Creole Identity in the Caribbean and the U.S." In *Gardens and Cultural Change: A Pan-American Perspective,* edited by Michel Conan and Jeffrey Quilter, 26–46. Washington, DC: Dumbarton Oaks, 2007.

Edwards-Ingram, Ywone. "Medicating Slavery: Motherhood, Health Care, and Cultural Practices in the African Diaspora." PhD dissertation, College of William and Mary, 2005.

Gamble, David. *The Wolof of Senegambia.* London: International African Institute, 1957.

Gibbs, Patricia. "Slave Garden Plots and Poultry Yards," Colonial Williamsburg Foundation Research Publication. At http://research.history.org/Historical_Research/Research_Themes/ThemeEnslave/SlaveGardens.cfm.

Greene, Wesley. "Research on 18th Century Gardens," Colonial Williamsburg Foundation Research Publication. At www.history.org/history/cwland/resrch1.cfm.

Hatch, Peter J. "Thomas Jefferson's Favorite Vegetables." In *Dining at Monticello: In Good Taste and Abundance,* edited by Damon Fowler, 55–64. Chapel Hill: University of North Carolina Press, 2005.

Heath, Barbara J. "Bounded Yards and Fluid Boundaries: Landscapes of Slavery at Poplar Forest." In *Places of Cultural Memory: African Reflections on the American Landscape,* proceedings of National Park Service conference, May 9–12, 2001. At http://www.nps.gov/crdi/conferences/conflinks.htm.

"Slave Gardens or Huck Patch. Early American Gardens," A Museum in a Blog. At http://americangardenhistory.blogspot.com/search/label/Slave%20Garden%20or%20Huck%20Patch.

Twitty, Michael W. "Purposeful Patches: The Gardening Plots of Enslaved African Virginians." *The Tiller* (Fall 2007): 6–10.

Twitty, Michael W. "Flavors of Slavery and Freedom." *Edible Chesapeake* (Spring 2009): 22–23.

Weaver, William Woys. *Heirloom Vegetable Gardening.* New York: Henry Holt and Company, 1997.

MICHAEL W. TWITTY

GOURDS. During the era of slavery, gourds were commonplace throughout the American South, the Caribbean, and the slave societies of Central and South America. Enslaved African Americans used dried gourds constantly because they were durable, useful, and easy to grow. They also were biodegradable, disappearing into the earth like other plant matter. Therefore, while archaeologists on slave sites discover pots, **shells**, **buttons**, knives, and other resilient objects, they rarely find clear evidence of gourds. As a result, scholars are only beginning to realize what a large role gourds played in the daily life of slaves.

Gourds belong to the cucurbit family of plants, which includes winter squash, summer squash, and pumpkins. The bottle gourd (*Lagenaria siceraria*), also called "the white-flowered gourd," has large flowers that open up at night to be pollinated by moths. The vine grows rapidly with little cultivation in warm climates throughout the world, so it was one of the earliest plants domesticated by humans. Its ovoid or long-necked fruit, which is a hard shell containing hundreds of seeds, varies in size and shape and can be put to numerous uses.

Africans brought to the Western Hemisphere as slaves were already familiar with gourds, and they found that Native Americans had been growing and using gourds for centuries. The plant seems to have originated in Africa and spread to Asia. Some have speculated that gourds floated across the Atlantic from Africa to the Americas in pre-Columbian times. But recent DNA studies of ancient gourd remains in Ecuador suggest that New World gourds arrived from Asia, perhaps brought by humans as long as 10,000 years ago, well before the domestication of plants for food.

Besides gourds and various other cucurbits, native inhabitants of tropical America also had an unrelated tree (*Crescentia cujete*). Occasionally called a gourd tree, it produces a globular fruit with a hard, woody shell slightly thinner and less porous than a bottle gourd. The fruit, almost as big as a softball, is best known through the *maracas*, or rattles, used by Latin American musicians. When the Old and the New Worlds came together in the Caribbean more than 500 years ago, the confusion regarding these separate fruits was immediate, since the Spanish referred to both the tree and the gourd vine with the Spanish noun *calabaza*, which became *calabash* in English.

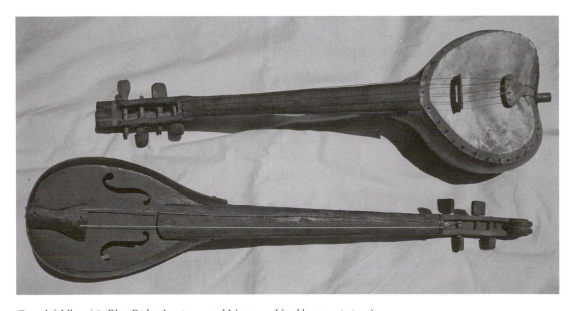

Gourd fiddles. (© Blue Ridge Institute and Museum. Used by permission.)

Drinking from Gourds

On Nicey Kinney's Georgia plantation, slaves used gourds as drinking containers and dippers:

> De bestest water dat ever was come from a spring right nigh our cabin and us had long-handled gourds to drink it out of. Some of dem gourds hung by de spring all de time and dere was allus one or two of 'em hangin' by de side of our old cedar waterbucket. Sho', us had a cedar bucket and it had brass hoops on it; dat was some job to keep dem hoops scrubbed wid sand to make 'em bright and shiny, and dey had to be clean and pretty all de time or mammy would git right in behind us wid a switch. Marse Gerald raised all dem long-handled gourds dat us used 'stid of de tin dippers folks has now, but dem warn't de onliest kinds of gourds he growed on his place. Dere was gourds mos' as big as waterbuckets, and dey had short handles dat was bent whilst de gourds was green, so us could hang 'em on a limb of a tree in de shade to keep water cool for us when us was wukin' in de field durin' hot weather.

Source: George P. Rawick, eds. *The American Slave: Georgia Narratives*, Vol. 13. Westport, CT: Greenwood Press, 1972.

The word "calabash" became the generic term for gourds among early European newcomers, who lacked the knowledge or interest to differentiate the fruit of the tree from that of the vine. Arrivals from Africa made use of both, building on their prior familiarity with gourds, which had figured constantly in both their folklore and their daily life. In much of West Africa, decorated gourds, along with **baskets**, served as the primary containers. They ranged in size from small drinking cups to huge bowls, often carried on the head, that could hold vegetables or milk. Bottle gourds also made fine canteens, since water permeating slowly through the shell evaporates, keeping the water inside cool. In fishing communities, West Africans used gourds as floats for their nets, and everywhere gourds served as resonators for creating a wide variety of string and percussion instruments.

All these uses continued among Africans in the New World and were augmented by other innovations that developed from necessity or learned from American Indians. As slavery expanded in the West Indies, Africans learned to put fireflies inside a gourd pierced with small holes, making it into a lamp, and they used gourds to bail out their **canoes** and sailboats. In Haiti, gourds became a common medium of exchange; one denomination of Haitian currency is still called a "gourd." In America, slaves in the Chesapeake region used small "darning gourds" to hold the fabric in place when mending clothes, and workers in the Carolinas turned gourds into bird houses to attract purple martins, aggressive birds that would scare hawks away from the **chickens** and devour bothersome mosquitoes and barnyard insects.

Everywhere, rural African Americans used long-handled dipper gourds, known as drinking gourds, to dip water from streams and wells. And like the American Indians, blacks in the South used large bushel gourds with a hole cut at the small end, near the stem, as buckets for hauling water. Gourds were used to keep **rations** of food and could be used in place of other crockery and utensils. But the gourd made its greatest impact on the material culture of the Americas through the introduction of African musical instruments. Different parts of the New World absorbed and adapted diverse African instruments—the birimbau and the marimba in Latin America, the **banjo** in North America. Large dipper gourds could be fashioned into gourd-bodied banjos, and over time the banjo gained a foothold in parts of the Caribbean and on North American plantations, in part because slave **drums** were often forbidden by law. The gourd-conscious Hausa of Nigeria played a "molo," which usually had three strings, and in the Congo-Angola region, Kimbundu speakers referred to a stringed musical instrument as *mbanza*. This latter term predominated in the New World, perhaps because it bore some resemblance to *bandore*, a variant of the word *pandore*, meaning an English-style lute. It passed into Brazilian Portuguese as *banza*, into Jamaican English as *banja*, and into Virginia English as "banjar." Thomas Jefferson wrote that black slaves had introduced "the Banjar, which they brought hither from Africa."

A unique watercolor, "The Old Plantation" (owned by the Colonial Williamsburg Foundation), was reportedly painted on a plantation in the Charleston, South Carolina, area in the late 18th century and shows slaves dancing to music played on a carved gourd banjo. Johann David Schoepf, a German naturalist who visited South Carolina in the 1780s, noted that a common "musical instrument of the true Negro is a *Banjah*. Over a hollow calabash (*Cucurb lagenaria L.*) is stretched a sheep-skin, the instrument lengthened with a neck, strung with 4 strings." Schoepf decided this unfamiliar creation "gives out a rude sound," but he reported that in "America and on the islands they make use of this instrument greatly for the dance."

Because the gourd vine grew rapidly and then withered quickly, it often appeared in black folklore and sermons as an emblem of fickleness. In the Old Testament, Jonah is grateful for the cool shade of a gourd vine, but it only lasts a brief time (Jon. 4:6–10). Black writer Zora Neale Hurston made use of this image in her 1934 novel, *Jonah's Gourd Vine*.

During slavery times, the gourd became an emblem of freedom for slaves escaping to the North by following the North Star, which is located near the constellation known as the Big Dipper. Since slaves used gourds for dippers, they sang a song called "Follow the Drinking Gourd" to instruct others on the path to freedom. Northerners opposed to slavery adopted the same symbol, and gourds appear in several paintings of black subjects by white artists, such as *A Southern Cornfield* (1861) by Thomas Waterman Wood, and *Near Andersonville* (1865–1866) by Winslow Homer. When ex-slaves began forming Equal Rights Leagues in North Carolina in 1865, *The Freedmen's Journal* reported that new chapters sprang up as quickly as "a gourd in the night."

See also Clothing; Gardens.

FURTHER READING

Epstein, Dena. *Sinful Tunes and Spirituals, Black Folk Music to the Civil War.* Urbana: University of Illinois Press, 1977.
Greene, Wesley. "A Discussion of 18th-century Curcurbits," Colonial Williamsburg Foundation Research Publication. At www.history.org/history/CWLand/resrch12.cfm.

Northup, Solomon. *Twelve Years a Slave: Narrative of Solomon Northup, a Citizen of New-York, Kidnapped in Washington City in 1841, and Rescued in 1853.* Auburn, NY: Derby and Miller, 1853. Documenting the American South. At http://docsouth.unc.edu/fpn/northup/northup.html.

Schöpf, Johann David. *Travels in the Confederation, 1783–1784.* Translated and edited by Alfred J. Morrison. New York: Benjamin Franklin, 1968.

PETER H. WOOD

GRAVES. Slaves were buried in rural burial grounds, where evidence of traditional folk customs can be found, or in urban contexts such as **cemeteries** of **benevolent associations**, funeral homes, or other organizations, where the graves take on a more Euro-American or Creole appearance.

Rural and Plantation Burial Grounds

The earliest graves of African Americans are generally those of slaves, often found on Southern plantations. In these rural burial grounds, many of the graves of slaves may be unmarked or marked with unconventional items, such as metal pipes. Some graves may be marked with memorial plants, such as cedars, yucca, daffodils, snowbells, or other heirloom plants.

Graves may appear untended, because these rural burial grounds largely did not participate in the Euro-American "beautification of death" movement. A distinctive characteristic often remarked on by researchers is the prevalence of grave goods found on African American graves. These items may include bottles, some still filled with liquid, possibly **medicine**, ceramics, lamps, furniture, and other items associated with the individual during life. At least one early source refers to these items as "necessities." Many of these items have been removed from graves, either during scheduled "cleanup" or by theft. Others have been buried in the soil and may not be immediately apparent.

Accounts of early plantation burials are uncommon. They describe simple **coffins**, made on the plantation by enslaved carpenters that were unpainted, unlined, and lacked coffin hardware. Coffins, however, were likely a European influence and many 18th-century burials probably lacked coffins. According to **slave narratives**, by the Civil War, plantation carpenters made wooden coffins, sometimes painted black, and lined with black and white calico.

While some bodies were wrapped in **cloth** or a shroud—a practice reported by a host of African cultures, such as the Wolof of the Senegambia, Sierra Leone–Liberia region, Gold Coast, Bight of Benin, and Niger Delta region—many others were interred in clothes. African accounts of shrouds are generally from the 17th century, and these groups may have been influenced by Catholic and Islamic groups, making it difficult to distinguish precontact behavior.

Burials typically occurred at night, perhaps reflecting the inability to take time off from work, although it may be just as likely that night burials were the specific choice of the enslaved Africans because there would be less white oversight. Evidence indicates that, in New York, enslaved African Americans preferred nighttime burials, with the result that in 1722 a law was enacted to prohibit burials except during the day.

Burying the Dead

Robert Shepherd from Georgia remembered that bodies were laid out on cooling boards and wrapped in sheets while the coffin was built:

> When one did die, folks would go 12 or 15 miles to de buryin'. Marster would say: "Take de mules and wagons and go but, mind you, take good keer of dem mules." He never seemed to keer if us went—fact was, he said us ought to go. If a slave died on our place, nobody went to de fields 'til atter de buryin'. Marster never let nobody be buried 'til dey had been dead 24 hours, and if dey had people from some other place, he waited 'til dey could git dar. He said it warn't right to hurry 'em off into de ground too quick atter dey died. Dere warn't no undertakers dem days. De homefolks jus' laid de corpse out on de coolin' board 'til de coffin was made. Lordy Miss! Ain't you never seed one of dem coolin' boards? A coolin' board was made out of a long straight plank raised a little at de head, and had legs fixed to make it set straight. Dey wropt 'oman corpses in windin' sheets. Uncle Squire, de man what done all de wagon wuk and buildin' on our place, made coffins. Dey was jus' plain wood boxes what dey painted to make 'em look nice. White preachers conducted de funerals, and most of de time our own Marster done it, 'cause he was a preacher hisself. When de funeral was done preached, dey sung *Harps From De Tomb*, den dey put de coffin in a wagon and driv slow and keerful to de graveyard. De preacher prayed at de grave and de mourners sung, *I'se Born To Die and Lay Dis Body Down*. Dey never had no outside box for de coffin to be sot in, but dey put planks on top of de coffin 'fore dey started shovellin' in de dirt.

Source: George P. Rawick, ed. *The American Slave: Georgia Narratives*, Vol. 13. Westport, CT: Greenwood Press, 1972.

Some slave owners prohibited the use of **drums** to announce the burial, while others discouraged singing, which they thought was "heathenish."

Accounts generally describe large assemblages, with individuals from surrounding plantations participating. The nature of the gathering, however, varies considerably from account to account. There are accounts from the Barbados where the burial procession was marked by "mirth and joy," with no "weeping or bewailing." Some accounts from the South mention the singing of hymns. Differences may be the result of various religious influences; where Christianity was dominant, the enslaved may have altered their customs; where Christianity had less of an impact, more African-based customs continued.

The burial grounds were set apart from the main house, although often not far from the slave settlement. Located on less productive plantation land, these burial grounds often are located on prime development tracts, often in proximity to water.

Some burials in the Barbados were not made in burial grounds, but rather under house floors. At least one such grave has also been identified in South Carolina.

Burials typically were made in an east-west orientation. Although this often is attributed to Judeo-Christian influences, a vast number of sun-worshiping cultures recognize that the sun gives life, going back to the Egyptians. Some have suggested that east-facing burials may suggest an intentional orientation to Africa. No evidence supports one supposition over the others.

There are also "abnormal" burial positions. Several accounts record individuals being buried facedown to prevent the return of the spirit. There are similar accounts of individuals buried north-south, or "cross-wise with the world." South Carolina has an oral tradition that those dying of drowning are buried where the tide can wash over the grave.

Even while in use, these burial grounds appeared unkempt and covered with trees and brambles. Graves might be marked with wood planks (headboards), sticks or branches, brick, or occasionally a small marble stone.

The burial grounds begun in slavery continued to be used after emancipation, largely because of the strong association with ancestors. As a result, these graveyards often contain far more burials than initially thought or suspected. It is also not uncommon for more recent burials to intrude into earlier ones. While repugnant to white society, in African American culture, the desire to be with one's ancestors was a driving force that maintained the use of "filled" grounds. Often the burial grounds were limited in size by surrounding white owners.

Many of the burial grounds were never formally deeded by their white owners. That, coupled with the appearance of "abandonment," has resulted in numerous court cases as African American graves and burial grounds are found in areas marked for development. In South Carolina, court cases have occurred or are occurring in Beaufort, Charleston, and Georgetown counties. Outcomes favoring the preservation of the graves are never certain, and many states do not require archaeological removal of burials. Instead, graves typically are removed by funeral homes and others unskilled in the recovery of skeltonized human remains and their associated artifacts. This has significantly affected the ability of professional archaeologists and bioanthropologists to learn more about African American graves and mortuary practices.

Urban Burial Grounds and Practices

During the antebellum period, cities such as Charleston, South Carolina, and Petersburg, Virginia, with large populations of free persons of color had burial grounds begun by various African American associations, benevolent associations, and **churches**. Descriptions are even less common for these burials than for those on plantations, but the few available reveal considerable variation. As in plantation burial grounds, individual graves generally were not marked, although wood boards or posts were used. Marble markers might be found, reflecting on the virtues of a good "servant," and clearly erected by the owner of the slave. Perhaps because of closer oversight or the more confined conditions, these urban burial grounds appear to be more carefully laid out.

For most urban enslaved African Americans, however, burial grounds were little more than disposal locations. For example, Charleston, South Carolina, had five burial grounds used by African Americans between 1746 and 1860. As each became filled, a new one was created and the old was "abandoned," with the sale of the property for new housing lots.

There is no mention of burial goods or other traditional black African practices openly associated with these burials, perhaps because of the strict white oversight faced by both free and enslaved African Americans in the urban setting.

Burial Associations

Confronted by racism, poverty, and uncertainty, African Americans sought to ensure a good burial through a variety of benevolent associations. Some, such as the Brown Fellowship in Charleston, South Carolina, trace roots back to the early antebellum period. A number were organized in urban areas across the South before the Civil War. Many more were organized after emancipation, with different "bury leagues" or cooperative societies forming in both urban and rural areas. Members paid a small sum on a regular basis with the promise of a respectful burial upon death. Typically a coffin, hearse, and other accoutrements were provided.

Magicoreligious Beliefs

While many beliefs may be inferred from the scant historical accounts, the best evidence comes from late 19th- and 20th-century folklore and oral history studies. Although virtually all of these were conducted by whites and therefore may exhibit varying degrees of bias, they do provide rich information on the importance of the cemetery and burial in African American culture.

A large number of accounts have been collected concerning the importance of grave dirt, or goofer dust. Its powers varied depending on when collected and whose grave from which it was obtained. Equally important in much rootwork was the use of human bones, including hand bones and the skull.

Another theme running through African American oral tradition is the "plat-eye" or evil spirit not given appropriate respect during burials. The plat-eye is able to take on various shapes and haunts both the graveyard and those still alive. The use of blue paint on many Low Country houses is based on its ability to keep the plat-eye and other spirits away.

Archaeological and Bioanthropological Studies

The most impressive, and thorough, examination of an African American cemetery is that conducted by the Howard University African American Burial Ground Project. Between 1991 and 2006, the project investigated in detail the "rediscovery" of the New York African Burial Ground in 1989 during the construction of a federal office building. As a result of the work, 419 enslaved Africans and their descendants were made available for detailed bioanthropological study before they were reinterred. The study incorporated historical research, demographic analysis, analysis of the coffin remains and associated artifacts, and a detailed examination of the skeletal remains.

The work incorporated studies of childhood health; use of the teeth to examine issues of disease, diet, and nutritional inadequacy; evidence of infectious disease; indications of arthritic and traumatic damage; and growth and development indicators found in children and young adults. In addition, the study incorporated DNA analysis, revealing that a variety of West and West Central African states and empires were represented in the burials. The use of chemical analysis, with strontium isotope analysis and analysis of lead, helped determine where individuals were born and grew up. Among other results, the study found that infant mortality was high—higher than for the white population—and that overall life expectancy was short and few adults lived to old age. During life, the adults were subjected to extreme work stresses, with much degenerative joint disease in both men and women.

No other research project has had funding to compare with the New York Burial Ground Project, yet important studies of African American populations have taken place in a number of southern states, including South Carolina, Georgia, Arkansas, Mississippi, Louisiana, and Texas.

See also Charms; Conjure Bags; Fetishes.

FURTHER READING

Blakey, Michael L., and Lesley M. Rankin-Hill. *The New York African Burial Ground: Skeletal Biology Final Report.* 2 vols. Washington, DC: Howard University, 2004.

Browning, James B. "The Beginnings of Insurance Enterprise among Negroes." *Journal of Negro History* 22 (4) (1969): 417–432.

Conner, Cynthia. "'Sleep on and Take Your Rest': Black Mortuary Behavior on the East Branch of the Cooper River, South Carolina." MA thesis, University of South Carolina, 1989.

Handler, Jerome S., and Frederick W. Lange. *Plantation Slavery in Barbados: An Archaeological and Historical Investigation.* Cambridge, MA: Harvard University Press, 1978.

Hogue, S. Homes, and Jeffrey S. Alvey. *Final Report on Archaeological Burial Recovery at Pepper Hill 1 Cemetery. 22LO998, Lowndes County, Mississippi.* Mississippi State: Cobb Institute of Archaeology, 2006.

Hyatt, Harry Middleton. *Hoodoo – Conjuration – Witchcraft – Rootwork: Beliefs Accepted by Many Negroes and White Persons These Being Orally Recorded Among Blacks and Whites.* Vol. 4. St Louis, MO: Memoirs of the Alma Egan Hyatt Foundation, 1974.

Medford, Edna Greene, ed. *The New York African Burial Ground: History Final Report.* Washington, DC: Howard University, 2004.

Nichols, Elaine, ed. *The Last Miles of the Way: African-American Homegoing Traditions, 1890-Present.* Columbia: South Carolina State Museum, 1989.

Owsley, Douglas W., and Charles E. Orser Jr. *An Archaeological and Physical Anthropological Study of the First Cemetery in New Orleans, Louisiana.* Baton Rouge: Department of Geography and Anthropology, Louisiana State University, 1984.

Peter, Duane E., Marsha Prior, Melissa M. Green, and Victoria G. Clow, eds. *Freedman's Cemetery: A Legacy of a Pioneer Black Community in Dallas, Texas.* 2 vols. Austin: Texas Department of Transportation, 2000.

Peterkin, Julia. *Roll, Jordan, Roll.* New York: Robert O. Ballou, 1933.

Rathbun, Ted A., and Richard H. Steckel. "The Health of Slaves and Free Blacks in the East." In *The Backbone of History: Health and Nutrition in the Western Hemisphere,* edited by Richard H. Steckel and Jerome C. Rose, 208–225. Cambridge: Cambridge University Press, 2002.

Rose, Jerome C., ed. *Gone to a Better Land: A Biohistory of a Rural Black Cemetery in the Post-Reconstruction South.* Fayetteville: Arkansas Archaeological Survey, 1985.

Trinkley, Michael, Debi Hacker, and Sarah Fick. *The African American Cemeteries of Petersburg, Virginia: Continuity and Change.* Columbia, SC: Chicora Foundation Research Series 55, 1999.

MICHAEL TRINKLEY

GUINEAS. Introduced in 1663 during the reign of Charles II of England, the "guinea" **coin** represented a new denomination in the nation's monetary system. The coins were so named because much of the gold used to produce them came from the Gold or "Guinea" Coast of West Africa and was provided by the Royal African Company, which had been granted a monopoly of the Africa trade from 1672 until 1698. Coins produced from African gold bore the company's distinctive emblem below the monarch's head: an elephant or elephant and a castellated howdah, an ornate canopied seat used for riding on elephants and camels.

All coins of this denomination, whether or not they bore the insignia of the Royal African Company, came to be known as guineas. And because the company grew so prominent in the slave trade—to the extent that England was second only to Portugal and Brazil as the foremost exporter of slaves to the New World by the 17th century's end—guineas came to be associated with the traffic in human chattel. Another reason why the coins were linked to the slave trade may have been that some of the same English entrepreneurs who originally were involved in mining African gold along the Guinea Coast later abandoned that venture to pursue what became a more lucrative trade in the seizure and export of native peoples from the adjacent Bight of Benin, which came to be known as the Slave Coast.

Guineas are approximately 25 millimeters in diameter, about the size of a U.S. quarter. Initially valued at 20 shillings, the coin increased in value to 30 shillings in 1694 before settling at 21 shillings for most of the 18th century. Each guinea contains slightly less than a quarter ounce of pure gold, which, at 2009 prices would be worth about $250 in bullion value alone. The coins also were produced in one-half, two, and five guinea denominations, containing nearly an eighth, a half, and one and a quarter ounces of pure gold, respectively. Beyond their intrinsic gold value, guineas are highly prized by collectors of rare coins who pay tens of thousands of dollars for the best and scarcest specimens. Among the most prized examples are those bearing

English guinea coin with the head of Charles II, 1677. (The Colonial Williamsburg Foundation. Gift of the Lasser Family.)

the elephant or elephant and castle emblems, symbols of a time when England ruled the seas and the Sub-Saharan peoples and resources of Africa were fair game for exploitation.

FURTHER READING

Manning, Patrick. "The Impact of the Slave Trade on the Societies of West and Central Africa." In *Transatlantic Slavery: Against Human Dignity*, edited by Anthony Tibbles, 97–104. London: National Museums and Galleries on Merseyside, 1995.
Richardson, David. "Liverpool and the English Slave Trade." In *Transatlantic Slavery: Against Human Dignity*, edited by Anthony Tibbles, 70–76. London: National Museums and Galleries on Merseyside, 1995.
Seaby, Peter. *The Story of British Coinage*. London: B. A. Seaby, 1985.

SAM MARGOLIN

GUITARS. The guitar played only a small role as a slave instrument, which is in sharp contrast to its dramatic rise in popularity at the end of the 19th century and its dominating role in American music by the mid-20th century. In contrast, **fiddles** accompanied the first European settlers to the New World. Slaves from Africa arrived with fresh memories of single- and double-string **gourd** fiddles that led to its early adoption by slave musicians. It was soon joined by the fretless **banjo**, an instrument with unclear origins but common precedents in Africa and Europe. With a fretless neck, the construction of either instrument remained with the skills of a local luthier with access to materials required. The fretted neck of the guitar was difficult to create without instruction and access to designs. Guitars were uncommon among northern Europeans who saw them as a unique part of Spanish culture in the 17th and 18th centuries. It is likely that the earliest use of guitars in the New World was in those parts of North America under Spanish control, although the English guitar, which is related to the cittern, could be found in the former British colonies of North American beginning in the last quarter of the 18th century. In the early 19th century, guitars began to be manufactured in a way that made them accessible to the American market, and a rage for the guitar swept America starting in the 1830s, following the fashion in England. Professional guitarists toured the country performing in the European style during the 1830s and 1840s. Those looking to keep up with musical innovations likely purchased guitars to show they could stay current with fashion. This rage even caught up free blacks, such as William Johnson (1809–1851), a barber in Natchez, Mississippi, whose diary shows his striving for just such status and includes a reference to his purchase of guitar strings for his fiancée, also a free black, in the 1840s.

Besides the issue of the fretted neck, these early guitars were strung with gut strings that could not produce the kind of volume that would make the instrument viable outside the parlor. Guitarists did appear in some early 1850s minstrel shows, but they were a peripheral instrument to the banjo, fiddle, bones, and tambourine that supplied the crux of the show's music.

The slave experience with the guitar was probably closer to that of Liza Mention, of Beech Island, South Carolina, who recalled string bands composed of fiddles and banjos at the local dances but not any of the cheap mass-produced guitars that were commonplace by the time she was interviewed in 1937. In another case, former slave Harriet Jones from North Carolina remembered how the slave-owning Fulbright family participated in a Christmas party for the house servants that included dancing and the singing of Christmas songs with accompaniment of guitar, banjo, and fiddle. When the master and the mistress went to **slave quarters** to oversee the Christmas dance of field slaves, Jones recalled only the sounds of banjo and fiddle, implying that the guitar was essentially a store-bought trophy, the instrument of the house servants.

The Works Progress Administration (WPA) Federal Writers' Project narratives make scarce mention of the guitar. An index of instruments mentioned by name in the WPA narratives compiled by musicologist Robert B. Winans finds only 15 references to guitars in comparison with 106 for the banjo and 205 for the fiddle. The preponderance of those 15 references comes from three contiguous Mississippi counties, Copiah, Rankin, and Simpson, in the southwest portion of the state. According to Simon Durr of Copiah County, slaves from his plantation were given **passes** to attend frolics at other plantations with music provided by fiddle and guitar. Slaves from Simpson County consistently described fiddle and guitar accompaniment for dancing. The frolics occurred on Saturdays, in woods lit by large bonfires, and ran late into the night. The bands were fronted by a caller who called the steps while the bands played "Molly Put the Kettle On" and "Turkey in the Straw." Set dances, those directed by the caller, were augmented with buck dancing. In one case, the slave master allowed the building of a large shaded platform for slave dances. Simpson County alone produced nine references to fiddle and guitar with one each from Rankin and Copiah. Another reference appears across the Mississippi River from Natchez in Black River Louisiana where slaves on the Kilpatrick family plantation also had a fiddle and guitar group to provide music for the Saturday night frolics.

Until the early 1920s, the banjo was the instrument commonly paired with the fiddle across the rural South including Mississippi. The cluster of guitar players in southern Mississippi is a clear anomaly. Still references appear to other slave guitarists, even in other parts of Mississippi. The uncle of former slave Evergreen Richardson played guitar on a plantation in the central county of Madison County, which was about 60 miles south of Carroll County, home to one of the most popular guitar and fiddle groups of the 1920s.

Although southern Mississippi including Natchez was under the control of Spain from 1779 to 1798, nothing links this governance with the use of guitars in this area. In the capital of Spanish America, New Orleans, however, a clear and continued Spanish influence had an apparent impact on the use of the guitar in that city. New Orleans had a long tradition of string band music that included the guitar, with violin, mandolin, and string bass. Brass and reed musicians doubled on a string instrument, which allowed them to perform in a wide variety of social contexts. This included music for social gatherings and serenading. The earliest proto-jazz groups combined horns and strings and exclusively used guitarists.

Perhaps western Kentucky is the most interesting region in terms of guitar playing and its long-term influence on American culture. Two WPA interviewees from this region, Tinnie Force and Elvira Lewis, describe banjo and guitar groupings, but they make no mention of the fiddle. It is likely that there were fiddlers and that they simply were outside of the interviews or the interviewee's memory.

African American musicians, starting during Reconstruction, adopted the guitar and rapidly developed a plethora of styles that continue to reverberate across 21st-century American culture. Uncommon during slavery, the guitar did not carry the stigma of bondage associated with the fiddle and banjo and came to a place of dominance in the 20th century.

FURTHER READING

Epstein, Dana J. *Sinful Tunes and Spirituals: Black Folk Music before the Civil War* Urbana: University of Illinois Press, 1977.

Noonan, Jeffery J. *The Guitar in America: Victorian Era to Jazz Age.* Oxford: University of Mississippi Press, 2009.

Rawick, George, ed. *The American Slave: A Composite Autobiography*, Westport, CT: Greenwood Press, 1972–1979.

Winans, Robert B. "Black Instrumental Music Traditions in the Ex-Slave Narratives." *Black Music Research Newsletter* 5, no. 22 (Spring 1982): 2–5.

JARED SNYDER

GUMBO. Gumbo, from the Bantu word for **okra**, is a soup or stew thickened with okra and served over **rice** that originated in 18th-century Louisiana. Gumbo usually contains two or more meats or seafood. Okra has a slimy consistency that serves as a thickening agent. Rice flour also could be used to thicken a gumbo. Some historians believe that gumbo is an adaptation of French bouillabaisse.

Among the most distinct characteristics of gumbo are the key ingredients that reflect an international blending of culinary traditions from France, Africa, Spain, the Caribbean, Germany, and Native Americans. Two-thirds of the slaves in Louisiana were brought from the Senegambia region of West Africa by the French slave trade. The people from the Senegal Valley cultivated rice, **indigo**, and **cotton**. These were key cash crops in colonial Louisiana. Barrels of rice seed and okra, among other African foodstuffs, were carried through the Middle Passage with thousands of slaves who knew how to cultivate these crops. By 1720, rice became an important **food** staple and an abundant crop in the Lower Mississippi Delta. Many slaves kept small kitchen **gardens** where they raised vegetables, including okra and **herbs**, to supplement their meager weekly **rations** of salt pork and a peck of **corn**meal. Some slaves raised **pigs** and **chickens**. Slaves supplemented their diet with foods foraged in nearby forests, bayous, and rivers, including small game, **fish and shellfish**, and sassafras leaves. Most of these ingredients found their way into a gumbo.

Filé is originally a Native American seasoning made from ground sassafras leaves that can serve as a thickening agent as well as a seasoning in gumbo. Another key ingredient that distinguishes gumbo from other soups or stews came from Spain and is called the "Holy Trinity," which is a sautéed mixture of onion, celery, and green pepper. It is still prepared to this day as the start of a gumbo. Spices and red pepper added flavor to gumbo, a technique that came from Africa and the Caribbean. German settlers who brought their knowledge of sausage making to the region introduced another kind of meat into gumbo. Combinations of okra, vegetables, fish, pork, or chicken scraps, and seasoning that were simmered for long hours in an iron kettle produced gumbo served over steamed rice. Gumbo was served in many Big Houses and in **slave quarters**. Enslaved cooks used whatever appropriate ingredients were available to prepare gumbo.

See also Cast Iron Pots.

FURTHER READING

Folse, John. *The Encyclopedia of Cajun and Creole Cuisine*. Baton Rouge, LA: Chef John Folse and Company Publishing, 2005.

Genovese, Eugene D. *Roll, Jordan, Roll: The World the Slaves Made*. New York: Vintage, 1976.

Kiple, Kenneth F., and Kriemhild Coneé Omelas, eds. *The Cambridge World History of Food*. Cambridge: Cambridge University Press, 2001.

Tucker, Susan, ed. *New Orleans Cuisine: Fourteen Signature Dishes and Their Histories*. Jackson: University Press of Mississippi, 2009.

JULIA ROSE

H

HAIR AND HAIRSTYLES. The structure of the hair of African and African-descended people is characterized by an intense curl pattern that is called "kinky" or "nappy." The forms of styling and concealment of this intricately textured hair are an eloquent, visual language through which the experience of black women and girls, particularly, can be "read."

African Background

Complex hair cultures that centered in the symbolism of the head and used various forms of carving, sculpting, and molding developed over many centuries in West Africa. By the time of the trans-Atlantic slave trade, West African hairstyles had become a sculptural form of body art as well as a form that required maintenance. Although challenged by the intricacy of the kink, women in these cultures were pleased by the excellent sculptural qualities of coarse, malleable hair. They frequently reduced the thick, amorphous mass of hair and organized it into compact units—beautiful geometric shapes that contained philosophical and social meanings. The picks used to create these hairstyles were finely carved from wood and the handles often decorated. Wood and fiber masks and figurines made out of clay, wood, and metal bearing artful hair forms were other key elements in these highly integrated, material cultures.

Women's and girls' hairstyles signified conditions such as age, marital, and social status, as well as grief and initiation into secret societies. A communal art form, as one could not create a precise or complex style on one's own head, the care of the hair also had spiritual dimensions. For example, in the Mende culture, the working space where the hair was styled had to be cleared of tensions and be full of harmony to achieve a successful pattern.

Bound Heads in Bondage

Enslaved and resettled in North America, African women generally did not have the tranquility and luxurious license to leisurely gather and painstakingly beautify one another, but vestiges of the African practices survived in the enslaved community.

Laboring for the master from sunup to sundown and maintaining the slave community from sundown to when they went to bed, black women generally resorted to

Hairdressing for Special Occasions

Gus Feaster, formerly enslaved in South Carolina, recollected that "some o' de old men had short plaits o' hair":

> De gals come out in de starch dresses fer de camp meeting. Dey took dey hair down out'n de strings fer de meeting. In dem days all de darky wimmens wore dey hair in string 'cep' when dey 'tended church or a wedding. At de camp meetings de wimmens pulled off de head rags, 'cept de mammies. On dis occasion de mammies wore linen head rags fresh laundered. Dey wore de best aprons wid long streamers ironed and starched out a hanging down dey backs. All de other darky wimmens wore de black dresses and dey got hats from some dey white lady folks; jes' as us mens got hats from our'n. Dem wimmens dat couldn't git no hats, mostly wore black bonnets. De nigger gals and winches did all de dressing up dat dey could fer de meeting and also fer de barbecue.

Source: George P. Rawick, ed. *The American Slave: South Carolina Narratives*, Vol. 2. Westport, CT: Greenwood Press, 1972.

Sarah Felder remembered that, in Mississippi, "Ebery Sunday we hed ter wrap hair."

Source: George P. Rawick, ed. *The American Slave: Mississippi Narratives*, Supp. Ser. 1, Vol. 7, Part 2. Westport, CT: Greenwood Press, 1978.

simple, expedient means of maintaining their hair and routinely covered their heads with a kerchief or **cloth**. After the fall harvest season and on Sundays, however, field-working women had some time for personal maintenance. Urban-dwelling female slaves also had some respite on Sunday. So, in addition to factors of time and intensive labor, other factors worked against the continuation of African hair care traditions among enslaved women.

The integrated material cultures that supported African hair care practices had been decimated. Without the use of smoothly carved hair implements, some enslaved women resorted to raking the head with the farm utensil used to card sheep's wool. However, the close combing and precise parting—essential to artful styling—was not possible with the bulky carding tool.

Another factor in the decline of African hair culture within the enslaved community was the disparagement of the "lower" African physical type by whites. Ideas and images of "higher and lower races" began to proliferate in American opinion in the 1790s when a spate of treatises on physical variations among the races began appearing in England and the United States. This racist disdain discouraged the creative manipulation and public projection of kinky hair.

As the image of the African physical character depreciated in the public view and the bristling character of the hair was ridiculed, as evidenced by the proliferation of pickaninny and black-face-type **caricatures** in print media, and whites' pervasive and derisive description of the hair as "wool," black women came to dislike and reject the lively character of their hair and were motivated further to conceal it.

The custom of covering the head, particularly among urban mulatto women, also was reinforced by the forcible restriction of these women's ability to assert their beauty, project a public allure, and compete with white women for the attention of white men. Forbidden to show their luxuriant tresses, mulatto women in the Louisiana territory developed the artfully tied and shaped "tignon" head wrapping, which evolved into a chic accessory, subverting its basic purpose.

After becoming an integral part of enslaved women's personas, certain types of head coverings became principal symbols of respectability. Reminiscent of the social coding in African hair forms, in some areas of the American South, head coverings also were symbols of married status.

In coastal South Carolina, the fresh, white turban signified the status of the trusted, chief house servant—the "mammy." The brilliant whiteness of the mammy's turban was official balm in the plantation manor, obliterating the tensions that accompanied a kinky-haired black women's entrance into the formal company of whites. Second to the turban as a symbol of respectability in the hierarchy of female slave head coverings was the often-colorful bandanna. Like the turban, the bandanna was tied at the forehead with the ends tucked in but was a more snug covering than the higher, thicker, and more authoritative-appearing turban that was created from larger swaths of cloth. Like the turban, house servants wore the bandanna.

Compared with house servants, female fieldworkers could exercise more options in the appearance of the head and were able to work without covering their hair. In photographs and illustrations, however, black women at work in the fields generally appear with their hair covered by simple rags. These women devised sleek, graceful ways of wrapping the rags. A small piece of cloth was pulled to the back of the head and tied with the ends tucked neatly inside to form a snug cap. Women in agrarian West African cultures did not wear their hair tightly bound while working and sweating in hot weather, so the head-covering custom among black women fieldworkers was attributable to more than factors of utility, such as keeping dirt and crop debris out of hair and the rigors and deprivations of slavery.

In addition to these social and pragmatic factors, other motives influenced the practice of enslaved women concealing their hair. The economic significance of the head covering in the slave woman's persona was pointed out by a former enslaved man who, when interviewed for the 1930s Federal Writers' Project, recalled: "Just before dese here speculators would get to a town or plantation . . . dey stop the crowds . . . and make de womens wrap up dey heads with some nice red cloth so dey all look in good shape to de man what dey gwine try to do business with."

While vestiges of the communal aspects of traditional African hair care continued in slavery, much of the artistry and symbolism was lost. In addition to the functional constraints of enslavement, geographic factors contributed to the enslaved women's loss of African types of hair care practices. Their West African ancestors had settled near streams, rivers, and oceans, and water had become an important symbolic and functional element in women's hair care and beauty. Ritual baths, massaging the cleansed head and body with perfumed oils, belief in river spirits that appear as dazzlingly beautiful women, and aesthetics and styles based on the freshness of the hair and tidiness of the scalp were integral parts of the West African feminine grooming practice. In contrast, enslaved women often lacked access to flowing bodies of water.

Descriptions of enslaved women's hair care practices appear infrequently in the African American **slave narrative** and oral history collections and in historiography and fiction about slavery, but scattered accounts in these sources provide glimpses of hair care practices. In recalling hair care practices on a Georgia plantation for a Federal Writers' Project interview, a former slave described a confined, insect-infested situation:

> On Sundays, the old folks [adults] stayed home and looked one another's heads over for nits and lice. Whenever they found anything, they mashed it twixt they finger and thumb and went ahead searching. Then the woman's wrapped each other's hair the way it was to stay fixed 'til the next Sunday.

The wrapping referred to encircling sections of hair with thread or string. To wrap the hair, a woman would part the hair in blocks. Then she gathered, according to the thickness of the hair, a few strands or many, and secured the section of hair by tying a piece of thread or string around it at the end. The wrapped lengths of hair were connected with string or hung loose like braids. This technique kept the hair in place and smooth. Enslaved women's braided and wrapped hair forms were typically simple, functioning for purposes of utility rather than fashion and style.

A former resident of a southern Louisiana plantation recalled a style that was smoothed by being rolled up for several days but was still vibrant: "The girls dress up on Sunday. All week they wear they hair all roll up with cotton they unfold from the cotton boil. Sunday come they comb the hair out fine. No grease on it. They want it naturally curly." Memories of string-wrapped hair evoked joy in the former slave, Peter Clifton:

> I meets Christina and seek her out for to marry. Dere was somethin' about dat gal day I meets her, though the hair had about a pound of cotton tread it in, dat just attracted me to her like a fly will sail 'round and light on a 'lasses pitcher.

Often the heads of black women were doubly wrapped—first with the string wrappings and then by a kerchief. In *Mamba's Daughters* (1929), novelist DuBose Heyward, who had spent years observing the black people of Charleston, graphically describes the hairstyle of an old black female character of the 1900s who had lived during the antebellum era and who had "not been born to the dignity of the kerchief." Her hair was

> divided into a dozen or more equal tufts. Each of these was tightly wrapped with string, commencing at the tip and ending at the scalp; the collection, resembling rope ends, was drawn together and united in a tight knob on the crown. The general effect was as though an enormous gray tarantula had settled upon the head, and was holding on tightly with outstretched legs.

Keeping the hair restrained and untangled, the string wrappings primarily functioned as devices of maintenance, not style. One black woman reported that the style also was to "make um grow." Like kerchiefs and turbans, string-wrappings were a provisional response to the problematic image of kinky hair in a society that deemed, as an essential feature of feminine beauty, long, soft tresses.

Varieties of Braids

Young black girls normally wore their hair uncovered, either braided, string-wrapped, or short and loose in the style that later would be called a close "Afro." Considered unseemly for women, wiry, kinky braids could assume an amusing, animate character of cuteness when worn by little girls. Consequently, braids were an outstanding part of the "pickaninny" caricature, a familiar figure of 19th-century American popular culture. With her "woolly" hair braided in "sundry little tails, which stuck out in every direction," Topsy, originally appearing in Harriet Beecher Stowe's 1852 novel *Uncle Tom's Cabin*, was the most famous of the pickanniny figures.

Typically, however, the hair of young black girls was not worn in wildly erratic ways. A common, easily maintained style was the simple box-braid. The often very short hair was parted into four or six squares, braided, and the tiny braids vertically connected by sticking the end of the top braid into the top of the lower braid. This style was easier to create than the other common braided style that resembled patterns formed by growing crops that came to be known as "cane rows" or "cornrows." In the latter style, the braided row is created through the continuous motion of the stylist's hands down or across the head; additional strands are picked up and incorporated into the row as the hands move along the head.

Black people living on the coasts and the islands off the coasts of South Carolina, Georgia, and Florida retained comparatively more complex African behavior than did enslaved blacks living inland, and some of this was manifested in the hair culture of the coastal and Sea Island–enslaved women.

One of the most elaborate examples of the hair care practices of enslaved women is seen in an ivory bust of a young black woman who lived at the Retreat Plantation on St. Simons Island, Georgia. The neck base of the sculpture is carved with the legend: "Nora August, slave, age 23 years. Purchased from the market, St. Augustine, Florida, April 17, 1860. Now a free woman." An anti-slavery medallion is carved on the neck. It says: "Am I not a man and a brother?" Above the medallion is carved: "Sold east of plaza, 1860." The sculpture is part of the Sea Island Company Collection, St. Simons Island, Georgia.

The sculpture of August has thick, kinky hair that is divided into five sections and braided into dense, thin rows; each section is molded into raised, pyramidal-shaped wedges that form a starfish-shaped pattern in back. The top three sections of the hair converge into three braids that are formed into a cord-wrapped crown at the top front of the head. The two sections of the lower back of the head converge into a single, cord-wrapped, U-shaped braid at the nape of the neck. The even, intricate detail of the hair indicates that the parting and braiding of Nora's hair were done by a woman or girl with considerable practice in creating such styles. The sculptural wedge structure is reminiscent of the treatments of hair on figures carved in traditional West African cultures.

Little is known about the specific circumstances out of which the hairstyle was produced except that August was either an enslaved worker on the Retreat Plantation or a recent contraband arrival. It is unclear whether the style was entirely a direct African retention or the spontaneous, creative response of two black women to the sculptural potential of thick, kinky hair. A likely assumption is that it was a combination of both impulses. One aspect of the style of braiding used in August's hairstyle was a technique long and extensively used by African women: the continuous weaving of the hair into parallel rows, that is, "cornrowing."

Presented to the nurses at Darien, Georgia, in 1865, the sculpture was carved from life at Retreat Plantation, which was occupied by Union troops and used as an army hospital and camp for contraband slaves. Clearly apparent in the form are two inspirations: the inspiration of the hair stylists to articulate a black women's distinctive beauty through an intricately detailed hair form and the inspiration of the sculptor to work a piece of ivory, probably indigenous to Africa and a medium difficult to carve, into fine detail to produce a lasting portrait of a regal, self-possessed, newly emancipated woman.

See also Headwraps, Tignons, and Kerchiefs.

FURTHER READING

Boone, Sylvia Arden. *Radiance from the Waters: Ideals of Feminine Beauty in Mende Art.* New Haven, CT: Yale University Press, 1986.

Genovese, Eugene D. *Roll, Jordan, Roll: The World the Slaves Made.* New York: Random House, 1976.

Harris, Juliette, and Pamela Johnson, eds. *Tenderheaded: A Comb-Bending Collection of Hair Stories.* New York: Pocket Books, 2001.

Herkovits, Melville. *The Myth of the Negro Past.* New York: Harper and Row, 1941.

Morrow, Willie Lee. *400 Years without a Comb.* Rev. ed. San Diego, CA: Morrow's Marketing, 1985.

Rawick, George P., ed. *The American Slave: A Composite Autobiography.* Westport, CT: Greenwood Press, 1972–1979.

White, Shane, and Graham White. *Stylin': African American Expressive Culture from Its Beginnings to the Zoot Suit.* Ithaca, NY: Cornell University Press, 1998.

JULIETTE HARRIS

HEADWRAPS, TIGNONS, AND KERCHIEFS. Slaves wrapped their heads or wore head-coverings such as tignons and kerchiefs. These types of headwear were viewed with wonder or with derision by slaveholders and other whites, for they were structured differently from other types of headwear worn during slavery. At times, headwraps were colorful and configured in stylish ways so that they completely covered the **hair**. The wrapping and tying of hair was carried over from Africa, as a traditional way to represent beauty, enclose **charms**, and seal intentions about health and well-being.

Representations of enslaved women have featured them with headwraps. The "mammy," usually an enslaved female, who served as a nursemaid or a cook in a slaveholder's main house, was regularly identified in publications as someone who wore a headwrap. Some enslaved women may have been forced to cover their hair to avoid competing with the mistress in the arena of beauty. Materials that could be used for headwraps and handkerchiefs were included in plantation supplies given to slaves.

Enslaved men sometimes wore headwraps, as did children. In the 1830s, Fanny Kemble (1809–1893), an English actress who married a Southern plantation owner in Georgia, found it strange that slave babies were wearing headwraps. Apparently, their parents were trying to protect the babies from crawling insects as well as the cold air, thus preventing illnesses. Perhaps, based on beliefs about how early a child's hair should be combed or cut, the hair may have been left uncombed and covered.

Slaves literally and practically used their heads to lighten their loads. The common West African practice of transporting goods on the head was popular, too, in the Americas. Here slaves, including pregnant women, carried a wide range of things such as live animals, furniture, and agricultural produce in this manner. Wrapping the head or using wrapped-cloth pads helped to facilitate such transport by lessening the pressure of the weight.

Headwraps were not simply easy or quick solutions to hair care for the enslaved. Wrapping and tying the head ensured that it was protected, empowered, and invested with both secular and spiritual meanings. These practices helped the slaves to nurture both self and community.

FURTHER READING

Needlework picture with the figures of a white woman and a black woman wearing a headwrap. Catherine Fairfax with Chloe at Mounteagle, attributed to Ann Culpepper Fairfax, Alexandria, Virginia, ca. 1805, appliquéd wool, cotton, and linen fabrics, wool embroidery thread, and beads on a wool ground. (The Colonial Williamsburg Foundation. Purchased with partial gift funds from "Jeannine's Sampler Seminar.")

Edwards-Ingram, Ywone. "Medicating Slavery: Motherhood, Health Care, and Cultural Practices in the African Diaspora." PhD diss., College of William and Mary, 2005, 201–207.

Griebel, Helen Bradley. "The West African Origin of the African-American Headwrap." In *Dress and Ethnicity: Change Across Space and Time*, edited by Joanne B. Eicher, 207–226. Oxford: Berg Publishers, 1995.

Kemble, Frances Anne. *Journal of a Residence on a Georgian Plantation in 1838–1839*. 1863. Reprint, Savannah: Library of Georgia, 1992.

Simkins, Anna Atkins. "Function and Symbol in Hair and Headgear Among African American Women." In *African American Dress and Adornment: A Cultural Perspective*, edited by Barbara M. Starke, Lillian O. Holloman, and Barbara K. Nordquist, 166–171. Dubuque, IA: Kendall/Hunt Publishing Company, 1990.

YWONE EDWARDS-INGRAM

HERBS. An herb is a nonwoody plant used for its medicinal, culinary, or aromatic value. In American folklore and enslaved African American communities, an herb also could include parts of trees and common weeds. In both Western Europe and West and Central Africa, the notion of special herbs that were gathered for these purposes was a part of daily life in rural communities that were largely self-reliant and had limited access to spices,

medicines, and perfumes. When these cultures encountered Native American traditions, this unique interpretation of the landscape was reinforced as foreign plants mixed with native ones in a new body of herbal knowledge. As enslaved Africans and their descendants worked at creating new Afro-Creole cultures from New England south to Texas and into the central interior, each community had its approach to growing, gathering, and making use of such plants to heal, feed, disinfect, and provide fragrance.

Herbs familiar to the contemporary Western world were well known in historic West and Central Africa. Some were native to Africa and Asia; others were introduced by Arab traders from North Africa and Europeans trading in enslaved persons and gold who settled on the coast. Others were completely native to Africa and would be introduced into the Americas with the slave trade.

Herbalism was an essential part of daily life. While specific people in the community were charged with healing, and therefore knew hundreds of herbal plants, remedies, and combinations, most West and Central Africans grew up collecting and learning the uses of common plants necessary for daily life. Among the Ewe, herbs were collected to disinfect and sweeten **gourds** and earthenware **pottery**; others were used to prevent infection in wounds or purify the body or, in the case of initiatory or religious ceremonies, the soul. In traditions analogous to those of southern and eastern Asia, sacred herbs were grown around temple compounds, others were made into special teas for consumption for both physical and spiritual imbalances, and others were specially selected to flavor foods while also acting as medicinal cures.

In what is now Ghana and Nigeria, for example, indigenous species of the basil plant were incorporated into both traditions of spiritual purification and food preparation. Thyme was used as a disinfectant and important ingredient in healing. European traders and explorers noted the dispersion of herbs as a part of West African life. Swedish botanist Adam Afzelius (1750–1837), traveling in what is now Sierra Leone, recorded sage, purslane, and thyme in the gardens of villagers there. Mint was incorporated into the teas and aromatic culture of the Sahel and Senegambia, having been brought from Morocco and other parts of the Islamic world. Special herbs collected from the bush were steeped for sacred herbal baths, burned to expel insects, or included as part of power objects such as amulets, **charms**, or offerings made to divine forces. In the words of Harriet Collins, a formerly enslaved woman, the idea that certain healing traditions came from Africa guaranteed their confidence and sense of authenticity in the enslaved community: "My mammy larned me a lots of doctorin' what she larnt from old folkses from Africy, and some de Indians larnt her. . . . All dese doctorin' things come clear from Africy, and dey allus worked for Mammy and for me, too."

When enslaved Africans came to what would become the United States, they encountered both exotic and familiar herbs as a result of their contact with the Islamic and European worlds. They also found plants native to the northeastern and southeastern woodlands and coastline that were members of the same botanical families as those in West Africa. Those plants introduced with the slave trade dispersed around the South and the eastern seaboard, further linking enslaved blacks with ancestral traditions. Whatever their origin, enslaved blacks gained a reputation for their interest in and usage of herbs. Without these herbs, blacks could not accomplish much of the necessary healing because of the expense and the class and racial status of blacks in slave societies. Without such herbs, the foodways of enslaved people also would have been much blander, their spiritual traditions would have lacked a central component, and lives often lived in misery and challenging conditions would not have known the fragrance of these plants.

This relationship with plants and the landscape provided a source of conflict and empowerment for enslaved communities. On the one hand, certain enslaved healers were rewarded with emancipation for providing herbal cures for ailments and snake-bites; and on the other hand, herbalism was condemned for its connections with traditional African religious practices and most especially with its connection to knowledge of poisons. In colonial-era Williamsburg, blacks were banned from practicing as apothecaries, and traditional methods of healing were occasionally outlawed or placed under stringent control by legal authorities. "Pizens" (poisonous substances) were used to rebel against slavery and were a subtle form of retaliation. Attempts at poisonings, and successful murders of whites from New York to Virginia to North Carolina to Louisiana, all point to the use of tuckahoe, oleander, and devil's shoestring among other toxic herbs to seek revenge against the forces of African American oppression.

Herbal traditions in enslaved communities borrowed heavily from those of their European masters. European settlers of the period favored culinary herbs such as lovage, parsley, sage, thyme, sweet marjoram, savory, borage, and horseradish. Early African American **gardens** included cuttings of rosemary, mint, catnip, pennyroyal, sage, balm, and various types of roses. Basil was grown for export in Virginia as early as the 1770s, and this may have some connection with the large West African population there. In Louisiana, among other parts of the South, basil was associated with good luck and was grown by the doorway to discourage negative forces and bring good luck. Sage tea was boiled for fevers or flux. In the Upper South, mint tea crossed the ocean from Senegambia, and mint-flavored beverages have retained their popularity in the region into the 21st century. Garlic was used to expel parasitic worms from the body. Many herbs were used in this capacity because of the lack of hygiene. Enslaved children often were required to eat with their hands in unsanitary conditions. Parasitic worms from animal or human waste consistently infected the ground and eating troughs from which enslaved children were fed.

A number of traditional herbs and plants that were similarly used for healing have been found among the archaeological remains of Thomas Jefferson's Poplar Forest. Bedstraw, carpetweed, cherry dock, goosefoot (lamb's quarters), mallow, nightshade, ragweed, smartweed, vervain, and poppy were recovered from the **slave quarters** at the site. Some of these herbs may have been edible potherbs; others provided infusions used for teas and soaking liquids used to soothe external ailments. Similarly, a number of important medicinal and spiritual herbs, including comfrey, mullein, mayapple, wormseed, tansy, pokeweed, and Sweet William, that originated in enslaved communities in the 18th and 19th centuries continued to be used in African American communities in Virginia into the early 20th century. Herbs, especially fragrant ones such as basil, rosemary, lavender, and roses, often were rubbed on or placed between safeguarded clothing as a means of deodorizing or perfuming special clothing. Herbs not only healed the enslaved body and spirit but also provided a sense of humanity despite the utter poverty and degradation that the enslaved people often had to endure.

Both men and women had access to and participated in herbalism in enslaved communities, but for women, the use and value of herbs was especially important in matters of healing, beginning with childbirth and continuing through child rearing and general family health care. In Georgia, Aunt Darkas was remembered as a blind woman who "could go ter the woods and pick out any kind of root or herb she wanted." Polly Shine recalled that "Maser would get us a Negro mama, and she doctored us from herbs she got out of the woods." Enslaved women were particularly valued for their role as midwives and healers of childhood illnesses and "women's troubles." Indeed, the brutalities of slavery gave rise to the use of some herbs and plants such as pennyroyal and cotton root as abortifacients. "Conjure women," midwives, and "doctors" were essential persons of the social landscape, drawing their personal and communal power from the herbs that they grew and gathered around them.

FURTHER READING

Ball, Charles. *Slavery in the United States: A Narrative of the Life and Adventures of Charles Ball.* New York: Published by John S. Taylor, 1837. Documenting the American South. At http://docsouth.unc.edu/neh/ballslavery/menu.html.

Edwards-Ingram, Ywone. "Medicating Slavery: Motherhood, Health Care, and Cultural Practices in the African Diaspora." PhD diss., College of William and Mary, 2005.

Heath, Barbara J. "Bounded Yards and Fluid Boundaries: Landscapes of Slavery at Poplar Forest." In *Places of Cultural Memory: African Reflections on the American Landscape,* Proceedings of National Park Service conference, May 9–12, 2001. At http://www.nps.gov/crdi/conferences/conflinks.htm.

Mellon, James. *Bullwhip Days: The Slaves Remember.* New York: Avon Books, 1990.

Westmacott, Richard. *African-American Gardens and Yards in the Rural South.* Knoxville: University of Tennessee Press, 1992.

MICHAEL W. TWITTY

HOECAKES. Hoecakes are a simple unleavened bread of ground **corn**, water, and occasionally salt formed into a round or oblong cake and baked until browned, usually over an open fire. Tradition holds that slaves cooked hoecakes on large gardening **hoes** during days spent in the fields, and the cooking method gave the dish its name. Whether the term "hoe" refers to the tool used for cultivation or a specialized large flat kitchen implement is unclear, however. The association of hoecakes with the garden hoe baking method became solidified in 19th-century cookbooks and life accounts, especially after Reconstruction. The term "hoecake" typically refers to the Southern version of corn and water bread, but similar breads existed throughout the United States under the names ashcake, Johnny cake, crackling bread, and bannock. Sometimes different names indicate a shift in preparation practice or the inclusion of additional ingredients. Ashcakes were prepared by placing the dough near or directly in ashes to cook and were sometimes covered with cabbage leaves. Crackling bread benefited from the addition of small bits of meat left over from rendering of pork fat during the butchering process. The term "bannock" originates from the English combination of water and grain baked into bread.

Hoecake is the only term for corn bread that suggests the type of tool used in the baking process. Slaves could have used large garden hoes by leaning the metal blade toward the fire and placing the cake on the side exposed to heat. The hoe also may have been removed from the long wooden handle and used like a griddle. In this method, the hoe would sit directly on top of a small fire or coals and the cakes would be flipped to bake evenly. If hoes specifically were made for baking, the pan would sit on top of the fire and the cakes were cooked in a similar manner. Using garden hoes would have allowed field hands to carry only a few items to the fields each day to both work and prepare a meal.

Although the origins of hoecakes are associated with slaves, simple cornmeal breads were eaten by a diverse swath of the U.S. population. The practice of making simple breads and cakes can be found in all of the cultures that came to settle in the Americas. Native Americans were the first to use corn for bread and the tradition likely passed to colonists and slaves early during the colonial period. While the English would have related this to bannock, Spanish, French, African, and Dutch culinary traditions all had their own versions of simple breads. Through the Atlantic slave trade, the Portuguese transported American maize to West Africa in the 16th and 17th centuries, and African slaves were likely exposed to corn before their forced passage to the American colonies as a result. The weekly **rations** of corn that slaves typically received in the United States would have been a familiar staple to make bread. Hoecakes were only one among many corn dishes regularly consumed by the enslaved population.

See also Food and Foodways.

FURTHER READING

Cofield, Rod. "How the Hoe Cake (Most Likely) Got Its Name." *Food History News* 76 (2008): 1, 6–7.

Covey, Herbert C., and Dwight Eisnach. *What the Slaves Ate: Recollections of African American Foods and Foodways from the Slave Narratives.* Santa Barbara, CA: ABC-CLIO, 2009.

Opie, Frederick Douglass. *Hog & Hominy: Soul Food from Africa to America.* New York: Colombia University Press, 2008.

LAURA RUSSELL PURVIS

HOES. The hoe was the most widely used agricultural implement in the plantation world. This simple tool—a broad, steel-edged blade fixed to the end of a long wooden handle—was the enslaved field hand's badge of office.

The hoe was not something with which the early European settlers in North America were familiar; in northern Europe, it was the plough that was used habitually to break the soil. But the plough was not an option open to Native Americans who had no draft animals. They relied instead on fire-hardened digging sticks, to which blades fashioned from clam shells or animal bones were sometimes added, enabling cultivators to scoop soil into mounds in which seeds could be planted. Early English settlers in the Chesapeake, who were not well provided with draft animals, adopted this Native American practice when they began to grow tobacco and corn. Because the English could draw on the European tradition of iron and steel making, which Native Americans could not, they were able to import hoes with metal blades that were far more robust than the makeshift items used in Native American systems of agriculture. A preference for the hoe as the primary instrument of tillage, established early on in the settlement of the Chesapeake, was strengthened when Virginia's planters turned to enslaved Africans as field hands, as they did decisively in the 1680s. West Africans, who knew ferrous metallurgy but lacked draft animals, were well used to the metal-bladed hoe; it was an ancestral tool for them.

In the 18th-century plantation, hoes were almost always imported from Britain. The leading British manufacturers had the capacity to produce them in huge numbers. The

Wrought-iron broad hoe head of the type used to cultivate tobacco, probably American, 1750–1860. (The Colonial Williamsburg Foundation.)

Crowley firm in the North East of England could turn out over 11,000 hoes a week in the 1750s. Colonial metalworkers could not match such speed and volume. Vast numbers of hoes were needed because the market underwent tumultuous growth as the enslaved population of the English-speaking colonial world increased exponentially. It was a market that had to be replenished annually, for it was taken for granted that a hoe would be worn out after a year's labor.

Hoes were made in various forms. There was a fundamental distinction between the broad hoe and the narrow. The first, whose blade might measure as much as seven or eight inches across, was used to turn over the soil; the other was employed to chop back weeds. Each type came in various sizes, ranging from 0, suitable for a child slave, through 4 or 5, heavy models for prime field hands. Already, at the start of the 18th century, British manufacturers differentiated between the Virginia hoe, which was intended for **tobacco** cultivation, the Carolina hoe, which was adapted for the **rice** fields of the Low Country, and several types of hoes destined for the **sugar** islands of the Caribbean.

The hoe was a tool of the plantation frontier. It was most heavily employed in the growing of tobacco in the Tidewater and in the first phase of rice cultivation in South Carolina. Changes in agricultural practice reduced its relative importance toward the end of the 18th century. The shift from tobacco to grain made by many Chesapeake planters led to the increased use of the plough after 1750. Similarly, the spread of tidal irrigation through the Low Country in the second half of the 18th century made the hoe less conspicuous than it had been in South Carolina's formative years. In that earlier period, an endless round of hoeing had taken up the Low Country summer; under the new regime of tidal irrigation, greater use was made of controlled floods to suppress weed growth in rice fields.

But while the demand for hoes slowed in Chesapeake and South Carolina, new markets opened up in the Cotton South in the early 19th century. Indeed, the hoe played a fundamental role in the advance of cotton cultivation across Alabama and Mississippi in the 1820s and 1830s. The first crops were raised on hastily cleared fields that were littered with stumps and roots. The plough could not operate in such conditions; the hoe had to serve. Only in the 1840s did a concerted turn to ploughs occur. By this time, hoes were being produced by Northern industrialists who had acquired a capacity for bulk production that colonial artisans had lacked. The emergence of specialized producers, like the Scovil Hoe Company of Higganum, Connecticut, pushed foreign manufacturers out of the U.S. market.

The North may have profited from the escalating demand for farm tools in the South, but Yankee observers were not impressed by Southern reliance on the hoe. They took it to be an apt symbol of what they saw as the slovenliness of Dixie agriculture. Maine physician and abolitionist Charles Grandison Parsons (1807–1864) scoffed at the crudity of the hoes ("as heavy as the woodman's axe!") he claimed to have seen while traveling through the South in 1852–1853. Noted landscape architect Frederick Law Olmsted (1822–1903), contrasting the efficient bustle of Northern agriculture with the torpor of the slave South, enlarged on the point. Overly bulky tools were attributable to the reckless work habits that slavery encouraged:

> I am assured that, in the careless and clumsy way they must be used by the slaves, anything lighter or less rude could not be furnished them with good economy, and that such tools as we constantly give our laborers, and find profit in giving them, would not last out a day in a Virginia corn-field. . . .

Ironically, this was an issue on which Southern planters found some common ground with their Northern critics. Manufacturers in the North, it was complained, produced substandard articles for the Southern market.

The stigmatization of the hoe as primitive instrument, which reached its climax in the years preceding the outbreak of the Civil War, was the culmination of a lengthy process, one that had begun in the mid-18th century when Chesapeake planters began to swap tobacco growing for the cultivation of wheat, abandoning the hoe for the plough in the process. As this was the Revolutionary era, the change of implement began to be imbued with ideological meaning. The plough was held up as an emblem of sturdy republican virtue. It became the proud embodiment of a new nation, featuring eventually on no fewer than 16 state seals. The hoe, which had hitherto had no particular negative connotation, correspondingly became an emblem of servility. Yet it was the hoe that had been the foundation of American agriculture from its earliest days. In the South, it long remained so.

See also Hoecakes.

FURTHER READING

Evans, Chris. "How Sweden Went Global and Carolina Got Its Hoes. An Atlantic Tale." *Common-place* 7:1 (October 2006). At http://www.common-place.org/vol-07/no-01/evans/.

Flinn, M. W. *Men of Iron: The Crowleys in the Early Iron Industry.* Edinburgh: Edinburgh University Press, 1962.

Parsons, Charles Grandison. *Inside View of Slavery: or A Tour Among the Planters.* Boston, 1855.

CHRIS EVANS

HOMINY. Hominy is maize (**corn**) that has been treated and cooked so that the germ and outer hull are removed. It was a method of preparing the corn developed by indigenous Native Americans so that it was more easily digestible, and it had the added benefit of converting niacin and vitamin B into a more absorbable form. Unlike the untreated corn consumed in West and Central Africa that led to a number of nutritional deficiencies and diseases, hominy, combined with other foodstuffs such as legumes, in many cases soup beans, butter beans, or black-eyed peas, was the basis of a fairly balanced diet. Both blacks and whites ate hominy as part of their daily diet. Using

Large wooden mortar used to pound corn into hominy, Virginia, 1800–1900. (The Colonial Williamsburg Foundation.)

large ears of white "Virginia Gourdseed" corn and later varieties, enslaved communities were constantly in the process of preparing hominy, known as "beating" hominy.

The mortars and pestles used for beating corn, lye barrels, and large iron pots known as "hominy pots" became part and parcel of the **slave quarters**' material culture. The sound of beating hominy, day and night, was a constant in the quarter just as the pounding of millet, **rice**, and sorghum had been in West Africa. Hominy, corn mush, and other similar foods took the place of the bland, starchy grain preparations eaten with spicy sauces or **stews** or bits of meat or **fish** as the main meal of the day in West Africa. Hominy often was eaten communally out of the pot it was cooked in. It left a familiar white film on everything it touched.

In the 17th and 18th centuries, hominy was eaten as the main meal several times a day. According to J. F. D. Smyth who traveled in the Middle Colonies in the middle of the 18th century and wrote in 1784 of his experiences in America after returning to England:

> He [an enslaved person] is called up in the morning at day break, and is seldom allowed time enough to swallow three mouthfuls of homminy, or hoe cake, but is driven out immediately to the field to hard labour;. . . . About noon is the time he eats his dinner, and he is seldom allowed an hour for that purpose. His meal consists of homminy and salt, and, if his master be a man of humanity, he has a little fat, skimmed milk, rusty bacon, or salt herring to relish his homminy or hoe cake. . . . They then return to severe labour, which continues in the field until dusk. . . . It is late before he returns to his second scanty meal. . . .

According to William Hugh Grove, an English traveler who visited Virginia in 1732:

> (Corn) Tis the only support of the Negroes, who Roast it in the Ear, Bake for Bread, and Boyl it when Hulled, and Like our buttered wheat, the Children and better sort breakfast with it and make farmity. The first they call Homny and the Latter Mush. To Hull it they Beat it in a Mortar as the Scots do their Barley.

"Old Dick," an enslaved man from 18th-century Virginia, said,

> I was put to work at the hoe, I was up an hour before sun, and worked naked till after dark. I had no food but Homony, and for fifteen months did not put a morsel of any meat in my mouth, but the flesh of a possum or coon. . . .

Making Hominy

Sarah Thomas, a formerly enslaved woman from Mississippi, described the hominy-making process as such:

> It wuz made by putting oak ashes in a barrel wid holes in de bottom and pouring water over dem ashes and whut dripped through made a strong lye. Den dey husked de corn and put it in dat lye to boil till it swell up and wuz tender and husks come off and lef' the corn purty and white. Den dey washed it through several waters till it wuz clean.

Sources: George P. Rawick. *The American Slave: Mississippi Narratives*, Supp. Ser. 1, Vol. 10, Part 5. Westport, CT: Greenwood Press, 1978.

Peter Bruner, a formerly enslaved man from Kentucky, remembered beating hominy:

> At nights he [the master] would have me to beat hominy. This hominy was beat out of corn. It was beat in a mortar a large piece of timber similar to a water bucket. They had a pestle to beat the hominy with. By the time I would get this beaten it would be about 10:30 o'clock and the next duty I was to perform was to go and wake my mistress up in order for her to see if it was fine enough. Then I would return and next time beat it into meal. Then I would have to go and get another peck of corn and beat it, and by the time I had accomplished this it would be about 1 o'clock. I think that was good bedtime.

Sources: Peter Bruner. "A Slave's Adventures toward Freedom. Not Fiction, but the True Story of a Struggle." Documenting the American South. http://docsouth.unc.edu/neh/bruner/bruner.html.

Hominy was bland and boring, but filling. If enslaved people were lucky, it was seasoned with a bit of preserved or salted pork or a piece of fatback, or it was enjoyed with black-eyed peas or other cowpeas, often called "hominy beans." Many enslaved people, especially those from the Chesapeake and its diaspora, recalled eating hominy late into antebellum slavery. James V. Deane from southern Maryland reported that the food for a cornshucking party on his tobacco plantation included "supper at twelve, roast pig for everybody, apple sauce, hominy and corn bread." Another man from the same area recalled, "our food consisted of bread, hominy, black strap molasses and a red herring a day." Adeline Hodge of Alabama described a feast of **chickens** eaten with "dem good ol' cushaws an' lye hominy, too."

See also Cast Iron Pots; Food and Foodways; Pigs and Pork.

FURTHER READING

Gibbs, Patricia A. "Re-Creating Hominy: The One-Pot Breakfast Food of the Gentry and Staple of Blacks and Poor Whites in the Early Chesapeake," in *The Cooking Pot: Proceedings*, Oxford Symposium on Food & Cookery. London: Prospect Books, 1988.

Hilliard, Sam Bowers. *Hog Meat and Hoecake: Food Supply in the Old South, 1840–1860*. Carbondale: Southern Illinois Press, 1971.

Hudson, Charles. *The Southeastern Indians*. Knoxville: University of Tennessee, 1989.

Morgan, Philip D. *Slave Counterpoint: Black Culture in the Eighteenth-Century Chesapeake and Lowcountry*. Chapel Hill: University of North Carolina Press, 1998.

Rawick, George P. *The American Slave: Kansas, Kentucky, Maryland, Ohio, Virginia and Tennessee Narratives*, Vol. 16. Westport, CT: Greenwood Press, 1972.

Vlach, John Michael. *By the Work of Their Hands: Studies in Afro-American Folklife*. Charlottesville: University of Virginia Press, 1991.

Weatherford, Jack. *Indian Givers: How the Indians of the Americas Transformed the World*. New York: Fawcett Columbine, 1988.

MICHAEL W. TWITTY

HOPPIN' JOHN. Hoppin' John is a dish combining cowpeas, usually black-eyed peas, and **rice**. It is particularly associated with the Carolina Low Country and Georgia Sea Islands but is found in other forms throughout the Lower South. It is a dish based on culinary traditions brought by enslaved Africans from West and Central Africa and specifically relates to similar dishes found in Senegambia.

In the rice-growing region from lower North Carolina to upper Florida, vast quantities of Carolina Gold rice were cultivated for export. Broken or unpolished rice that was not sold was given to the enslaved community as an addition to their **rations**. Cowpeas, a crop of African origin that came to the South during the slave trade, came in a diverse array of forms and colors, including brown, black, blue-gray, red, and white, as well as the familiar black-eyed form. All of these separately or together were boiled and spiced with "Negro pepper" and mixed with broken rice and salt **fish** or pork to form a tasty dish. The dish became associated with New Year's Day in African American folk tradition and came to symbolize good luck owing to black-eyed peas as traditional West African symbols of the Creator's guidance and protection, wealth, and fertility. The word for black-eyed pea in Yoruba, for example, is a pun on the words for "tradition," "beauty," and "good character." In Senegal, black-eyed peas by themselves or cooked in a dish are given as alms to beggars. Hoppin' John was first recorded in Sarah Rutledge's cookbook *The Carolina Housewife* in 1847 and called for red (field) peas boiled, then steamed, with rice. The dish is related to other culinary creations that started in West and Central Africa and the enslaved community, including **hominy** and black-eyed peas, red beans and rice, Limpin' Susan (**okra** and rice), and greens and rice. Hoppin' John was a convenient one-pot meal, taking full advantage of the limited utensils available in the ordinary enslaved household.

See also Pigs and Pork.

FURTHER READING

Gamble, David. *The Wolof of Senegambia*. London: International African Institute, 1957.

Harris, Jessica B. *The Welcome Table: African American Heritage Cooking*. New York: Fireside, 1995.

Harris, Jessica B. *Iron Pots and Wooden Spoons: Africa's Gifts to New World Cooking*. New York: Fireside Press, 1999.

Rutledge, Sarah. *The Carolina Housewife*. 1847. Columbia: University of South Carolina Press, 1979.

Walker, Sheila S. "Everyday Africa in New Jersey: Wonderings and Wanderings in the African Diaspora." In *African Roots/American Cultures: Africa in the Creation of the Americas*, edited by Sheila Walker, 45–80. Lanham, MD: Rowman and Littlefield Publishers, 2001.

MICHAEL W. TWITTY

HORSES. Until well into the 20th century, Americans relied on horses as a major mode of transportation. Whether ridden singly or grouped together in a team to pull a wagon, a carriage or a stagecoach, horses hauled people and supplies over long and short distances. Animals were expensive and needed to be maintained. To sustain the horses' strength and health, they required daily care. Many slaveholders, even when they possessed few other slaves, assigned individuals specifically to take care of their horses, **mules**, and livestock.

Enslaved individuals who worked with horses were described variously as ostlers, hostlers, grooms, and stable hands. Daily care of the horses included putting out hay, **corn** or feed, carrying buckets of water at least twice a day, and mucking out the stalls, as well as exercising the horses, grooming them with a brush or curry comb, and putting them out to pasture in good weather. Slaves who worked at public livery stables performed much the same work. Stable hands also were responsible for maintaining, cleaning, and polishing the tack, including the leather saddles, harnesses, reins, bits,

Horse Racing

Former slave Henry Coleman was a jockey and raced horses in South Carolina:

When I wuz a young fellow I used to race wid de horses. I wuz de swifes runner on de plantation. A nigger, Peter Feaster, had a white horse of his own, and de white fokes used to bet amongst de selves as much as $20.00 dat I could outrun dat horse. De way us did, wuz to run a hundred yards one way, turn around and den run back de hundred yards. Somebody would hold de horse, and another man would pop de whip fer us to start. Quick as de whip popped, I wuz off. I would git sometimes ten feet ahead of de horse 'fore dey could git him started. Den when I had got de hundred yards, I could turn around quicker dan de horse would, and I would git a little mo' ahead. Corse wid dat, you had to be a swift man on yer feets to stay head of a fas horse. Peter used to git so mad when I would beat his ole horse, and den all de niggers would laf at him kaise de white fokes give me some of de bettin money. Sometimes dey would bet only $10.00, sometimes, $15 or $20. Den I would race wid de white fokes horses too. Dey nebber got mad when I come out ahead. After I got through, my legs used to jus shake like a leaf.

Source: George P. Rawick, ed. *The American Slave: South Carolina Narratives*, Vol. 2. Westport, CT: Greenwood Press, 1972.

Black attendant with Captain Beckwith's horse at the headquarters of the Army of the Potomac, Brandy Station, Virginia, ca. 1864. (Library of Congress.)

and stirrups. An archaeological study of the Rich Neck Slave Quarter in Williamsburg, Virginia, which dates to the mid-18th century, recovered remnants of harness-related gear, including buckle, rings, chains, and hook fragments from the **slave quarters**. Stable hands usually maintained whatever carts, wagons, or coaches were owned by the slaveholder, although blacksmiths were required for more complicated repairs or to shoe the horses. Slaves also saddled up the horses for riding by slaveholders and their guests and then cooled the horses down and put them back in the stables after they returned. The slaves sometimes accompanied their masters on trips to care for the horses.

Horses typically were kept in stables, and in urban environments enslaved workers frequently lived within them. The Aiken-Rhett House (built 1817) in Charleston, South Carolina, includes a stable with six stalls, wooden pegs for storing the tack, a hay loft, and an adjoining carriage house at the end of a brick work yard. The stable's second floor contains a series of small rooms for enslaved workers.

Some enslaved African Americans took advantage of their position in the stable. In a letter George Washington (1732–1799) wrote to his farm manager in 1793, he pronounced a young slave named Cyrus "very unfit I believe to be entrusted with horses, whose feed there is strong suspicions he misapplies. . . ." At the same time, Washington also accused his slaves of "suffering my horses to be rode at unseasonable hours in the night without your knowledge or that of the overseers."

The slaves working with horses who had their owners' trust were the jockeys. Wealthy Southerners who bred and raced racehorses used their slaves, both adolescents and adults, as jockeys and trainers. These individuals enjoyed such privileges as a more flexible work schedule and some personal freedom. Although races were sometimes informal, enslaved jockeys also wore uniforms, similar to those worn today, and carried their owners' colors. Born on Maryland's Eastern Shore, William Green became a jockey for his owner, Edward Hamilton. Green remembered that his master "kept a great number of fine noble horses, with a number of race horses; and being the right size for a rider, he took me to ride races." After Green became a fervent Christian, he asked Hamilton to give him another job because he did not want to be exposed to the gambling that often accompanied horse racing, and Hamilton complied.

See also Blacksmith Shops.

FURTHER READING

Franklin, Maria. "An Archaeological Study of the Rich Neck Slave Quarter and Enslaved Domestic Life," Colonial Williamsburg Foundation Research Publication, 2004. At http://research.history.org/Files/Archaeo/ResPubs/RNSQ%20report.pdf.

George Washington to William Pearce, Philadelphia, December 22, 1793. Papers of George Washington, Library of Congress.

Green, William. *Narrative of Events in the Life of William Green, (Formerly a Slave.) Written by Himself.* Springfield, MA: L. M. Guernsey, 1853. Documenting the American South. At http://docsouth.unc.edu/neh/greenw/menu.html.

KYM S. RICE

I

INDIGO. Indigo is one of the world's oldest dyes as well as a popular blue pigment. The most common dye in West Africa, indigo became popularized in the Americas in the mid-18th century. Slaves grew indigo plants, produced the dye, and colored **cloth**. The process of producing indigo proved less taxing than **rice** production, but the respite for slaves proved brief because the indigo industry in the United States collapsed with the American Revolution.

Indigo formed a crucial part of the slave trade. Asian indigo-dyed fabrics came to Europe for reexport to West Africa as essential **barter** for slaves. These slaves provided much of the labor on the indigo plantations in the West Indies and Americas. The end product crossed the Atlantic for use in Europe.

The slaves who produced indigo likely had considerable familiarity with the dye. Indigo has been exceedingly fashionable in every part of the world since ancient times. Many of the slaves in America came from West Africa, which is also the center of **textile** activity in the African continent, in the 21st-century countries of Nigeria, Ghana, Senegal, Ivory Coast, and Mali. It is quite possible that slaves who produced indigo in the Americas had produced it in Africa.

The popularity of indigo as a source of income brought the indigo industry to the Americas. Every ethnic group in the Americas experimented with indigo, beginning with the Dutch in New York. However, no one had any success in producing indigo until the 18th century. In the late 1740s, Eliza Lucas Pinckney (1722–1793) of South Carolina developed indigo as a cash crop. Pinckney came to South Carolina from the West Indies, where indigo production was common. At the age of sixteen, left in charge of her family's plantations and her ailing mother, Pinckney perfected a method of cultivating indigo in the swampy South Carolina tidewater. Indigo replaced rice as a major cash crop as export demand for the latter stagnated. The indigo industry, although centered in South Carolina, also existed in Georgia, Virginia, Alabama, Louisiana, and Florida.

In French-owned Louisiana, the French government encouraged indigo production in the 1720s by sending seed over from the West Indies. Advisers from West Indian plantations helped many plantation owners build indigo factories in the lower Mississippi valley around New Orleans. These plantations produced 70,000 pounds of

---

Making Indigo

Emma Tidwell from Arkansas grew indigo and made dye:

We planted indigo an hit growed jes like wheat. When hit got ripe we gathered hit an we would put hit in a barrel an let hit soak bout er week den we would take de indigo stems out an squeeze all de juice outn dem, put de juice back in de barrel an let hit stay dere bout nother week, den we jes stirred an stirred one whole day. We let hit set three or four days den drained de water offn hit an dat left de settlings an de settlings wuz blueing jes like we have dese days. We cut ours in little blocks. Den we dyed clothes wid hit. We had purty blue cloth. De way we set de color we put alumn in hit. Dat make de color stay right dere.

Source: George P. Rawick, ed. *The American Slave: Arkansas Narratives*, Vol. 10, Parts 5 & 6. Westport, CT: Greenwood Press, 1972.

---

indigo annually by 1750. In the second half of the century, the quality of the product improved and more than 240,000 pounds of dye were produced, all by slave labor. When the Spanish assumed control over Louisiana in 1763, many settlers were enticed to the region by the prospect of making riches from indigo. Up to 550,000 pounds were sold annually in the 1790s. Increased competition from Guatemala,

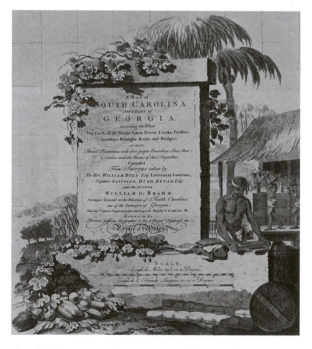

Detail of cartouche illustrating indigo production. From "A Map of South Carolina and Georgia," 1757. (The Colonial Williamsburg Foundation.)

exhaustion of the soil, insect damage, and the upheavals caused by the American Revolution effectively killed the industry by the early years of the 19th century.

Indigo promised to improve the working conditions for slaves. It involved toiling on dry land instead of swamps, with the labor less physically intensive although requiring precision. Slaves who worked with indigo often had body parts turn blue from handling the dye, and they remained that way as long as they worked on the plantation. For every five acres of indigo, four workers were required.

These workers used different sources to make indigo. More than 300 plant species produce the indigo dye, and many processes were used to make it. Indigo is insoluble in water and must be reduced (the process of removing oxygen) and dissolved in an alkaline solution before it will adhere to fabric. When a fabric has been soaked in the dye solution long enough to absorb the potential color, the material is removed and hung to dry. Exposure to the air causes reoxidation and turns the greenish shade to blue. The dye then has been absorbed by the fibers of the fabric and is again water-insoluble. Indigo is one of the most colorfast of natural dyes and the color retains its hue for decades.

The process of making indigo is exacting and repetitive, and different plant sources required different treatments. In the method most popular in South Carolina, the plants were placed in a series of three adjoining vats after harvesting. The plants remained in the first vat until they had oxidized. When the resulting liquid reached the right consistency and odor, it was transferred to the second vat to be aerated by agitating paddles. The blue liquid drained into the third vat where it sat until a muddy substance settled to the bottom. After the remaining liquid was drained off, the semisolid remainder was placed in linen bags to drain further and then it was placed into boxes to form into cakes. The cakes were dried in sheds, cut into cubes, and packed into barrels for shipment.

American indigo yielded a weaker blue than dyes from Africa or the West Indies. A common shade of blue required 50 cakes of African or West Indian indigo but more cakes of American indigo, hence more expense. A dark shade of indigo-dyed fabric could require as many as 150 cakes, thereby demonstrating the wealth of the owner.

Dying the cloth was labor-intensive and tedious. As in the African tradition, mud kilns often were used for the preparation of mordant ash, with any cracks in the thick walls repaired before each use. Layers of wood, from dry sticks to green boughs, were layered on top of a sieve that lay about a foot from the top of the kiln. Balls formed of old ash from the salt-ash pots and wood ash from house cooking fires then were placed on top of the sticks. When these formed a big pile, rising above the walls of the kiln, the sticks were ready to be lighted. The fire was kept burning for about 10 to 12 hours or until all the wood turned to ash. The ash was collected continuously, to be formed into balls that were left to dry. When all the wood had burned, the kiln was left to cool for a night and a day. To prepare the alkaline solution, the dyer used a pot with a hole in the bottom placed over another pot. Ash was placed in the top pot to act as a sieve and water was poured over the ash. As the water drained, it took salt with it, and then the salt water was transferred to the dye pot. The indigo cakes, broken up, were placed in a pot with the alkaline water poured over them. The mixture was left to stand for about three days and occasionally stirred. As the water was absorbed by the cloth, more water was added. The dye would keep for only about five days before developing an unpleasant odor that could pass to the cloth being dyed. The cloth was dipped three or four times for a few minutes and then left to dry in the sun. The series of dippings and dryings was repeated to achieve the desired color. Dyed cloth was never rinsed but instead drip-dried.

The technique often used with indigo, tie and dye, was also employed by the slaves. Tie and dye, practiced throughout the world, likely came to America through both African and European sources. Tie and dye is a resist method of patterning fabric that is achieved by withholding dye from certain areas of the fabric. This leaves the original undyed area as a background for the design of the dyed area, or vice versa.

The onset of the French and Indian War in 1756 increased demand for American indigo because the French were no longer selling to the American or British markets. The British placed a bounty on the product, thereby increasing profits for planters and prompting more planters to grow indigo. Indigo became such a source of wealth that almost every successful professional man in the Low Country supplemented his income by planting it. A South Carolina planter reportedly could fill his bags with indigo and ride to Charleston to buy a slave with the contents, exchanging a pound of indigo for a pound of a slave. By the eve of the American Revolution, Charleston indigo planters alone pounded more than a million pounds of indigo or 35 percent of South Carolina's total exports.

The high price for indigo translated into a high price for slaves. In 1754, the governor of South Carolina lamented that slaves cost more to purchase in his state than in any other because of the indigo demand. The prices did not remain high for long, however. When the American Revolution began, the British market for indigo disappeared along with the British bounty. Other markets proved impossible to develop. By 1780, planters largely abandoned indigo in favor of rice, although a few small growers produced it until the Civil War. Worldwide, indigo lasted as a popular natural dye until the introduction of synthetic dyes in the 20th century.

FURTHER READING

Balfour-Paul, Jenny. *Indigo*. Chicago: Fitzroy Dearborn, 1998.
Goldstone, Lawrence. *Dark Bargain: Slavery, Profits, and the Struggle for the Constitution*. New York: Walker, 2005.
Pettit, Florence H. *America's Indigo Blues: Resist-Printed and Dyed Textiles of the Eighteenth Century*. New York: Hastings House, 1974.
Polakoff, Claire. *Into Indigo: African Textiles and Dyeing Techniques*. New York: Anchor Books, 1980.

CARYN E. NEUMANN

IRONWORK. Ironworking was a highly developed skill among African peoples, especially those inhabiting the region from the west edge of Burkina Faso to Gambia and the Atlantic Ocean. Africans from this region, brought as slaves to the New World, played an important role in shaping American culture, including significant contributions to the architectural ironworking traditions of the American south, especially in Charleston, South Carolina, and New Orleans, Louisiana.

South Carolina planters particularly sought slaves from **rice**-growing Senegal-Gambia and the Gold Coast, and a large number of Africans from the Congo-Angola region entered the colony during the formative period of the 1730s. In New Orleans, the French brought enslaved Africans from Senegal, Whydah, and Angola, and both the Spanish and French exchanged Indians for blacks from the West Indies, where West African slaves dominated.

Surviving architectural ironwork from these early days continues to be a point of pride for Charleston and New Orleans residents and dominates their architecture up to the present day. In Charleston, lampposts and lamps, gates, railings, storefronts, boot scrapers, window grilles, and sign brackets made of wrought iron contribute to the city's unique architectural experience. New Orleans, especially the historic *Vieux Carré*, is renowned for its ornate wrought iron on railings, grilles, and gates. Throughout the urban and the rural south, **blacksmith shops** turned out well-made hardware and tools for the farm and home such as latches, hinges, **nails**, agricultural implements, and cooking equipment, as well as andirons, tongs, and shovels for fireplaces.

Wrought iron is a medium which allowed skilled slaves to apply their knowledge, experience, and imagination. Although the full history of this creative and dynamic process remains undiscovered, elements of the story are now emerging. Blacksmithing was one trade in which slaves incorporated African influences into European ironworking traditions, and it flourishes as an Afro-American craft in Charleston and New Orleans up to the present day.

Charleston

During the 18th and the first half of the 19th century, slaves constituted the majority of South Carolina's population. It was the only Southern state to reopen the foreign slave trade from 1803 to 1807, and slaves were brought in huge numbers to its major seaport in Charleston. While most slaves were resold to nearby plantations, some remained in the city to be integrated into the urban slave system, becoming an important element of Charleston life.

Most slaves who mastered ironworking lived in urban surroundings. In fact, urban slavery held more advantages for the slave than rural situations because enslaved individuals in a city had more opportunity to become involved in various trades. Sometimes slaves acquired skills and training from their owners. Christopher Werner, the German ironworker who designed Charleston's famous Sword Gate originally made for the city's guard house in 1838 but later installed on Legare Street, owned five slaves who carried out his commissions. Of these black craftsmen, Toby Richardson is the best remembered, and may possibly be responsible for many works designed by Werner including the Sword Gate. Masters often hired out their slaves to different craftsmen, allowing them to increase their knowledge and experience. Many slaves hired themselves out in their free time, with the profits earned split with their masters or used to buy freedom. Charleston became a central destination for many former slaves who had received or purchased their freedom and were looking for better opportunities to develop their skills and earn a living. Among those free blacks were blacksmiths, carpenters, bricklayers, shoemakers, tailors, seamstresses, painters, wheelwrights, and silversmiths.

Widespread involvement of free and enslaved African Americans in the ironworking industry caused some white laborers to feel the pinch of competition from blacks and they successfully petitioned the General Assembly to restrict training opportunities for blacks. These laws had little impact, however, and black artisans continued to prosper in the ironworking trades.

Charleston's free black class, which numbered only 586 in 1790, grew to 3,622 by 1860. In the 1848 city census, free African Americans were recorded in more than 50 different occupations. The records also show that among ironworkers, almost complete parity had been achieved between blacks and whites. Of 89 smiths, 45 were white, 40 were slave, and 4 were listed as "free persons of colour." Two years later, some 16 free blacks listed their trade as blacksmith. As a result of their skill in ironworking and their abilities as businessmen, many slaves were able to earn enough money to purchase their freedom. The tradition of African American employment in ironworking in Charleston persisted after the Civil War; in the 1870 census, African American workers accounted for 54 percent of listed blacksmiths.

New Orleans

There was a radical difference between the treatment of slaves on rural plantations and their treatment in urban New Orleans. New Orleans' slaves were generally better fed, clothed, and housed than their rural counterparts. This privileged situation allowed them easier access to training and to acquire the skills necessary to play an important role in the New Orleans economy.

It is commonly thought that New Orleans ironwork was largely crafted by skilled slaves during the antebellum period. However, sparse records relating to the involvement of slaves in this craft has prompted a long debate among scholars regarding the source of New Orleans' architectural ironwork. Some argue that although the early ironwork was designed by craftsmen in New Orleans, the work was produced and imported from Seville, Spain. Other scholars assign the manufacture of much of the French Quarter ironwork in the shop of the famous Jean Lafitte (ca. 1776–ca. 1823), "the pirate of the Gulf."

Lafitte himself mentioned in his journal that he constructed a blacksmith shop in New Orleans in 1805. A 1930s brochure by Mrs. Philip Werlein describing New Orleans iron railings states that "one story that seems well authenticated is that a great many of the best [railings] were made in the work shop of the famous pirates Jean and Pierre Lafitte in St. Philip Street." The brochure also says: "Other of the older residents remember a little shop on St. Louis Street which made a specialty of these same iron railings. All agree that the majority were the work of the skilled slaves brought to the city from St. Domingo where they had been well trained in the art." Slaves shipped to Louisiana were not identified on the slave registers by trade, but this does not mean that there were no skilled slaves among those that were transported to America. Slave owners knew that enslaved Africans had the capacity to acquire new European-style skills and that Africans had long traditions of skilled workmanship, including ironworking.

Beginning in French colonial Louisiana, authorities actively advocated the training of blacks in ironworking. In fact, the value of a slave skilled as an artisan was greatly increased, and many masters paid white artisans to train their slaves to be hired out for income as skilled laborers. Lafitte and his partner accordingly accepted slaves as apprentices in their shop. Although these craftsmen's names remain unknown, it is evident that during the antebellum period, slaves and free blacks spent their days in blacksmith shops, forging the decorative architectural ironwork so commonly identified with the city of New Orleans. The decorative balconies, window grills, and gates produced by such firms as Leeds, Geddes and Shakespeare, Baumiller and Gaudwin, Malus, or Urtubies should be recognized as the products of African American artisans because these firms owned slaves and employed free blacks in their workshops.

See also Slave Badges.

FURTHER READING

Baldwin, William P. *The Early Iron Work of Charleston*. Charleston, SC: History Press, 2007.

Blassingame, John W. *Black New Orleans, 1860–1880*. Chicago: University of Chicago Press, 1973.

Christian, Marcus. *Negro Ironworkers in Louisiana, 1718–1900*. Gretna, LA: Pelican, 1972.

Edgar, Walter. *South Carolina: A History*. Columbia: University of South Carolina Press, 1998.

Hall, Gwendolyn Midlo. *Africans in Colonial Louisiana: The Development of Afro-Creole Culture in the Eighteenth Century*. Baton Rouge: Louisiana State University Press, 1992.

Joyner, Charles. *Down by the Riverside: A South Carolina Slave Community*. Urbana: University of Illinois Press, 1984.

Lyons, Mary E. *Catching the Fire: Philip Simmons, Blacksmith*. Vancouver: University of British Columbia Press, 2000.

Morgan, Philip D. *Slave Counterpoint: Black Culture in the Eighteenth-Century Chesapeake and Lowcountry*. Chapel Hill: University of North Carolina Press, 1998.

Powers, Bernard E., Jr. *Black Charlestonians: A Social History, 1822–1885*. Fayetteville: University of Arkansas Press, 1994.

Vlach, John Michael. *Charleston Blacksmith: The Work of Philip Simmons*. Athens: University of Georgia Press, 1981.

Vlach, John Michael. *The Afro-American Tradition in Decorative Arts*. Athens: University of Georgia Press, 1990.

Vlach, John Michael. *By the Work of Their Hands: Studies in Afro-American Folklife*. Charlottesville: University Press of Virginia, 1991.

RAZIKA TOUATI KHELIFA SENOUSSI